The
METAMORPHOSES
of OVID

BOOKS BY ALLEN MANDELBAUM

POETRY

Journeyman, 1967

Leaves of Absence, 1976

Chelmaxioms: The Maxims, Axioms, Maxioms of Chelm, 1978

A Lied of Letterpress, 1980

The Savantasse of Montparnasse, 1988

VERSE TRANSLATIONS/EDITIONS

Life of a Man by Giuseppe Ungaretti, 1958

Selected Writings of Salvatore Quasimodo, 1960

The Aeneid of Virgil, 1972 (National Book Award, 1973), 1981

Selected Poems of Giuseppe Ungaretti, 1975

Inferno of Dante, 1980

Purgatorio of Dante, 1982

Paradiso of Dante, 1984

Ovid in Sicily, 1986

Ungaretti and Palinurus, 1989

The Odyssey of Homer, 1990

The
METAMORPHOSES
of OVID

A New Verse Translation by
Allen Mandelbaum

A Harvest Book
Harcourt Brace & Company
San Diego　New York　London

Detail of *From the Garden* from the Lightner Museum Series
© 1993 Anna Tomczak/Swanstock

"My Eyes" from *Ovid in Sicily* translated by Allen Mandelbaum, copyright 1986.
Reprinted by permission of The Sheep Meadow Press.

Excerpts from *Savantasse of Montparnasse* translated by Allen Mandelbaum,
copyright 1987. Reprinted by permission of The Sheep Meadow Press.

Library of Congress Cataloging-in-Publication Data
Ovid, 43 B.C.–17 or 18 A.D.
[Metamorphoses. English]
The metamorphoses of Ovid/a new verse translation by Allen
Mandelbaum.—1st ed.
(A Harvest Book)
p.   cm.
ISBN 0-15-170529-1
ISBN 0-15-600126-8
1. Metamorphosis—Mythology—Poetry.   2. Mythology, Classical—
Poetry.   I. Mandelbaum, Allen, 1926–   II. Title.
PA6522.M2M36   1993
873'.01—dc20   93-8118

Designed by Lisa Peters
Printed in the United States of America
First Harvest edition 1995
A B C D E

*This translation of
Ovid's seamless song is inscribed to
my brother in law and in love, Leonard Feldman,
and my sister, Rayma.*

CONTENTS

The
METAMORPHOSES
of OVID

BOOK I

MY SOUL WOULD SING of metamorphoses.
But since, o gods, you were the source of these
bodies becoming other bodies, breathe
your breath into my book of changes: may
the song I sing be seamless as its way
weaves from the world's beginning to our day.

Before the sea and lands began to be,
before the sky had mantled every thing,
then all of nature's face was featureless—
what men call chaos: undigested mass
of crude, confused, and scumbled elements,
a heap of seeds that clashed, of things mismatched.
There was no Titan Sun to light the world,
no crescent Moon—no Phoebe—to renew
her slender horns; in the surrounding air,
earth's weight had yet to find its balanced state;
and Amphitrite's arms had not yet stretched
along the farthest margins of the land.
For though the sea and land and air were there,
the land could not be walked upon, the sea
could not be swum, the air was without splendor:
no thing maintained its shape; all were at war;
in one same body cold and hot would battle;
the damp contended with the dry, things hard
with soft, and weighty things with weightless parts.

A god—and nature, now become benign–
ended this strife. He separated sky
and earth, and earth and waves, and he defined
pure air and thicker air. Unraveling
these things from their blind heap, assigning each
its place—distinct—he linked them all in peace.
Fire, the weightless force of heaven's dome,
shot up; it occupied the highest zone.
Just under fire, the light air found its home.

Latin [1–28]

The earth, more dense, attracted elements
more gross; its own mass made it sink below.
And flowing water filled the final space;
it held the solid world in its embrace.
When he—whichever god it was—arrayed
that swarm, aligned, designed, allotted, made
each part into a portion of a whole,
then he, that earth might be symmetrical,
first shaped its sides into a giant ball.
He then commanded seas to stretch beneath
high winds, to swell, to coil, to reach and ring
shorelines and inlets. And he added springs
and lakes and endless marshes and confined
descending streams in banks that slope and twine:
these rivers flow across their own terrains;
their waters sink into the ground or gain
the sea and are received by that wide plain
of freer waters—there, they beat no more
against their banks, but pound the shoals and shores.

At his command, the fields enlarged their reach,
the valleys sank, the woods were clothed with leaves,
and rocky mountains rose. And as the sky
divides into two zones on its right side,
with just as many to the left, to which
the hottest zone is added as a fifth,
the god provided regions that divide
the mass the heavens wrap, and he impressed
as many zones upon the earth. Of these,
the middle zone, because of its fierce heat,
is uninhabitable; and thick snows
cover two outer zones; between them he
aligned two other regions, and to these
he gave a clement climate, mixing heat
and cold. Above, the air extends; and for
as much as earth is heavier than water,
so is the air more ponderous than fire.
He ordered fog and clouds to gather there—

Latin [29–54]

in air—and thunder, which would terrify
the human mind; there, too, the god assigned
the winds that, from colliding clouds, breed lightning.

Yet he who was the world's artificer
did not allow the winds to rule the air
unchecked, set free to riot everywhere.
(But while each wind received a separate tract,
it still is difficult to curb their blasts,
to keep the world, which they would rend, intact:
though they are brothers, they forever clash.)
Eurus retreated toward Aurora's lands,
into the Nabataeans' kingdom and
to Persia, where the rays of morning meet
the mountain crests. And Zephyrus now went
to shorelines warm with sunset, in the west.
To Scythia, beneath the northern Wain,
swept horrid Boreas. Incessant rain
and mists that drench the southlands opposite—
this was the work of Auster. The god placed
above these winds the ether, without weight,
a fluid free of earth's impurity.

No sooner had he set all things within
defining limits than the stars, long hid
beneath the crushing darkness, could begin
to gleam throughout the heavens. That no region
be left without its share of living things,
stars and the forms of gods then occupied
the porch of heaven; and the waters shared
their dwelling with the gleaming fishes; earth
received the beasts, and restless air, the birds.

An animal with higher intellect,
more noble, able—one to rule the rest:
such was the living thing the earth still lacked.
Then man was born. Either the Architect
of All, the author of the universe,

in order to beget a better world,
created man from seed divine—or else
Prometheus, son of Iapetus, made man
by mixing new-made earth with fresh rainwater
(for earth had only recently been set

apart from heaven, and the earth still kept
seeds of the sky—remains of their shared birth);
and when he fashioned man, his mold recalled
the masters of all things, the gods. And while
all other animals are bent, head down,
and fix their gaze upon the ground, to man
he gave a face that is held high; he had
man stand erect, his eyes upon the stars.
So was the earth, which until then had been
so rough and indistinct, transformed: it wore
a thing unknown before—the human form.

That first age was an age of gold: no law
and no compulsion then were needed; all
kept faith; the righteous way was freely willed.
There were no penalties that might instill
dark fears, no menaces inscribed upon
bronze tablets; trembling crowds did not implore
the clemency of judges; but, secure,
men lived without defenders. In those times,
upon its native mountain heights, the pine
still stood unfelled; no wood had yet been hauled
down to the limpid waves, that it might sail
to foreign countries; and the only coasts
that mortals knew in that age were their own.
The towns were not yet girded by steep moats;
there were no curving horns of brass, and no
brass trumpets—straight, unbent; there were no swords,
no helmets. No one needed warriors;
the nations lived at peace, in tranquil ease.
Earth of itself—and uncompelled—untouched

by hoes, not torn by ploughshares, offered all
that one might need: men did not have to seek:
they simply gathered mountain strawberries
and the arbutus' fruit and cornel cherries;
and thick upon their prickly stems, blackberries;
and acorns fallen from Jove's sacred tree.
There spring was never-ending. The soft breeze
of tender zephyrs wafted and caressed
the flowers that sprang unplanted, without seed.
The earth, untilled, brought forth abundant yields;
and though they never had lain fallow, fields
were yellow with the heavy stalks of wheat.
And streams of milk and streams of nectar flowed,
and golden honey dripped from the holm oak.

But after Saturn had been banished, sent
down to dark Tartarus, Jove's rule began;
the silver age is what the world knew then—
an age inferior to golden times,
but if compared to tawny bronze, more prized.
Jove curbed the span that spring had had before;
he made the year run through four seasons' course:
the winter, summer, varied fall, and short
springtime. The air was incandescent, parched
by blazing heat—or felt the freezing gusts,
congealing icicles: such heat and frost
as earth had never known before. Men sought—
for the first time—the shelter of a house;
until then, they had made their homes in caves,
dense thickets, and in branches they had heaped
and bound with bark. Now, too, they planted seeds
of wheat in lengthy furrows; and beneath
the heavy weight of yokes, the bullocks groaned.

The third age saw the race of bronze: more prone
to cruelty, more quick to use fierce arms,
but not yet sacrilegious.

□   □   □

Latin [101–27]

                                    What bestowed
its name upon the last age was hard iron.
And this, the worst of ages, suddenly
gave way to every foul impiety;
earth saw the flight of faith and modesty
and truth—and in their place came snares and fraud,
deceit and force and sacrilegious love
of gain. Men spread their sails before the winds,
whose ways the mariner had scarcely learned:
the wooden keels, which once had stood as trunks
upon the mountain slopes, now danced upon
the unfamiliar waves. And now the ground,
which once—just like the sunlight and the air—
had been a common good, one all could share,
was marked and measured by the keen surveyor—
he drew the long confines, the boundaries.
Not only did men ask of earth its wealth,
its harvest crops and foods that nourish us,
they also delved into the bowels of earth:
there they began to dig for what was hid
deep underground beside the shades of Styx:
the treasures that spur men to sacrilege.
And so foul iron and still fouler gold
were brought to light—and war, which fights for both
and, in its bloodstained hands, holds clanging arms.
Men live on plunder; guests cannot trust hosts;
the son-in-law can now betray his own
father-in-law; and even brothers show
scant love and faith. The husband plots the death
of his own wife, and she plots his. And dread
stepmothers ply their fatal poisons; sons
now tally—early on—how many years
their fathers still may live. Now piety
lies vanquished; and the maid Astraea, last
of the immortals, leaves the blood-soaked earth.

□   □   □

Latin [127–50]

And in this age, not even heaven's heights
are safer than the earth. They say the Giants,
striving to gain the kingdom of the sky,
heaped mountain peak on mountain mass, star-high.
Then Jove, almighty Father, hurled his bolts
of lightning, smashed Olympus, and dashed down
Mount Pelion from Mount Ossa. Overwhelmed
by their own bulk, these awesome bodies sprawled;
and Earth soaked up the blood of her dread sons;
and with their blood still warm, she gave their gore
new life: so that the Giants' race might not
be lost without a trace, she gave their shape
to humans whom she fashioned from that blood.
But even this new race despised the gods;
and they were keen for slaughter, bent on force:
it's clear to see that they were born of blood.

When Jove, the son of Saturn, saw this scene
from his high citadel, he groaned; recalling
Lycaon's recent monstrous meal (a feast
the other gods had yet to hear about),
his heart was filled with anger such as Jove
can feel—a giant rage. And he convoked
a council of the gods; they came at once.

On high there is a road that can be seen
when heaven is serene: the Milky Way
is named—and famed—for its bright white array;
to reach the regal halls of mighty Jove,
the Thunderer, the gods must take this road.
On either side there range the homes of those
who are the noblest of the gods, the most
illustrious and powerful: their doors
are open wide; their halls are always thronged

Latin [151–72]

(the lesser gods have homes in other zones).
And if this not be too audacious, I
should call this site high heaven's Palatine.

And now, within the marble council hall,
the gods were seated. Throned above them all,
and leaning on his ivory scepter, Jove—
three times and then a fourth—shook his dread locks
and so perturbed the earth and seas and stars.
Then, opening his angry lips, he said:

"Now, more than ever, I am plagued, beset
by cares in governing the world; I faced
those horrid Giants, with their snake-shaped feet;
each monster, with the hundred hands he had,
was ready to assail the sky, to seize
these heavens—but that challenge was much less
than what confronts us now. For, in the end,
however fierce they were, those Giants all—
when they attacked—formed part of one same pack.
But now I must contend with scattered men;
throughout the world, wherever Nereus' waves
resound, I shall destroy the mortals' race.
I swear on the infernal streams that glide
beneath the woods of Styx, that I have tried
all other means; and now I must excise
that malady which can't be cured: mankind—
lest the untainted beings on the earth
become infected, too. I have half-gods
and rustic deities—Nymphs, Satyrs, Fauns,
and woodland gods who haunt the mountain slopes:
we've not yet found them fit for heaven's honors,
but let's ensure their safety on the lands
we have assigned to them. Can you, o gods,
believe they are secure when I myself,
who am the lord of lightning and your lord,
met with the trap Lycaon set for me—
Lycaon, famed for his ferocity?" □ □ □

Latin [173–98]

All shouted, keen to hear who had been guilty
of such a sacrilege: even as when
an impious band was fierce in its attempt
to blot the name of Rome and, to that end,
shed Caesar's blood; and all of humankind,
faced with calamity, was horrified,
the whole world shuddering. And you, Augustus,
are no less pleased by all the firm devotion
your people show to you than Jove was then
to hear the gods outcry on his behalf.

But Jove, with word and gesture, curbed the uproar;
when they had quieted, his words once more
could break the silence in the hall: "Be sure—
he has already paid the penalty.
But I'll tell you his crime and punishment.
I'd heard about this age of infamy;
and hoping to disprove such tidings, I
descended from Olympus' heights; I went
from land to land, a god in human guise.
Just now, it would be useless to describe
each sacrilege I found—upon all sides:
the truth was far, far worse than what I'd heard.
And I had crossed Mount Maenala's dread slopes,
home of wild beasts; I passed Cyllene's peak
and chill Lycaeus' pine grove. So I reached
the region and the uninviting home
of the Arcadian tyrant. Dusk had fallen,
and night was soon to follow. I'd made known
I was a god, and an Arcadian crowd
began to worship me. At first Lycaon
just jeered at all their pious prayers, but then
he said: 'I mean to test him; let us see
if he, beyond all doubt—infallibly—
is god or man.' This was the test he'd planned:
by night—with me asleep—treacherously
to murder me. And not content with that,
he seized a hostage the Molossians

Latin [199–226]

had sent to him; Lycaon cut his throat;
some of the still warm limbs he boiled in water,
and some he roasted on the fire. No sooner
had he set these before me as my meal
than I, with my avenging lightning bolt,

struck down his home, which caved in on itself—
walls worthy of their owner. He ran off
in panic, and when he had reached the fields,
within the stillness, he began to howl:
he tried to utter words—to no avail.
Wrath rises to his mouth; he foams; and just
as he was always keen on slaughter, now
he turns against the sheep; indeed he's pleased
to shed more blood. His clothes are changed to fur,
his arms to legs: he has become a wolf.
But he keeps traces of his former shape.
His hair is gray; he has the same fierce gaze;
his eyes still glitter, and he still presents
a savage image. Yes, one house collapsed;
but it was more than one I should have smashed.
Wherever earth extends, fierce Fury reigns!
A vast cabal of crime—that's what I see.
Let them all pay the proper penalties
without delay. For such is my decree."

Some of the gods approve Jove's words with shouts,
inciting him still more; some indicate
assent with silent signs. In any case,
complete destruction of the human race
saddens them all. What aspect would earth take
once it was stripped of men? Who'd offer incense
upon the altars? Had Jove planned by chance
on wild beasts as earth's sole inhabitants
and overlords? Such were the things they asked.
Their king was quick to set their fears at rest:
he would take care of everything; he swore
a new race, one far different from the first,
emerging wondrously, would share the earth.   □   □   □

Latin [227–52]

And now, as Jove was just about to hurl
his thunderbolts at the whole earth, he stayed
his hand: he was afraid that all those flames
might set the sacred sky ablaze, ignite
the world from pole to pole. He brought to mind
that, in the book of fates, this was inscribed:
a time would come when sea and land would burn,
a conflagration that would overturn
the palace of the sky—in fact destroy
the stunning fabric of the universe.
And so Jove set aside his lightning bolts
forged by the Cyclops; in their stead he chose
another punishment: he planned to drown
the race of men beneath the waves: he'd send
a deluge down from every part of heaven.
At once, within the caves of Aeolus,
Jove shuts up Boreas and other gusts
that might disperse the clouds. But he frees Notus,
who flies out on drenched wings: his awesome face
is veiled in pitch-black darkness, and his beard
is heavy with rainclouds, and water flows
down his white hairs; dark fog rests on his brow;
his wings and robes are dripping. Suddenly
his vast hands press against the hanging clouds;
and from the sky, rain pours as thunder roars.
Then Iris, Juno's messenger—her robes
are many-colored—fetches water, fuels
the clouds with still more rain. The crops are felled;
the wretched farmer weeps as he sees all
his hopes forlorn, in ruins on the ground—
the labor of the long years—useless, gone.

But angry Jove is hardly satisfied
with just the waters of his realm on high:
he needs his azure brother's aid, his waves—
and Neptune offers help without delay.

Latin [253–75]

That lord of waters summons all his rivers;
they hurry to his halls. This is his speech:
"The time is late. No long harangues. In brief:
Set all your forces free—that's what we need!
Open your gates and let your currents speed:

loosen the reins; don't slow or stay your streams!"
So he commands. His river-gods disband;

returning to their homes, they all unleash
their founts and springs; and these rush toward the sea.
Neptune himself lifts high his trident, strikes
the earth: it shakes and, as it shudders, frees
a pathway for the waters. As they leap
across their banks, they flood the open fields;
orchards and groves, and herds, and men and homes,
and shrines and all the sacred things they hold
are swept away. And if some house remains
in place despite the fury it has faced,
the rising waters overtop the roof;
the towers can't be seen beneath the eddies.
Between the sea and land one cannot draw
distinctions: all is sea, but with no shore.

One man seeks refuge on a hill, another
rows in his curving boat where, just before,
he'd plowed; one sails across his fields of grain
or over the submerged roof of his villa;
sometimes an anchor snags in a green meadow;
sometimes a curving keel may graze the vines.
Where grateful goats had grazed along the grass,
the squat sea-lions sprawl. And undersea,
the Nereids, amazed, stare hard at cities
and homes and groves; through woodlands, dolphins roam;
they bump against tall branches, knock and shake
oak trees. The wolf now swims among the sheep;
the waves bear tawny lions, carry tigers;
the boar is swept along—his lightning force
is useless; and the stag's swift legs can't help;

   . . .

Latin [276–306]

the bird that searched so long for land where he
might rest, flight-weary, falls into the sea.

By now the heights are buried by sea swells;
the surge—a thing no one has seen before—
beats on the mountaintops. Most men are drowned
among the waves; and those who have escaped,
deprived of food, become starvation's prey.

The land that lies between Boeotia
and Oeta's fields is Phocis—fertile land
as long as it was land, but now a mass
the sudden surge had changed into a vast
sea-tract. There, Mount Parnassus lifts, star-high,
its two steep peaks that tower over clouds.

And here (the only place the flood had spared)
Deucalion and his wife, in their small skiff,
had landed. First, they prayed unto the nymphs
of the Corycian cave, the mountain gods,
and Themis—she, the goddess who foretells
the future, in those early days, was still
the keeper of the Delphic oracle.

One could not point to any better man,
a man with deeper love for justice, than
Deucalion; and of all women, none
matched Pyrrha in devotion to the gods.
And when Jove saw the flooded world—by now
a stagnant swamp—and saw that just one man
was left of those who had been myriads,
that but one woman had escaped the waves—
two beings who were pious, innocent—
he rent the clouds, then sent out Boreas
to scatter them; the sky could see again
the land, and land again could see the heavens.   □   □   □

Latin [307–29]

The fury of the sea subsided, too.
And Neptune set aside his three-pronged weapon;
the god of waters pacified the waves
and summoned sea-green Triton, bidding him
to blow on his resounding conch—a sign
for seas and streams to end the flood, retreat.
And Triton, as he rose up from the deep—
his shoulders shell-encrusted—held his conch:
a twisting hollow form that, starting from
a point, then spiraled up to a wide whorl—
the conch that, when it's sounded in midsea,
reechoes on the shores to west and east.
Now, too, when Triton drew it to his lips—
wet with sea brine that dripped from his soaked beard—
and, just as Neptune ordered, blew retreat,
the sound reached all the waters of the sea
and those that flow on land—and having heard
his call, they all obeyed: they curbed their course.
The rivers fall back, and the hills emerge;
the sea has shores once more; the riverbeds,
however full their flow, now keep it channeled;
the land increases as the waters ebb;
the soil can now be seen; and then, at last,
after that long night, trees show their bare tops
with traces of the flood—slime on their boughs.

The world had been restored to what it was.
But when Deucalion saw earth so forlorn,
a wasteland where deep silence ruled, a bare
and desolate expanse, he shed sad tears
and said to Pyrrha:

       "O my wife, dear sister,
the only woman left on earth, the one
to whom I first was linked as a dear cousin
and then as husband, now we are together
in danger: all the lands both east and west
are empty now—and we alone are left:

Latin [330–355]

the sea has taken all the rest. And we
may not survive: we have no certainties—
that vision of the clouds still haunts my mind.
How would you feel, sad heart, if you'd survived
the fatal flood, but I had lost my life?
How would you, all alone, have borne the fear?
With whom would you—alone—have shared your tears?
For if the sea had swallowed you, dear wife,
I, too—believe me—would have followed you
and let the deluge drown me, too. Would I
were master of the arts my father plied;
then I, son of Prometheus, would mold
and so renew mankind—its many tribes.
But now the race of men has been reduced—
so did the gods decree—to me and you:
We are the last exemplars."

So he said;
together they shed tears and then resolved
to plead with the celestial power, to pray
unto the sacred oracle for aid.
Then, side by side, they went without delay
to seek the waters of Cephisus' stream;
although its waters were not limpid yet,
the river flowed along its normal bed.
They took some water and, upon their heads
and clothing, sprinkled it, then turned their steps
to holy Themis' shrine. The roof was grimed
with pallid moss, the altars had no flame.
They reached the temple steps, and there they both
kneeled down, bent to the ground; in awe, they kissed
the cold stones, saying: "If the gods are pleased,
by righteous prayers, and their wrath can be
appeased, then tell us, Themis, by what means
the ruin of our race can be redeemed;
and, kindest goddess, help this flooded world."
The goddess had been moved; her oracle
gave this response: "Now, as you leave the temple,

Latin [355–81]

cover your heads and do not bind your clothes,
and throw behind you, as you go, the bones
of the great mother.''

                    They are stunned, struck dumb;
and Pyrrha is the first to break their long
silence: she says she cannot do as told;
with trembling voice she begs the goddess' pardon,
but she cannot offend her mother's Shade
by scattering her bones. Again, again,
they ponder all the oracle had said;
those words—obscure and dark—leave them perplexed.
At last, Prometheus' son speaks words that would
allay the fears of Epimetheus' daughter:
"I may be wrong, but I think Themis' answer
did not involve impiety or ask
for any sacrilege. By the great mother,
the earth is meant; and bones, I think, mean stones,
which lie inside earth's body. It is these
that we must throw behind us as we leave.''

Her husband's explanation solaced Pyrrha;
yet hope was not yet firm—for, after all,
they both were doubtful of the oracle.
But what is wrong in trying? They set out;
they veil their heads, they both ungird their clothes;
and they throw stones behind them as they go.
And yes (if those of old did not attest
the tale I tell you now, who could accept
its truth?), the stones began to lose their hardness;
they softened slowly and, in softening,
changed form. Their mass grew greater and their nature
more tender; one could see the dim beginning
of human forms, still rough and inexact,
the kind of likeness that a statue has
when one has just begun to block the marble.
Those parts that bore some moisture from the earth
became the flesh; whereas the solid parts—

whatever could not bend—became the bones.
What had been veins remained, with the same name.
And since the gods had willed it so, quite soon
the stones the man had thrown were changed to men,
and those the woman cast took women's forms.
From this, our race is tough, tenacious; we
work hard—proof of our stony ancestry.

The other animals—arrayed in forms
of such variety—were born of earth
spontaneously; the torrid sun began
to warm the moisture that the flood had left
within the ground. Beneath that blazing heat,
soft marshes swelled; the fertile seeds
were nourished by the soil that gave them life
as in a mother's womb; and so, in time,
as each seed grew, it took on its own form.

So, when the Nile, the stream with seven mouths,
recedes from the soaked fields and carries back
its waters to the bed they had before,
and slime, still fresh, dries underneath the sun,
the farmers, turning over clods, discover
some who are newly born, who've just begun
to take their forms, and others who are still
unfinished, incomplete—they've not achieved
proportion; and indeed, in one same body,
one part may be alive already, while
another is a lump of shapeless soil.
For, tempering each other, heat and moisture
engender life: the union of these two
produces everything. Though it is true
that fire is the enemy of water,
moist heat is the creator of all things:
discordant concord is the path life needs.

□   □   □

Latin [409–33]

And when, still muddy from the flood, the earth
had dried beneath the sunlight's clement warmth,
she brought forth countless living forms: while some
were the old sorts that earth had now restored,
she also fashioned shapes not seen before.

And it was then that earth, against her will,
had to engender you, enormous Python,
a horrid serpent, new to all men's eyes—
a sight that terrified the reborn tribes:
your body filled up all the mountainside.

That snake was killed by Phoebus; until then
he had not used his fatal bow except
to hunt down deer and goats in flight: he smashed
that monster with innumerable shafts,
a task that left his quiver almost bare
before the Python perished in the pool
of poisoned blood that poured out of his wounds.
To keep the memory of his great feat
alive, the god established sacred games;
and after the defeated serpent's name,
they were called Pythian. Here all young men
who proved to be the best at boxing or
at running or at chariot racing wore
a wreath of oak leaves as their crown of honor.
The laurel tree did not exist as yet;
to crown his temples, graced by fair long hair,
Phoebus used wreaths of leaves from any tree.

————————

Now Daphne—daughter of the river-god,
Peneus—was the first of Phoebus' loves.
This love was not the fruit of random chance:
what fostered it was Cupid's cruel wrath.
For now, while Phoebus still was taking pride
in his defeat of Python, he caught sight

Latin [434–55]

of Cupid as he bent his bow to tie
the string at the two ends. He said: "Lewd boy,
what are you doing with that heavy bow?
My shoulders surely are more fit for it;
for I can strike wild beasts—I never miss.
I can fell enemies; just recently
I even hit—my shafts were infinite—
that swollen serpent, Python, sprawled across
whole acres with his pestilential paunch.
Be glad your torch can spark a bit of love:
don't try to vie with me for praise and wreaths!"
And Venus' son replied: "Your shafts may pierce
all things, o Phoebus, but you'll be transfixed
by mine; and even as all earthly things
can never equal any deity,
so shall your glory be no match for mine."

That said, he hurried off; he beat his wings
until he reached Parnassus' shady peak;
there, from his quiver, Cupid drew two shafts
of opposite effect: the first rejects,
the second kindles love. This last is golden,
its tip is sharp and glittering; the first
is blunt, its tip is leaden—and with this
blunt shaft the god pierced Daphne. With the tip
of gold he hit Apollo; and the arrow
pierced to the bones and marrow.

                              And at once
the god of Delos is aflame with love;
but Daphne hates its very name; she wants
deep woods and spoils of animals she hunts;
it is Diana, Phoebus' virgin sister,
whom she would emulate. Around her hair—
in disarray—she wears a simple band.
Though many suitors seek her, she spurns all;
she wants to roam uncurbed; she needs no man;
she pays no heed to marriage, love, or husbands.

Latin [455–80]

Her father often said: "You're in my debt:
a son-in-law is owed me." And he said:
"You owe me grandsons." But his daughter scorns,
as things quite criminal, the marriage torch
and matrimony; with a modest blush

on her fair face, she twines her arms around
her father's neck: "Allow me to enjoy
perpetual virginity," she pleads;
"o dear, dear father, surely you'll concede
to me the gift Diana has received
from her dear father." And in fact, Peneus
would have agreed. O Daphne, it's your beauty
that will prevent your getting that dear gift.
Your fair form contradicts your deepest wish.

Phoebus is lovestruck; having seen the girl,
he longs to wed her and, in longing, hopes;
but though he is the god of oracles,
he reads the future wrongly. Even as,
when grain is harvested, the stubble left
will burn, or as the hedges burn when chance
has led some traveler to bring his torch
too close, or to forget it on the road
when he went off at dawn, so Phoebus burns,
so is his heart aflame; with hope he feeds
a fruitless love. He looks at Daphne's hair
as, unadorned, it hangs down her fair neck,
and says: "Just think, if she should comb her locks!"
He sees her lips and never tires of them;
her fingers, hands, and wrists are unsurpassed;
her arms—more than half-bare—cannot be matched;
whatever he can't see he can imagine;
he conjures it as even more inviting.
But swifter than the lightest breeze, she flees
and does not halt—not even when he pleads:
"O, daughter of Peneus, stay! Dear Daphne,
I don't pursue you as an enemy!
Wait, nymph! You flee as would the lamb before

the wolf, the deer before the lion, or
the trembling dove before the eagle; thus
all flee from hostile things, but it is love
for which I seek you now! What misery!
I fear you'll stumble, fall, be scratched by brambles
and harm your faultless legs—and I'm to blame.
You're crossing trackless places. Slow your pace;
I pray you, stay your flight. I'll slow down, too.
But do consider who your lover is.
I'm not a mountain dweller, not a shepherd,
no scraggly guardian of flocks and herds.
Too rash, you don't know whom you're fleeing from;
in fact, that's why you run. I am the lord
of Delphi's land, and Claros, Tenedos,
and regal Patara. Jove is my father.
Through me, all is revealed: what's yet to be,
what was, and what now is. The harmony
of song and lyre is achieved through me.
My shaft is sure in flight; but then there's he
whose arrow aimed still more infallibly,
the one who wounded me when I was free
of any love within my heart. I am
the one who has invented medicine,
but now there is no herb to cure my passion;
my art, which helps all men, can't heal its master."

He'd have said more, but Daphne did not halt;
afraid, she left him there, with half-done words.
But even then, the sight of her was striking.
The wind laid bare her limbs; against the nymph
it blew; her dress was fluttering; her hair
streamed in the breeze; in flight she was more fair.

But now the young god can't waste time: he's lost
his patience; his beguiling words are done;
and so—with love as spur—he races on;
he closes in. Just as a Gallic hound
surveys the open field and sights a hare,

Latin [505–34]

and both the hunter and the hunted race
more swiftly—one to catch, one to escape
(he seems about to leap on his prey's back;
he's almost sure he's won; his muzzle now
is at her heels; the other, still in doubt—
not sure if she is caught—slips from his mouth;
at the last instant, she escapes his jaws):
such were the god and girl; while he is swift
because of hope, what urges her is fear.
But love has given wings to the pursuer;
he's faster—and his pace will not relent.
He's at her shoulders now; she feels his breath
upon the hair that streams down to her neck.
Exhausted, wayworn, pale, and terrified,
she sees Peneus' stream nearby; she cries:
"Help me, dear father; if the river-gods
have any power, then transform, dissolve
my gracious shape, the form that pleased too well!"
As soon as she is finished with her prayer,
a heavy numbness grips her limbs; thin bark
begins to gird her tender frame, her hair
is changed to leaves, her arms to boughs; her feet—
so keen to race before—are now held fast
by sluggish roots; the girl's head vanishes,
becoming a treetop. All that is left
of Daphne is her radiance.

                    And yet
Apollo loves her still; he leans against
the trunk; he feels the heart that beats beneath
the new-made bark; within his arms he clasps
the branches as if they were human limbs;
and his lips kiss the wood, but still it shrinks
from his embrace, at which he cries: "But since
you cannot be my wife, you'll be my tree.
O laurel, I shall always wear your leaves
to wreathe my hair, my lyre, and my quiver.
When Roman chieftains crown their heads with garlands

Latin [534–60]

as chants of gladness greet their victory,
you will be there. And you will also be
the faithful guardian who stands beside
the portals of Augustus' house and keeps
a close watch on the Roman crown of oak leaves.
And even as my head is ever young,
and my hair ever long, may you, unshorn,
wear your leaves, too, forever: never lose
that loveliness, o laurel, which is yours!"

Apollo's words were done. With new-made boughs
the laurel nodded; and she shook her crown,
as if her head had meant to show consent.

In Thessaly there is a deep-set valley
surrounded on all sides by wooded slopes
that tower high. They call that valley Tempe.
And the Peneus River, as it flows
down from Mount Pindus' base—waves flecked with foam—
runs through that valley. In its steep descent,
a heavy fall, the stream gives rise to clouds
and slender threads of mist—like curling smoke;
and from on high, the river sprays treetops;
its roar resounds through places near and far.
This is the home, the seat, the sanctuary
of that great stream. And here, within a cave
carved out of rock, sat Daphne's father, god
and ruler of these waters and of all
the nymphs who made their home within his waves.
And it was here that—though they were unsure
if they should compliment or comfort him—
first came the river-gods of his own region:
Enipeus, restless river; poplar-rich
Sperchios; veteran Apidanus
and gentle Aeas and Amphrysus; then
the other, distant rivers came—all those

Latin [561–81]

who, on whatever course their currents flow,
lead down their wayworn waters to the sea.

The only missing god was Inachus.
He had retreated to his deepest cave,
and as he wept, his tears increased his waves;
the disappearance of his daughter, Io,
had left him desperate. He did not know
if she was still alive or with the Shades;
he could not find her anywhere, and so
he thought that she was nowhere; in his heart
his fears foresaw things devious and dark.

Now it was Jove who had caught sight of Io;
she was returning from her father's stream,
and Jove had said: "O virgin, you indeed
would merit Jove and will make any man
you wed—whoever he may be—most glad.
But now it's time for you to seek the shade
of those deep woods" (and here he pointed toward
a nearby forest); "for the sun is high—
at its midcourse; such heat can't be defied.
And do not be afraid to find yourself
alone among the haunts of savage beasts:
within the forest depths you can be sure
of safety, for your guardian is a god—
and I am not a common deity:
for I am he who holds within his hand
the heavens' scepter: I am he who hurls
the roaming thunderbolts. So do not flee!"
But even as he spoke, she'd left behind
the pasturelands of Lerna, and the plains
around Lyrceus' peak, fields thick with trees.
Then with a veil of heavy fog, the god
concealed a vast expanse of land; Jove stopped
her flight; he raped chaste Io.

□   □   □

Latin [581–600]

Meanwhile Juno,
from heaven's height, had chanced to cast her eyes
on Argus' center; she was stupefied
to see that hovering clouds, in full daylight,
had brought about a darkness deep as night;
she knew that this could not be river mist
or fog that rises up from the damp soil.
So Saturn's daughter looked around to see
just where her Jove might be—so frequently
she'd caught him sneaking or, more flagrantly,
at play. And since he wasn't in the sky,
she said: "I am mistaken or betrayed";
and then, descending from the heavens' height,
she stood upon the ground and told the clouds
that they must now recede.

Jove had foreseen
his wife's arrival; he had changed the daughter
of Inachus: she now was a white heifer.
And even as a heifer she was lovely.
Great Juno—grudgingly—praised the cow's beauty,
then asked who was her owner, where did she
come from, what herd did she belong to—all
as if she were aware of nothing. Jove,
contriving, said the earth had given birth
to this fine heifer—hoping that would stop
his wife's barrage. And Juno asked to have
the heifer as a gift. What should he do?
It would be cruel to consign his love;
but if he kept her, he would just raise doubts.
On one side, shame keeps urging: Give her up.
Love, on the other side, insists: Do not.

Love could have overcome his shame, but if
he should refuse so slight, so poor a gift
to one who was his sister and his wife,
he'd have to run a disconcerting risk,
since Juno could conclude that, after all,

Latin [601–21]

this heifer was no cow. So, in the end,
the goddess got her rival as a present.
Yet Juno still suspected treachery;
to ward off any wiles, she now entrusted
the heifer to Arestor's son; for Argus
was gifted with a hundred eyes, and he
would sleep with only two of those eyes shut
at any time, in turn—the rest he left
awake and watchful. He was Io's guardian;
no matter where he turned, he always kept
some eyes on her; though he might turn his back,
he still had her in view. By day he let
the heifer graze; but when the sun had set,
he locked her in and tied, around her neck,
a shameful halter. She was always fed
on leaves from trees and bitter herbs, and slept
upon the ground—and it was often bare
of grass; poor Io drank from muddy streams
and, when she tried to lift her arms to plead
with Argus, found she had no arms to stretch;
and when she tried to utter some lament,
nothing but lowings issued from her lips,
a sound that she was frightened to emit—
her own voice frightened her.

                  And Io reached
the shores on which she had so often played,
the river banks of Inachus; she stared
at her strange horns reflected in the waves,
and at her muzzle; and she fled, dismayed
and terrified. Not even Inachus
and all his Naiads knew just who she was;
but she would trail her father and her sisters
and let them touch her as she sidled up
to be admired. Once, old Inachus
had plucked some grass and held it out to her:
she licked her father's hands, and tried to kiss
his palms, and then began to weep; and if

Latin [621–47]

she could have uttered words, she would have told
her name and wretched fate and begged for aid.
Instead of words, it's letters that she traced
in sand—she used her hoof: so she revealed
her transformation—all of her sad tale.
"What misery!" cried Inachus; he clasped
her horns and neck; and snow-white Io moaned.
"What misery!" he wailed. "Are you my daughter,
the one whom I have sought through all the world?
My sorrow at the loss of you was less
than in my finding you; and now there's silence;
my words receive no answer, only sighs
and lowing—these must serve as your reply.
To think that—unaware, oblivious—
I was intent on all your wedding rites,
your marriage torch, and I was hoping for
a son-in-law and then grandsons. But now
it is a bull whom you must wed; you'll bear
a bull as son. And I can't kill myself,
however deep my grief: sad fate indeed
to be a god: the gate of death is closed
against me; I am doomed to bear this sorrow
eternally."

                And while her father mourned,
Argus, the many-eyed, came up, and drove
old Inachus away; her guardian grabbed
poor Io; and to other pasturelands,
he thrust her. Then he sat upon a peak
and, from that height, kept all the fields in sight.

But now the ruler of the gods cannot
endure his Io's suffering so much;
he summons Mercury, the son that Jove
had by the shining Pleiad; he instructs
his son to murder Argus. And at once,
with his winged sandals, Mercury flies off;
within his hand, he grasps the potent wand

Latin [647–72]

that can bring sleep; his cap is on his head.
And so arrayed, the son of Jove descends—
down from his father's fortress high in heaven
to earth. He sets aside his cap, his wings;
the wand is all he keeps but makes it seem
a shepherd's crook; and then, in rural guise,
along stray paths, the son of Maia drives
some goats he'd rustled from the countryside;
and as he goes, upon the reeds he'd tied
together—rustic pipes—he plays a song.

And Argus is entranced by those strange sounds:
"Whoever you may be," he says, "sit down
beside me on this rock; no other spot
can offer richer grass to all your flock;
and there is perfect shade for shepherds here."

So Mercury joins Argus on the rock
and whiles away the time with varied talk;
he plays upon the reeds—with that he hopes
that Argus' watchful eyes will drop their guard.
But Argus tries to ward off languid sleep;
and though some of his eyes have shut, he keeps
the rest awake and watchful. And indeed,
since pipes had been invented recently,
he asks how that invention came about.

The god replied: "On the cool mountainside
of Arcady, among the woodland nymphs
whose home was in the forest of Nonacris,
one was most famous—she whom they called Syrinx.
And more than once that nymph had been pursued
but had eluded all the guile and wiles
of Satyrs and the many gods who dwell
in shaded woods or on the fertile fields.
For like Diana, goddess of Ortygia,

Latin [672–94]

she was a devotee of chastity;
and she dressed like Diana, so that one
might well have thought she was Latona's daughter—
except for this: Diana bore a bow
of gold, while Syrinx' was of cornel wood.
Despite that difference, she was often taken
to be Diana. And one day, as she
was coming back from Mount Lycaeus, Pan
caught sight of Syrinx. He—whose head was wreathed
with sharp pine needles—said . . ."

                                And much was left
to tell: how Syrinx, scorning all his pleas,
fled through the barren waste until she reached
the placid, sandy stream of Ladon: here
the river blocked her flight, and so she begged
her sister water nymphs to change her shape.
And Pan, who thought that he had caught the nymph,
did not clutch her fair body but marsh reeds;
and he began to sigh; and then the air,
vibrating in the reeds, produced a sound
most delicate, like a lament. And Pan,
enchanted by the sweetness of a sound
that none had ever heard before, cried out:
"And this is how I shall converse with you!"
He took unequal lengths of reeds, and these
Pan joined with wax: this instrument still keeps
the name Pan gave it then, the nymph's name—Syrinx.

When Mercury was just about to tell
these things, he saw that Argus' hundred eyes
had given in to sleep; they all were closed.
At once he checks his talk; and to abet
the power of sleep, with his enchanted wand
he touches lightly Argus' drowsing eyes;
and then, unhesitatingly, he strikes

Latin [695–717]

the watchman with a sword curved like a scythe;
he strikes the nodding head just where the neck
and body join; he knocks it off the rock
and sends it tumbling, bleeding, down the steep
descent, and stains the cliffside with that blood.

O Argus, you lie low; the light that glowed
in many pupils now is spent; one night
alone now holds in sway your hundred eyes.

And Juno took the hundred eyes of Argus
and set them on her sacred bird: she filled
the feathers of the peacock's tail with jewels
that glittered like the stars. And then the goddess
unleashed her rage; she struck her Grecian rival
at once: she sent a Fury to harass
poor Io's eyes and mind; she pierced her breast
with an invisible, relentless goad;
she drove the frightened girl across the world—
a fugitive.

　　　　　And nothing else was left
for way-worn Io on her endless path
but to seek refuge on your banks, o Nile.
And there she knelt and, drawing back her head,
lifted her eyes—she had no other way
to plead or pray—up to the stars, with moans
and tears and wretched lowings, as if she,
beseeching Jove, asked him to end her grief.
At that, Jove threw his arms round Juno's neck;
he begged his wife to end this punishment.
"You need not fear the future," so he pledged;
"she'll never cause you harm or grief again—"
and as his witness for the oath he'd sworn,
it was the Stygian marsh he called upon.
Now Io, with the goddess' rage appeased,
regains the form she had before: she sheds
the rough hairs on her body, and her horns

Latin [717–40]

recede; her round eyes shrink, her mouth retracts,
her arms and hands appear again; and each
of Io's hoofs is changed into five nails.
There's no trace of the heifer that is left,
except the lovely whiteness of her flesh.
Content that just two feet now meet her needs,
the nymph stands up but hesitates to speak
for fear that, like a heifer, she will low;
then, timidly, she once again employs
the power of speech she had—for so long—lost.
And now she is a celebrated goddess,
revered by crowds clothed in white linen: Isis.

Her son was Epaphus, and it's believed
that she gave birth to him from great Jove's seed;
he shares his mother's shrines in many cities.
The peer of Epaphus in temperament
and age was Phoebus' son, young Phaethon.
Once, Phaethon—so proud to have the Sun
as father—claimed that he was better born
than Epaphus, who met that claim with scorn:
"Fool, do you think that all your mother says
is true—those lying tales that swelled your head?"
And Phaethon blushed: ashamed, the boy was forced
to check his scorn; he hurried off at once
to tell Clymene of that calumny:
"And, mother, what will cause you still more pain,
is this: I, who am frank, so prone to pride,
was tongue-tied. I am mortified—ashamed
that I could be insulted in this way—
yet not rebut the charge! So, if in truth
my lineage is heavenly, provide
the proof of my high birth, and justify
my claim to have a father in the sky!"
That said, he threw his arms around her neck
and begged her, by his own life and the life

of Merops, whom she'd married now, and by
his sisters' nuptial torches, for some sign—
so certain that it could not be denied—
that he indeed was born of Phoebus' line.

Clymene—though it is not clear if she
was swayed by Phaethon's appeal or felt
more rage at the foul charge against herself—
stretched out both arms to heaven; as she turned
her eyes to the bright sun, Clymene cried:
"By all the radiance and light of one
who sees and hears us now, I swear, dear son,
that you are born of this same Sun who stands
before you as the world's great guardian.
If what I say is false, then let this be
the last time that I gaze at him, indeed
the last time that I see a new day dawn.
But you yourself can see your father's house:
the place from which he rises lies quite close
to our own land. So Phaethon, you can,
if you so wish, go there yourself and ask
the Sun directly for the proof you want."

He leaps with joy—he's heard his mother's words:
imagining the sky, his mind is stirred.
He crosses his own Ethiopia;
he passes India, the land that lies
beneath the solar fires of the sky;
and soon the boy has reached the very place
from which his father rises: Phoebus' palace.

Latin [763–79]

BOOK II

THE SOARING PALACE of the Sun, with all
its giant columns, was ablaze with gold
and bronze, as if aflame; its pediments
were crowned on high with polished ivory;
and glowing silver graced the double doors.

But even such materials could not match
the grace and power of the artist's craft.
For, on those double doors, in high relief,
Vulcan had carved the world's wide sphere, the reach
of all the seas that circle the dry land,
and, too, the skies that overhang earth's span.
The sea has blue-gray gods: shown with his horn,
Triton; and Proteus, lord of shifting forms;
and, as his many mighty arms press down
on the enormous backs of whales, Algaeon.
There Doris and her daughters are arrayed:
some Nereids swim among the waves; some stay
along the shoals and dry their damp green hair;
still others ride on fishes. And their features
are not alike, yet not unlike—as sisters
indeed should be. And on the land, one sees
men and their cities; woods, wild beasts, and streams;
and Nymphs and other rural deities.
Over these scenes, the artist carved on high
the image of the heavens bright with light:
the zodiac—with six signs on the right,
and six that stand upon the left-hand side.

The road was steep, but when the boy had reached
the palace, he went straight to face the Sun;
he wanted to dispel all doubts, to learn
if Phoebus was indeed his father, but—
while still somewhat far off—he had to halt:
the light was dazzling—he could not draw close.
There, on a throne where fiery emeralds glowed,
sat Phoebus, in his regal purple cloak;
and Day and Month and Year and Century

Latin [1–25]

stood right and left of him; spaced equally,
the Hours, too, were seen. There, flower-crowned,
stood Spring; and naked Summer, wreathed with stalks
of grain; and Autumn, stained with trodden grapes;
and glacial Winter, with his stiff white locks.

There, with his eyes that oversee all things,
the Sun, down from his towering throne, could see
his son bewildered by this strange new scene.
He said: "Dear Phaethon, what brought you here?
What are you seeking in this fortress—why
come here, o son I never shall deny?"
The boy replied: "O you, the common light
of this vast world, o Phoebus, who are my
own father—if you say I have the right
to use that word, and if it is no lie,
a false guise that Clymene used to hide
her shame—remove my doubt, give me some proof,
o Father, that I am your son in truth!"

Then Phoebus set aside the dazzling rays
that wreathed his head; he had his son draw near
and said, embracing him: "I have no cause
to say you are not mine; Clymene's words
about your birth are true. To set you free
of any doubts, ask what you will of me:
whatever gift you want, you shall receive.
And may the pool of Styx on which gods swear,
the pool my eyes have never seen, now be
the witness of my promise." Just as soon
as Phoebus' words were done, young Phaethon asked
to have his father's chariot—for one day,
to guide its wingèd horses on their way.

Three and four times the god shook his bright head;
repenting of his promise, Phoebus said:
"If you ask this, my words indeed were rash!
Oh, if I could retract what I have pledged!
Believe me, son, this is the only gift

Latin [25–52]

I wish I could refuse you. But at least
I have to try dissuasion. What you seek
is too unsafe: it never would befit
your strength, your age—your tender years. For fate
made you a mortal, but what you request
is not a mortal's task. Though you're too young

to gauge what it involves, even the gods
would never dare to face a test so hard.
Each god is free to do as he desires,
but none can guide this chariot of fire
except for me; not even he who rules
immense Olympus, he whose deadly force
hurls savage thunderbolts, can keep on course
my chariot. And who's more great than Jove?
The road starts off so steeply that my steeds
must struggle hard, though they are fresh from sleep;
midway, it runs so high across the sky,
that even I am often terrified—
my heart is rocked with terror and dismay
as I see earth and sea far, far below;
and in descent, the course needs firm control—
it plunges, sheer: then even Tethys, she
who, at my journey's end, always receives me
into her waves, is anxious lest I fall
headlong. And add to this the heavens' own
unending, wheeling round that draws along
the steep stars on its dizzying, swift course.
My path runs counter to the skies' rotation;
I am the only one who can resist
its impetus, a thrust that overcomes
all else. But just imagine your own self
in my place. Can you hope to keep on course?
Can you withstand the poles' compelling force?
Won't heaven's hurtling motion bear you off?
Perhaps you think you'll find the sacred groves
and cities of the gods along that road—
and temples rich with gifts. Instead, you'll meet
insidious snares and traps and savage beasts.

Latin [52–78]

And though you may hold firm and not mistake
your way, you'll have to face the horns of Taurus,
the bow of Sagittarius, and the jaws
of the ferocious Lion; you must cross
the Scorpion, who curves his cruel arms
to one side while, out to the other, stretch
the Crab's extended claws. You cannot check
these horses: there is fire in their chests—
it fuels their mouths' and nostrils' blazing breath!
It's hard enough for me to rule those steeds
when their ferocious spirits feel such heat:
their necks rebel against the reins. My son,
be careful lest the gift you'd have me grant
prove fatal: while there still is time, relent—
don't ask for such a task. The surest proof
that I'm your father is my fear for you.
Look at my face! And would you could inspect
my heart and learn what cares a father bears!
And, finally, look round you carefully:
what wealth the world arrays! What wonders grace
the sky and earth and sea; you need but choose
whatever you may want—and it is yours!
I won't refuse you anything! But this—
and this alone—don't ask of me: a gift
that will not gain you fame, but suffering.
My son, what you now seek is not a blessing,
but punishment. Why do you throw your arms
around my neck and coax me—senselessly?
Don't doubt it: you'll have anything you wish
(I've sworn it on the waters of the Styx).
But I implore you: make a wiser choice!"

His warning now is done. But Phaethon
resists his father's plea: the boy insists;
he longs to guide the chariot. And Phoebus,
who stalled the boy as long as possible,
must grant what had been asked; he leads his son
to the high chariot—the gift of Vulcan.

Latin [79–106]

The axle was of gold, of gold the pole;
the wheels had rims of gold, and silver spokes
stretched from the hubs. Arrayed along the yoke,
topaz and gems, reflecting Phoebus, glowed.

And while—amazed—audacious Phaethon
gazed at this splendid handiwork, alert
Aurora, as the east shone, opened wide
her purple gates, her halls rich with rose light.
The stars retreat; their ranks are driven off
by Lucifer, who is the last to leave
his station in the sky.

               When Phoebus saw
that Lucifer was gone, that all the world
was tinged with red, and that the moon's slim horns
had faded, he commanded the swift Hours
to yoke his steeds. And they were quick to bring
the fire-breathing team from the high stalls:
those stallions—fed upon ambrosial nectar—
had clanking bits and bridles. Phoebus then
anointed his son's face with sacred ointment,
that it might stand the heat's ferocity;
upon his head he set the flaming rays;
and, sighing anxiously again, again—
foreseeing a calamity—he said:

"Dear boy, although I know you won't turn back,
at least heed this advice. Avoid the lash;
just hold the reins hard fast. These horses need
no urging on to speed: your only task
will be to hold in check their racing feet.
And do not try to ride straight through the sky's
five zones: there is a curving, slanting road
that stays inside the limits of three zones—
a course that does not cross the southern pole
and not the northernmost. That is your path:
you cannot miss the tracks my wheels have left.

Latin [107–33]

And so that earth and heaven may receive
in just and equal measure their due heat,
don't ride too high, and do not sink too low:
too high—and heaven's halls will burn; descend
too low—and earth will meet its flaming end.

And do not let your wheels veer too far right:
avoid the writhing Serpent on that side,
just as, upon the left, you are to shun
the stars that form the Altar. Keep your run
along a course between those constellations.
I leave the rest to Fortune: may she help
and guide you better than you do yourself.
Now, even as I speak, damp Night has reached
her goal upon the farthest western shore.
We can't delay; our call has come; bright Dawn
has put to flight the shadows—they are gone.
Hold fast the reins; but if you still can change
your mind, forget my chariot—accept
the counsel that I gave you, while there's time
and you're on solid ground, and not yet launched
in ignorance—a dilettante—upon
the course you've chosen—your unhappy lot.
Let me bring light unto the world, the light
that you can see in safety—from the earth!"

Too late: with his young body, Phaethon
has leaped into the chariot: he takes
his place with pride. Rejoicing, he holds fast
the reins—and thanks his hesitating father.

Meanwhile the four winged horses of the Sun,
Eous, Aethon, Pyrois, and Phlegon,
neighing, fill the air with flames: their hooves
are pawing now; they pound the exit gate.
As soon as Thetis—knowing not what fate
awaits her grandson—has unbarred the way,
now free to cross the sky's immensity,
the horses sprint ahead; and through the air,

Latin [134–58]

they drive their hooves; they cleave the clouds; they lift
themselves upon their wings; they pass beyond
the winds of Eurus—east winds that are born
in that same sky-zone where the chariot starts.
But now the weight those horses bear is light;
the pressure of the yoke is far more slight
than they are used to. Lacking proper ballast,
ships roll and rock among the waves—unbalanced:
so did that chariot leap through the air,
tossing on high, as if it had no rider.
The team can sense the difference: those four—
berserk—desert their customary course:
no rule, no order governs their wild rush.
The boy is terrified: he does not know
how to apply the reins he took on trust;
he does not know what is the charted road—
and even if he knew, he's lost control.

Then, for the first time ever, the Sun's rays
inflamed the northern Bears, who tried—in vain—
to plunge into the sea's forbidden waves.
The Serpent, too, was driven wild: he lies
close to the icy pole: and numbing cold
had always kept him lazy, lumpish, slow,
until that blazing heat stirred his strange frenzy.
You, too, Bootes—so the tale is told—
however sluggish, struck by terror, fled—
though slowed down by the oxcart that you drag.

Sad Phaethon looked down from heaven's heights
at earth, which lay so far, so far below.
He paled; his knees were seized by sudden fright;
and there, within the overwhelming light,
a veil of darkness fell upon his eyes.
Would he had never touched his father's steeds!—
so he repents. Would he had not received
proof of his origins, would that his plea
had been refused. If only he had been

a son of Merops! Like a ship that's tossed
and battered by the blasts of Boreas—
a ship whose captain has renounced the helm
and now depends upon the gods and prayers—
such was the chariot of Phaethon.

What's to be done? Behind his back lies much
of his sky-track, but more still lies ahead.

His mind is measuring both distances.
Westward, he sees the goal his fate forbids;
behind, there lies the east. He can't decide
his course; he's numb with fear; he does not grip
the reins hard fast nor let them dangle, slack;
he does not even know the horses' names.
And more, across the speckled skies, he sees
things strange, the monstrous figures of fierce beasts:
the boy is terrified.

There is a point
just where the Scorpion's curving pincers form
a pair of bows: his tail and arms stretch out
to either side—the space they occupy
is wide enough to span two constellations.
And when the boy beholds the Scorpion
steeped in black venom, threatening to strike
with his hooked point, he's stunned; frozen with fright,
he loses grip; the reins fall slack; they slide
and graze the horses' backs; those four feel that;
they dash, off course—their way depends on chance—
through unknown regions of the air; unchecked,
they follow random impulse; they collide
with stars embedded in the sky; they drag
the reeling chariot on pathless tracts.
Now they rush upward; now they hurtle down,
approaching earth. The Moon is thunderstruck—
she sees the stallions of her brother course
below her own. The clouds are scorched: they smoke.
Earth's highest parts catch fire first: the soil
is drained of moisture; parched, it cracks; the fields

Latin [184–212]

are blanched; the trees are ravaged, stripped of green;
and, serving to efface itself, ripe grain
provides the fuel that abets the blaze.

Yet these were but small griefs. For greater still
was the destruction of huge towns and walls,
whole regions and their peoples. Woods and peaks
catch flame: Mount Athos, Taurus in Cilicia,
and Oete, Tmolus, and parched Ida (once
so rich with springs); and Helicon, the slopes
on which the virgin Muses had their home;
and Haemus, in those days not yet beneath
the sway of Orpheus. Etna now is one
vast pyre, with fire added to its flames;
both of Parnassus' summits are ablaze,
and Eryx, Cynthus, Othrys, Rhodope
(at last, no longer snow-capped), Dindymus,
and Mimas, Mycale, and—famous for
the sacred worship on its heights—Cithaeron.
And Scythia is not reprieved despite
its frigid climate; and the Caucasus
is now aflame, as Ossa is, and Pindus,
and that peak higher than them both—Olympus;
the towering Alps and cloud-crowned Apennines.

The boy can see earth blaze upon all sides;
he cannot bear the torrid air he breathes,
much like the fiery gusts from some deep furnace;
his feet can feel his chariot's white heat.
The ashes and the swirling sparks are fierce;
thick smoke has shrouded him; as black as pitch,
the darkness hems him in; he does not know
where he is heading, where he is; his team
of horses sweep him on—just as they please.

The Ethiopians—so it is said—
became black then as blood rushed to their skins;
and it was then that Libya became

a desert, all her moisture dried; then, too,
the nymphs, their hair disheveled, mourned the loss
of springs and lakes—Boeotia cannot find
the fount of Dirce; Argos, Amymone;
and Corinth seeks in vain Pirene's waves.
Nor are the streams with ample channels, those
whom fate had given shores set far apart,
exempt: even the center of the Don
is steaming now; and so is old Peneus;
in Teuthras' land, Caicus; and the swift
Ismenus; and the Xanthus, destined now
to burn a second time; tawny Lycormas;
Meander, winding playfully along
its curving course; the Mela in Mygdonia;
and Taenarus' Eurotas. Babylonian
Euphrates also blazes, and Orontes,
Thermodon, Ganges, Phasis, and the Danube.
Alpheus boils; Sperchios' banks are scorched:
the golden sands borne by the Tagus' course
have melted; and the singing swans that throng
the Lydian waters suffocate upon
Cayster's waves. The Nile flees, terrified,
out to edges of the earth; it hides
its head—and it is hidden yet; and all
its seven mouths are parched and clogged with dust;
its seven riverbeds are stripped of waves.
The Hebrus and the Strymon share that fate,
as do the Rhine, the Rhone, the Po, as well
as Tiber, who is meant to rule the world.

At every point the soil has gaping cracks;
light penetrates the world below; it strikes
with fear Avernus' ruler and his wife.
The sea shrinks; where, just now, the tracts of waves
spread wide, the dry sands spread; and peaks that once
were covered by the sea, jut here and there—
new islands in the scattered Cyclades.
The fish retreat into the deepest seas,

Latin [237–65]

and arching dolphins can no longer dare
to leap—as usual—into the air.
The corpses of sea-calves float on their backs.
They say that Nereus, Doris, and their daughters
sought refuge in their caves; but even these
were far too hot to bear. And Neptune tried—
three times—to lift his fierce face and his arms
above the waves; and he—three times—could not
endure the blazing air. And mother Earth,
around whom all the waters crowded close
(the waters of the sea and the parched springs
that on all sides were seeking some asylum
within her darkest innards), raised her face—
scorched to the neck—and, wearily, at last
lifted her hand up to her brow and shuddered,
shaking all things; and when she'd settled back
(a little lower than she'd been before),
her words were stifled as she begged: "Great lord
of all the gods, if I indeed deserve
this fate, and it's decreed, do not delay
your thunderbolts! If I am meant to face
a death by fire, let it be your flames
that strike me down—for that would mitigate
my ruin. Even speech is hard for me—
just opening my lips" (a gust of smoke
had almost choked her). "See, my hair is singed:
how many ashes blur my eyes, my face!
Is this how you repay me—the reward
for my fertility, my patient work?
It's I who bear the harrow and hooked plow;
yearlong, I get no rest; I furnish leaves
to feed the beasts and harvests for mankind,
their peaceful food; and I, for you, provide
incense. But even if I've earned this end,
what suffering have the waters merited?
What has your brother Neptune done? Why has
the sea, the realm that fell to him by lot,
shrunk so, retreating farther from the sky?

Latin [265–92]

And if your brother's plight and mine do not
move you, then pity your own heaven's fate.
Look here, look there: smoke runs from pole to pole!
If they should fall, your halls will also topple!
You see how even Atlas has to struggle:
he bears the white-hot axis on his shoulders—
but he is close to giving up. If all
three realms are ruined—sea and land and sky—
then we shall be confounded in old Chaos.
Save from the flames what's left, if anything
can still be saved. Think of the universe!"

Here Earth fell silent—and, in any case,
she could no longer stand the savage flames,
nor utter other words. And she withdrew
into herself—into her deepest caves,
recesses closest to the land of Shades.

Then the Almighty Father, calling on
the gods as witnesses (and, above all,
on Phoebus, who had lent that chariot),
declares that if he does not intervene,
all things will face a dread catastrophe.
He climbs to heaven's highest point, the place
from which he sends his cloud banks down to earth,
from which he moves his thunder and deploys
his bolts of lightning. But he does not bring
his clouds, his downpours: thunder serves his cause;
and after balancing a lightning bolt
in his right hand, from his ear's height he throws
that shaft at Phaethon; and it hurls him out
of both his chariot and his life; the god
quells fire with savage fire! Maddened now,
the horses, rearing back, tug free their necks.
Unyoked, they crack their gear and race away.
Here, bits and bridles fall, and there the axle
is torn free from the pole; elsewhere, the wheels

. . .

and spokes are scattered—far across the sky,
the battered remnants of that chariot fly.

And as the flames devour his ruddy hair,
young Phaethon plummets down; he pivots round
his burning body, trailing in the air
the sort of track that one can sometimes see
when—through clear skies—a star will seem to fall
but then, in fact, does not. And he lands far
from his own country; in another part
of the earth's span, the waves of the great Po
now bathe the boy's scorched face. There, in the west,
the Naiads bury Phaethon's body, burned;
upon his stone they carve these lines of verse:

> HERE PHAETHON LIES:
> HIS DARING DROVE THE BOY TO DRIVE
> HIS FATHER'S CHARIOT: HE TRIED
> AND FAILED. BUT IN HIS FALL HE GAINED
> THE DEATH OF ONE SUPREMELY BRAVE.

Meanwhile his father, Phoebus, in despair,
hid his own face; the world, for one full day—
if we believe what ancient stories say—
was left without a single ray of sun.
The only light came from the conflagration:
that way, at least, the fires served some need.
But Clymene, once she had spoken all
that can be said when such disaster falls,
went wild; she tore her robes; across the world
she wandered, searching for his lifeless body
at first, and then his bones; and these she found
at last along the foreign riverbank
where they'd been buried. Clymene lay prone
upon that grave; her warm tears bathed the stone
on which she read his name; beside the Po,
with her bared breasts, she warmed his sepulcher.

□   □   □

Latin [317–39]

And joining Clymene in her lament,
her daughters, the Heliades, now wept
sad tears (the useless gift one gives the dead).
They beat their breasts; stretched out upon his tomb,
by night, by day, they called upon him—though
their brother could not hear their words of sorrow.

Four times the moon had linked its crescent's tips,
and still, as they had done before, the sisters
(for repetition made lament a habit)
were mourning, when the eldest, Phaethusa,
who wanted to lie prone along the ground,
complained: she said her feet were growing stiff.
And when the fair Lampetia tried to help
her sister, she—Lampetia herself—
was fastened by the force of sudden roots.
And a third sister, even as she tore—
despairing—at her hair, clutched nothing more
than leaves. Another cried that shoots had shackled
her shins; another, that her arms were now
slim boughs. And while the sisters wonder, bark
enfolds their groins and, step by step, their bellies,
their breasts, their shoulders, then their hands; and all
that's left uncovered are their mouths that call
upon their mother.

What is she to do?
She's driven here and there, as panic strikes,
bestowing kisses while there still is time.
But that is not enough: and so, she tries
to wrench her daughters' bodies from the trunks,
and with her hands she breaks the tender boughs.
But just as Clymene does this, as if
she had inflicted a live wound, blood drips.
"No, no, I pray you, mother!" so each cries,
hurting, "I pray you, save me! When you rip

Latin [340–62]

this tree, it is my body that you tear.
Farewell . . ." At these last words, the bark closed up.
And from these new-made boughs, the tears that drip
are amber: it will harden in the sun.
The stream's clear waters bear that amber off,
and it will then adorn young wives in Rome.

Cycnus, the son of Sthenelus, had witnessed
this strange change. He was kin to Phaethon
but, even more, was linked by deep affection.
He put aside his kingship—he, in fact,
was ruler of the tribes and mighty towns
of all Liguria. He went to weep
along the Po's green banks, where now the three
sisters of Phaethon were new-made trees.
But as he wept, his voice grew faint, his hair
was hid beneath white plumage, and his neck
grew longer, stretching outward from his chest.
A membrane knit together reddened fingers;
wings wrapped around his sides; a pointed beak
replaced his mouth. For Cycnus had become
a swan—a strange new bird, who does not trust
his wings to seek the sky of Jove, as if
that bird recalled the cruel lightning bolt
the god had hurled. And so the swan seeks out
still pools and broad lakes; hating all that's fiery,
he chooses water—fire's contrary.

And meanwhile, Phaethon's father, in despair,
without his radiance (as he appears
when he is in eclipse), detests the day
and light and his own rays: the god gives way
to sorrow—and to sorrow, he adds rage.
He will not serve the world: "In every age,

Latin [362–85]

from first to last, I've had no rest! Enough!
I'm weary of my endless rounds," he says,
"my unrewarded toil. Let someone else
now guide the chariot that bears the light!
If none will do that, and the gods confess
they can't, let Jove himself take on that task!
And when he plies my reins, at least for once
he'll have to set aside the thunderbolts
he uses to strip others of their sons.
Then he will learn firsthand what savage force
is in those fire-footed steeds: he will
admit that he who could not guide them well
did not deserve to die." So said the Sun.

And all the gods crowd round him: suppliant,
they pray that he may yet relent, not let
the world be plunged into the dark. And Jove
offers excuses for the bolt he cast,
although—such is the way of kings—he adds
threats to his pleas.

        The Sun then yokes his team—
they still are terrified, still wild. He grieves
and goads; he plies the lash ferociously
as he denounces them—he feels those steeds
are guilty in the death of his dear son.

————————

But the Almighty Father now inspects
his heaven: he goes round the battlements
to see if any sector has by chance
been weakened by the fire's violence.
And when he sees that they have all held fast
and kept the strength they had in ages past,
he goes to see the earth—how human tasks
and matters are proceeding. He attends,
above all, to Arcadia, the land

Latin [385–405]

most dear to him. There he restores the flow
of springs and rivers: they resume their course.
He gives the soil its grass again; the trees,
their leaves; the injured forests now grow green
at his command.

        And as Jove came and went,
renewing that dear land, he saw a nymph,
a virgin of Arcadia, Callisto;
at once a flame erupted in his bones.
She was not one of those whose days were spent
in carding softened wool, nor was she bent
on elegant new ways to dress her hair.
Her robe was fastened by a simple clasp;
a plain white headband held her flowing hair.
When she held fast a bow or slender lance,
she seemed Diana's warrior—in fact,
no nymph who roamed the slopes of Maenalus
was dearer to the goddess than Callisto.
But favor shown today can fade tomorrow.

The sun was high—it had just passed mid-course—
when the young nymph sought shade within a forest
whose ancient trees no ax had ever touched.
Callisto slid her quiver off her shoulder,
unstrung her bow, and stretched out on the grass;
she used the painted quiver as her pillow.

No sooner had he seen the weary girl—
alone, defenseless—than Jove told himself:
"This turn is one my wife won't learn about!
But even if she were to hear of it,
this prize, in truth, is worth a fit or two
of Juno's anger!" And Jove then assumed
the aspect of Diana and her clothes.
He said: "O virgin, dearest friend, what slopes
have you been hunting on?" The girl leaped up
from her green resting-place as she replied:

Latin [406–28]

"Welcome, o goddess, you whom—even if
Jove's self should hear me—I prize over him!"
He smiled, quite pleased to hear himself preferred
to his own self; and then he kissed the nymph
in fervent fashion—not as virgin's lips
are usually kissed. And even as
the girl was just about to tell him where
she had been hunting, he—quite carnally—
broke in, embracing her; and in that act
the god revealed himself. Yes, she fought hard—
as much as any woman can when caught
(o Juno, had you seen Callisto then
you'd think of her in kinder terms): she fought,
but what girl—who, in fact, of any sort?—
could ever break the grip of the great Jove!

A victor, Jove returns to heaven. She
now loathes that forest, hates the grove of trees
that witnessed her disgrace, that infamy;
she almost leaves behind—in her retreat—
her quiver with its arrows, and the bow
she'd propped against a bough.

                                    Just then, Diana,
together with her followers, comes down
the slopes of Maenalus; and she is proud
of all the game they've caught. Diana sees
Callisto; she calls out. At first the nymph
runs off, afraid that this might be great Jove
returning in disguise. But when she sees
that other nymphs are coming forward, she
takes heart; she knows this is not trickery
and joins her friends. But it is hard indeed
to show one's face without appearing guilty!
She scarcely lifts her eyes; she does not stand
beside the goddess, as she always did,
nor does she take her place as the chief nymph;
she now is silent, but her blushes speak.

Latin [428–50]

And if Diana had not been a virgin,
there were a thousand signs she could have read;
the nymphs had sensed the truth—or so it's said.

Since then, nine months had gone by—to the day.
Diana had been hunting; but the rays
shed by the Sun, her glowing brother, made
the goddess weary, and she sought the shade
of cool woods watered by a murmuring brook
that flowed across a sandy bed. The place
delighted her. Diana dipped her toes
into the stream—and that, too, pleased her so.
She said: "No one can see us! Shed your clothes!
Let's bathe!"

       Callisto blushed. They all disrobed—
she was the only one who would delay.
And since she hesitates, the other nymphs
snatch off her robe—she's naked now, her shame
is plain to see. "Be off!"—the goddess cries—
"Do not defile this sacred spring!" With that
the girl is banished from Diana's band.

Though Juno had long since sensed all of this,
the goddess held off her harsh punishment
until the time was ripe. Now it had come;
there was no reason to delay: in sum,
her rival, adding wound to wound, had borne
a boy, Arcas. As soon as Juno turned
her eyes and angry mind to this, she cried:
"As if I had not had enough, this, too,
was needed: you, adulteress, bore this fruit—
a son; the wrong you've done me now is known
to all—the living proof of how my Jove
behaved! But, shameless, you shall pay; I'll take
from you the shape that gives both you and, too,
my husband such delight."

▢   ▢   ▢

Latin [451–75]

So Juno said,
and then she caught Callisto by the hair
in front and pulled her, face down, to the ground.
The girl stretched out her arms, imploring pity:
but those same arms began to sprout rough, shaggy
black hairs; her hands began to curve and lengthen
into hooked claws—they now were feet; the face
that Jove had so admired now was changed
to lumpish jaws; that she might not implore,
the gift of speech was taken from her: hoarse,
her throat could only utter angry growls—
a frightening sound. And yet, though now a bear,
she still retains the mind she had before,
and shows her suffering with endless moans:
she lifts her hands, though they are hands no more—
up to the sky and stars; she means to say—
though without speech—that Jove had not kept faith.
How often, too afraid to lie at rest
on lonely forest slopes, Callisto roams
outside the home and through the fields that once
were hers! How often is she chased along
the rocks by barking dogs, for she who was
a hunter has become the hunted one—
a frightened fugitive. When beasts draw near,
she hides, forgetting how she now appears;
although she is a she-bear, she still fears
the sight of bears along the mountain slopes
and shudders when the wolves approach, although
Lycaon, her own father, is a wolf.

———

Time passed: the grandson of Lycaon, Arcas,
who had no knowledge of his mother's fate,
was close to sixteen. He was hunting game,
seeking the likeliest of lairs, and stretching
tight nets around the woods of Erymanthus,
when suddenly he chanced upon his mother.

Latin [476–500]

She froze, surprised; she seemed to recognize
her son. And Arcas drew back, terrified:
her fixed eyes stared and stared—he did not know
just who that she-bear was; when she gave signs
of drawing closer, Arcas poised to pierce
her chest with his death-dealing shaft, but Jove,
all-powerful, stayed Arcas' hand: he checked
that horrid crime; he snatched the two of them
and, with a swift wind, swept them up to heaven
and set them in the sky, a close-set pair
of constellations: Great and Little Bear.

But Juno, when she saw her rival shine
among the stars, was furious: she went
down to the sea, to visit white-haired Tethys
and ancient Ocean, whom the gods revere.
When they asked Juno what had brought her there,
she answered: "If you wish to know why I,
the queen of gods, have left the sky and come
down to the waves, this is the reason why:
another has usurped my place on high!
And you can say I'm feeding you some lie
if, when the world is darkened by black night,
you do not see two stars—those two have just
been honored by the highest place above
(to torment me): the point they occupy
is where the farthest, shortest circle rings
the axis' highest point. What happens now?
What fear can I inspire if I bring
such benefits to my worst enemies?
What power can I summon if I seek
revenge and those whom I would punish end
as did that nymph—who now is made a goddess!
My Jove may even go as far as this:
to take away that bestial face, restore
the form she had before (he did just that
for Io)! And, in fact, why doesn't he
drive Juno off and give that girl my bed?

Latin [500–526]

So easily arranged—and he'd be glad
to have Lycaon as a father-in-law!
But you who've nurtured me, if you are touched—
hurt by the way in which I have been scorned—
do not allow the Bear—that constellation
which gained the heavens through adultery—
ever to set into your blue-green sea;
prevent that slut from tainting your pure stream."

The sea-gods granted her entreaty. Juno,
mounting her agile chariot, reached the sky
once more, drawn by her bright peacocks, adorned
so recently with the slain Argus' eyes.
And when those peacocks changed array, then, too,
the raven, that loquacious bird, changed hue—
most suddenly—from white to black. His plumage
was once as silvery-white as any dove's;
indeed his feathers' color could have matched
the color of the geese whose loud alert
would later serve to save the Capitol;
it even matched the river-loving swans'.
The raven, Phoebus' sacred bird, was changed
because his tongue was far too talkative:
once white, that bird is now white's opposite.

In all of Thessaly there was no girl
more lovely than Coronis of Larissa.
O god of Delphi, you loved her as long
as she was chaste or, better, hid her sins.
But Phoebus' bird, discovering what she'd hid—
her infidelity—sped off at once,
an unrelenting spy, to tell his lord.
The crow, who loves to gossip, flapped his wings
and, following the raven, was most keen

Latin [526–48]

to hear it all, to learn why he was flying
to Phoebus; when the raven told his tale,
the crow enjoined him:

     "Do not scorn my warning:
I tell you there's no profit in this journey.
Consider what I used to be—and see
what I am now: it was fidelity
that ruined me. Just listen to my story.

"Once, long ago, a child was born without
a mother: he was Erichthonius
(born from the soil where Vulcan's seed had fallen,
brushed off Minerva's leg when she had foiled
the god in his attempt to ravish her).
Minerva hid him in a basket woven
of reeds from Attica; and she entrusted
this basket to the biform Cecrops' daughters
but, in consigning it, gave this strict order:
those three girls never were to look inside it.
Now I was hidden, perched on the thin boughs
of which so many grew on a high elm;
I spied on them, to see what they would do.
Two, Pandrosos and Herse, did not breach
the goddess' order; but the third, Aglauros,
rebuked her sisters, saying they were cowards;
and she undid the knots. Within the basket,
they found a baby boy and, too, a serpent
stretched out beside him! And I told the goddess
what I had seen. What was my recompense?
I was degraded by Minerva: she
no longer favored me as her attendant;
the rank I had was given to the night-owl!
My fate should serve as warning for all birds:
do not court trouble; curb your tongue, your talk.

"And, if you think the tale I told is false—
and say Minerva never sought me out

as her attendant, and I forced myself
upon her—why then, go and ask the goddess.
Minerva now may be displeased with me,
but she'll admit I was her favorite,
the one whom she herself had chosen. This
is how that came to be: a well-known story.

60

"My father was a king, the famed Coroneus
of Phocis; and I was a lovely princess
with many suitors (do not laugh at this!).
My beauty was my ruin. For, in fact,
while I was walking on the shoreline sands,
as I still do, the sea-god saw me and
grew hot with love; his pleas and honeyed words
were useless; he made ready to use force.
He chased me; as I ran, I left behind
the hard-packed sands and staggered wearily
along the soft and yielding shore—in vain;
then I invoked both gods and men. My voice
could reach no mortal. But, a virgin, I
did stir the virgin goddess with my plea.
And as I stretched my arms out toward the sky,
they started to grow darker, sprouting feathers.
I tried to free my shoulder, flinging off
my robe; but it, too, had become a cloak
of feathers, rooted deeply in my skin.
I tried to beat my bared breast with my hands:
but I, by now, had neither hands nor breast.
I ran, but now my feet no longer sank
into the sands; I skimmed along the ground,
then I flew off, on high, into the sky:
there I was taken by Minerva as
her stainless, blameless comrade.

                              "But by now
to what does all my serving her amount?
I am supplanted by Nyctimene,
one who became an owl because of her

Latin [567–90]

outrageous sin. Have you not heard men speak
of what is known to all of Lesbos—how
Nyctimene defiled her father's bed?
And as a bird, yet conscious of her crime,
she flees men's eyes and flees the light: she hides
for shame among the shadows; she has been
cast out by all and exiled from the sky."

So said the crow, and yet the raven cried:
"And may her fate be yours, too; I despise
your warnings, all your empty prophecies."
That said, he flew ahead, and found Apollo,
and told him of Coronis: just how she
had lain beside a youth in Thessaly.
And when the god heard of that treachery,
his laurel wreath fell off his head; his face,
his lyre's quill, and his complexion changed;
his heart was swollen, hot with wrath; he readied
the weapons that he always kept at hand:
he tied the cord at both ends to his bow,
which he drew taut, and then let fly a shaft
that pierced Coronis' breast, the breast he'd pressed
so often and so tightly to his chest—
a flawless shot that no one could deflect.
The girl was struck; she groaned; and as she drew
the arrow out, a jet of red blood bathed
her fair white limbs. Coronis said: "Before
I paid with death, I could have given birth.
Instead we two must die as one." Her life
and blood streamed out; her body, stripped of soul,
was soon invaded by a lethal cold.

Apollo does repent—but it's too late:
A lover, he now hates his harsh revenge;
he curses his own self for having let
his anger lash; he hates the bird who forced
upon him knowledge of the crime that brought
. . .

such grief; he hates his bow, he hates his hand,
and, with that hand, he hates his hasty shafts.
He tries to warm Coronis' lifeless body;
he turns in vain to useless remedies,
the arts of medicine—as if he could

inflict defeat on death. No thing could help;
and when Apollo saw that they were set
to light the pyre, to let the final fire
consume Coronis' flesh, from his heart's depth
the lover moaned (but did not weep, for tears
must never bathe the faces of the gods);
he moaned as does the cow who sees the hammer,
lifted as high as the right ear, crash down,
resounding as it pounds the hollow temples
of her own suckling calf.

        Yet when Apollo
had poured perfumes on his beloved's breast—
with no hope that she might delight in them—
and had performed the offices that she,
however guilty, did deserve in death,
he could not bear the thought of his own seed—
his son—reduced to ashes in the pyre.
So, from Coronis' womb, Apollo snatched
the unborn child and carried him away
to biform Chiron's cave. As for the raven,
who hoped he would receive some recompense
for having told the god the truth, Apollo
expelled him from the ranks of the white birds.

————————

Meanwhile the centaur Chiron swelled with pride:
he now was foster-father of a child
of godly stock: and he was glad to face
the task of raising Aesculapius—
a task but, too, an honor.

▫ ▫ ▫

Latin [615–34]

     Now the daughter
of Chiron comes; her reddish hair falls thick—
a mantle—on her shoulders. She was born
to Chiron by the nymph Chariclo on
the banks of a swift river, and her mother
had called the child Ocyrhoe (the Greek
for "rapid flow"). The girl was quick and apt:
she'd learned her father's art; but not content
with that, she also learned prophetic chants.
And when she saw her father's ward, her soul
was seized by vatic frenzy; there—enclosed
within her breast—a godly fire glowed.
She cried:

     "O child, grow strong! You are to be
the healer of the world: how often shall
your skills save mortal bodies' life and health!
And you shall have the right to resurrect
the dead, a gift that Jove will then resent;
and when you've done this once (though he's your own
grandfather), he will hurl his thunderbolt
to thwart your doing it again; and you,
a god, shall then become a bloodless corpse;
but from a corpse you shall be changed once more
into a god: the fate you've known before
is to repeat itself.

     "You, too, dear father,
fated from birth to live eternally,
shall one day long to die; for you shall be
tormented by a dreadful serpent's venom
that, through a wound, will spread throughout your body—
an endless agony—till, mercifully,
the gods free you from immortality;
and death can take you. The three Fates will splice
the thread of what was once your endless life."

▫ ▫ ▫

Latin [635–54]

But there was more she had to prophesy.
And from her deepest heart Ocyrhoe sighed,
and tears ran down her cheeks; she said: "The Fates
have checked my speech. I am allowed to say
no more; they will not let me use my voice.
What good was there in having learned this art,
if now it only draws the wrath of gods
against me? Would I not be better off
without the power to predict the course
of days to come? I can already sense
that they are stripping all my human semblance;
I am already pleased to feed on grass;
and I already feel the urge to dash
across wide fields: a mare—that is the form
I now am taking on, a body like
my father's! Must I change in full? And—why?
My father's form is only half equine!"

The last part of her speech was scumbled, blurred,
and soon one lost all sense that there were words
at all: her voice did not yet seem a mare's—
more like the voice of one who mimes a mare.
But soon her whinnying came clear and true;
along the ground her arms began to move
like legs; her fingers fused, and her five nails
were wrapped in horn: her hands were now light hooves.
Her hair, which had hung loose across her shoulders,
now, on her right, became a flowing mane.
Her voice, her image—both had suffered change;
and, too—as Hippe—she gained a new name.

————————

And Chiron, son of Philyra, shed tears;
o Phoebus, he called out to you in vain:
you could not stay the mighty Jove's decree;
and even if you could, you were away,
still mourning for Coronis as you roamed

through Elis and Messenia. In those days
you wore a sheepskin cloak; and shepherdlike,
your left hand held a rustic staff; your right,
a pipe whose seven reeds were all unequal.

And while you mourned the love you'd lost, you sought
sweet consolation from your tender pipes;
they say that your untended herd went off—
your cattle strayed into the fields of Pylos.
And there the son of Maia, Mercury,
caught sight of Phoebus' cows and, craftily,
drove them into a wooded hiding place.

No one had seen this theft except for one
old man whom all his neighbors knew as Battus,
the guardian of rich Neleus' grazing lands
and groves and splendid herd of prized broodmares.
Afraid of Battus' chatter, Mercury
drew him aside and said—persuasively:
'Now, my fine friend—whoever you may be—
if anyone, by chance, should come to seek
his herd, just say that you have never seen
these cows; and you can count on this reward:
just pick the sleekest cow—and she is yours."
And Battus got—at once—the cow he chose,
and said: "My friend, be sure—your herd is safe.
That stone which you see there will sooner tell
about your theft than faithful Battus will."

The son of Jove then made as if to leave;
but he came back soon after—though transformed
in voice and guise. "O farmer, have you seen
some cattle pass this way?" he asked; "I need
your help; don't hide the facts, for all that herd
was stolen from me. Come now, if you tell
the truth, you'll get a cow and her fine bull."
And tempted by that doubled recompense,
the old man answered: "You will find them there—

below these mountains." Mercury laughed loud
and said: "Would you betray me to myself?
You rascal, to my face, have broken faith!"
And then the god transformed the faithless chest
of Battus to hard stone. Down to today
they call that rock a touch (or telltale) stone,
although the stone itself had been no spy.

Then Mercury, who bears the magic wand,
flew off on level wings. And from on high,
in flight, he saw the land Minerva loves:
Athenian fields and the Lyceum's grove.
That chanced to be the very day on which
chaste virgins celebrate Minerva's feast:
upon their hands, in baskets flower-ringed,
they bear their pure and holy offerings
up to Minerva's hill, her sanctuary.
And even as the winged god saw below
the young Athenian girls returning home,
he did not fly ahead but circled them.

Just as the swift kite-hawk, on catching sight
of innards when a bull is sacrificed,
will wait and hover just as long as, round
the altar, he can see the faithful crowd;
not daring to swoop low, he yet stays close
on high: he tips his wings and wheels above
his prey—he's greedy; he is full of hope:
just so the swift god of Cyllene wheeled
in steady rings around the sacred hill.

And just as Lucifer is brighter than
the other stars, and as the golden moon
in turn is far more bright than Lucifer,
so did fair Herse, gem of the procession,
outshine the other girls, all her companions.   □   □   □

Latin [703–25]

Her beauty had amazed the son of Jove;
as Mercury hung in the sky, fierce love
swept through him with a force that matched the heat
of lead shot from a Balearic sling:
a missile flying through the air that grows
more incandescent as it soars below
the clouds and finds a fire it had not known.
He changes course; he leaves the sky and falls
to earth; nor does the god disguise himself:
he is quite sure his form will win the girl.
He has good reason to be confident,
yet he attends to these refined details:
he smooths his hair; and he adjusts his cloak
so that its folds fall gracefully and show
its golden border; and he takes much care
to see that, in his hand, he holds the wand
that can enchant with sleep or drive it off;
on his sleek feet his winged sandals glow.

King Cecrop's palace had three inmost rooms,
adorned with ivory and tortoiseshells.
O Pandrosos, the right-hand room was yours;
the left was where Aglauros slept; between
the two stood Herse's room. The first to see
the god approaching was Aglauros: she
dared ask him who he was, what brought him there.
And this was Mercury's reply: "I'm he
who flies across the air as emissary
of Jove; he is the god who fathered me.
I won't invent some lie; I only hope
you won't betray your sister—even as
I trust you will be pleased to be the aunt
of one whom I shall father. What I want
is Herse. Help me, I am sick with love."

Aglauros looked at him as avidly
as—only recently—her eyes had peeped
into the basket that contained the secret

Latin [726–49]

of golden-haired Minerva; and the girl
asked Mercury, as payment for her help,
for heaps of gold. Meantime, she made him leave.

Aglauros earned Minerva's cruel gaze,
and the deep sigh the warrior-goddess gave
was violent: her breast and her breastplate—
her aegis—quaked. And after all, this same
young girl (Minerva now recalled) profaned
the casket that contained Minerva's secret.

Despite the orders of the goddess, she
had seen the child born without mother, one
engendered by the god of Lemnos, Vulcan,
out of the earth. And now that same girl planned
to win the gratitude of Mercury
and of her sister, and—most greedily—
to gain great heaps of gold—a tidy fee.

Minerva hurried to the house of Envy:
a squalid den that dripped with gore, a filthy,
secluded cavern in a deep-set valley:
it knows no sun, no breath of wind—a grim
and frozen place forever gripped by sloth;
within that space, there is no kindly hearth.
And it is always full of dense, dark fog.

The virgin warrior-goddess reached that cave;
she stood before the door (for she was not
indeed allowed to enter such a place)
and struck it with her pointed javelin.
At last the door flew open.

                              There within,
she saw that Envy was intent upon
a meal of viper flesh, the meat that fed
her vice. Minerva turned aside her eyes.
But Envy sluggishly rose from the ground,
leaving the half-chewed dregs of serpents' flesh

Latin [749–72]

and coming forward with her faltering steps.
And when she saw the splendid goddess dressed
in gleaming armor, Envy moaned: her face
contracted as she sighed. That face is wan,
that body shriveled; and her gaze is not
direct; her teeth are filled with filth and rot;
her breast is green with gall, and poison coats
her tongue. She never smiles except when some
sad sight brings her delight; she is denied
sweet sleep, for she is too preoccupied,
forever vigilant; when men succeed,
she is displeased—success means her defeat.
She gnaws at others and at her own self—
her never-ending, self-inflicted hell.

Despite Minerva's hatred and disgust,
she speaks brief words to Envy: "Now you must
infect with venom one of Cecrops' daughters:
I mean Aglauros." She adds nothing else.
Then, with her lance as lever to add thrust,
the goddess leaves the ground behind, flies off.

When Envy's grim eyes see the goddess leave,
she mutters, sad that now she has to please
Minerva. Then she grips her staff, wrapped round
with thorny boughs, and, cloaked in a dark cloud,
goes off: she tramples any field she crosses;
she scorches grass and blights the green treetops;
her breath infects all people, houses, towns.
At last she reaches Athens: she can see
its citadel, the height above a city
of intellect and wealth and festive peace;
and it is hard for Envy not to weep,
since there is nothing there that calls for tears.

But, entering the room of Cecrops' daughter,
she does Minerva's bidding: Envy touches
Aglauros' breast with her rust-colored hand;

Latin [772–98]

she breathes a horrid poison—much like pitch—
into the girl; it penetrates her bones
and lungs. And that the venom may be strong—
and never falter—Envy sets before
Aglauros' eyes the image of her sister
wed joyfully to such a handsome god.
So Envy heightened Herse's happy lot.

Incited by these images, Aglauros
begins to feel the bite of secret grief;
by night, by day, she longs, she moans; she's worn
away, a slow decay, like ice that's pierced
by fitful sunrays. She is now undone
by Herse's happiness, a course that mimes
a fire beneath a heap of thorny weeds:
they don't go up in flames; they are consumed
by faint but never-ending heat. At times
she wants to die—never to see the sight
of Herse's joy; at times she wants to speak
to Cecrops, her stern father—to defeat
the sin of Herse and her Mercury.

But then the girl decides on this: she sits
at Herse's threshold—she will not admit
the god when he returns. Mercury begs
for entry—all his words are sweet and soft;
he tries to calm her. But she cries: "Be off!
I will not leave until you've left this house!"
"Agreed!" was his quick answer. Then he struck
the figured door with his compelling wand;
the door flew open. And Aglauros tried
to rise; but now the limbs that bend when we
would sit, are gripped by sluggish heaviness:
she cannot budge; she cannot stand: her knees
are stiff; a chill climbs to her fingertips;
her veins have lost their blood—they pale; and as
a cancer, which cannot be cured, attacks
the healthy parts, advancing from the sick,

Latin [799–826]

so does that fatal chill move limb by limb;
it makes its way into her breast; it blocks
her vital pathways, and her breath is choked.
She does not even try to speak; but had
she tried, her voice would not have found a path:
by now her neck has turned to stone; her mouth
has hardened, too. She is a seated statue,
bloodless—and yet that statue is not white:
Aglauros' soul gives it a black, black hue.

Now that he's taken his revenge upon
Aglauros' impious words and thoughts, the son
of Maia leaves the town that takes its name
from great Athena. Once again, he makes
his way to heaven on his outspread wings.

And when he was in heaven once again,
his father, Jove, draws him apart and says
(though not revealing to his son the cause
for all of this—that is, the call of love):
"My son, who always faithfully fulfill
whatever I may ask, do not waste time;
glide down to earth—be swift as usual—
and find the land from which your mother's star
is seen on high along the left-hand skies
(the men who live there call that country Sidon).
You'll see a herd (the king's own cattle) grazing
far off, on a green hillside; drive that herd
down to the shore."

He spoke—at once his words
were acted on: the herd was headed shoreward.
That beach was where the daughter of the king,
Europa, always played with her companions.

□   □   □

Latin [827–45]

Now, majesty and love do not go hand
in glove—they don't mix well. And so, great Jove
renounced his solemn specter: he—the lord
and father of the gods—whose right hand holds
his massive weapons, three-pronged lightning bolts,
the king whose simple nod can shake the world—
takes on the semblance of a bull; among
the herd he lows; he mingles with the heifers;
he roams the tender grass—a handsome presence.
He's white—precisely like untrodden snow,
like snow intact, untouched by rainy Auster.
His neck has robust muscles; from his shoulders,
his dewlap hangs. His horns, it's true, are small,
but so well wrought, one would have thought a craftsman
had made them; they were more translucent than
pure gems. His brow has nothing menacing;
his gaze inspires no fear. He seems so calm.

Agenor's daughter stares at him in wonder:
he is so shapely, so unthreatening.
At first, however, though he is not fierce,
she is afraid to touch him. Then she nears,
draws closer, and her hand holds flowers out
to his white face. Delighted, as he waits—
a lover—for still other, greater joys,
he kisses her fair hands—no easy test
to check his eagerness, delay the rest.
And now the great bull sports along the grass,
and now he stretches snow-white flanks along
the golden sands. Her fear has disappeared,
and now he offers to the girl his chest,
that she might stroke him with her virgin hand;
and now his horns, that she might twine them round
with garlands. At a certain point, Europa
dares to sit down upon his back: the girl
is not aware of what he is in truth.
And then, as casually as he can,
the god moves off, away from the dry sands;

Latin [846–70]

with his feigned hooves, he probes the shallows, then
advances even farther; soon he bears
his prey out to the waves, the open sea.

Europa now is terrified; she clasps
one horn with her right hand; meanwhile the left
rests on the bull's great croup. She turns to glance
back at the shore, so distant now. Her robes
are fluttering—they swell in the sea breeze.

Latin [871–75]

BOOK III

Cadmus · Actaeon ·

Semele · Tiresias · Narcissus & Echo ·

Pentheus

BUT HIS FALSE SEMBLANCE soon is set aside:
on reaching Crete, Jove shows his own true guise.
Meanwhile the father of the ravished girl,
not knowing what had taken place, commands
Cadmus, his son, to find Europa or
to suffer exile from Agenor's land—
a cruel threat, but born of love!

And so
he roamed the world in vain; what man could hope
to bring to light the secret loves of Jove?
Agenor's son stays on his wandering path—
far from his home, far from his father's wrath.
And he consults Apollo's oracle:
he wants to find where it is best to settle.
The oracle replies: "You'll meet a heifer
in a deserted place—a cow that never
has worn the yoke or drawn a curving plow.
You are to follow in that heifer's tracks;
and where she stops to rest upon the grass,
you are to build your walls and call that land
Boeotia." As soon as Cadmus left
the grotto of Castalia, he saw
a heifer—with no herdsman—passing by:
upon her neck she bore no servile sign.
He follows—carefully—the heifer's path
and offers to Apollo silent thanks
for showing him the way he was to take.
The heifer now had forded the Cephisus
and crossed the fields of Panope. She halted;
and as she lifted heavenward her brow
from which two tall horns spread, she filled the air
with lowings; she looked back on those who now
were close behind; she kneeled; then, on her side,
she rested on the grass. The grateful Cadmus'
lips kissed this foreign land—so did he greet
these fields he'd never seen before, these peaks.
But then, for the libations to complete

Latin [1–26]

the sacrifice he now would offer Jove,
he needed living water from a spring:
and this he sent his servingmen to seek.

An ancient forest lay at hand: no ax
had ever violated it. A mass
of rocks, a grotto forming a low arch,
stood there among dense shrubs and pliant boughs;
and from that cave abundant waters gushed.
That grotto served a serpent as his den—
a serpent that was sacred unto Mars.
He had a golden crest; his eyes flashed flames;
and all his body was puffed out with poison.
He had three tongues that flickered, and his teeth
were set in three rows. And into this wood
the luckless men of Tyre now made their way.
They lowered urns into the grotto's waters;
their pitchers splashed and clattered, and the dark-
blue serpent, hissing horribly, thrust out
his head from the deep cave. Their hands were quick
to drop the urns; their blood ran cold; fear-struck,
they trembled suddenly. The serpent twists
and twines his body into scaly knots:
he darts and flashes; in a giant arch,
he rises through the unresisting air
to half his height; and all the forest lies
beneath his gaze; and you could see his size—
a mass to match the Snake that stands between
the two Bears. He is quick to spring upon
the men of Tyre: whether they prepare
to fight or just take flight or—paralyzed
by fear—do nothing, he attacks them all.
His fangs kill some, and some his crushing coils,
and some he kills with his infested breath.

The sun had reached its zenith; shadows now
were at their thinnest. Cadmus, wondering
what's kept his comrades back, sets out in search.

Latin [26–52]

He has a shield of lion's hide, a lance
with gleaming iron tip, and a javelin—
and, better than all arms, his daring soul.

On entering the woods, he sees his friends'
cadavers—and the giant victor licking
the horrid wounds with bloody tongue. Cadmus
cries out: "My faithful friends, I shall avenge
your death or die beside you!" Saying that,
he lifts a massive rock with his right hand
and, straining to his utmost, heaves it at
the serpent. Such a blow would surely have
smashed in the sturdiest of walls with all
its tallest towers; but the snake was left
unscathed: the scales of his dark hide—much like
a hard cuirass—repelled the crashing rock.
Yet they're not tough enough to stand against
the javelin; it strikes his flexing spine
just at the middle coil; its iron tip
drives deep into his innards. Mad with pain,
the snake twists back his head, he sees his wound;
his teeth grip tight the shaft; and even as
his body shakes, at last he frees the shaft;
but in his bones the iron tip holds fast.
At that, his wrath can only grow. The veins
along his throat are swollen; his dread jaws
are flecked with white foam; even as they scrape
along the ground, his scales resound; the breath
that issues from his Stygian cave infects
the air. He writhes in giant coils, and then
he stiffens like a towering trunk, erect,
or, like a swollen river, thrusts ahead,
smashing the trees with his onrushing chest.

Agenor's son gives way a bit; his shield
of lion's hide repels the snake's attack;
his thrusting spearhead holds those jaws in check.
The angry serpent snaps at the hard shaft—

Latin [52–83]

no use, his teeth are caught on the hard tip.
Down from his poisonous palate, blood now drips,
staining the green grass, but the wound can't take
its full effect: the snake draws back his neck—
the shaft cannot sink deep. Yet now at last,

Agenor's son draws closer, planting fast
the shaft into the serpent's throat until
the snake, in his retreat, meets at his back
an oak tree: Cadmus spears both tree and neck.
Beneath the serpent's mass, the oak tree bends;
and at the lashing of his tail, it groans.
The victor looks at the defeated hulk;
but suddenly he hears a voice (although
he can't tell where it comes from, it is heard):
"Why, Cadmus, do you stare at that slain snake?
You, too, will be a snake at whom men gaze."

There, Cadmus, pale, his senses gone, dismayed,
stood—with his hair erect, on end—afraid.
But then Minerva came, that warrior's aid;
she glided from the sky and ordered him
to plow the ground and then to plant within
the earth the viper's teeth: these were to be
the seeds of men to come. And he obeyed;
and even as he pressed his plow—as she
had bid him do—he scattered the snake's teeth
within the ground: from such seed, men would spring.
At that—a thing beyond belief—the ground
began to stir, and from the furrows sprang
spear-tips, then casques with waving plumes, and next,
shoulders and chests, and weapon-bearing arms:
a harvest crop of warriors with shields.
Just so, on holidays, the theater's
backdrop is raised and human forms appear:
one sees the faces first, then—slowly—all
the rest, as rolling upward steadily,
full forms appear until, at the stage-edge,
their feet are planted. ▫ ▫ ▫

Latin [84–114]

                    Frightened at the sight
of these new enemies, Agenor's son
prepared his weaponry. But "Set those down!"
one of the race sprung from the ground cried out;
"This is a civil strife! Do not intrude!"
That said, with his hard sword, in hand-to-hand
combat he struck a brother born of earth,
then fell himself beneath a javelin
flung from afar. He who had touched that shaft
was also quick to fall; he soon gave up
the breath he had received so recently.
And battle frenzy soon had seized them all;
each at the other's hand, those brothers fell:
their wounds were mutual. Now those young men,
destined to such brief lives, beat with their chests
against their mother earth, warmed with their blood.
Five youths alone were left alive: Echion
was one of these. Warned by Athena, he
cast down his weapons to the ground: he sought—
and made—a pact of peace with his four brothers.
All five were at his side when—to fulfill
the orders of Apollo's oracle—
the stranger come from Sidon, on the soil
the god had promised to him, founded Thebes.

And Thebes has flourished: even in your exile,
o Cadmus, you might seem content and tranquil:
the parents of your wife were Mars and Venus;
and she, Harmonia, has given you
dear sons and daughters, and dear grandsons, too,
past boyhood now. But it is surely true
that we must never count a man as blessed
until we see his final day, his death.
O Cadmus, in the midst of all your gladness,
the cause of your first sorrow was Actaeon:
for strange horns sprouted on your grandson's brow,

Latin [115–39]

and then his blood was lapped by his own hounds.
But if you probe with care, you will not blame
your grandson; for the one to fault is Fate—
there is no crime in making a mistake.

A mountainside was where it all began.
All morning, young Actaeon and his friends
had hunted, killing beasts of every sort;
and now the mountain slopes were stained with blood.
But noon had come; all shadows had grown short;
the sun was at the midpoint of his course.
And to his hunting band that roamed across
the pathless slopes, Actaeon spoke calm words:
"Our nets and spears are soaked with wild beasts' blood;
we've had good luck, my comrades: that's enough.
Aurora on her saffron chariot
will bring a new day; we'll renew the hunt.
But Phoebus now stands high, a point that lies
midway along his path across the sky;
he cracks the fields with scorching heat; it's time
to stop: come, carry back our knotted nets."
They do as asked: they interrupt the chase.

A valley lay nearby: in its dense woods,
the pointed cypress and the pitch-pine stood.
That site was called Gargaphia, a grove
Diana, goddess who wears tucked-up robes,
held sacred. And within the deepest shade,
the innermost recess, there lay a cave
most perfect. Though no mortal art had shaped
that grotto, Nature's craft can imitate
the ways of art; here she had shaped an arch
of what was native there—of porous rock
and of light tufa. To the right, there glowed
a clear, thin spring that widened as it flowed
into a pool surrounded by a meadow.
And here, when she was weary of the chase,
the virgin goddess of the woods would bathe

her limbs within the crystalline, cool waves.

On this day, too, Diana reached her cave;
and to her armor-bearing aide, she gave
her lance, her quiver, and her unstrung bow.
And when she sheds her robe, another holds
what she had put aside; two nymphs unbind
the sandals from her feet, while Crocale—
the daughter of Ismenus—more adept
than they are, gathers up Diana's hair,
where it trails loose upon the goddess' neck,
and knots it neatly, although Crocale's
own hair hangs free. And Psecas, Phiale,
and Ranis, Nephele, and Hyale
fill ample urns with water, which they pour
over Diana, daughter of the Sun.

And while the goddess, as she's always done,
was bathing in her pool, Cadmus' grandson,
now that his hunting tasks had been postponed,
had chanced, while wandering, to reach that grove,
a place he did not know: and now he found
the sacred cave, for Fate would have it so.
No sooner had he come into that grotto,
whose walls were sprayed with water from the spring,
than all the naked nymphs on seeing him—
a male—beat on their breasts. They filled the grove
with sudden cries; they crowded round Diana,
trying to hide her body with their own.
But taller than her nymphs, above the rest,
the goddess could be seen—up from the neck.

Diana, so dismayed, without her clothes,
upon her cheeks displayed the colors shown
by clouds when struck aslant by sunlight or
by Dawn—the color crimson. Though her band
of nymphs pressed close around her, she did turn
aside, avert her face; she had at hand

Latin [164–88]

no arrows—shafts she would have liked; instead,
she used just what she had: Diana took
and flung the water, and his face was drenched.
And as she cast the water of revenge
that soaked the young man's hair, the goddess said,
in words that were an ominous presage:
"Now go, feel free to say that you have seen
the goddess without veils—if you can speak."
There were no other threats. But then she set
a long-lived stag's horns on the head she'd drenched;
she made his ear-tips sharp, stretched out his neck,
and changed his hands to feet, arms to long legs,
and cloaked his body with a spotted hide.
That done, timidity was added on.

And now Autonoe's heroic son
takes flight and, as he races, he's amazed
at how much speed he has. Then, when he sees
his features and his horns in a clear stream,
he tries to say "Poor me" but has no words.
He moans—that's all his voice can summon now—
and tears flow down a face that's not his own.
But while he stands in doubt, he sees his hounds—
and they sight him. The first to bark aloud:
the Cretan dog, Ichnobates, so quick
to scent a quarry; and the Spartan dog,
Melampus. Then the others in the pack,
swift as the wind, rush to attack: Laelaps,
fierce Theron, and the stout Nebrophonus;
Dorceus, Pamphagus, Oribasus—
all three Arcadian dogs; swift Pterelas,
keen Agre, and Hylaeus, battling dog—
just lately he'd been ripped up by a boar;
Harpyia with her two pups; Nape born
of a she-wolf; Polmenis, who—before—
had served as shepherd dog; and with thin flanks,
the Sicyonian Ladon; Canace
and Dromas, Sticte, Tigris, Alce; Leucon,

whose coat was white as snow, and Asbolus
with pitch black hairs; and famed for sturdiness,
stout Lacon, and the racing hound, Aëllo;
and Thous, and Lycisce with her brother,
Cyprius; Melaneus and Harpalos,
who in the middle of his black brow bore
a white sign; shaggy Lacne; and two brothers,
Agriodus and Labrus—though their father
was Cnossian, their mother was from Sparta;
Hylactor, with his piercing bark; and others—
to tell their names in full would be past measure.

That pack is keen for prey: along the crags
and cliffs and rocks so hard to cross, where paths
are rough and where there is no path at all,
they rush. On those same slopes where he once gave—
he now is given—chase: he has to race
away from his own hounds. He wants to shout,
"I am Actaeon! Don't you recognize
your master?" But his heart has been denied
all speech. Their barking echoes through the sky.

While Melanchoetes is the first to fix
his fangs in his own master's back, the next
is Theridamas, while the one to clutch
his shoulder fast is Oresitrophos.
Those three had started later than the rest
but, by a mountain shortcut, had outstripped
the others. Now they check their master's flight,
till all the pack collect and sink their fangs
into his body; there is no place left
to wound. Actaeon groans. And though the sounds
he utters are not human, they are not
the sounds a stag could voice. He fills the heights
he knows so well with his laments and cries;
he sinks down on his knees; he seems to plead;
dismayed, his eyes look round, he would beseech
like those who hold their arms outstretched, in need.

Latin [218–41]

But since Actaeon's friends are ignorant
of what had happened, all his hunting band—
as usual—incite the savage pack
with cries. They miss Actaeon; they look round
to see where he could be; they call aloud
his name—and each outdoes the other's shouts
(Actaeon hears his name and turns around).
But when they see he's absent, they complain;
they say that laziness keeps him away;
he's missed the spectacle that ends the chase—
the sight of such a splendid stag at bay.
He would, in truth, be absent, but he's here;
he would delight to see—not feel and fear—
the sight of his own hounds' ferocity.

Upon all sides, his hounds have hemmed him in;
they sink their muzzles into every limb—
the flesh of their own master in false guise
as stag. Diana was not satisfied
until, so mangled, young Actaeon died;
for—so they say—that was the destiny
the quiver-bearing goddess wished to see.

Men heard his fate—and disagreed: some thought
Diana was too cruel, too unjust;
while others said her action, though severe,
was worthy of a virgin so austere.
Both sides brought suasive arguments to bear.
And only Juno neither blamed nor cleared
Diana: she was simply glad to hear
that now Agenor's house had met disaster.
The rage that Juno's rival had provoked
was aimed at all who shared Europa's blood.

———————

A newer hurt is added to the old,
for Semele—so Juno has been told—

Latin [242–60]

is pregnant with the seed of mighty Jove.
And Juno hones her tongue; she means to brawl,
but then she asks: "What have I gained for all
my reprimands to him, my bitter quarrels?
It's not my Jove but Semele herself
whom I must strike, if I am rightly called
great Juno; if my right hand justly holds
the jeweled scepter, if I am the queen,
the sister, and the wife of Jove (at least
his sister), I shall ruin Semele.
But, then again, if she is quite content
with something furtive—just a passing thing—
the insult to my bed would be quite brief.
But who could swallow that? She has conceived!
And now she runs about—that's all I need—
with her full womb to show her guilt; she seeks
to be a mother thanks to Jove's own seed—
a gift that I myself have scarce received.
She trusts her beauty that much! How deceived
she'll be: I am not Saturn's daughter if
she does not finish in the waves of Styx—
there Jove himself must let my rival sink!"

Then, rising from her throne, she wraps herself
within a saffron cloud; and to the house
of Semele she goes. Just at the threshold,
she lets the cloud dissolve—but not before
she's taken on the counterfeited form
of an old woman, whitening the hair
that frames her temples, furrowing her skin
with wrinkles; as she makes her way, her limbs
are huddled, bent; her steps are tottering.
Her voice is also aged: Beroe
from Epidaurus, nurse of Semele—
that is the one whom Juno has become.
And in that guise, the goddess greets the girl;
they chatter, touching many things, until
Jove's name crops up. And the old woman sighs

Latin [260–80]

and says: "I pray it's Jupiter himself,
but I'm afraid to take such things on trust.
So many men, pretending to be gods,
through guile and wiles, insinuate themselves
into the beds of chaste and modest girls.

But even if he's Jove, that's not enough.
If he is Jove in truth, then have him prove
his love is true. He comes to mighty Juno
in all his force and splendor; even so,
in force and splendor have him visit you.
Yes, ask him to embrace you—and to show
the might and majesty that Juno knows:
let him display his powers when he comes."

Such were the words of Juno. They persuade
the girl, who did not know what fate awaits
a mortal woman caught in the embrace
of Jove when all his powers are arrayed.
And so, when Jove comes down to her, the girl
asks him to grant one gift to her—although
she does not name that gift. And Jove replied:
"Whatever you may want, I'll not refuse.
And to assure you that my pledge is true,
I swear it by the sacred Styx, an oath
that calls upon a godhead so supreme
that all the deities must stand in fear
before the flow of that torrential stream."

She's glad to get a gift that will bring evil:
in being free to choose at will, the girl
will die because her lover must comply.
She asks: "I want to see you in the guise
you take when you embrace Saturnia."

Jove, even as she speaks, would curb her words;
but he's too slow, too late to cut her short;
her hasty words have reached the air. He groans:
she can't withdraw her wish, nor he his oath.

Latin [280–98]

So Jove, in deepest sadness, now ascends
to heaven's heights; he gives a sign, and mists
assemble; he adds clouds and lightning mixed
with gusting winds and—last—the thunderbolts
and flames that no one can evade. But Jove
attempts to mute his force as best he can.
He sets aside the bolt of fire that felled
Typhoeus of a hundred hands—a shaft
too fierce; instead he takes a lighter bolt,
in which the Cyclops' hands had mixed less wrath,
less fury, fire, and menace: "Second Shafts"
is what the gods have called such weaponry.
With these in hand, he visits Semele.
Her mortal body can't withstand the flash
of force so heavenly; that nuptial gift
consumes her flesh; she is reduced to ash.

The babe, not fully formed as yet, was snatched
(if what is told is true) out of her womb,
then sewed up in the thigh of Jove, his father,
until, his full time come, the boy was born.
The one who cared, in secret, for the infant
was Ino, his maternal aunt; but later
he was entrusted to the Nysan nymphs.

_____

On earth, things followed all of Fate's decrees,
and even twice-born Bacchus' infancy
was passing tranquilly. The story goes
that meanwhile, in his home on high, great Jove,
his spirits warmed by nectar, set aside
his heavy cares and jested pleasantly
with Juno—she was also idle then.
"The pleasure love allots to you," he said,
"is greater than the pleasure given men."
But she contested that. And they agreed
to let Tiresias decide, for he

knew love both as a woman and a man.

Tiresias had once struck with his staff
two huge snakes as they mated in the forest;
for that, he had been changed—a thing of wonder—
from man to woman. Seven autumns passed,
and still that change held fast. But at the eighth,
he came upon those serpents once again.
He said: "If he who strikes you can be changed
into his counter-state, then this time, too,
I'll strike at you." His stout staff dealt a blow;
and he regained the shape he had before,
the shape the Theban had when he was born.

And when he had been summoned to decide
this jesting controversy, he took sides
with Jove. The story goes that Juno grieved
far more than she had any right to do,
more than was seemly in a light dispute.
And she condemned to never-ending night
the judge whose verdict found her in the wrong.
But then almighty Jove (though no god can
undo what any other god has done),
to mitigate Tiresias' penalty,
his loss of sight, gave him the power to see
the future, pairing pain with prophecy.

———————

Tiresias was famous: far and near,
through all Boeotian towns, they asked the seer
for counsel; none could fault his prophecies.

The first to test him was Liriope,
a nymph the river-god Cephisus had
caught in his current's coils; within his waves
he snared the azure nymph—and had his way.
And when her time had come, that lovely nymph

gave birth to one so handsome that, just born,
he was already worthy of much love:
Narcissus was the name she gave her son.

And when she asked the augur if her boy
would live to see old age, Tiresias
replied: "Yes, if he never knows himself."
For many years his words seemed meaningless;
but then what happened in the end confirmed
their truth: the death Narcissus met when he
was stricken with a singular, strange frenzy.

For when he reached his sixteenth year, Narcissus—
who then seemed boy or man—was loved by many:
both youths and young girls wanted him; but he
had much cold pride within his tender body:
no youth, no girl could ever touch his heart.

One day, as he was driving frightened deer
into his nets, Narcissus met a nymph:
resounding Echo, one whose speech was strange;
for when she heard the words of others, she
could not keep silent, yet she could not be
the first to speak. Then she still had a body—
she was not just a voice. Though talkative,
she used her voice as she still uses it:
of many words her ears have caught, she just
repeats the final part of what she has heard.

It's Juno who had punished Echo so.
Time after time, when Juno might have caught
her Jove philandering on the mountaintops
with young nymphs, Echo, cunningly, would stop
the goddess on her path; she'd talk and talk,
to give her sister nymphs just time enough
to slip away before they were found out.
As soon as Juno had seen through that plot,
she menaced Echo: "From now on you'll not

Latin [345–66]

have much use of the voice that tricked me so."
The threat was followed by the fact. And Echo
can mime no more than the concluding sounds
of any words she's heard.

When Echo saw
Narcissus roaming through the lonely fields,
she was inflamed with love, and—furtively—
she followed in his footsteps. As she drew
still closer, closer, so her longing grew
more keen, more hot—as sulfur, quick to burn,
smeared round a torch's top bursts into flame
when there are other fires close to it.
How often, as she tracked him, did she pray
that she might tempt him with caressing words
and tender pleas. But she cannot begin
to speak: her nature has forbidden this;
and so she waits for what her state permits:
to catch the sounds that she can then give back
with her own voice.

One day, by chance, the boy—
now separated from his faithful friends—
cried out: "Is anyone nearby?" "Nearby,"
was Echo's answering cry. And, stupefied,
he looks around and shouts: "Come! Come!"—and she
calls out, "Come! Come!" to him who'd called. Then he
turns round and, seeing no one, calls again:
"Why do you flee from me?" And the reply
repeats the final sounds of his outcry.
That answer snares him; he persists, calls out:
"Let's meet." And with the happiest reply
that ever was to leave her lips, she cries:
"Let's meet"; then, seconding her words, she rushed
out of the woods, that she might fling her arms
around the neck she longed to clasp. But he
retreats and, fleeing, shouts: "Do not touch me!
Don't cling to me! I'd sooner die than say

Latin [366–91]

I'm yours!"; and Echo answered him: "I'm yours."
So, scorned and spurned, she hides within the woods;
there she, among the trees, conceals her face,
her shame; since then she lives in lonely caves.
But, though repulsed, her love persists; it grows
on grief. She cannot sleep; she wastes away.
The sap has fled her wrinkled, wretched flesh.

Her voice and bones are all that's left; and then
her voice alone: her bones, they say, were turned
to stone. So she is hidden in the woods
and never can be seen on mountain slopes,
though everywhere she can be heard; the power
of sound still lives in her.

         And even as
Narcissus had repulsed that nymph, he scorned
the other nymphs of waves and mountains and,
before that, many men. Until, one day,
a youth whom he had spurned was led to pray,
lifting his hands to heaven, pleading: "May
Narcissus fall in love; but once a prey,
may he, too, be denied the prize he craves."

There was a pool whose waters, silverlike,
were gleaming, bright. Its borders had no slime.
No shepherds, no she-goats, no other herds
of cattle heading for the hills disturbed
that pool; its surface never had been stirred
by fallen branch, wild animal, or bird.
Fed by its waters, rich grass ringed its edge,
and hedges served to shield it from the sun.

It's here that, weary from the heat, the chase,
drawn by the beauty of the pool, the place,
face down, Narcissus lies. But while he tries
to quench one thirst, he feels another rise:
he drinks, but he is stricken by the sight

Latin [392–416]

he sees—the image in the pool. He dreams
upon a love that's bodiless: now he
believes that what is but a shade must be
a body. And he gazes in dismay
at his own self; he cannot turn away
his eyes; he does not stir; he is as still
as any statue carved of Parian marble.
Stretched out along the ground, he stares again,
again at the twin stars that are his eyes;
at his fair hair, which can compare with Bacchus'
or with Apollo's; at his beardless cheeks
and at his ivory neck, his splendid mouth,
the pink blush on a face as white as snow;
in sum, he now is struck with wonder by
what's wonderful in him. Unwittingly,
he wants himself; he praises, but his praise
is for himself; he is the seeker and
the sought, the longed-for and the one who longs;
he is the arsonist—and is the scorched.

How many futile kisses did he waste
on the deceptive pool! How often had
he clasped the neck he saw but could not grasp
within the water, where his arms plunged deep!
He knows not what he sees, but what he sees
invites him. Even as the pool deceives
his eyes, it tempts them with delights. But why,
o foolish boy, do you persist? Why try
to grip an image? He does not exist—
the one you love and long for. If you turn
away, he'll fade; the face that you discern
is but a shadow, your reflected form.
That shape has nothing of its own: it comes
with you, with you it stays; it will retreat
when you have gone—if you can ever leave!

But nothing can detach him from that place:
no need for food, no need for rest. He's stretched

Latin [416–38]

along the shaded grass; his eyes are set—
and never sated—on that lying shape.
It is through his own eyes that he will die.
He lifts himself a little, then he cries—
his arms reach toward the trees that ring that site:
"O woods, you are the ones to testify:
among your trees so many lovers hide
their grief. Do you remember anyone
in your long life—those many centuries—
whose love consumed him more than mine wastes me?
I do delight in him; I see him—yet,
although I see and do delight in him,
I cannot find him (love confounds me so!).
And there's another reason for my sorrow:
it's no great sea that sunders him from me,
no endless road, no mountain peak, no town's
high walls with gates shut tight: no, we are kept
apart by nothing but the thinnest stretch
of water. He is keen to be embraced;
my lips reach down: I touch the limpid wave,
and just as often he, with upturned face,
would offer me his mouth. You'd surely say
that we could touch each other, for the space
that separates our love is brief. Come now,
whoever you may be! Why cozen me,
you boy without a peer in all this world!
When I would seek you out, where do you go?
My age, my form don't merit scorn: indeed,
the nymphs were lavish in their love of me.
Your gaze is fond and promising; I stretch
my arms to you, and you reach back in turn. I smile
and you smile, too. And, often, I've seen tears
upon your face just when I've wept, and when
I signal to you, you reply; and I
can see the movement of your lovely lips—
returning words that cannot reach my ears.
Yes, yes, I'm he! I've seen through that deceit:
my image cannot trick me anymore.

Latin [438–63]

I burn with love for my own self: it's I
who light the flames—the flames that scorch me then.
What shall I do? Should I be sought or seek?
But, then, why must I seek? All that I need,
I have: my riches mean my poverty.
If I could just be split from my own body!
The strangest longing in a lover: I
want that which I desire to stand apart
from my own self. My sorrow saps my force;
the time allotted me has been cut short;
I die in my youth's prime, but death is not
a weight; with death my pain will end, and yet
I'd have my love live past my death. Instead,
we two will die together in one breath."

Such were his words. Then he returns, obsessed,
to contemplate the image he had left:
his tears disturb the water; as he weeps,
they fall upon the surface. What he seeks
is darker, dimmer now—as if to flee.
"Where do you go?" he cries. "Do not retreat;
stay here—do not inflict such cruelty.
Let me still gaze at one I cannot touch;
let sight provide the food for my sad love."

As he laments, he tears his tunic's top;
with marble hands he beats his naked chest.
His flesh, once struck, is stained with subtle red;
as apples, white in one part, will display
another crimson part; or just as grapes,
in varied clusters, when they ripen, wear
a purple veil. But when the water clears
and he sees this, it is too much to bear.
Just as blond wax will melt near gentle fire,
or frost will melt beneath the sun, just so
was he undone by love: its hidden flame
consumes Narcissus: now he wastes away.

□   □   □

Latin [464–90]

His color now has gone—that mix of white
and ruddiness; he's lost his sap and strength,
all that has been so beautiful to see:
there's nothing left of the entrancing flesh
that once had won the love of Echo. Yet,
faced with the sight of him, she feels deep pity;
each time he cries "Ah, me!" the nymph repeats
"Ah, me!"; and when he flails his arms and beats
his shoulders, she repeats that hammering.
His final words at the familiar pool,
when once again he gazed into the waves,
were these: "Dear boy, the one I loved in vain!"
And what he said resounded in that place.
And when he cried "Farewell!," "Farewell!" was just
what Echo mimed. He set his tired head
to rest on the green grass. And then dark death
shut fast the eyes that had been captured by
the beauty of their master. Even when
the world below became his home, he still
would stare at his own image in the pool
of Styx. His Naiad sisters, in lament,
as offering for their brother, cropped their hair.
The Dryads also wept. That choir of grief
was joined by Echo as she mimed their sounds.
They had prepared the pyre, the bier, the torches;
but nowhere could they find Narcissus' body:
where it had been, they found instead a flower,
its yellow center circled by white petals.

And once his prophecy had come to pass
and all the towns of Greece had heard of that,
renown—well earned—now crowned Tiresias.
The only one among the Greeks to scorn
the seer was Pentheus; he—Echion's son—
despised the gods and mocked the auguries
of old Tiresias; he even mocked

the prophet for his dwelling in the dark—
his blindness. But the white-haired seer just shook
his head and answered, saying: "You indeed
will wish that you had been denied this light,
for then, made blind as I am blind, you might
not have to see the rites of Bacchus. I
foresee the day—and it is soon to come—
when Bacchus Liber, son of Semele,
shall come. If you don't worship that new god,
you will be torn into a thousand parts—
your scattered limbs tossed round about; your blood
will foul the woods and stain your mother and
your mother's sisters. This will come to pass.
You will not honor the new god; and then
you will complain that, in my blindness, I
saw far too well."

                              His words were not yet done,
when Pentheus chased him out. But what the seer
had said was true. His presage soon fell due.

Now Bacchus has arrived; fanatic cries
ring out across the fields; for these new rites,
a mix of men and matrons and young wives,
the nobles and the commons, leave behind
the town; they rush and crowd. "What heats your minds
with this insanity?"—so Pentheus tries
to check them—"Why this frenzy? Are your minds
askew? Mars' serpent was your parent: can
you now succumb to clanging cymbals and
the flute of crooked horn, the cheap deceits
of magic? How can you, who did not fear
the swords of war, the trumpets, tight-held spears,
arrayed and keen—now be defeated by
this wine-incited madness, these shrill cries
of women, obscene crowds, and futile drums?
What sorry sight could leave me more amazed?
You elders, you who sail the long seaways,

Latin [515–38]

who brought your wandering household gods to this
transplanted Tyre—would you now permit
all this to fall—without defending it?
Or you, young men much closer to my years,
men far more fit for gripping armor than
for lifting high the thyrsus—helmets suit
your heads much more than tender garlands do.
I ask you this: remember, you're the seed
of one whose serpent strength was such that he—
although alone—crushed many. In defense
of his own pool and fountain, he met death:
come now, defend your name, your fame. He killed
brave warriors, but you need only rout
a coward crowd to save your father's land.
If Thebes is fated to a life so brief,
then I should rather see these great walls breached
by warriors and battering rams: at least
I'd hear the clash of iron, the roar of flames.
We would be wretched then, but not ashamed;
lament would be our lot, but we would not
have need to hide our blame; there would be tears,
but we would be unstained. But now our Thebes
will fall before an unarmed boy. He has
no warcraft and no horsemen, no sharp shafts;
his only arms are tresses soaked in myrrh,
soft garlands, garments rich with purple dyes
and gold embroidery. Just stand aside
a moment, and I'll force him to confess
that he's no son of Jove, and all his rites
are counterfeit. And if Acrisius
was resolute—for he had nerve enough
to scorn the empty godhead and to shut
the gates of Argos in his face—need I
and all of Thebes be cowed when he arrives?
Be quick"—so did he spur his slaves—"go now:
bring this intruder here to me—in chains!
And don't delay."

□   □   □

Latin [539–63]

           Though Cadmus tried to sway
his grandson, as did Athamas and all
his family, no council could dissuade
the mind of Pentheus. They can't stay his rage;
their calls for calm don't check him—they abet
the force they would repress: so have I seen
a torrent—there where nothing curbed its course—
flow rather peacefully—no rage, no roar;
but where it had been dammed—where giant stones
and tree trunks blocked its path—it boiled and foamed;
resistance only made its fury grow.

And now his slaves return, bloodstained and scarred—
and when their master asks where Bacchus is,
they say they have not seen him; then they add:
"We caught this follower of his, this priest
who serves his sacred rites." And they push forward
a man whose hands are tied behind his back.
He's an Etruscan devotee of Bacchus.

The eyes of Pentheus stare in fury, yet
he does not kill him on the spot but asks:
"O you who now will die and, with your death,
will serve to warn the others, tell me this:
your name, your parents' names, your land, and why
you are a votary of these strange rites."

The prisoner shows no fear as he replies:
"Acoetes is my name, Maeonia
my country, and I come from humble folk.
My father left no fields for me to till,
no sturdy oxen, and no woolly flocks—
in sum, no cattle. He himself did not
have much—no more than line and hook and rod:
he would catch fish and draw them—leaping—up.
That craft was all his wealth, and when he passed
his skill to me, he said:
    ▫ ▫ ▫

Latin [564–88]

'You are to have
my craft; you are my follower, my heir.'
And when he died, he left me nothing more
than the expanse of waters. This is all
that I can call my patrimony. Soon—
that I, for all my days, not be confined
to nothing but those shoals—I learned to guide
a ship: I taught my hands to steer. My eyes
upon the stars, I learned to recognize
the rainy constellation of the Goat,
Taygete, the Hyades, the Bears;
I learned the ways of winds and their directions,
what harbors offer ships the surest shelter.
By chance, as I was headed out for Delos,
thrust off my course and toward the coast of Chios,
with well-plied oars we rode and reached the land:
agile, we leaped out onto the wet sands;
and there we spent the night. As soon as dawn
began to redden in the sky, I woke;
I showed my crewmen where they were to go
to find and fetch fresh water. Meanwhile, I
remained behind upon a rise, to see
what wind was promising; then I called back
my comrades as I headed for the ship.
Opheltes led the others, shouting: 'Here
we are!' Across the sands he tugged a boy,
a trophy (so he called him), whom he'd found
in a deserted field: a boy whose form
could match the loveliness of a young girl.
That boy, like one who's stunned by wine and sleep,
can hardly follow him along the beach:
he sways and staggers. As I stare at him,
his clothes, his face, his gestures—nothing seems
to mark him as a mortal. Sensing that,
I tell my friends: 'I do not know which god
is hidden in this body, but I know
that in this body there's a deity.
Be friend to us, whoever you may be:

Latin [589–613]

assist us in our journey and forgive
these men who captured you.' 'You need not pray
for us,' says Dictys—one whom none outraced
in climbing to the topmost mast and then,
with rope held fast, in sliding down again.
And Libys said that he was right; so did
fair-haired Melanthus, he who manned our prow
as lookout; and Alcimedon agreed,
and Epopeus, he whose voice marked time—
when we were rowing, he would spur us on.
They all agree: unheeding, greedy, they
are keen to profit from so fair a prey.
At that, I shout: 'But I will not permit
such sacrilege; I'll not defile this ship;
we will not take a god as plunder: I
am in command; it's I who must decide.'
I block the boarding plank; then Lycabas
is furious; he was the man most reckless
of all the crew: for a ferocious crime
he had been driven out from Tuscany.
As I resist his force, his tough fists pound
my throat; I would have toppled overboard,
had I not gripped a rope that broke my fall.
The godless crew applauds that blow. At last,
Bacchus (for he indeed is Bacchus), just
as if the ruckus had awakened him,
and wine no longer dimmed his mind, cries out:
'What are you doing? Why this brouhaha?
Come tell me, sailors, why I'm here—and where
you're taking me.' But, 'There's no need to fear,'
says Proreus; 'simply tell us where you want
to sail, and there we'll let you disembark.'
'Then head for Naxos,' Bacchus answers him;
'that is my home; you will be welcome there.'
And, by the sea and all the gods, those cheats
all swear to do just that; they order me
to set the sails upon our painted ship.
Since Naxos lies upon our right, I head

Latin [613–40]

that way. Opheltes cries: 'Have you gone mad?
What are you doing now?' And most of them,
with nods and winks and some with whispers, let
me understand that I am to tack left.
Amazed, I say: 'Then someone else must take
the helm.' I'll have no part in their foul plot.
My crewmen curse me out; they will not stop
their muttering. And one, Aetalion,
says: 'Do you think that it is you alone
on whom our safety must depend?' That said,
he comes and takes my place; he does not head
for Naxos; he turns left instead. At that,
the god, prepared to mock them now, as if
he had seen through their fraudulence at last,
high on the curved stern, eyes the sea; then he
feigns tears and says: 'The shore you promised me
is not the coast I see. What did I do
to earn this punishment? What glory can
you, sailors, win—for you are all grown men—
in tricking me, a boy? I'm one against
so many of you.' I, long since, had wept;
but that foul band derides my tears; they beat
the waters still more quickly with their oars.
And by that god himself I swear to you
(for there is none more near to us than Bacchus)
that what I have to tell you now is just
as true as it's incredible. Midsea,
the ship stands still as if in some dry dock.
But, stupefied, they still persist. They beat
with oars, they spread the sails, they try to speed
in one way or another. Ivy creeps
and twines around the oars; its upward reach
clings to the mast and, spiraling, impedes
the sails with heavy clusters. Bacchus now,
with grapes in clusters garlanding his brow,
waves high a wand that's wreathed with ivy leaves:
around him, tigers, lynxes (all of these
are phantom forms—as are the company

of savage spotted panthers). All the crew,
impelled by madness or by terror, leap
down from the deck into the sea. The first
whose body starts to darken and to bend
is Medon—I can see his spine curve in.

And Lycabas asks him: 'What kind of monster
are you becoming?' But as he asks this,
his own jaws spread, his nose is squashed, his skin
grows hard and scaly. Lybis, as he tries
to budge the blocked oars, sees his hand shrink in,
but none could call them hands—they now are fins.
Another, as he reaches out to catch
a cable that is twisted, finds he has
no arms; his crippled body plunges back
into the sea; the tail that ends his body
curves like a crescent moon. Upon all sides,
they leap and dive; the sea spray showers high;
I see them now emerge and now sink back;
they have devised a playful dance; they draw
the water into their wide nostrils, then
they blow it out again. Along the deck
where, just before, there were some twenty men
(the crew that ship could carry), I was left
alone. I shuddered, cold with fear, and not
aware of what I did; but then the god
encouraged me: 'Do not lose heart, sail on
to Naxos.' Once I reached that coast, I joined
the cult of Bacchus, following his rites.''

"We've showed much patience," Pentheus said; "we've heard
all of your endless tale—which wound its way
so that my anger might, through such delay,
wind down. But now, you slaves be quick. Don't wait;
his fate is savage torture; send him down
into the night of Styx." Tyrrhenian
Acoetes, carried off at once, was locked
within a sturdy dungeon. But as they
prepared their instruments of cruel torture—

Latin [669–98]

the irons in the fire—it is said
that, of their own accord, the doors flew open,
and, of their own accord, with no one there
to loosen them, the chains fell from his arms.

But Pentheus, unrelenting, goes himself—
he sends no messenger—to see the place
where the Bacchantes choose to celebrate
their sacred rites: Cithaeron. And the mount
resounds with strident chants and howls and shouts.
As an excited stallion, when he hears
the brazen trumpet sound the battle call,
is keen to join the clash, so Pentheus, when
he hears those long-drawn cries pulse through the air,
grows hot: that clamor reignites his wrath.

Midway along the mountain-side there lies
a clearing; although ringed by woods, that site
stands free of trees. And here, as Pentheus spies
the sacred rites with his profaning eyes,
the one who is the very first to sight
Echion's son—just as she is the first
to rush against him madly, and the first
to hurl a thyrsus at him—is his mother.
"Come, come, my sisters, both of you!" she shouts.
"A giant boar is roaming on our slopes:
I must tear him apart." Against him rush
all that mad crowd, attacking from all sides:
he's trembling—yes, he's trembling now, his speech
is much less violent; he blames himself,
admits that he has sinned. But he is pierced
with bitter wounds. He cries: "Autonoe,
my dear aunt, help me now, you must recall
Actaeon's shade—have mercy!" She does not
remember her Actaeon; and she shreds
his right arm, and fierce Ino rips his left.
That sorry wretch has no arms left with which
to plead. He lifts the stumps: "O mother, see!"

Latin [698–725]

Agave, seeing that, just howls; she shakes
her head, her hair, tears off his head, and yells,
as she lifts high his head: "This, comrades, spells
our victory—our work!" The wind is not
more swift in stripping leaves from some tall tree
when, touched by autumn's chill, they hang loosely,
than were those vile hands, tearing Pentheus' body.

The fate of Pentheus serves as warning: now
the Theban women, bearing incense, crowd
these new rites; at these holy shrines, they bow.

BOOK IV

———

B<small>UT</small> <small>MINYAS'</small> <small>DAUGHTER</small>, his Alcithoe,
will take no part in Bacchus' sacred orgies:
she even dares to say he's not Jove's son.
Her sisters share in her impiety.

The priest has given orders: there will be
a Bacchic festival: all women-servants
must be relieved from labor on that day;
they and their mistresses are all to wrap
the hides of animals around their breasts,
loosen the bands that bind their tresses, and
wear garlands on their heads, and in their hands
hold fast the leafy thyrsus. And he adds
that any who would slight the deity
will face the unrelenting Bacchus' wrath.

They all obey: the matrons and young wives
desert their looms and baskets, set aside
their labors; burning incense, they invoke
Bacchus and also call him Bromius,
Lyaeus, and the twice-born, and the one
who has two mothers, blazing lightning's son—
and Nyseus, and Thyoneus the unshorn,
Lenaeus, and the planter of the vine
that brings such joy, Nyctelius, as well
as father Eleleus, and Euhan, Iacchus,
and all the endless other names you bear,
through town on town in all of Greece, o Liber.
For you are blessed with endless youth: you are
eternally a boy; high heaven's star—
the handsomest of all; your face is like
a virgin's when you don't display your horns.
You've won the Orient; its farthest bounds
are yours, where sun-scorched India is bathed
by Ganges. You, the god men venerate,
killed sacrilegious Pentheus and Lycurgus,
the one who plied the two-edged battle-ax;
it's you who seized the Tuscans—you who cast

Latin [1–23]

their bodies overboard. Your chariot
rolls heavily across the mountaintops;
it's drawn by lynxes, and it has bright reins.
Bacchants and satyrs follow in your wake,
together with Silenus: that old man
is drunk; he staggers, leaning on his staff—
or hardly keeps his seat upon the back
of the bent ass he rides. And where you pass,
young men and women chant and clamor—glad.
Palms beat the tambourines, bronze cymbals clash,
long flutes of perforated boxwood add
their strident music. Theban women cry:
"Be with us now, o merciful and mild!"
observing, as the priest had asked, your rites.

And only Minyas' daughters stay at home;
they violate the holy day; the tasks
Minerva sets are theirs: close to the loom,
they give their household women work to do.
They thumb the twisting threads, they spin their wool.
And one, whose thumb is agile, as she draws
a thread, says to her sisters: "Let us now—
while others stop their work to join the crowd
upon this so-called feast day—on our part
(since we are great Minerva's votaries,
and she is a much finer deity),
lighten the useful labor of our hands
with varied talk; our ears are idle; let
each take her turn at telling tales, so that
the hours may seem less tedious to those
who listen." And to this they all agree:
they say that she should be the first to speak.

But she, who knows so many fables, finds
it hard to choose the tale that's best to try.
O Dercetis of Babylonia, shall
the change you suffered be the tale she tells?
For you—the Palestinians are convinced—

Latin [24–46]

found all your limbs were veiled by scales: as fish,
it's pools that you were driven to inhabit.
Or should she speak of Dercetis' great daughter,
Semiramis, the queen who had to wear
white feathers and, as dove, spend her last years
perched on high towers? Or recount instead
how, using chants and potent herbs, a Naiad
transformed the bodies of young boys? She changed
those boys into mute fishes—until fate
forced her own self to take that same sad shape.
Or how the mulberry, which once had borne
white berries, now has such dark fruit, because
it has been touched by blood? This last seems best:
it's not a tale that many know as yet.
So even as she weaves, she tells her story:

"The house of Pyramus and that of Thisbe
stood side by side within the mighty city
ringed by the tall brick walls Semíramis
had built—so we are told. If you searched all
the East, you'd find no girl with greater charm
than Thisbe; and no boy in Babylon
was handsomer than Pyramus. They owed
their first encounters to their living close
beside each other—but with time, love grows.
Theirs did—indeed they wanted to be wed,
but marriage was forbidden by their parents;
yet there's one thing that parents can't prevent:
the flame of love that burned in both of them.
They had no confidant—and so used signs:
with these each lover read the other's mind:
when covered, fire acquires still more force.

"The wall their houses shared had one thin crack,
which formed when they were built and then was left;
in all these years, no one had seen that cleft;

Latin [46–67]

but lovers will discover every thing:
you were the first to find it, and you made
that cleft a passageway which speech could take.
For there the least of whispers was kept safe:
it crossed that cleft with words of tenderness.
And Pyramus and Thisbe often stood,
he on this side and she on that; and when
each heard the other sigh, the lovers said:
'O jealous wall, why do you block our path?
Oh wouldn't it be better if you let
our bodies join each other fully or,
if that is asking for too much, just stretched
your fissure wide enough to let us kiss!
And we are not ungrateful: we admit
our words reach loving ears.' And having talked
in vain, the lovers still remained apart.
Just so, one night, they wished each other well,
and each delivered kisses to the wall—
although those kisses could not reach their goal.
But on the morning after, when firstlight
had banished night's bright star-fires from the sky
and sun had left the brine-soaked meadows dry,
again they took their places at the cleft.
Then, in low whispers—after their laments—
those two devised this plan: they'd circumvent
their guardians' watchful eyes and, cloaked by night,
in silence, slip out from their homes and reach
a site outside the city. Lest each lose
the other as they wandered separately
across the open fields, they were to meet
at Ninus' tomb and hide beneath a tree
in darkness; for beside that tomb there stood
a tall mulberry close to a cool spring,
a tree well weighted down with snow-white berries.
Delighted with their plan—impatiently—
they waited for the close of day. At last
the sun plunged down into the waves, and night
emerged from those same waves. □ □ □

Latin [68–92]

"Now Thisbe takes
great care, that none detect her as she makes
her way out from the house amid the dark;
her face is veiled; she finds the tomb; she sits
beneath the tree they'd chosen for their tryst.
Love made her bold. But now a lioness
just done with killing oxen—blood dripped down
her jaws, her mouth was frothing—comes to slake
her thirst at a cool spring close to the tree.
By moonlight, Thisbe sees the savage beast;
with trembling feet, the girl is quick to seek
a shadowed cave; but even as she flees,
her shawl slips from her shoulders. Thirst appeased,
the lioness is heading for the woods
when she, by chance, spies that abandoned shawl
upon the ground and, with her bloodstained jaws,
tears it to tatters.

       "Pyramus had left
a little later than his Thisbe had,
and he could see what surely were the tracks
of a wild beast left clearly on deep dust.
His face grew ashen. And when he had found
the bloodstained shawl, he cried: 'Now this same night
will see two lovers lose their lives: she was
the one more worthy of long life: it's I
who bear the guilt for this. O my poor girl,
it's I who led you to your death; I said
you were to reach this fearful place by night;
I let you be the first who would arrive.
O all you lions with your lairs beneath
this cliff, come now, and with your fierce jaws feast
upon my wretched guts! But cowards talk
as I do—longing for their death but not
prepared to act.' At that he gathered up
the bloody tatters of his Thisbe's shawl
and set them underneath the shady tree
where he and she had planned to meet. He wept

and cried out as he held that dear shawl fast:
'Now drink from my blood, too!' And then he drew
his dagger from his belt and thrust it hard
into his guts. And as he died, he wrenched
the dagger from his gushing wound. He fell,

supine, along the ground. The blood leaped high;
it spouted like a broken leaden pipe
that, through a slender hole where it is worn,
sends out a long and hissing stream as jets
of water cleave the air. And that tree's fruits,
snow-white before, are bloodstained now; the roots
are also drenched with Pyramus' dark blood,
and from those roots the hanging berries draw
a darker, purple color.

      "Now the girl
again seeks out the tree: though trembling still,
she would not fail his tryst; with eyes and soul
she looks for Pyramus; she wants to tell
her lover how she had escaped such perils.
She finds the place—the tree's familiar shape;
but seeing all the berries' color changed,
she is not sure. And as she hesitates,
she sights the writhing body on the ground—
the bloody limbs—and, paler than boxwood,
retreats; she trembles—even as the sea
when light wind stirs its surface. She is quick
to recognize her lover; with loud blows
she beats her arms—though they do not deserve
such punishment. She tears her hair, enfolds
her love's dear form; she fills his wounds with tears
that mingle with his blood; and while she plants
her kisses on his cold face, she laments:
'What struck you, Pyramus? Why have I lost
my love? It is your Thisbe—I—who call
your name! Respond! Lift up your fallen head!'
He heard her name; and lifting up his eyes

. . .

Latin [116–45]

weighed down by death, he saw her face—and then
he closed his eyes again.

              "She recognized
her own shawl and his dagger's ivory sheath.
She cried: 'Dear boy, you died by your own hand:
your love has killed you. But I, too, command
the force to face at least this task: I can
claim love, and it will give me strength enough
to strike myself. I'll follow you in death;
and men will say that I—unfortunate—
was both the cause and comrade of your fate.
Nothing but death could sever you from me;
but now death has no power to prevent
my joining you. I call upon his parents
and mine; I plead for him and me—do not
deny to us—united by true love,
who share this fatal moment—one same tomb.
And may you, mulberry, whose boughs now shade
one wretched body and will soon shade two,
forever bear these darkly colored fruits
as signs of our sad end, that men remember
the death we met together.' With these words,
she placed the dagger's point beneath her breast,
then leaned against the blade still warm with her
dear lover's blood. The gods and parents heard
her prayer, and they were stirred. Her wish was granted."

That tale was done. Another had begun:
this time the teller is Leuconoe—
the pause is brief before the second story.

She speaks; her sisters listen—silently:
"Even the one who guides and shepherds all
with glowing light—the Sun—has been enthralled
. . .

Latin [145–70]

by love. His loves are what I now shall tell.
The first to witness the adultery
of Mars and Venus—it is said—was he;
for he's the god who is the first to see
all things. The Sun was shocked, and he told Vulcan—

the son of Juno, and fair Venus' husband—
the when and where of all those furtive meetings.
And Vulcan's mind and hands gave way: he dropped
what he was working on. But once the shock
was over, he began, with subtle care,
to fashion slender chains of bronze—so thin,
the net and snare they formed could not be seen.
There was no fine wool thread, no spiderweb
that hangs down from a ceiling, that could be
compared with his thin net's transparency.
The slightest touch, the least of movements, was
enough to set the web to work. And then,
around that bed, he draped it cunningly.

"When Venus and her lover went—together—
to bed, they both were soon entwined by that
amazing trap and Vulcan's craft: the net
had caught them in the act—the pair had clasped.
At once, the god of Lemnos opened wide
the ivory doors, so that he could invite
the other gods to see that obscene sight,
such shame enchained. At this, one deity,
not given to solemnity, said he
would hope and pray that such obscenity
and shame might be his lot. His wish provoked
the laughter of the gods: all heaven spoke,
for many days, of this—told and retold.

"But Venus wants revenge: she can't forget
the spy who had informed: the Sun had wrecked
her secret love, and she would pay him back

Latin [170–92]

in kind. Son of Hyperion, what now?
Your beauty, your bright color, your bright rays
are useless. Yes, your fires heat all the earth,
but you yourself have now been set aflame.
Though you are charged with watching everything—
for all the world deserves your scrutiny—
you have confined your eyes: you want to see
one girl—and nothing else—Leucothoe.
You rush to rise within the eastern sky,
and you are slow to sink into the sea.
Too early and too late—you stretch your stay
to gaze upon that girl, and your delay
prolongs the winter days. But then, at times,
your light has failed; your heart is dark, and so
your rays are darkened, too; and fear takes hold
of mortals. And you are not dark because
the moon, drawn close, has interposed itself
between the earth and you: it's love that leaves
your face so wan and weak. It's she alone
you love; you have forgotten all the rest:
you shun the mother of Aeaean Circe—
however lovely—and the girl of Rhodes;
and Clytie—who, though you scorn her, hopes
to win your love—now suffers terribly.
Leucothoe sweeps clean your memory.
She is the daughter of Eurynome—
the fairest woman in the land of spices—
but when the girl had grown to womanhood,
just as her mother's beauty was unmatched,
so did the daughter's loveliness surpass
her mother's. Orchamus, her father—he
was seventh in old Belus' dynasty—
was now the king of all the Persians' cities.

"Beneath the heavens of Hesperia
lie pastures fit for horses of the Sun—
not fields of grass but of ambrosia:
when their hard daily tasks are done, they can

refresh their weary bodies and restore
the force they need to labor. As they graze
on those celestial fields, as Night now takes
her turn of toil, the Sun himself assumes
the semblance of Eurynome: he comes
to his beloved's inner room. He finds
twelve household women hard at work; around
Leucothoe, by lamplight, each one whirls
a spindle as she twists fine threads of wool.
And even as the Sun embraces her,
as would a mother a beloved daughter,
he says: 'I have to speak of private matters.
You, women, leave: I need some privacy—
a mother's right.' This, they obey: no one
is left to witness what he wants. The Sun
announces: 'I am he who measures out
the year; I am the one who sees all things;
and, too, because of me, the earth can see
all things: I am the world's eye. Do be sure,
the sight of you has pleased me.' Struck by fear,
in shock, she drops her wool, drops her distaff.
Even her fear becomes her. He can't wait:
he takes his own true form, his glittering shape.
That sudden vision finds her still afraid,
but godly radiance is just too great.
And she—unable to protest—submits.

"But Clytie was jealous (for the Sun's
love of Leucothoe was more than warm).
Incensed, she told the world, and she informed
her rival's father: she defamed her name.
And in the face of his fair daughter's shame,
the king is cruel: though his daughter prays,
beseeching mercy, even as she claims—
her arms stretched to the Sun—that she was raped
against her will, he pays no heed, inflicts
a brutal burial in a deep ditch;
the sand heaped over her is heavy, thick.   □   □   □

Latin [216–40]

"But then the Sun, with penetrating rays,
soon perforates that heat, a passageway
through which, poor nymph, your head might yet work free.
But it's too late: you cannot lift your head,
Leucothoe; the heavy mass of sand
had crushed you; there you lay, a bloodless corpse.

"And nothing that the one who guides swift steeds
had ever suffered since the fiery death
of Phaethon had brought him deeper grief.
He tried indeed, deploying all the heat
his rays could summon, to revive and warm
your limbs, which death had chilled; but foiled by fate,
instead he spread around your burial place
a fragrant nectar. After long lament,
he said: 'Fate may be contrary, and yet
you are to reach the sky.' Her body, steeped
in sweet celestial nectar, suddenly
melted away; a liquid fragrance drenched
the earth: and then a shrub of sweet incense
lengthened its roots within the soil and rose
until its top broke through the burial mound.

"But Clytie—though love might justify
her jealousy, and jealousy provide
some cause for telling what the Sun had tried
to hide—is sought no longer by the bright
light-giver; he still shuns her company,
her body. Clytie had madly risked—
and lost; but she cannot resign herself.
And now the nymph begins to waste away:
naked, upon the naked earth, by day
and night she sat, disheveled, her head bare:
she touched no food, no drink; her only fare
was dew and tears; she never left that spot;
and all she did was stare—she watched the god,
keeping his face in view, his path across
the sky. At last—they say—the soil held fast

Latin [241–66]

her limbs: and weirdly pale, she changed in part
into a bloodless plant: another part
was reddish; and just where her face had been,
a flower, much like a violet, was seen.
Though held by roots that grip, forever she
turns toward the Sun; she's changed, and yet she keeps
her love intact."

The tale was now complete;
now all of them had heard that prodigy.
Some sisters said such things could never be,
while others were convinced that anything
was in the power of true deities—
but surely Bacchus was not one of these.

When all their talk was done, Alcithoe—
whose turn to tell a story now had come—
running her shuttle swiftly through the threads
upon her loom, said: "Daphnis' love is too
well known to be retold: that shepherd boy
of Ida, whom a nymph—as her revenge
against a rival—turned to stone; so sharp
are wounds that pierce a jealous lover's heart.
Nor shall I tell how Sithon, when the laws
of nature had been overturned, was now
a woman, now a man—ambiguous.
Nor how the faithful friend of the boy Jove
has now become hard metal; nor how those
Curetes sprang from heavy rains; nor how
Crocus and Smilace were changed to flowers.
I set these tales aside: to charm your mind,
it is a newer tale that I'll recite.
You'll hear just how Salmacis' fountain gained
so much ill-fame, why it can enervate
the limbs of any man: who dares to bathe
within its waves is rendered soft and weak.

Latin [266–87]

Although that fountain's power is well known,
its cause has been revealed to few alone.

"Within the caves of Ida, Naiads nursed
a little boy, the son of Hermes and
the Cytherean goddess. In his face
one saw his father and his mother traced:
his name—Hermaphroditus—linked their names.
Three-times-five years had passed, and now he left
his Ida—mountain that had nurtured him.
The toils of traveling were lightened by
his curiosity; for him, the sight
of unknown lands and rivers brought delight.
The Lycian towns were also on his way,
as were the Carians, who lived beside
the Lycians. Here he saw a gleaming pool—
so clear that one could see the very bottom.
No marsh reeds and no random weeds had clogged
its waters, and no spiky rushes marred
the surface: it was clear. And it was ringed
by meadows: ever fresh, that grass was green.
Those waters were a Naiad's home, but she
had little taste for hunting, archery,
or racing with her feet—the only nymph
who never was inclined to join the swift
Diana's company. Her sisters—so
they say—would urge her: 'Do take up the bow
or javelin, Salmacis; it is best
to vary ease with tougher tasks—hard tests.'
But hardships did not draw her; she took up
no spear, no colored quiver, and she shunned
the hunt. Instead, she bathes her lovely limbs
in her own pool: there, with a boxwood comb,
she often smooths her hair; that she may see
what best becomes her, she consults the waves;
and now, in a transparent robe, she rests
along the tender leaves, the tender grass,
or—often—gathers flowers. And by chance,

just when the boy had come, she was among
the flowers. What she saw, she wanted: him.

"Though eager to approach him, she held back.
She needed calm, and so she smoothed her dress
and studied what expression would seem best;
she would have nothing mar her loveliness.
Then she began with this: 'Dear boy, you are
most worthy to be taken for a god;
and if a god, you must be Cupid; if
you are a mortal, they are surely blessed—
those who gave birth to you. Much happiness
must be your brother's; and most fortunate,
your sister, if you have one, and the nurse
who gave you suck; but blessed above them all
must be your promised bride—if there's a girl
whom you have graced with such great dignity!
If that's the case, let us love furtively.
But if you have no bride as yet, choose me;
together, on one bed, we two can wed.'

"Then she fell still; he blushed (in truth, the boy
was ignorant of love). But that blush just
made him more handsome; for his color was
like that of apples on a sun-drenched tree,
or ivory when painted, or the tone
the moon takes when, beneath its whiteness, glows
some redness—and the brazen cymbals clash
in vain, trying to ward off the eclipse.
But she can't stop; again, again the nymph
pleads for his kisses, even if they are
the sort a sister gets; she was about
to fling her arms around his ivory neck,
when he cried out: 'Enough! If you don't stop,
I'll leave and you—alone—can keep this spot.'
Salmacis shuddered, and 'Dear stranger, I
will yield this place to you' was her reply.
At that, she feigned departure—but she kept

Latin [315–38]

her eyes upon him, always turning back.
Then, hiding in a nearby thicket, she
crouched low among the hedges, on her knees.
He—thinking he was now alone, not seen—
roams freely round the meadow; and he bathes
from toe to heel his feet within the waves,
which come to welcome him, as if in play.
Charmed by the warm, caressing pool, he slips
his thin clothes from his slender body. This—
his naked form—indeed ignites Salmacis:
the Naiad's eyes are glittering, much like
the image of the Sun when—facing him—
a mirror mimes the rays of his bright disk.
The Naiad cannot wait; she can't delay
delight; she aches; she must embrace; she's crazed.
With hollow palms he claps his sides, then dives
with grace into the waves; his left, his right
arms alternating strokes, he glides; the light
shines through the limpid pool, revealing him—
as if, within clear glass, one had encased
white lilies with the white of ivory shapes.

" 'I win—now he is mine!' the Naiad cries.
She flings her clothes aside, and then she dives,
as he had done, into the waves; he tries
to fend her off, but she insists; her grip
is firm; against his will she snatches kiss
on kiss; she feels his chest; upon all sides
she fondles him. At last, although he strives
to slip away, he's caught, he's lost; she twines
around him like a serpent who's been snatched
and carried upward by the king of birds—
and even as that snake hangs from his claws,
she wraps her coils around his head and feet,
and with her tail, entwines his outspread wings;
or like the ivy as it coils around
enormous tree trunks; or the octopus
that holds its enemy beneath the sea

Latin [339–66]

with tentacles, whose vise is tight. But he,
who does indeed descend from Atlas' line,
won't yield; what she desires he still denies.
At that, her body presses fast, and as
she clutches him, she cries: 'However hard
you try, you won't escape, you wayward one!
O gods, do grant my plea: may no day dawn
that sunders him from me, or me from him.'
Her plea is heard; the gods consent; they merge
the twining bodies; and the two become
one body with a single face and form.
As when one grafts a twig around a bough
and wraps the bark around them, he will see
those branches, growing to maturity,
unite: so were these bodies that had joined
no longer two but one—although biform:
one could have called that shape a woman or
a boy: for it seemed neither and seemed both.

"And when he saw just what the pool had done,
how he who was a man had now become
a half-man—one whose limbs had lost the force
they had before he plunged—as he stretched out
his hands, Hermaphroditus, though deprived
of manly voice, now cried: 'Do grant this gift,
dear father and dear mother, to the son
who carries both your names: whoever comes
into this pool as man, may he emerge
a half-man; at these waters' touch, may he
be weakened, softened.' And they heard his plea;
moved by their biform son, his parents poured
into the pool a potion that endowed
those waters with a pestilential power."

———————

The tale was done—but not the sisters' scorn
for Bacchus; and their weaving still went on,

Latin [367–90]

the desecration of his holy day.
But—suddenly—they heard a roar invade
their room: a roaring—hoarse and harsh—of drums,
invisible, and flutes with curving horns,
and tintinnabulating gongs. The room
was steeped in saffron, myrrh—in sweet perfume.
What happened then was most incredible:
the wefts turned green; and all the hanging cloth
began to sprout with boughs, as ivy does;
a part became grapevines; where threads had been,
now twining tendrils grew; along the warp,
vine leaves began to sprout; the purple hue
that had adorned rich fabrics passed into
a purple hue that colored clustered grapes.
Indeed, the hour had come when it is hard
to say that it's still day or it is dark,
when an uncertain light trespasses on
the boundary of night. And suddenly,
the walls began to tremble and the lamps—
oil-fed—to flare up, and the palace seemed
ablaze with ruddy flames, while phantom beasts
were roaring. Now the sisters rush to seek
some hidden corner, any place to keep
the flashing flames away; but smoke invades
the halls. And as the sisters try to hide,
their limbs—grown smaller now—are covered by
a membrane, just as thin wings cloak their arms.
Within the dark, they cannot see just how
they've lost their former shape. Though they can show
no feathered plumage, their transparent wings
sustain them; and when they attempt to speak,
the sounds they utter fit their shriveled shapes;
and each to each, they grieve in thin, thin squeaks.
They do not haunt the houses, but the woods;
since they detest the day, they fly by night.
It is from twilight that their name derives,
for bats are often called the Vesperites.

□   □   □

Latin [390–415]

Through all of Thebes, the name of Bacchus now
had gained great fame; his mother's sister, Ino,
would praise him everywhere, that men might know
the new god and the powers he had shown.
Of all her sisters, it was she alone
who'd not been struck by any grief except
her sorrow for her sisters' fate. But Juno
could not endure the happiness of Ino:
the pride she took in Athamas, her husband,
and in her children and the god she'd nurtured—
was just too much for Juno. And she thought:
"When he, the bastard son of Semele,
was hurt, he brought his force to bear—transformed
those sailors from Maeonia and plunged
that crew into the sea; he drove a mother
so mad that she could tear apart the guts
of her own son; and he cloaked Minyas' daughters
with weird wings: and am I to be denied
the force to right a wrong? Am I confined
to nothing more than tears? No, no, it's he
who teaches me what my response must be
(it's right to learn from one's own enemy)."

Beneath the shadows cast by somber yews,
there is a path that, sloping downward, moves
through voiceless silences—the road that leads
to the infernal world, where sluggish Styx
exhales its fog and mists. Those who descend
along that path are phantoms: recent Shades—
those dead whom proper burial has graced.

No thing within that wasteland can escape
the wan and wintry chill. In that vast space,
the new-come souls are slow to find their road
that leads to somber Pluto's heartless halls—
his palace in the capital of Hell.

Latin [416–38]

That capital is spacious; open gates
are everywhere, a thousand entryways;
and even as the sea ingathers all
the rivers of the earth, so are all Shades
received within that space: it's not too strait
for any throng—with so much room for all,
it never seems to crowd. These Shades are wan,
lifeless, with neither flesh nor bones; while some
flock to the forum, others fill the halls
of Pluto, king of the abyss; some souls
would imitate the arts and skills they plied
when, in the upperworld, they were alive.

And Juno, Saturn's daughter, having left
her home in heaven, dared to take that path
down to the underworld—her hate, her wrath
were so intense. She passed the entrance gate,
and there, beneath her sacred body's weight,
the threshold groaned; and Cerberus, who'd raised
his three heads high, barked loud—three mouths as one.

The goddess summoned the ferocious Furies,
Night's daughters, unrelenting deities.
Before a prison barred by adamant,
the Furies sat—three sisters combing black
snakes twining through their hair. That place is called
the House of the Harassed. There Tityos
stretches across nine acres, offering
his vitals to the vulture's rending beak.
You, Tantalus, can never quench your thirst;
and, hanging over you, the fruits elude
your grasp. Ixion whirls upon his wheel—
pursuing and in flight from his own self.
And Danaus' fifty daughters, those who wed
and killed their fifty cousins, are condemned
to an unending task—again, again
to fetch new water for their riddled jars.

□   □   □

Latin [439–63]

Though Juno's daughter glares at all of them,
it is Ixion whom she stares at most;
then, as her eyes catch Sisyphus, she asks:
"And why must he endure unending pain,
while Athamas, his brother, can lay claim

to an imposing palace, though he shows,
as does his wife, such endless scorn for me?"
And she explains the reasons for her wrath
and for her visit here—and what she wants:
she'd have the dynasty of Cadmus fall,
she wants the Furies to drive Athamas
insane—she'd have him stained with some foul act.
With mingled prayers and promises, commands,
she spurs the Sisters to abet her cause.
When Juno's plea was done, Tisiphone—
disheveled as she was—shook her gray locks,
pushed back the snakes that straggled down her face,
and said: "There's no need to explain at length.
What you would have us do, consider done.
Leave this unpleasant kingdom, and return
to heaven's air—much sweeter than our own!"

So Juno, glad, went back to her high home.
And just as she reentered heaven, Iris,
daughter of Thaumas, purified the goddess:
she washed away the stains of Styx with rain.

And fierce Tisiphone was quick to act;
at once she seized a torch—it was blood-soaked;
then, putting on a bloodied crimson cloak,
she wrapped a snake around her waist and left.
And at her side went Sorrow, Terror, Dread,
and Madness, with his eyes askew, awry.
She reached the Theban threshold. It is said
the doorposts trembled at the sight of her.
Ino and Athamas were terrified:
they tried to flee. The Fury blocked their way:
she stretched out arms entwined with snakes; she shook

Latin [464–92]

her locks; the serpents stirred and crackled—some
coiled round her shoulders; others, sliding down
her breast, emitted hisses, vomited
their putrid spit, and darted out their tongues.
Then from her hair, the Fury tore a pair
of vipers; and with pestilential care,
she threw them. They began to glide across
the breasts of Ino, chest of Athamas;
the fetid breath they spewed did not inflict
wounds on their bodies, but it did infect
their minds—a dread assault. Tisiphone
had also brought a horrid potion: froth
from Cerberus' jaws, the Hydra's venom, wild
hallucinations, dark forgetfulness,
and wrath and tears and love of slaughter—all
of these were mixed and mingled with fresh blood,
then boiled in a bronze caldron as she stirred
the potion with a stalk of green hemlock.
While fear held fast those two, the Fury poured
this brew into their breasts, and it infused
their inmost hearts with madness. Taking up
her torch, she whirled it round—a speeding gyre
where flame met flame to form a wheel of fire.
Her work was done: Tisiphone had won.
Now she returned to Pluto's spectral realm
and there untied the snake that bound her waist.

Then Athamas, the son of Aeolus,
insane, cried out to all within his halls:
"Come, comrades, spread the nets within these woods!
I've seen a lioness with her two cubs!"
And he, in frenzy, tracked his wife as if
she were a wild beast to be chased; he snatched
his son, Learchus, from her breast—the boy
was smiling, arms outstretched. And Athamas
whirled him around as one would whirl a sling,
and then—ferocious—dashed the infant's head
against a rugged rock. And Ino—crazed

Latin [492–519]

by grief or by the poison that had seeped
into her innards—howled; in disarray,
her hair disheveled, as she fled, she bore
in her bare arms her little Melicerta
and shouted: "Bacchus! Bacchus!" And when Juno
heard Bacchus' name, she laughed and said: "O Ino,
see if your foster-son can help you now!"

Above the sea there loomed a promontory;
the pounding waves had hollowed out its base—
the waters there were shielded from the rain.
But at its top, the cliff rose high and sharp
and jutted out across the open sea.
And Ino—with the strength that madness brings,
free of all fears—was quick to climb that peak;
and with her young son in her arms, she leaped
down from that height into the deep. Where she
struck hard, the waters whitened with the foam.

But Venus, pitying the unjust fate
that had befallen her granddaughter, Ino,
spoke to her uncle with these suasive words:
"O god of waters, you whose force commands
a kingdom only heaven can surpass,
Neptune, I know I plead for a great kindness;
but may you, in your mercy, pity these—
so dear to me—who now, as you can see,
are cast into the vast Ionian:
receive them as two new sea-deities.
The deep owes something of its own repute
to me—if I was formed from foam in truth,
rising midsea (my name in Greek is proof)."
And Venus' prayer was answered: Neptune gave
to Ino and her son new names, new shapes;
rid of their mortal parts, they both were changed
into new gods—revered sea-deities.
Palaemon was the name the son received,
and Ino now became Leucothoe. ▫ ▫ ▫

Latin [520–42]

The Theban women who were Ino's friends
had followed her as closely as they could;
they saw her final footprints at the edge
of that steep cliff and—sure she had met death—
they mourned the house of Cadmus, beat their breasts,
and tore their hair, their robes; and taking Juno
to task, they said she was unjust, too cruel
in punishing her rival. But the goddess
resented their rebukes. "And now the chief
mementos of my cruelty will be
you Theban women, you yourselves," she said—
and did. The woman who loved Ino most
cried out: "I'll follow her—like my dear queen,
I'll leap into the sea." But as she tried
to leap, she could not move at all: her feet
were fastened to the rock. A second tried
to beat her breast as she had done before—
but now she felt her lifted arms grow hard.
A third, who'd stretched her hands out toward the waves,
was frozen in that stance, a stony change.
Another, as she gripped her hair and tried
to tear it from her head, could feel her fingers
grow stiff in that same gesture. Each one kept
the pose in which she had been caught. But some
were changed to birds, and even now—along
that stretch of sea—their wingtips skim the waves:
they have been called Ismenides, a name
they take from the Ismenus, Theban stream.

But Cadmus does not know that both his daughter
and grandson have become sea-deities.
Too much despair, too many signs of grief,
misfortunes, heap on heap, have left the king
a slave to sorrow; he who founded Thebes
now leaves his city—as if this ill fate
did not have him as target, but the place.

Latin [543–67]

Together with his wife, he wandered long
until, at last, he reached Illyria.
Weighed down by years and woes, those two recalled
the early trials that had beset their house
and their own troubles. Cadmus then spoke out:
"That serpent I transfixed when we first came
from Sidon—you remember him, the snake
whose teeth I scattered on the ground, the seed
from which we saw a strange crop sprout—was he
a sacred serpent? If the gods' intent
in all they have inflicted is revenge
for that, then may I, too, become a snake:
let me be stretched into a serpent's shape."

No sooner was this said than—like a snake's—
his belly stretched, and he could feel the scales
that sprouted on his toughened skin; his body
grew darker and was marked by blue-gray spots.
He fell, face down, upon his cheeks; his legs
were gradually linked in one same form
that—drawn out—ended in a slender point.
His arms were left, and while they still remained—
even as tears stained his still-human face—
he stretched those arms and cried: "O my poor wife,
come, come, draw closer; just as long as I
can claim some remnant of my self, touch me:
hold fast my hand, while it is still my limb—
before the snake invades the whole of me!"
He wanted to say more, but suddenly
his tongue was split, and every time he tried
to utter some lament, he hissed—and that
was all the voice that nature let him keep.
His wife struck her bare breast and cried: "Stay! Stay!
O my sad Cadmus, shed this monstrous shape!
What's happening? Where are your feet? Where are
your shoulders and your hands, your face? I speak—
but everything you are keeps vanishing.
Why, gods of heaven, not inflict on me

Latin [567–94]

the form that he has taken: let me be
a serpent, too!" These were her words. He linked
his dear wife's face and slid between her breasts
as if he knew them well; and he caressed
Harmonia, seeking her familiar neck.

Their comrades (those who'd journeyed out with them)
looked on in horror. But she only stroked
the crested dragon's slippery neck: at once
there were two snakes with intertwining folds,
who glided off into the nearby woods
to hide themselves. And even to this day
that pair do not flee men and don't attack.
Mild serpents, they remember who they were.

Yet Cadmus and Harmonia can take
some comfort: even in their serpent shape
they are consoled by Bacchus' godly state;
now India, converted, venerates
their grandson; and Achaia celebrates
his rites in crowded shrines.

                              One king alone,
Acrisius, the son of Abas, born
of the same stock as Cadmus (but the line
that stemmed from Belus, rather than Agenor),
still warred upon the new god, still denied
that Bacchus was a son of Jove—divine.
Within Acrisius' city, his walled Argos,
the new god was not welcome—even as
Acrisius held that Perseus, born of Danae,
Acrisius' daughter, was no son of Jove,
conceived within a godly shower of gold.
But soon enough—such is the force of truth—
the king reversed himself, accepting Bacchus
as deity, and Perseus' claim as just.   □   □   □

Latin [594–614]

By then, the first had been received in heaven;
the other, Perseus, was already cleaving
the soft air with his whirring wings, returning
triumphant, bearing Gorgon's head; and as
the son of Danae flew above the desert sands
of Libya, from the memorable spoils
of serpent-haired Medusa, drops of blood
fell to the earth; and these the ground absorbed,
and then gave life to snakes of varied sorts.
And that's why Libya is snake-infested.

From Libya, Danae's son was driven by
the warring wind—now here, now there, much like
a rain cloud; he surveyed the lands that lay
below; three times he saw the northern Bears;
three times he saw the pincers of the Crab.
Winds bore him east, and then they bore him west.
The day was fading now; he was afraid
to fly by night; descending from the sky,
he reached Hesperia, the land of Atlas.
There he might rest a while before the star
of morning stirred Aurora's fires and she
led out the flaming chariot of the day.

This Atlas, son of Iapetus, was massive;
no man could match his stature. And no land
lay farther west than his domain—earth's edge
and sea span that received the panting steeds
and weary chariot of the Sun that set.
He had a thousand flocks, and he could claim
as many herds; they grazed on his green plain
at will: no neighbors bordered his domain.
And he had trees with gleaming golden leaves
that covered golden boughs and golden fruit—
the apples of the three Hesperides.

□   □   □

Latin [614–38]

"My lord," said Perseus, "if you prize high birth,
I'd have you know that I am born of Jove;
or if you would applaud amazing feats,
you surely will esteem what I've achieved!
Please let me be your guest—I need to rest."

But Atlas was not ready to forget
an ancient prophecy that he had heard
from Themis of Parnassus. She had said:
"The day will come, o Atlas, when your trees
will be despoiled of all their gold; and he
who gains that prize will be a son of Jove."
For fear of that, he had enclosed his orchards
with sturdy walls; and as his guardian,
Atlas had chosen an enormous dragon—
and banned all strangers from his boundaries.
To Perseus, too, he said: "Be off: you boast
of mighty deeds and say you're born of Jove—
all lies; and fables cannot help you now."
And adding force to menace, Atlas tried
to thrust back Perseus—who held his ground,
while mingling heated words with words of calm.

But when, at length, he found he could not match
the strength of Atlas (how could any man?),
the son of Danae cried: "For you, I seem
to be a thing so trivial, so mean—
for that I shall requite you with this gift!"
At that, he turned his back to Atlas—and
held up Medusa's head with his left hand.
Great Atlas now became a mountain-mass
as huge as he had been; his beard, his hair
were changed to woods; his shoulders and his arms,
to ridges; what had been his head was now
a mountaintop; his bones were changed to stones.
That done, in all his parts his form grew still
more huge—such was your will, o gods; his head
supported all of heaven and its stars.

Latin [639–62]

But now the winds had once again been shut
in their eternal jail by Aeolus,
the son of Hippotas; now Lucifer,
bright star of morning who awakens men
to labors, lit the heavens. Once again,
the son of Danae took up his wings,
tied them to both his feet and, in its sheath,
bound his hooked sword around his waist; he cleaved
the limpid air that his winged sandals beat.

Around him and below lay countless lands
and peoples—Perseus did not stop for them.
At last, he saw the Ethiopians' home,
the realm of Cepheus. There ferocious Ammon
had ordered innocent Andromeda
to suffer for her mother's insolence.
Andromeda was tied to a rough rock;
and when he saw her, Perseus would have thought
she was a marble statue, were it not
for a light breeze that stirred her hair, and warm
tears trickling down her cheeks. He was struck dumb;
a flame—its force was strange—swept through his limbs;
her beauty gripped him—he almost forgot
to beat his wings, to keep his airborne course.

And when he had descended to the earth,
the son of Danae said: "You don't deserve
these chains; the bonds that you should wear are those
that bind devoted lovers. May I know
why you are captive here?" She held her tongue
at first—a virgin, she would never dare
address a man; she would have held her face
between her hands—if she had not been tied.
She did the only thing she could: her eyes
were filled with tears. But even as she cried,

. . .

Latin *[663–85]*

he pressed her for an answer; to avoid
his thinking that her silence meant to hide
some crime for which she had to pay this price,
she told the visitor her country's name
and hers; and then Andromeda explained
the sin her mother had committed when
she dared to boast of her own loveliness
(Cassiope had claimed that she surpassed
even the beauty of the Nereids).
She'd not yet finished telling him of this,
when waves surged loud and, over the immense
sea surface, rose a monster—a wide tract
of sea was covered by that dragon's chest.
Andromeda cried out. Beside the rock,
her father and her mother, overwrought
(both grieving, but her mother with more cause),
can offer nothing more than their despair;
they cling to her chained body. But the stranger
exclaims: "There will be time for tears—but later:
now precious little time is left to save her.
If I should seek your daughter as my wife—
I, Perseus, son of Jupiter and Danae,
to whom, when she was prisoned by her father,
the god descended in a fecund shower
of gold—I, Perseus, I who have defied
the Gorgon with her serpent tresses, I
who dare to ride the air with beating wings—
should I not be the one you would prefer
above all others as your son-in-law?
To those great gifts that are already mine,
I now shall try—with gods as my allies—
to add another claim: I want to save
your daughter; if my bravery succeeds,
I'll have her as my wife. Is that agreed?"
Both Cepheus and Cassiope accept
that pact (who could refuse it?), and they plead
with Perseus to be quick: they promise him

. . .

Latin [685–705]

their daughter and a kingdom in addition.
And now—just as a speeding ship will cleave
the waters with its driving, pointed beak,
as oarsmen's sweating arms are bent on speed—
so did the monster, with his thrusting chest,
roll back the waves; and now he is in reach:
the space that separates him from the reef
is like the space a whirling ball can cross
when catapulted by a Spanish sling.
Then, springing upward from the ground, where he
had dug his heels, young Perseus suddenly
leaped high into the clouds. Ferociously,
the monster rushed against the shadow cast
by Perseus on the surface of the sea.
And even as the sacred bird of Jove,
when it has sighted in an open field
a snake that stretches out its dappled back
beneath the sun, will swoop in swift attack—
but from behind, not frontally, so that
the snake cannot twist back its savage fangs—
the eagle grips its victim's scaly neck
with eager claws: just so did Perseus plunge;
down, through the empty air, he swooped headlong;
assailing from above the roaring beast,
he dug his curving blade unto the hilt
into the snake's right shoulder. That deep wound
drives Ammon's dragon wild; he now soars high
into the air, and now the monster dives
beneath the waves, and now he thrashes like
a savage boar, hemmed in and terrified,
encircled by a crowd of baying hounds.
The monster's fangs are eager; to escape
their poison, with his swift wings Perseus leaps
above, aside; and where he can, he strikes
against the monster's shell-encrusted back,
its flanks, and then its tail where it thins out
in fishlike form; his scythelike sword smites hard.
The monster vomits brine and purple blood.

Latin [705–29]

But Perseus' wings are soaked with sea spray now;
his sandals are too water-logged to trust;
and when he sights a shoal whose top juts out
in calm seas, and is hidden when it's rough,
it's there he takes his stand; from there he thrusts;
he grips the outer edges of the rock;
and with his right, again, again he strikes;
he drives his blade three times and then a fourth:
he sinks his sword into the monster's guts.

The shore, the houses of the gods on high—
applauding Perseus' feat—resound with cries
of joy. Cassiope and Cepheus, glad,
salute the hero as their savior,
their family's redeemer. Free of chains,
Andromeda moves forward—she, the cause
of his hard trial, is also his reward.
And Perseus, drawing water, cleanses now
the hands with which he'd won his victory;
and lest the snake-wreathed head of Phorcys' daughter
be damaged by the roughness of the sands,
the hero softens the hard ground with leaves;
and over these he spreads twigs of seaweed
that flower undersea: upon that bed,
the hero lays—facedown—Medusa's head.

The weeds he'd gathered were still fresh, alive,
and so their porous marrows could soak up
the Gorgon's power and, with that, grow hard:
their leaves and stems became so strangely tough.
Intrigued, the sea-nymphs gathered still more twigs
and watched that stunning metamorphosis.
Then, scattering those weeds as seed throughout
the waves, they multiplied those coral shapes.
And coral keeps that nature to this day:
the pliant weed that sways beneath the waves,
above the surface stiffens into stone.

□   □   □

Latin [729–52]

Now Perseus, using clouds of turf, heaps up
three altars: each meant for another god.
The altar to the left is Mercury's;
the altar to the right is yours, Minerva;
great Jove receives the altar at the center.
A cow is slaughtered for the warlike virgin;
and for the winged-foot god, a calf is slain;
for you, the greatest god, he kills a bull.
And then, without delay, the hero claims
Andromeda as wife: he seeks no dowry—
the girl alone rewards his victory.

And Love and Hymen shake the marriage torches,
and fires are fed by incense in abundance,
and garlands wreath the roofs, and lyres and flutes
and songs that echo everywhere bear witness
to glad exuberance. Flung wide, the portals
display the gilded palace—and the banquet
is sumptuous. King Cepheus' chieftains crowd.
When they have feasted well and drunk their fill
of Bacchus' gracious gift of wine, young Perseus
inquires about the region's life and ways.
And one of Cepheus' lords without delay
details the thoughts and habits of that place
and, having finished his description, says:
"Now, sturdy son of Danae, may I pray
that you retell what force and craft you used
when you subdued the Gorgon's snake-wreathed head."

Then Perseus told them how, beneath cold Atlas,
there was a shelter ringed by sturdy walls;
two sisters lived just at the entranceway;
those Graeae, Phorcys' daughters, shared one eye.
Through subtle wiles and guile, the son of Danae—
while one was passing that eye to the other—
stretched out his hand and intercepted it.

Latin [753–77]

He held it fast as he advanced across
uncharted, lonely tracts, across rough rocks
and horrid gullies, till he reached the house
of fierce Medusa and her sister Gorgons
(another set of daughters born of Phorcys).
Along the fields and paths where he had trekked,
he saw the forms of men and animals
who had been changed to stone because their gaze
had dared to spy upon Medusa's face.
But Perseus himself had found a way
to see the dread Medusa yet escape
the fate of others, for his left hand held
a shield of bronze reflecting her dread form.
And when deep sleep had overtaken her,
together with the snakes that wreathed her hair,
he cut that Gorgon's head off from the neck;
and from Medusa's blood two sons sprang up:
Chrysaor and the wingèd Pegasus.

And Perseus added to his tale the perils—
not fictive—he had faced in his long journey;
he told them, too, of all the seas and lands
that he had seen beneath him in his flight,
and of the stars he'd touched as his wings beat.
But when his voice fell still, that interval
allowed one of the lords to ask him why
the only one among the Gorgon sisters
whose hair was wreathed with serpents was Medusa.
The guest replied: "What you have asked deserves
retelling: listen now to my true words.
Medusa was astonishingly fair;
she was desired and contended for—
so many jealous suitors hoped to win her.
Her form was graced by many splendors, yet
there was no other beauty she possessed
that could surpass the splendor of her hair—
and this I learned from one who said he'd seen her.
Her beauty led the Ruler of the Sea

to rape her in Minerva's sanctuary
(so goes the tale). Jove's daughter turned aside
chaste eyes: the goddess hid her face behind
her aegis—but she made Medusa pay:
she changed that Gorgon's hair to horrid snakes.

And to this day, Minerva, to dismay
and terrify her foes, wears on her breast
the very snakes that she herself had set—
as punishment—upon Medusa's head."

BOOK V

BUT WHILE THE STALWART son of Danae told
the story of his feats, the royal halls
were filled with din and discord—not the sounds
of festive wedding songs, but the uproar
that rises at the start of savage quarrels.
What was a feast is now a bitter brawl:
one might well liken it to tranquil seas
that swell when winds—berserk—whip suddenly.

It's Phineus, the brother of the king,
who dared to start the strife: now—in the lead—
he brandishes his bronze-tipped ashen shaft;
he shouts: "I'm here! I want revenge! You snatched
my bride, but it is you whom I shall seize:
this time, no thing can save you—not your wings,
nor Jove appearing in a shower of gold."

But just as Phineus was set to strike,
King Cepheus cried: "What frenzy drives your mind?
How can you, brother, conjure such a crime?
Is this what Perseus deserves—the way
in which you would repay a guest so brave?
It's he who saved her life. He did not snatch
Andromeda from you: it was the wrath
of the immortal Nereids; it was
horned Ammon and that monster of the sea
who came to glut his belly on the flesh
of my own flesh. Yes, brother, it was they
who took Andromeda from you, when she
was doomed to die—unless your cruelty
wants just this thing, her death—that you might be
consoled at the expense of my own grief!
Beneath your very eyes, you saw her chained;
you were her uncle and her promised mate,
yet you did nothing then; you brought no aid.
How, then, can you outcry when someone saved
her life? Why, then, deny him what he's gained?
If winning her as wife seems such a prize,

Latin [1–25]

you should have sought to free her from that rock
where she was helpless, chained. You failed to act;
so let him keep what he has won: I've sworn
to give him his reward; if not for him,
I now would be a sorrowing old man.
And try to understand: the choice was not
between yourself and him; my choice was made
between yourself and death—her certain fate."

His brother did not answer; but in doubt,
not knowing which of two to strike, he stared
at each in turn: at Cepheus, and at Perseus.
Yet doubt did not last long; with all the force
of rage, he aimed his shaft at Perseus—
but missed the mark: his lance-head struck a couch.
There it held fast, but Perseus leaped at last
upon the cushions, grabbed the shaft, and cast
the lance straight back; it surely would have smashed
the chest of Phineus if—shamefully—
that wretch had not been quick enough to scurry
behind the altar, taking refuge there.
And yet that shaft had some effect; it struck—
full force—the face of Rhoetus; as he fell,
he wrenched the iron from his bone; he writhed;
he stained with blood the well-spread banquet table.
At that, the fury of the crowd could not
be checked; they hurled their shafts; some called for death
to Perseus and to Cepheus. But the king
had fled his palace, even as he called
on loyalty and justice and the gods
of hospitality as witnesses
that he had tried to stop that sacrilege.

And then warlike Minerva came to shield
her brother with her aegis, giving him
fresh courage. Now there was an Indian
among the guests—a youth called Athis, one
who had been born in Ganges' crystal stream;

Latin [26–47]

his mother was that river's nymph, Lymnaee.
His beauty was stupendous; and the boy—
sixteen years old, in full force—wore rich robes
that made him still more handsome, for his cloak
was purple fringed with gold; a golden chain
adorned his neck: a golden diadem
curved round his hair, which was perfumed with myrrh.
He was adept at hurling javelins
at distant targets, but he was still more
adept at bending bows. And even then,
while Athis was intent upon his bow,
the stalwart Perseus snatched the smoldering brand—
one he had taken from the altar's center—
and smashed the face of Athis, crushed his skull.

Now Athis' close, inseparable friend
was the Assyrian Lycabas, a man
whose love was true—a love he did not hide.
And when he saw that splendid face defiled
by blood, and saw his comrade breathe his last
beneath that cruel wound, he wept, then grasped
the bow his friend had bent. With that in hand,
he cried: "Now face a man! You won't rejoice
too long at your defeat of this poor boy:
a victory that earns you more contempt
than glory!" As he spoke, the sharp-tipped shaft
streaked from the bowstring, but—his aim was off—
within a fold of Perseus' robe, it stuck.
Acrisius' grandson turned on Lycabas
with that same scimitar which he had flashed
in killing the Medusa: this he plunged
into the chest of the Assyrian.
And dying, Lycabas, with eyes that swam
in darkness, turned to search for Athis and,
beside the body of the boy, collapsed
but bore this comfort even as he left
to join the Shades: he shared death with his friend.

□　□　□

Latin [48–73]

At that, Metion's son, Syenian
Phorbas, and Libyan Amphimedon—
too keen to join the fight—slipped on warm blood
that drenched a stretch of floor. And when they tried
to rise, the blade of Perseus slashed the throat
of Phorbas; then he drove his sword between
the other's ribs. But he did not employ
his blade to vanquish Eurytus, the son
of Actor, who held high a battle-ax,
broad and two-edged: instead, with both his hands,
he lifted up a giant bowl, embossed
with figures, and he smashed that mass against
the son of Actor. On his back, near death,
the fallen victim vomited red blood
and pounded with his head against the ground.

Then Perseus felled Caucasian Abaris;
and from the line of Queen Semiramis,
proud Polydegmon; and Lycetes, come
from the Sperchios' shores; and Clytus, Phlegyas,
and Helice, whose hair was never shorn.
That done, the hero treaded on the heaps
of dying men.

       And even Phineus
was now afraid to deal with Perseus
directly—so he cast his javelin;
but it was aimed in error, striking Idas,
who until now had—all in vain—abstained
from fighting, taking sides with neither part.
He stared at savage Phineus; in rage,
he cried: "Since I am forced to join this fray,
accept, o Phineus, the foe you made;
and with this blow, let your blow be repaid!"
He wrenched the javelin out of his flesh
but then, about to fling it back, collapsed:
no blood was left within the limbs of Idas.

◻ ◻ ◻

Latin [74–96]

Hodites (of the Ethiopians,
Cepheus alone could claim a higher rank)
fell, too—cut down by Clymenus. Hypseus
killed Prothoenor and, in turn, was killed
by one of Lynceus' line. Among them all,
there stood the old Emathion, a man
who fostered fairness and revered the gods.
His years forbade his taking up a lance,
and so he fought with words—assailed, attacked
that wretched battle as his trembling hands
embraced the altar. Chromis, with his sword,
struck off Emathion's head; and as it rolled
across the altar, half-alive, his tongue
still spat out maledictions till his breath,
amid the altar fires, breathed its last.

And then, at Phineus' hands, both Broteas
and Ammon—they were brothers—met their death
(though none had bested Ammon as a boxer,
what good can gauntlets do, when they meet swords?);
so, too, did Ampycus, a priest of Ceres,
his temples circled by a white headband.
You, son of Lampetus, not used to war
but to the peaceful work of voice and lyre,
had been invited to delight the guests,
to celebrate the wedding with your chants.
The son of Lampetus now stood apart,
an inoffensive plectrum in his hand,
when Pedasus said scornfully: "Your chant
is still not done; go, sing the rest before
the shades of Styx." That said, he pierced the bard's
left temple with his dagger. As he fell,
the dying fingers of the poet brushed
again across the lyre's strings; that touch,
by chance, gave voice to sad and shadowed chords.

That sight enraged Lycormas; to avenge
that death, he wrenched a robust wooden beam

Latin [97–120]

out from the doorpost; with full force he smashed
the nape of Pedasus, who then collapsed
along the ground, as does a butchered bull.
Cyniphian Pelates, on his part, tried
to wrench a plank out from the left doorpost,
but even as he tried, the javelin
of Corytus, born in Marmarica,
pierced his right hand and pinned him to the plank.
With Pelates held fast, the lance of Abas
impaled his side. He did not fall to earth;
but dying, there he hung down from the wood
to which his hand was nailed. And Melanéus,
a partisan of Perseus, also fell,
as did another, Dorilas, who held
the richest fields of Masamonia—
no one could match the acres he possessed
or gather more abundant heaps of incense.
Caught by a lance that had been shot aslant,
his groin was struck—and that's a fatal hit.
And when the Bactrian Halcyoneus,
the man who'd hurled that shaft, saw Dorilas
gasping, his eyes askew, about to die,
he cried: "Of all the plots that you possess,
this spot, where you now lie, is all that's left!"—
and left him, a cadaver, there.

                                But Perseus
was quick to seek revenge: he wrenched the shaft
out from the still-warm wound and hurled it back:
it hit Halcyoneus' nose, then drove
straight through his neck, protruding on both sides.
While Fortune favored him, he also killed
Clanis and Clytius: born of one mother,
they died of different wounds. The sturdy arm
of Perseus cast one ashwood lance that ran
through both of Clytius' thighs; the other shaft
caught Clanis in the mouth—he bit that lance.
And then, beneath the hands of Perseus fell

Latin [120–44]

both Celadon of Mendes and Astreus
(his mother was a Palestinian;
his father was unknown); and Aethion
(till then, adept at reading days to come
but cheated—this time—by a lying omen);
Thoactes, armor-bearer of the king;

and then Agyrtes, who'd earned infamy
for killing his own father. Perseus

is weary, but his enemies are many—
and they are bent on killing him alone.
Arrayed against him, from all sides they thrust:
they all support a cause that would insult
both worth and trust. The only ones who stand
together with him are King Cepheus (but
the king, however honest, has no force),
the new bride, and her mother—their laments
are loud enough and yet are lost among
the clash of weapons and the moans of those
who've fallen. Through the desecrated house,
Bellona pours out streams of blood, as she
incites again—again renews the strife.

And now where Perseus stands, he is hemmed in
by Phineus and a thousand of his men.
The shafts fly faster—to the left, the right—
than winter hail; they graze his ears, his eyes.
Against a great stone pillar, Perseus plants
his back and so protects it from attack;
he faces their assault, confronts his foes
as they press on against him. On the left,
it is Molpeus of Chaonia
who threatens; on the right, it is Ethemon
the Nabatean. Even as a tigress
who feels the bite of hunger, if she hears
the bellowing of two herds that appear
to come from different valleys, does not know
which herd to harry (she is hot for both),
so Perseus, now unsure of what is best—

Latin [144–67]

to strike against the right, against the left—
first wounds Molpeus' leg and is content
to let him flee; and now, he guards against
Ethemon, who allows no truce, but lifts
his blade in rage and tries to slice the neck
of Perseus; but he has not gauged his force
and cracks his sword against the column's stone.
The blade breaks off; against its owner's throat,
it slides, but it inflicts no fatal wound.
And there Ethemon stands; he trembles and—
a suppliant—lifts up his helpless hands.
And Perseus sinks the gift of Mercury,
his scimitar, into Ethemon's body.

But Perseus saw that all his strength might yet
be forced to yield before their crowded ranks.
He cried: "You have compelled me to this step:
from my own enemy, I must seek help.
If any here—by chance—are friends of mine,
let them avert their eyes!" And he raised high
the Gorgon's head. Then Thescelus cried out:
"Go! Let your magic frighten someone else!"
and set himself to hurl his deadly lance;
but he was frozen in that very act:
a marble statue. Ampyx stood nearby;
and with his sword he rushed to strike the chest
that held the mighty soul of Perseus;
but as he thrust, his right hand, now grown stiff,
could not move forward and could not move back.

And Nileus (one who falsely claimed that he
was born of Nile, the stream with seven mouths—
he even had the shapes of seven channels
engraved upon his shield, with some in gold,
and some in silver) cried: "Now, Perseus, see
the source from which I spring. You will derive
much solace when you reach the dead, the Shades,
for you'll have fallen at the hands of one

Latin [167–92]

who is so great a champion. . . ." But his words
were stifled in mid-speech; you would have said
his open mouth still tried to speak, and yet
words could not pass. Now Eryx scorned that pair;
he cried: "It's lack of courage, not the power
of Gorgon, that has made you stiff; let us
lay low this youth and his enchanted arms!"
He started his attack; the earth held fast
his feet; and he was halted, motionless—
a rock, the image of a man in armor.

All these indeed deserved the fate they met.
But Perseus had one friend, Aconteus,
who fought on his behalf, but chanced to stare
at Gorgon's head and hardened into stone.
Astyages, who thought Aconteus still
a living man, struck hard with his long sword
against the stony form. The sword gave out
a clanging sound; and while Astyages
was still dismayed by that, the very same
force overcame him, too; and on his face—
now stone—the look of wonder still remained.

It would take far too long were I to tell
the names of all the commoners who fell.
Two hundred men were left to carry on;
two hundred, seeing Gorgon, turned to stone.

Then Phineus was ready to repent—
at last—for having launched this unjust clash.
But what can he do now? As he looks round,
he sees the varied shapes, the forms he knows;
he recognizes all his men; he calls
on each by name for help; he can't believe
what his eyes see; he touches those most close—
and all are marble now. He turns away;
and to his side, he stretches out his hands
and arms—the gesture of a suppliant;

Latin [192–215]

and, ready to confess his guilt, he says:
"You are the victim, Perseus! Now set
aside that monstrous prodigy, that head
of your Medusa: it begets hard stone.
Whatever it may be, I beg, I plead:
put it away. It was not out of hate
for you—nor out of any lust to take
the kingship—that I fought: I only sought
to win my wife. You had more worth, but I
could claim that I came first. Yes, I was slow
to yield; for that, I now repent. Just grant
my life—and nothing more—to me: the rest
is yours to take and keep. You are the bravest."
As he said this, he did not dare to look
at him to whom he prayed. And Perseus
replied: "You are a coward, Phineus,
but this I can allow you, to be sure—
and it is a great favor (do not fear):
no one will ever harm you with a spear.
No, not at all, for I shall make of you
a monument that always will endure:
for age on age, within these very halls,
here in the palace of my father-in-law,
you will be seen by all; my wife will draw
some solace from the image of the man
who once had sworn that he would be her husband."

That said, he turned the face of Phorcys' daughter
to that side where, bewildered, Phineus
had turned. And Phineus, too, tried to avert
his eyes too late: his neck grew stiff, the tears
he shed were turned to stone. And looking so—
in marble now—he stayed: his face displayed
his cowardice, his pleading gaze; his hands
implored; the statue caught his cringing stance.

□   □   □

Latin [215–35]

Then back to Argos, city of his birth,
triumphant Perseus, with his bride, returned.
And though Acrisius did not deserve
a champion so worthy, he avenged
his father's father. Proetus, a usurper,
had driven out Acrisius, his brother,
and seized the citadel. But not his arms,
and not the stronghold he had stolen, helped
the cause of Proetus: he could not defeat
the savage gaze of Gorgon—grim, snake-wreathed.

But Polydectes, you, the king of small
Seriphus, still were harsh, implacable:
despite young Perseus' worth, his feats and trials,
your hatred of him, venomous and vile,
was endless. Yes, you even dared belittle
his slaying of Medusa; speaking ill,
you said it was invented, false—a fable.
But Perseus cried: "If you want proof, then I
will give it to you. Let the others hide
their eyes"—and with Medusa's head held high,
he left that skeptic bloodless, petrified.

Her brother, until now, had always had
Minerva at his side. But now she left.
Out from Seriphus, with a hollow cloud
to cloak her, passing Gyarus and Cythnus
upon her right, she took the shortest course:
over the sea, she reached the lands of Thebes
and Helicon, the virgin Muses' home.

□   □   □

Latin [236–54]

When she had come to rest upon those slopes,
she told the learned sisters: "I have heard
that you now have a new and wondrous fount
on Helicon: it burst out from the ground
beneath the winged Pegasus' hard hoof.
I've come to see this marvel: I was there
when, from Medusa's blood, that horse was born."
Urania replied: "No matter what
has drawn you to our home, you gladden us,
o goddess, with your visit. You can trust
the news you heard: we owe to Pegasus
our new, our sacred, spring." She led the goddess
to see that wonder.

And Minerva looked
at length at where the waters had sprung up
beneath the horse's hoof when it struck hard.
And then her eyes took in the ancient forests,
the inmost groves, the grottoes, and the flowers—
those countless points of color on the meadows.
She said the daughters of Mnemosyne,
in what they did and where they lived, were blessed.

"O goddess, if your merits had not won
for you much higher tasks than we perform,
you would have joined our band; and you are right
when you commend our home and praise our art,"
one sister answered; "we are fortunate—
as long as we can count on peace. But now
(when there's no viciousness that's not allowed)
we virgins find our minds are menaced by
all things; and always—there before our eyes—
we can recall the savage Pyreneus;
that scene of terror has not left me yet.
This cruel king, commanding Thracian ranks,
had captured Daulis and the lands of Phocys,

Latin [254–76]

and ruled with an unjust—an iron—hand.
While we were traveling toward Parnassus' shrine,
he saw us passing, and he recognized
just who we were and, feigning reverence
for us as deities, said with deceit:
'Stop here, you daughters of Mnemosyne;
don't hesitate; the sky is menacing,
the rain has started falling'—and indeed
it had. 'My house will shield you from the storm.
The gods have often entered humble homes.'
Persuaded by the weather and his words,
we entered, taking refuge in his hall.
But when the north wind won against the south,
and rain no longer fell, and shadowed clouds,
across a sky grown bright, were in retreat,
we all prepared to leave. But Pyreneus
was quick to shut the door: he wanted us—
by force. But putting on our wings, we fled.
And then, as if he could have followed us
across the air, he hurried to the top
of his tall fortress, shouting: 'Just as you
can travel through the air, so can I, too.'
He'd lost his mind. Down from that pinnacle,
he hurled himself; headfirst he fell; his skull
was smashed; and as he died, he stained the soil,
defiling it with his foul blood."

The Muse
was still not finished with her words, when through
the air, there came the sound of whirring wings
and, from the high boughs, voices offered greetings.
Minerva looked on high: she tried to find
what tongues had voiced those sounds, which seemed so like
the speech of humans—but it was magpies
she saw upon those branches. There were nine
who, all aligned, lamented their sad fate;

Latin [276–98]

whatever sounds they like, they imitate.
And as Minerva wondered, even as
a goddess speaks to goddess, one Muse said:

"Those whom you see have only recently
been added to the many families
of birds; they faced a contest, and they lost.
Their father was rich Pierus, the lord
of Pella; and they had Paeonian
Evippe as their mother. Nine times she
had called upon the powerful Lucina
for help, and nine times she had given birth.
Those stupid sisters—proud that they were nine
in number—traveled through Haemonia
and through Achaia, touching every town,
until at last they came to Helicon
and challenged us to match their art of song:
'O goddesses of Thespia, it's time
you stop beguiling the untutored mob
with counterfeited songs; for you are frauds.
If you are confident, compete with us!
Neither your voice nor art can match our own,
and we can match your numbers. If you lose,
then yield to us the spring of Pegasus
and Aganippe, too, your other fount;
and if you win, we will concede to you
the plains of all our broad Emathia
as far as our snow-clad Paeonia.
And let the nymphs be judges of this test!'

"Though it was shameful to contend with them,
there was more shame—we thought—in turning down
their challenge. So the Nymphs were called to judge:
they swore upon their streams and then sat down
on benches that were formed of porous stone.

□   □   □

Latin [299–317]

"Now all was ready; without drawing lots,
the one who'd been the first to challenge us
began. She sang the battle of the gods
and Giants; she—unjustly—glorified
the Giants and belittled the great gods.
She said that, when Typhoeus bounded up
from Earth's abyss, the gods on high were so
afraid that they ran off and did not stop
until, exhausted, they were taken in
by Egypt, at the point where seven mouths
divide the flow of Nile. And then she dared
to tell us that Typhoeus, son of Earth,
had reached their refuge; and to hide, the gods
took on deceitful shapes as camouflage:
'So Jove became a ram, the lord of flocks;
that's why the Libyan Ammon still is shown
with curving horns. The god of Delos hid
within a crow's shape, Bacchus in a kid,
and Phoebus' sister in a cat; the daughter
of Saturn took the form of a white heifer;
and just as Venus hid herself as fish,
Cyllene's god became a winged ibis.'

"With that, her song was done; her voice had been
accompanied by chords upon the strings.

"Now we—the Muses of Aonia—
were challenged to reply. But if your time
is short, and other cares call you away,
you may not want to hear the song we sang."
"No, no; you can be sure," Minerva said;
"I'll listen from the start until you end."
She sat down in the woodland's pleasant shade.
The Muse replied: "We chose Calliope;

for all of us, she would—as one—compete.
Our sister rose; her flowing tresses wreathed
with ivy, she began to pluck the strings;
and their vibrations joined her mournful chant:

" 'The first to furrow earth with the curved plow,
the first to harvest wheat, the first to feed
the world with food men cultivate in peace,
the first to bless the earth with laws—was Ceres;
all things are gifts she gave. I want to sing
of Ceres: may my offering be worthy—
this goddess surely merits poetry.

" 'The island mass of Sicily is heaped
upon a giant's body: underneath
its soil and stones Typhoeus lies—the one
who dared to hope for heaven as his kingdom.
He writhes; he often tries to rise again.
But Mount Pelorus (closest to the land
of the Italians) crushes his right hand;
his left is in Pachynus' grip, just as
his legs are in Mount Lilybaeum's grasp;
his head is pressed—vast Etna holds it fast.
Beneath this mountain, on his back, in rage,
Typhoeus' mouth spits ashes, vomits flames.
He often strives to heave aside the ground—
the towns and heavy peaks that pin him down.
Then earth quakes. As it trembles, even he
who rules the kingdom of the silent dead
is anxious, for the crust of Sicily
may split and a wide crack reveal things secret:
daylight might penetrate so deep that it
would terrify the trembling Shades. His fear
of such disaster led that lord of darkness
to leave his sunless kingdom. Mounted on
his chariot—it was drawn by two black stallions—
he carefully assessed the island mass.
When he was sure that there were no vast cracks,

Latin [338–62]

that Sicily was everywhere intact,
his fears were ended. Then, as Pluto rode
from site to site, down from her mountain slopes
of Eryx, Venus saw him. As she clasped
her winged son, Cupid, this is what she asked:

" ' "O you, my son, my weapon and my armor,
dear Cupid—you, my power—take those shafts
to which both gods and mortals must submit;
with one of your swift arrows pierce the chest
of Pluto—god who, when the lots were cast,
assigning the three realms, received the last.
You conquer and command sky-deities—
not even Jove is free from your decrees;
sea-gods are governed by your rule—and he
who is the god of gods who rule the sea.
And why should Tartarus elude our laws?
Why not extend your mother's power—and yours?
One-third of all the world is still not ours.
We have been slow to act, but indecision
has earned us nothing more than scorn in heaven.
And—son—if my authority should weaken,
then yours would suffer, too. Do you not see
how both Athena and the hunting goddess,
Diana, would defy me? And the daughter
of Ceres, if we let her choose, will be
like them: she is so bent on chastity.
But for the sake of all I share with you,
please join that goddess-girl, Proserpina,
to her great uncle, Pluto." This, she asked.
Love, opening his quiver—he respects
his mother—from his thousand shafts selects
the sharpest, surest shaft—the arrow most
responsive to the pressure of his bow.
Across his knee, the pliant bow is bent;
Love's hooked barb pierces Pluto through the chest.

□   □   □

Latin [362–84]

" 'Not far from Enna's walls there are deep waters.
That lake—called Pergus—hears a music richer,
more songs of swans, than even the Cayster
hears as its current courses. Tall hills circle
that lake. Woods crown the slopes—and like a veil,
the forest boughs abate the flames of Phoebus.
Beneath those leaves, the air is cool, the soil
is damp—with many flowers, many colors.
There spring is never-ending. In that grove
Proserpina was playing, gathering
violets and white lilies. She had filled
her basket and, within her tunic's folds,
had tucked fresh flowers, vying with her friends
to see which girl could gather more of them.
There Pluto—almost in one instant—saw,
was struck with longing, carried that girl off—
so quick—unhesitating—was his love.

" 'The goddess-girl was terrified. She called—
in grief—upon her mother and companions,
but more upon her mother. She had ripped
her tunic at its upper edge, and since
the folds were loosened now, the flowers fell.
So simple is the heart of a young girl
that, at that loss, new grief is what she felt.
Her captor urged his chariot, incited
his horses, calling each by name and shaking
the dark-rust reins upon their necks and manes.
He galloped over the deep lake and through
the pools of the Palici, where the soil
spews fumes of sulfur and the waters boil.
He reached that place where the Bacchiadae—
a race that came from Corinth, which is bathed
by seas upon two sides—had built their city
between two harbors of unequal size.

" 'Between the spring of Cyane and the spring
of Arethusa (which had flowed from Greece),

there is a stretch of sea that is hemmed in,
confined between two narrow horns of land.
Among those waves lived Cyane, Sicily's
most celebrated nymph, and she had given
her name to that lagoon. Above the eddies,
just at the center, Cyane rose, waist-high.
She recognized Proserpina and cried:
"Pluto, you cannot pass. You cannot be
the son-in-law of Ceres unless she
gives her consent. To ask is not to rape.
And if I may compare small things to great,
I, too, was wooed—by Anapis—but I
wed him in answer to his prayers and pleas—
he never used the terror you abuse."
That said, she stretched her arms upon both sides
to block his chariot. But Saturn's son
could not contain his anger any longer:
he spurred his terrifying stallions, whirled
his royal scepter with his sturdy arm.
He struck the very depths of Cyane's pool.
The blow was such that, down to Tartarus,
earth opened up a crater: on that path
he plunged to darkness in his chariot.

" 'But Cyane nursed an inconsolable—
a silent—wound that was incurable:
a sadness for the rape of Ceres' daughter
and for the violation of the waters
of her own pool—for Pluto's scorn and anger.
She gave herself to tears and then dissolved
into the very pool of which she had—
till now—been the presiding deity.
You could have seen the softening of her limbs,
the bones and nails that lost solidity.
Her slender hairs, her fingers, legs, and feet—
these were the first to join the waves. In fact,
the slenderest parts can sooner turn into
cool waters. Shoulders, back, and sides, and breasts

Latin [410–35]

were next to vanish in thin streams. At last,
clear water flows through Cyane's weakened veins,
and there is nothing left that one can grasp.

" 'Meanwhile, the heartsick Ceres seeks her daughter:
she searches every land, all waves and waters.
No one—not Dawn with her dew-laden hair,
nor Hesperus—saw Ceres pause. She kindled
two pinewood torches in the flames of Etna.
Through nights of frost, a torch in either hand,
she wandered. Ceres never rested. When
the gracious day had dimmed the stars, again
the goddess searched from west to east, from where
the sun would set to where the sun ascends.

" 'Worn out and racked by thirst—she had not wet
her lips at any spring along her path—
she chanced to see a hut whose roof was thatched
with straw. And Ceres knocked at that poor door,
which an old woman opened. When she saw
the goddess there and heard her ask for water,
she gave her a sweet drink in which she'd soaked
roast barley. While the goddess drank this brew,
a boy came up to her; and scornful, rude,
he laughed and said she drank too greedily.
Offended, Ceres stopped her sipping, threw
the brew and all of its pearl-barley grains
full in his face. So—soaked—his face soon showed
those grains as spots; his arms were changed to claws;
a tail was added to his altered limbs.
And that his form might not inflict much harm,
the goddess shrank him, left him small—much like
a lizard, and yet tinier in size.
This wondrous change was watched by the old woman,
who wept to see it, even as she tried
to touch the transformed shape: he scurried off
to find a place to hide. The name he got

. . .

Latin [435–61]

is suited to his skin: the starry newt—
a beast that glitters with his starlike spots.

" 'To tell the lands and seas that Ceres crossed
would take too long: the world was not enough
to satisfy the searching mother. She
returned to Sicily, explored again
each part. She reached the pool of Cyane.
If Cyane had not been changed, she now
would have told Ceres all she knew; but while
she longs to speak, she lacks a tongue to tell.

" 'Yet Cyane transmitted one sure clue:
upon the surface of her waters floats
the girdle that Proserpina had worn;
that girdle—one that Ceres knew so well—
had chanced to fall into the sacred pool.
No sooner had she recognized that sign,
than Ceres—as if now, for the first time,
she knew her daughter had been stolen—tore
her unkempt hair; her hands beat at her breast
again, again. She did not know as yet
just where her daughter was, but she condemned
all lands. She said they were ungrateful and
unworthy of the gift of harvests she
had given them—above all, Sicily,
the place that showed the trace of the misdeed.
And there, in Sicily, she—without pity—
shattered the plows that turned the soil; her fury
brought death to both the farmers and their cattle.
She spoiled the seeds; she ordered the plowed fields
to fail; she foiled the hope and trust of mortals.
Now Sicily's fertility—renowned
throughout the world—appears to be a lie:
as soon as grass is in the blade, it dies,
undone by too much rain or too much sun.
The stars and winds bring blight; the greedy birds
devour the seed as soon as it is sown;

the crop is blocked by chokeweeds, tares, and thorns.
Then Arethusa, whom Alpheus loved,
lifted her head above her waters—these
had flowed to Sicily from Grecian Elis.
She brushed her dripping hair back from her brow
and said: "O Ceres, mother of the girl
you seek throughout the world, you, mother of
earth's fruits and grain, forgo your fury, end
your devastating violence. This land
does not deserve your scourging: it was forced
to yield before the bandit's brutal course.
And I do not beseech you on behalf
of my own homeland. I was not born here:
I come from Pisa, in the land of Elis.
My origins were there—yet Sicily
is dearer to me than all other countries.
I, Arethusa, have a newfound home:
sweet Sicily is now my country—and,
kind Ceres, may your mercy save this island.

" ' "Why I have left my homeland, why I crossed
so vast a stretch of sea until I touched
Ortygia—there will yet be time enough
to speak of that, a time when you are free
of cares, a moment of tranquillity.
But I can tell you now my journey's path:
earth, opening a chasm, let me pass.
I flowed through caverns deep below the surface,
then—here—I lifted up my head again,
again I saw the stars I had forgotten.
But in my passage underneath the earth
among the eddies of the Styx, I saw
Proserpina with my own eyes: she was
downcast, still somewhat touched by fear—and yet
she was a queen within that world of darkness,
the powerful companion—mighty mistress—
of Pluto, tyrant of the underworld."

□   □   □

Latin [485–508]

" 'Hearing these things, the mother, Ceres, stood
as motionless as stone. Long moments passed:
her mind seemed lost. When that paralysis
of fear had given way to grief no less
oppressive, Ceres, on her chariot,
rode toward the upper air. With shadowed eyes,
her hair disheveled, hate-inflamed, she cried:
"For one who is of both your blood and mine,
o Jupiter, I come to plead with you.
Though I, her mother, do not matter, you
at least can care to save your daughter—I
should hope your care will not be any less
because she owes her birth to me. Our daughter,
after so long a search, is found—if one
can speak of finding when it just confirms
the loss more certainly, when finding means
no more than merely knowing where she is.
As for his theft of her—that I can bear—
he only has to give her back! My daughter
is mine no longer, but you cannot let
a robber win her as his wife—through theft."

" 'Then Jupiter replied: "We share the care
and tenderness we owe to our dear daughter.
But if we would have things named properly,
then we must speak of love, not injury
or robbery. We should not be ashamed
of Pluto as a son-in-law—if only
you, goddess, would consent to that. Were he
to lack all else, it is no meager thing
to be the brother of a Jupiter!
But he, in fact, has many other splendors:
the portion of the world assigned to him
is, after all, a kingdom, only less
than what my portion is—and only chance
assigned this part to me and that to him.
In any case, if you are so intent
on separating them, Proserpina

Latin [509–30]

can see the sky again—on one condition:
that in the world below, she has not taken
food to her lips. This is the Fates' edict.' "

" 'These were his words. And yet, though Ceres wanted
to bring her daughter back, the Fates prevented
Proserpina's return, for she had broken
her fast: the girl, in all her innocence,
while she was wandering through a well-kept garden
within the underworld, from a bent branch
had plucked a pomegranate. She had taken—
peeling away its pale rind—seven seeds
and pressed them to her lips. No one had seen
that act of hers—except Ascalaphus
(the son, they say, that Orphne—not the least
famous among Avernus' nymphs—conceived
out of her love for Acheron, and bore
within the dark groves of the underworld).
He saw her taste those seeds: denouncing her,
he thwarted her return to earth. She moaned—
the queen of Erebus. Then, in revenge,
she changed that witness. He was made a bird
of evil omen: on his head she poured
waters of Phlegethon. Enormous eyes
and beak and feathers now are his. Deprived
of what he was, he now wears tawny wings;
his head is swollen, and his nails grow long
and hook back, forming claws; and it is hard
for him to move the feathers that now sprout
upon his sluggish arms. He has become
the bird that men detest—that would announce
calamities. He is the lazy screech-owl,
bringer of bitter auguries to mortals.

" 'Ascalaphus indeed seems to have earned
his punishment—his tongue was indiscreet.
But, Achelous' daughters, why do you,
as Sirens, have birds' feathers and birds' feet—

and features like a girl's? Is it because
you, Sirens skilled in song, had been among
the band of friends who joined Proserpina
when she was gathering spring flowers near Enna?
For after you—in vain—had searched all lands
for her, so that the waves might also witness
that search for one you loved, you voiced a plea
to be allowed to glide above the sea,
using your arms as oars to beat the air.
You found the gods were well disposed to answer:
your limbs were wrapped—at once—in golden feathers.
But you were mesmerizing, suasive singers,
born to entrance the ears; and that your lips
not lose that gift, each one of you was left
with young girl's features and a human voice.

" 'And what did Jupiter do then? Between
his brother Pluto and his grieving sister,
he has to strike a balance: he divides
the turning year into two equal portions.
Proserpina is shared by the two kingdoms:
the goddess is to spend six months beside
her husband, and six months beside her mother.
At once, the goddess' face and spirit alter:
her brow, which until then seemed overcast
even to somber Pluto, now is glad,
just as, when it defeats the dark rainclouds,
the sun appears—victorious and proud.

———————

" 'Generous Ceres, now at peace—at last
she has her daughter back—returns to ask
you, Arethusa, why you fled from Greece
and why you have become a sacred spring.
The waves fall still. Their tutelary goddess
raises her head above the depths; and after
her hands have twisted dry her damp green tresses,

Latin [553–75]

she tells the tale of how—long since—Alpheus,
the river-god of Elis, longed for her.

" ' "I was," she says, "one of the nymphs who live
in the Achaean woods. I was intent
on tracks and trails and setting hunting nets—
no nymph had greater passion for such tasks.
I never wanted to be known for beauty—
I thought my courage was conspicuous,
but all my fame was for mere loveliness.
One day—no day that I forget—I made
my way back from the forest of Stymphalus.
That day was hot—but twice as hot for me:
the hunting had been hard, and I was weary.
I came upon a stream. Unmurmuring
and unperturbed it glided, crystalline—
so clear down to the riverbed that one
could count each pebble there. That stream was so
transparent that it did not seem to flow.
Along the riverbanks the slopes received
the shadows cast by gray-white willow trees
and poplars nourished by those waters—shade
that was the gift of nature. I drew near.
And first I bathed my feet, then I went in
up to my knees. But now I wanted more
cool water: I undid my dress. I left
my soft gown draped on a bent willow branch;
naked, I plunged into the stream; and while
I strike those waters in a thousand ways,
dividing, joining, splashing as I play,
my arms withdrawing, plunging in—I hear
the strangest murmur rising from the depths.
I seek the nearest riverbank—in fear.
'Where do you flee so quickly, Arethusa?'
Alpheus, from his waters, called to me.
'Where do you flee so quickly?'—so did he
again speak hoarsely. I could only flee
without my dress—left on the other shore.

Latin [576–602]

My nakedness only inflames him more.
He hurries after me; naked, I seem
to him that much more ready for the taking.
I race; he—fiercely—presses after me:
even as doves with trembling wings will flee
the hawk, and hawk pursue the frightened doves.

" ' "I passed Orchomenus, Psophis, Cyllene,
the vales of Maenalus, chill Erymanthus,
and Elis; I sustained my pace; Alpheus
did not outrace me. But I could not match
his strength: my speed was spent—it could not last
as long as his. Yet, over level fields
and wooded hills, across the spurs and rocks
no path had ever marked, I did not stop.
The sun was at my back, and I could see
a giant shadow stretch ahead of me—
perhaps a phantom fashioned by my fear;
but I could surely hear his dread footsteps,
and I could feel his massive panting breath
upon the band that clasped my hair. As I
collapsed, exhausted by that course, I cried:
'Diana, save me! He is at my side!
I was your weapons' faithful guardian,
the huntress whom you chose to bear your bow,
the keeper of your quiver and your arrows.'

" ' "The goddess had been touched. And she detached
one cloud from a thick cloudbank, and she cast
that cloud around me. And when I was wrapped
in darkness, then Alpheus, ignorant
of where I was, searched in the mist—vainly.
Around the spot where she had hidden me,
he circled twice, and twice—unknowing—cried:
'O Arethusa, Arethusa!' I
was in the grip of what great misery!
Was I not like the lamb when it can hear
wolves howl around the fold? Or like the hare

Latin [602–28]

that, hidden by a hedge, can see the dread
muzzles of the dogs and dares not stir?

" ' "And yet Alpheus does not leave; aware
that I have stopped—no footprints trail beyond—
Alpheus probes the cloud that cloaks the ground.
I am beset. Cold sweat runs down my flesh;
My body rains dark drops, my hair drips dew,
and where I move my feet a pool is born.
In less time than it takes to tell you now
all that was happening, I am a spring.

" ' "But in those waters, he, the river-god
Alpheus, recognizes me, his love;
leaving the human likeness he had worn,
he once again takes on his river form,
that he might mingle with me. And the goddess
of Delos cracked a chasm through earth's crust:
I plunged into deep caverns, then was brought
here to Ortygia, dear to me because
its name is like the other name of Delos,
the island of Diana—and because
Ortygia is the place where, from below
the earth, up toward the air and sky, I flowed."

———————

" 'When Arethusa's tale had reached its end,
the goddess of fertility prepared
her chariot; she yoked her sacred pair
of dragons. With their bits held tight, she rides
upon the air, between the earth and sky.
Once at Athena's town, on touching ground,
she gives her chariot as well as seeds
of grain to young Triptolemus, and these
she'd have him scatter wide in many lands.
The youth flies over Europe and the breadth
of Asia; reaching Scythia, he descends.

Latin [628–49]

The ruler of that land is Lyncus, and
he enters the king's palace. When he's asked
to tell how he had come, and what and why
might be his name and country, he replies:
"My home is famous Athens; and my name,
Triptolemus. No ship has brought me here
across the waves; my feet did not cross land:
the air disclosed its roads to me; I bring
the gifts of Ceres; if you scatter these
across your spacious fields, they're sure to yield
rich harvests—cultivated, peaceful food."
And Lyncus, that barbarian, was struck
by envy; but that he might come to be
far-famed as a great benefactor, he
received his guest with hospitality.

" 'Yet when his guest was fast asleep, the king
attacked; his blade was just about to pierce
the chest of the Athenian when Ceres
transformed the Scythian king into a lynx,
then had Triptolemus ride off; across
the air, he drove her sacred dragon pair.'

"Calliope was done: her learned song,
sung with such skill, stopped here. The Nymphs, as one,
agreed: we goddesses of Helicon
had won. The losers could not stand their loss.
They shouted insults at us. As they scoffed,
Calliope replied: 'You challenged us:
for that alone, you merit punishment.
But now you dare to add your rude abuse.
Our patience is not endless: you would test
our anger, and our wrath will rage—unchecked.'
The sisters jeer and fleer; they scorn our threats;
but even as we warned them, when they lift
their hands to mock us, they now notice this:

Latin [650–70]

the feathers sprouting from their fingers and
the plumage covering their arms. And each
can see a sister's face with rigid beak
protruding now, and see new birds retreat
into the trees. And when they try to beat
their breasts, they all are borne by flapping wings;
they fly into the air as insolent
magpies, the mocking dwellers in the woods.
Yet, though they now are winged, their endless need
for sharp, impulsive, harsh, derisive speech
remains: their old loquacity—they keep."

Latin [671–78]

BOOK VI

Arachne · Niobe ·

Latona & the Lycian Peasants · Marsyas ·

Pelops · Tereus, Procne, Philomela ·

Boreas & Orithyia

THEIR TALE WAS DONE. And now the Muses won
Minerva's praise. She had listened carefully,
and she applauded all their artistry
in song—and justified what they had done
in striking down their rivals' spite and scorn.
But to herself she said: "To praise is less
rewarding than receiving praise: just as
the Muses punished the Pierides,
so, too, must I exact a penalty
from anyone who dares disparage me."
Her mind was set, intent on punishing
Arachne, for the goddess had indeed
heard that the Lydian girl would not concede
Minerva's mastery in working wool:
she claimed that she surpassed the goddess' skill.

Arachne was renowned—but certainly
not for her birthplace or her family.
Her father, Idmon, came from Colophon;
he dyed her porous wool with Phocaean purple.
Her mother now was dead; but like her husband,
she was lowborn: in sum, a simple couple.
Arachne's home was in a humble village,
Hypaepa. Yet consummate work had won
the girl much fame: through all the Lydian towns,
her name was known. To see her wondrous art,
the nymphs would often leave their own vineyards
along Timolus' slopes, and water nymphs
would leave Pactolus' shores. One could delight
not only in her finished work but find
enchantment as her art unfolded: whether
she gathered the rough wool in a new ball,
or worked it with her fingers, reaching back—
with gesture long and apt—to the distaff
for more wool she could draw out, thread by thread—
wool that was like a fleecy cloud—or twisted
her agile thumb around the graceful spindle,
. ·. .

Latin [1–22]

and then embroidered with a slender needle,
one knew that she was surely Pallas' pupil.

And yet the girl denied this; and instead
of taking pride in following so fine
a mentor, she'd reply, as if offended:
"Let her contend with me; and if I lose,
whatever she demands of me, I'll do."
To warn the girl against such insolence,
Minerva took the form of an old woman:
the goddess put false gray hair on her temples;
to prop her tottering limbs, she gripped a staff
and, in that guise, approached the girl and said:
"Not all that old age offers is mere chaff:
for one, the years bestow experience.
Take my advice: it is enough to be
supreme among all mortals when you weave
and work your wool, but never do compete
with an immortal goddess. Go, beseech
Minerva's pardon for the words you spoke;
ask humbly and she will forgive your boast."
Arachne scowled; abrupt, aggrieved, morose,
she dropped her threads; and though she kept her hand
from striking out, her rage was clear—it showed
upon Arachne's face as she replied
to Pallas (who was still disguised): "Old age
has addled you; your wits are gone; too long
a life has left you anile, stale, undone.
Your drivel might appeal to your dear daughter-
in-law, if you have one, or else your daughter,
if you have one. As for advice, I can
advise myself. And lest you think your warning
changed anything, be sure of this: I am
still sure of what I said before. Your goddess—
why doesn't she come here? Why not accept
my challenge?" Pallas answered: "She has come!"
She cast aside disguise, showed her true form.

□　□　□

The nymphs bowed down before the deity,
as did the Lydian women. Only she,
Arachne, showed no fear; she stood unawed.
And yet, despite herself, her cheeks were flushed
with sudden red, which faded soon enough—
as when the sky grows crimson with firstlight,
but pales again beneath the bright sunrise.
Arachne still insists upon the contest:
her senseless lust for glory paves her path
to ruin—for the goddess does not ask
for a delay, or warn her anymore.

Now each is quick to take her separate place
and, on her loom, to stretch her warp's fine threads.
On high, onto a beam, each ties her web;
the comblike reed keeps every thread distinct;
sharp shuttles, with the help of fingers, serve
for the insertion of the woof; notched teeth
along the slay, by hammering, now beat
into their place weft threads that run between
the fleece that forms the warp.

                              Both women speed:
their shoulders free (their robes are girt about
their breasts), they move their expert hands; and each
is so intent that she ignores fatigue.
Into the web they've woven purple threads
of wool that has been dyed in Tyrian tubs,
and hues so delicate that they shade off
each from the other imperceptibly—
as, when a storm is done, the rays of sun
strike through the raindrops and a rainbow stains
with its great curve a broad expanse of sky;
and there a thousand different colors glow,
and yet the eye cannot detect the point
of passage from one color to the next,
for each adjacent color is too like
its neighbor, although at the outer ends,

Latin [44–67]

the colors shown are clearly different.

Each rival weaves her pliant golden threads
into her web—and traces some old tale.
Minerva chooses to portray the hill
of Mars, a part of Cecrops' citadel,
the icon of an ancient controversy—
which god would win the right to name the city.
There twice-six gods—and one of them is Jove—
majestic and august, sit on high thrones.
Each god is shown with his own well-known traits;
thus, Jove has regal features; and the god
who rules the sea stands tall; with his long trident
he strikes the hard stone cliff; and from that rock
a fierce horse leaps, as if to urge the city
to take the name of Neptune. When Minerva
shows her own self, she has a shield, a lance,
a helmet on her head; to guard her breast
there is her aegis. When the earth is struck
by her sharp shaft, an olive tree springs up,
pale green and rich with fruit; this prodigy
astonishes the gods; and finally,
we see Minerva crowned by victory.

To these, Minerva added at each corner—
so that the girl be warned of what awaits her
audacity—a painted scene of contest.
Each pictured warning had its own bright colors
and figures—each distinct—in miniature.
One corner shows the Thracian Rhodope
and Haemus: these are now bleak mountains, but
they once were mortals who—presumptuous—
took as their own the names of the highest gods.
The second corner shows the sorry fate
of the Pygmaean queen who challenged Juno:
defeating her, the goddess changed that queen
into a crane and had her war against
the very people who had been her subjects.

Latin [67–92]

The third displays Antigone, who once
dared set herself against great Jove's consort;
Queen Juno changed her shape, made her a bird.
Though she was daughter of the Trojan king,
Laomedon, that did not help: the girl
was forced to wear white feathers and compelled,
with clattering beak—a stork—to applaud herself.
The final corner pictures Cinyras
bereft of all his daughters, who had boasted,
too recklessly, of their great beauty: Juno
changed them into her temple's marble steps;
and clinging to those steps, King Cinyras
embraces what were once his daughters' bodies,
and weeps. Minerva, as a sign of peace,
around the border of her work, now weaves
a wreath of olive branches, and with that—
her sacred tree—she finishes her task.

Arachne's scenes displayed Europa fooled
by the feigned image of a bull: and you
would think that both the bull and waves were true.
The girl is shown as she looks back to land
and calls on her companions, even as,
in fear of spray, she timidly draws back
her feet. She also draws Asterie
gripped tightly by the eagle; she shows Leda,
who lies beneath the swan's wings. And she adds
those tales of Jove, who, in a Satyr's guise,
filled fair Antiope with twin offspring;
who, as Amphitryon, hoodwinked you, too,
Alcmena; who, become a shower of gold,
duped Danae; and in the form of fire
deceived Aegina, daughter of Asopius;
and as a shepherd, gulled Mnemosyne;
and, as a speckled snake, Proserpina.

And, too, she showed you, Neptune, in the guise
of a grim bull who takes the virgin daughter

of Aeolus; and as Enipeus, you
beget the Aloids; and as a ram
you bluff Bisaltes' daughter. The kind mother
of harvests, golden-haired, knew you as stallion;
whereas the mother of the winged horse—she
whose hair was wreathed with snakes—knew you as bird;
and when you took Melantho, you were dolphin.
And each of these—the actors and the settings—
is rendered to perfection by Arachne.
Here's Phoebus, too, dressed like a countryman,
and then she shows him decked out in hawk's feathers,
then, in a lion's skin: and we can see
how, in his shepherd's guise, he baited Isse,
the daughter of Macareus. And here is Bacchus,
who fools Erigone with his false grapes;
and we see Saturn, in a horse's shape,
begetting Chiron. Then, to decorate
her web's thin border at the edge, Arachne
fills it with flowers interlaced with ivy.

Not even Pallas, even Jealousy,
could find a flaw in that girl's artistry;
but her success incensed the warrior-goddess.
Minerva tore to pieces that bright cloth
whose colors showed the crimes the gods had wrought;
a boxwood shuttle lay at hand—with that,
three and four times she struck Arachne's forehead.
That was too much: the poor girl took a noose
and rushed—still bold—to tie it round her neck.
But when she saw Arachne hanging there,
Minerva, taking pity, propped her up
and said: "Live then, but, for your perfidy,
still hang; and let this punishment pursue
all who descend from you: thus, you must fear
the future—down to far posterity."
That said, before she left, the goddess sprinkled
the juices of the herbs of Hecate
over Arachne; at that venom's touch,

Latin [116–40]

her hair and then her eyes and ears fell off,
and all her body sank. And at her sides,
her slender fingers clung to her as legs.
The rest is belly; but from this, Arachne
spins out a thread; again she practices
her weaver's art, as once she fashioned webs.

All Lydia is stirred by this; the news
runs through the Phrygian cities; all around,
this is the sole event that men recount.

Now Niobe, before she wed, had lived
close to Mount Sipylus; and she had known
Arachne—they were both Maeonians.
Yet Niobe refused to learn just what
her countrywoman's fate might well have taught:
do not compete with gods, and do not boast.
Yes, there was much that could incite her pride:
her husband's art, the noble lineage
that both could boast, their regal wealth and might—
all these pleased Niobe, but her delight
and pride in her own children fueled far
more overweening arrogance in her.
One could have said that she was the most blessed
of mothers—had she not said so herself.

Now Manto, daughter of Tiresias,
went through the streets of Thebes: the prophetess
was driven by divine impulse. She said:
"Women of Thebes, come all and offer incense
and pious prayers before Latona's shrine,
to honor her and her two children: wreathe
your hair with laurel. So Latona speaks,
through me." And they obey. In all of Thebes,

. . .

Latin [141–62]

the women wreathe their brows with laurel leaves;
and they burn incense in the sanctuary,
reciting prayers.

          But Niobe comes forward
together with a crowd of followers;
her Phrygian robes are sewn with threads of gold:
she is as lovely as her wrath allows.
And as she moves her shapely head, her hair,
in waves down to her shoulders, undulates.
She halts; imposing, tall, with haughty eyes,
she casts her gaze at all around and cries:
"Have you gone mad? Would you, at the expense
of deities you've seen, now reverence
those gods whom you have only heard about?
Why is Latona worshipped at this shrine,
while you, to my divinity, have yet
to offer incense? I have Tantalus
as father, and he was the only mortal
the gods invited to their banquet table;
I have as one grandfather mighty Atlas,
he who sustains the heavens on his shoulders;
and Jove himself not only is my other
grandfather but the father of my husband.
The Phrygian tribes all stand in awe of me;
I am the queen of what was Cadmus' country;
these walls, which rose because my husband cast
a spell with his entrancing lyre—yes,
these walls and all the people they enclose—
are ruled by me and my beloved spouse.
Wherever I, within my palace, turn
my gaze, tremendous treasures meet my eyes.
My beauty, too, is worthy of a goddess.
Then add to this my children: seven sons
and just as many daughters—and quite soon,
I shall have sons- and daughters-in-law. Now,
do say if I have reason to be proud:
do dare prefer a Titaness to me—

Latin [163–86]

that daughter of Coeus—whoever he may be.
Remember this: Latona is the one
to whom the earth—bound as it is—refused
the least of places where she could give birth.
Not welcome in the sky, on earth, on sea,
your goddess was exiled from all the world,
until the isle of Delos pitied her
and said: 'On land, you are a wanderer,
and I shift places on the sea'—with that,
he gave Latona as a resting-place
his own unstable isle. There she became
the mother of two children—just one-seventh
of mine. I'm happy—that can't be denied.
And I'll stay happy—none can doubt that, too.
By now I have so many and so much,
that Fortune can't do harm: I am secure—
there's nothing I need fear. Even suppose
that some part of my brood—or better still,
my tribe—of children should be lost to me;
not even then would I be left to live
with just two children—all Latona has;
yes, she is near indeed to childlessness.
Go now, you've done enough for your Latona—
and take those laurel wreaths out of your hair!"

And they obey; their rites are cut in half.
Now all that they can do is venerate
Latona with words murmured inwardly.

Latona is indignant; on the peak
of Cynthus, this is how the goddess speaks
to her Apollo and Diana: "I,
your mother, proud that I gave birth to you,
I who, except for Juno, am supreme
among the goddesses, must now bear this:
one who would question my divinity!
If you, dear children, do not help me, I—
through all the centuries—will be denied

the honors of the altar. This is not
the only hurt that I resent: insult
was added unto sacrilege: she dared
to say—comparing you to her own brood—
that you were their inferiors. She said—
and this is something she will yet repent—
that I was childless in effect; her tongue
is—like the tongue of Tantalus, her father—
profane." And here she would have added more,
if Phoebus had not cut her short: "Enough!
A long complaint does nothing but delay
her punishment!" Diana said the same.
They glided swiftly through the air until,
concealed by clouds, they reached the citadel
of Cadmus.

And below the walls, nearby,
there stretched a plain, a broad and level field
that—passing and repassing—hard horse hooves
and pounding wheels had softened, evened out.
All of Amphion's seven sons are there;
some leap on their tough horses; their knees press
against the flanks adorned with purple cloth;
they ply their bridles bossed with golden studs.
The firstborn son, Ismenus, rides his horse
with bit and bridle round a circling course;
his bit is tugging at the foaming mouth,
when he cries out: "Ah, me!" Apollo's shaft
has just struck at the middle of his chest;
he lets the reins fall from his dying hands
and slides down slowly over the right flank.
Beside him, Sipylus, his brother, hears
the quiver rattle through the empty air;
and he begins to give full rein, to dash,
just as a captain, sighting dark cloudbanks,
foreseeing storms, spreads all his sails, to catch
even the wind's least breath. He gives full rein.
He gallops, but the shaft none can outrace

Latin [209–35]

has caught him; quivering, it strikes his nape;
and piercing through his throat, nude iron showed.
Bent forward as he is, he now rolls down
and over his swift horse's mane and legs;
his warm blood stains the ground. Poor Phaedimus
and Tantalus—who bore the name of his
grandfather—having finished riding, now
had turned to what is young men's shining contest;
and they are wrestling, straining chest to chest,
entwined together, when an arrow shot
from the taut bow drives through both sons at once.
They groan as one; as one, in pain, collapse
and strike the ground; their eyes bulge, fixed in death;
as one, the brothers breathe their final breath.
Alphenor sees them fall; he beats his breast
and weeps; he runs to lift them up; he clasps
cold bodies. In that pious act, he falls;
the god of Delos, with a fatal shaft,
has pierced him through the chest. And when they draw
the arrow out, part of his lungs comes, too,
stuck to the barbs; and with his blood, his life
pours forth. His long-haired brother, Damasicthon,
is struck by more than one wound: first, a shaft
hits him just where the lower thigh begins,
the hollow just behind the knee. As he
tugged at that shaft, a second arrow drove—
up to the feathers—through his throat: the rush
of blood expelled that arrow, spurting up:
its long and slender stream arched through the air.
The last, Ilioneus, stretched out his arms
in prayer, a useless gesture; he implored:
"Oh, spare me, all you gods"—he did not know
that he need not beseech them all. Apollo
was moved—but mercy came too late. The arrow
had left the bow already. Yet that son
died from a wound less harsh; it struck his heart—
but not too deeply.

□   □   □

Latin [236–66]

                   Niobe learned quickly
of this calamity: the news had spread,
the people grieved, and her own close friends wept.
She was dismayed, amazed at this display
of power—angry at the gods who dared
this much. Amphion, on his part, at once
drove through his chest a sword—and put an end
to both his days and torment. Niobe
was different now from that Queen Niobe
who just before this, at Latona's shrine,
had driven off the Thebans and had walked
the streets of Thebes with pride: that Niobe
was envied even by her friends, and this
was pitied even by her enemies!
She threw herself upon her sons' cold bodies
and—frenzied—gave the final kiss to each.
Then, lifting to the sky her livid arms,
she cried: "Feed, fierce Latona, on my grief
and sate your savage heart. My enemy,
you can exult: you've triumphed over me!
What triumph? Even in my misery,
I've more than you have in felicity:
despite these deaths, I still claim victory!"

As soon as that was said, one heard a taut
bowstring, a twanging that astonished all—
except for Niobe: calamity
had toughened her. Her seven daughters stood
with loosened hair, in robes of black, before
their brothers' biers. And one, while tugging out
the arrow that had struck her brother's guts,
sank down and died; her face collapsed against
the body of that brother. And another,
while trying to console her wretched mother,
fell silent suddenly and doubled over—
an unseen wound had made her lock her lips
until her soul had left. Another fell
while trying to run off. Another breathed

Latin [267–95]

her last upon a sister's corpse. One hid,
and one—who could be seen—was shuddering.

Six daughters now had died of different wounds.
The last was left. With all her body, all
her robes, her mother shielded her and cried:
"Do leave me one, my youngest, her alone!
I beg you, spare, of all my children, one!"
She prayed, and as she did, the one for whom
she prayed met death.

                        And Niobe now sat
childless, among cadavers—daughters, sons,
and husband; grief had made her stony, stiff.
The air is still, not even one hair moves,
her face is deathly pale; above sad cheeks,
her eyes stare motionless. Even her tongue
is frozen in her mouth; her palate now
is hard; her veins can pulse no more; her neck
can't bend; her arms can't move; her feet can't walk.
Within, her vitals, too, are stone. And yet
she weeps; and swept up in a strong whirlwind,
she's carried to her native land and set
upon the peak of Sipylus—and there
she weeps, and to this day her rock sheds tears.

—————————

Now, having witnessed this, the Thebans—all
the men and all the women—fear the gods'
retaliation; and with more devotion,
they now adore the two twins' awesome mother.
And since things recent call to mind things past,
the fate of Niobe led one to say:
"Just so, in Lycia's fertile fields, of old,
the peasants had to pay harsh penalties
for their disprizing the divinity
of great Latona. While it's true that tale

Latin [295–319]

is little known—for, after all, it's told
by country folk—it is extraordinary.
But I myself have visited that pool
and seen the site that saw the miracle.
In fact, my father, who was then too old
to face that journey, had entrusted me
to drive down some fine bullocks from that country;
and he had given me as guide a Lycian.
And while, with him, I roamed the grazing lands,
we came upon a lake; an ancient altar,
blackened by many sacrificial fires
and ringed by quivering reeds, rose from those waters.
My guide stood still and whispered fearfully:
'Have pity!' And I mimed him with: 'Have pity!'
I asked if this was once a Naiad's altar,
a Faun's, or else some local deity's.
My Lycian comrade answered: 'No, young man:
no mountain deity can claim this shrine.
The one who claims it as her own is she
whom Juno once had banished from the world.
She was the wanderer whose prayer for shelter
was answered by the wandering Delos when
it was a floating, shifting island mass.
There, even as she rested on two trunks,
a palm tree and an olive, she gave birth—
in spite of their stepmother—to a pair
of twins. And then—it's said—Latona fled
with her two infants, both of them divine,
in order to escape the wrath of Juno.
And hugging those two infants to her breast,
she came to Lycia, the Chimaera's land.
The sun was fiercely hot; the fields were scorched;
her journey had been long; her throat was parched;
she thirsted, for the heat did not abate;
her hungry babes had drained her breasts of milk.
Just then, she chanced to see a little lake
far off, in a deep valley, at the base;
and there the country folk were gathering reeds,

Latin [319–44]

bulrushes, and swamp grass. And when she reached
the banks and knelt along the ground to sip
cool water, all that rustic crowd would not
let Titan's daughter drink. She asked them: "Why
do you deny me this? All have a right
to water: Nature never has declared
that sun or flowing water or the air
is private property. When I drew near,
it was a public good I came to share;
nevertheless, I ask you as a favor
to give me some. I did not come to bathe
my limbs and weary body in your lake—
all that I wanted was to quench my thirst.
I speak, and yet my mouth is dry, my throat
is parched; the path my voice must take is hard.
For me, a sip of water will be nectar;
it's life and water I'll receive; for you,
in giving it to me, will give me life.
And, too, take pity on my infants—they
stretch out their little arms . . ." And then, by chance,
the children at her bosom did just that.
Who—hearing words so sweet—would not be moved?
But they, despite her prayers, still refused;
and then they added threats, and insults, too.
And as if that were not enough, they soiled
the water with their feet and hands, and jumped—
maliciously—to stir the bottom mud.
At that, Latona's wrath postponed her thirst.
Indeed, by now she pleads no more with these
unworthy folk: she does not choose to speak
as other than her goddess-self. She lifts
her hands to heaven, and she cries: "Live then
forever in that pool." Just as she wished
to have it, so it is. They love the water;
and now they plunge their bodies underneath
the surface of the pool's concavity;
now they thrust forth their heads, and now they swim
along the surface. And they often halt

Latin [345–73]

along the banks and often dive again
into the chilly depths. They still persist
in bickering shamelessly with their foul tongues;
and when they're under water, underwater
they try to curse each other. And their voices
are still hoarse, and their tumid cheeks swell up;
and those same bickerings puff out their jaws.
Their shoulders touch their heads, their necks have vanished.
Their backs are green; their bellies, which take up
most of their body, white; as new-made frogs,
they leap about within the muddy pool.' "

When he (whose name I do not know) was done,
and all had heard what happened to those Lycians,
another was reminded of a Satyr
who had contended with Latona's son:
a contest on the flute (one of the sort
Minerva had invented): he who won—
Apollo—punished him. The Satyr cried:
"Why do you tear me from myself? Oh, I
repent! A flute is not worth such a price."
He screams; the skin is flayed off all his form,
and he is but one wound; upon all sides,
his blood pours down; his sinews can be seen;
his pulsing veins glow with no veil of skin;
you could have tallied up his throbbing guts;
the fibers in his chest were clear, apparent.
The country Fauns, the woodland deities,
his brother Satyrs, and Olympus (he
whom Marsyas—even in his death throes—loved)
mourned him, as did all those who, on those slopes,
had shepherded their woolly flocks and herded
horned cattle. And the fertile soil was soaked
with tears that fell; and these, Earth gathered up
and drank them deep into her veins; then these
she changed into a watercourse and sent

Latin [373–98]

into the open air. From there the river,
within its sloping banks, ran down to sea:
it is called Marsyas—Phrygia's clearest stream.

But having heard these tales, the Thebans turned
back to the present; once again they mourn
Amphion and his children. They all blame
the mother; but one man, her brother Pelops—
so it is said—wept, too, for Niobe;
he drew aside his robe; he bared his chest
and showed his ivory shoulder on the left.
At Pelops' birth, this shoulder was of flesh
and bone and had the color of the right;
but then, it's said, his father cut up Pelops.
And when the gods had finished gathering
the pieces and poor Pelops was complete
once more, one part was missing still: the piece
between his throat and where the arm begins.
This they filled in with ivory, and so
he was again made whole.

                            The regions close
to Thebes now sent their chieftains; many kings
were urged to visit stricken Thebes, to bring
their words of solace, words of sympathy
for its calamity. And all these cities
brought comfort: Argos, Sparta, and Mycenae
from the Peloponnese; and Calydon
(Diana's wrath had not yet struck it down);
and Corinth, famed for bronze; Orchomenos,
the fertile land; and Patrae, proud Messene,
and flat Cleonae; Pylos, Neleus' city;
and Troezen, which was not yet ruled by Pittheus;
and all those other towns that are enclosed

Latin [398–419]

inside the Isthmus bathed by the two seas,
as well as those south of its outer coast.

And, Athens, only you—who would believe
that you would not pay homage unto Thebes!—

did not appear: you were beset by war;
barbarians—attacking from the sea—

were threatening your walls.

But you were saved
by Tereus, who had brought his troops from Thrace,
defeated the invaders, won great fame.
His wealth was great, his fighting men were many:
he had much power—and traced his line to Mars.
And so, Pandion, Athens' king, allied
himself to Tereus, giving him as bride
Pandion's daughter, Procne. But the patron
of weddings, Juno, was not present, nor
did Hymen or the Graces bless the pair.
The Furies were the ones who bore the torches
that they had stolen from a funeral;
it was the Furies who prepared the bed;
a sacrilegious screech-owl built its nest
and brooded on the rooftop, overhead.
It was beneath such signs that they were wed,
beneath such signs that they conceived a child.

Of course, all Thracians shared their happiness,
and they themselves were grateful to the gods.
Indeed, the Thracians made the day that saw
Pandion's daughter wed their mighty king
a yearly festival, just as they made
the day of Itys' birth a holiday.
How we, in judging things, are led astray!

Five autumns had already gone; the Sun
had led the wheel of years through five full turns,
when Procne spoke—endearingly—to Tereus:

"If you are somewhat fond of me, then either
send me to see my sister, or have her
come visit me in Thrace—you can assure
my father that her visit will be brief."
So Tereus had them launch his ship; with sails
and oars, he reached Piraeus, Cecrops' port.
Pandion's welcoming was warm, most cordial;
they joined right hands and wished each other well.

And Tereus had begun to tell just why
he'd come, and what his wife so wanted, and
to promise that her sister, if she went
to Thrace, would come home quickly, sound and safe,
when Philomela entered: she was dressed
magnificently, but her loveliness
was still more splendid, like a Naiad's or
a Dryad's when—so we are told—they roam
the deep woods, if they could be garbed as well—
as tastefully, as richly—as this girl.
That sight was quite enough; the flame of love
had taken Tereus, as if one had set
afire ripe grain, dry leaves, or a haystack.
It's true she's fair, but he is also spurred
by venery, an inborn tribal urge.
The vice inflaming him is both his own
and that dark fire which burns in Thracian souls.
His impulse was to buy his way to her,
to bribe her closest friends or faithful nurse
and then, when he'd corrupted them, to tempt
the girl himself, though that might cost his kingdom;
or else to ravish her, and then defend
his rape by waging unrelenting war.
There's nothing he'd not dare to do; his love
cannot be checked, his heart cannot contain
the flames within; and now the least delay
weighs heavily; his avid tongue again
repeats what Procne urged, but with those words
it is his secret need of which he speaks.

Latin [441–68]

Love makes him eloquent, and when his plea
might seem excessive, he is quick indeed
to say he's just relaying Procne's wish.
He even garnishes his plea with tears,
as if his wife had asked this, too, of him.

O gods, how dark the night that rules men's minds!
Precisely when he weaves his plot, he seems

a man most dutiful; he wins much praise
for what is wickedness. Does Philomela
not urge the visit even as he does?
She winds her arms around her father's neck,
entreating him to let her make the trip;
she says that it will do her good (but it
will do the opposite) to go and visit
her sister. Tereus watches her, and as
he looks, he feels delights that will be his;
those kisses and embraces that he sees
are food and fuel that goad his lechery;
she hugs her father—Tereus wishes he
were in Pandion's place—indeed if he
were Philomela's father he'd not be
less sacrilegious than he is. Pandion
gives way; he grants just what his daughters want.

And Philomela thanks him—poor thing, she
is glad—and what she thinks is victory
for both her sister and herself will be
a sad defeat.

       By now the Sun is left
with little more to do; his horses pace
along Olympus' slopes—their downward path.
A royal feast is readied; golden cups
now brim with Bacchus' gift. Then, as is just,
their bodies yield to peaceful sleep. But Tereus,
though Philomela has retired, lusts:
he can recall her face, recall her hands,
her gestures, and at will imagines what

Latin [469–92]

he's not yet seen; and in himself he feeds
the flames—his torment will not let him sleep.

Day breaks, and as his son-in-law prepares
to sail away, Pandion clasps his hand
and tearfully confides his daughter to him
and says: "Dear son-in-law, compelled by fond
and tender pleas, as both my daughters want
(and you, too, Tereus, wish), I now entrust
to you my Philomela; but I call
upon your loyalty, our binding ties,
and on the gods, as I enjoin you: guard
her lovingly, as would a father; send
my daughter back as quickly as you can;
for me, the least delay will seem so long:
in my old age, she is my consolation.
And Philomela, I do urge you, too,
if you indeed love me, return as soon
as possible (I miss your sister so—
I need no greater load)." And as he spoke
these final words, between his last requests
he kissed his Philomela, and he shed
soft tears. And then he asked them both to pledge
her quick return by offering their right hands;
he joined their hands together, and he begged
that they might bear his greetings to dear Procne
and his grandchild, whom he remembers always,
though they are distant. It is hard for him
to say farewell; he struggles with his tears,
and sobs—a sad foreboding stirs his fears.

Once Philomela is embarked upon
the painted ship, as Tereus' oars advance
across the sea, the land is left behind.
"I've won! What I have dreamed on now is mine!"
cries Tereus. That barbarian exults;
it's hard for him to hold off his delights.
His eyes are set on her, they never swerve;

Latin [492–515]

he's not unlike the sacred bird of Jove,
who, in his nest on high, sets down the hare
he's caught with his hooked claws; the captor stares—
his eyes are fixed upon his helpless prize.

The voyage now is done, and all have left
the weary ship and gone ashore. On land,
King Tereus drags the daughter of Pandion
into a hut that's hid in ancient woods:
and there he locks her up—she shakes with fear;
and pale, in tears, she asks to see her sister.
And he confesses to her his foul passion
and rapes her—she's a girl, and all alone;
again, again, she calls upon her father,
her sister, and—above all—the great gods.
She trembles like a lamb that's terrified,
that, wounded, cast off from a gray wolf's jaw,
cannot feel safe; or like a shuddering dove
whose feathers now are drenched in its own blood,
that still recalls the avid, clutching claws
that caught it. With her senses back, she tugs
at her disheveled hair; like one who mourns,
she beats her arms and then, with outstretched hands,
she cries:

        "What have you done, barbarian!
My father's plea and his fond tears, the love
my sister feels for you, and, too, my own
virginity; your bonds of marriage—none
of these could move you. All is now askew.
I am a concubine, and you've become
a bigamist: it's only right for Procne
to punish me like any enemy.
Why don't you, to complete your treachery,
tear out my soul? Would you had murdered me
before this wretched coupling! Then, at least,
my Shade would be unstained. But if the gods
of heaven see these things, if deities

Latin [516–43]

still have some power, if my loss of honor
does not mean all is lost, then you—someday—
will pay. I'll cast aside my shame, proclaim
your crime. If that be possible for me,
I'll tell my tale where many people crowd.
And if I'm shut up in these woods, I'll shout
unto the trees; I'll move the rocks to pity.
My tale will reach the heavens and—if they
are still in heaven—it will reach the gods."

Her words have angered him, but the fierce king
feels, too, a fear whose force can match his wrath.
Urged on by both these goads, he now unsheathes
the sword he carries at his side; he grabs
poor Philomela by the hair; he twists
her arms behind her back and binds her fast.
And Philomela offers him her throat—
she's seen the sword, and death is her dear hope.
But it's her tongue he seizes with a pincer;
and even as it calls upon her father,
protests and struggles hard to speak, he lifts
his blade and—without mercy—severs it.
Its root still quivers, while the tongue itself
falls to the ground; there, on the blood-red soil,
it murmurs; as a serpent's severed tail
will writhe, so did that tongue, in dying, twist
and try to reach its mistress' feet. Though this
indeed defies belief, it's said that Tereus
again, again, gave free rein to his lust
upon that mangled body.

After such
a foul exploit, he still was bold enough
to face his wife. And Procne asked at once
where her dear sister was. And Tereus groaned
and spun a cunning story of her death:
to make his fiction credible, he wept.
Then, from her shoulders, Procne tore away

Latin [543–67]

the robe whose ample border gleamed with gold;
she put on mourning clothes, and she erected
an empty sepulcher, to which she brought
expiatory offerings, the sort
of sacrifices that the Shades deserve—
but Philomela was not dead. And so
dear Procne mourned her sister's fate, although
there was no Shade to whom such rites were owed.

The Sun had passed through all the twice-six signs,
and now a full year's journey has gone by.
And what shall Philomela do? No flight
is possible: a guard had been assigned
to watch her; and around the hut, walls rise—
they are of solid stone; her lips are mute;
there is no way she can reveal the truth.
But desperation can indeed invent;
in misery the mind is keen. She hangs
a web upon a crude—a Thracian—loom
and, on a white background, weaves purple signs:
the letters that denounce the savage crime.
When that is done, she gives her servingwoman
the cloth—she's rolled it up—and, gesturing,
asks her to bring it to the queen. As bid,
but ignorant of what the message is,
the servingwoman takes the cloth to Procne.
The savage tyrant's wife, unrolling it,
soon reads her sister's tale, the dread misdeed,
and then—a fact that cannot be believed—
she does not speak: her mouth is blocked by grief.
Her tongue seeks words of scorn to match her wrath
but does not find them. Nor does Procne weep:
she sinks into herself, imagining
both licit and illicit penalties
she could inflict; revenge is what she needs.

The time had come for the triennial feast
of Bacchus, when the Thracian women meet

Latin [567–88]

by night, to celebrate their secret rites.
By night, the slopes of Rhodope resound
with clashing brazen cymbals; and by night,
the queen goes from her house; she is arrayed
just as the frenzied cult demands: her head
is wreathed with trailing vines; a deerskin hangs
from her left side; upon her shoulder rests
a light lance. As she strides the forest paths,
with crowds of followers behind her, Procne,
stirred by her sorrow's fury—and her rage
is awesome—feigns your frenzy, Bacchus. She
comes to the solitary stall at last.
She shrieks and howls, "Euhoe!," breaking down
the doors: she grasps her sister, dresses her
in a Bacchante's full array and hides
her face with ivy leaves; then, at her side
(her sister is amazed), hauls her away,
off to the palace, where she can be safe.
But when the wretched Philomela sees
the dwelling of the man of infamy,
she shudders, pale as death. But patient Procne,
once she has found a proper place, removes
the poor girl's Bacchic costume; she uncovers
her shamefaced sister and embraces her.
But Philomela will not lift her eyes;
she sees herself as an adulteress;
and staring at the ground, she tries to swear,
to call upon the gods as witnesses,
that she had been the prey of violence;
but after all, she has no voice—just gestures.

But Procne's rage can't be contained: she flames;
she scolds her tearful sister; she exclaims:
"No tears are needed here; it's time for steel,
or if you know of something harder still,
then give me that. I'm ready now to kill
in any way, however criminal:
I'll fire this palace with a torch and fling

Latin [588–614]

into the flames that artifex of sins;
or I'll cut out his tongue or else his eyes
and hack the limb that brought such shame to you;
I'll drive his soul out through a thousand wounds—
however horrible. But I have yet—
of all these deaths—to choose the end that's best."

Her words were not yet done when her dear son,
her Itys, entered. At the sight of him,
a notion strikes her; and with cruel eye,
she stares at her own son as she outcries:
"How closely you resemble him—your father!"
She says no more and, as her anger boils
within, begins to plan horrendous things.
It's true that when her son comes up to her
and greets her, as he throws his tiny arms
around her neck and, in his boyish way,
embraces her, she's moved, her wrath is tamed,
her eyes grow damp with tears she can't restrain.
But sensing that maternal love has swayed
her purpose, Procne turns aside her gaze
from Itys to her sister, thinking this:
"And why can he still speak endearingly,
while she is mute, her tongue cut out? If he
can call me mother, why can't she say 'sister'?
O, daughter of Pandion, do remember
the sort of man you married! Do you waver?
To pity such a husband is a crime!"

She does not hesitate; she drags her son
away, just as a tigress on the Ganges
hauls off a suckling fawn through the dark woods;
and when, in that vast palace, they have reached
a far-off room, while he, with hands outstretched,
already senses what his fate will be
and cries out, "Mother, Mother," while he tries
to throw his arms around her neck, her knife
strikes him—she does not turn aside her eyes—

Latin [615–41]

between his chest and side. That blow was quite
enough to kill. But Philomela strikes;
she hacks his throat. And then the sisters slice
his limbs, still quivering with some warm life.
Some pieces fill a boiling copper kettle,
and others sputter on the spit. His blood
drips everywhere in that secluded room.

Such is the feast to which his wife invites
the unsuspecting Tereus. She connives
to keep all their attendants and their slaves
away: the false pretext that she invents
is this—only a husband may partake
of such a sacred feast, an ancient rite
still celebrated in her own birthplace.
So, seated on his high ancestral throne,
he, Tereus, eats alone and, with his own
flesh, fills his belly; and his mind is so
completely ignorant of what he's done
that he calls out: "Bring Itys here—my son."
And Procne can't conceal her cruel delight;
and keen to be herself the one who tells
the news of this calamity, she cries:
"The one you want is with you now—inside."
He looks around and asks where Itys went;
and when mad Philomela rushes in—
her flowing hair is stained with butchery
and blood—against the father's face she flings
the bleeding head of Itys. There was never
a time when she longed so to have the power
of speech, to find the words to shout her joy.

The king of Thrace cries out—a giant shout;
he overturns the table, summoning
the snake-haired Sisters of the Stygian pit;
and now he wishes he could rip his chest
and rid his body of the horrid feast,
the innards he had swallowed; now he weeps

Latin [642–65]

and calls himself the miserable tomb
of his own son. And now, his sword unsheathed,
it is Pandion's daughters whom he seeks.

But you'd have said that those Athenians
had taken flight with wings. There, they are poised;
one sister wings her way into the dark woods,
the other rises to the roof—her breast
still bears the signs of their atrocious crime:
her feathers are bloodstained. And Tereus speeds—
spurred by his grief and need to seek revenge—
and he, too, changes form, becomes a bird,
a bird whose head is crowned with a stiff crest,
whose beak is huge, a long, protruding lance:
the hoopoe—ever ready to attack.

———————

Before old age had reached full term, Pandion,
undone by grief too great, has joined the Shades
of Tartarus. The king who takes his place,
his scepter is Erectheus; the domain
is his to rule. And it is hard to say
if he had gained more fame for his just ways
or for his bravery when war was waged.
He had four sons and just as many girls—
the grace that two of these displayed was special.
O Procris, when you married Cephalus,
grandson of Aeolus, to him you brought
felicity. But Boreas, who came
from Thrace, because of Tereus' crime was made
to wait; they kept him far from Orithyia,
that is, as long as he preferred to use
not force but pleas and prayers when he wooed.

But when his suasive words did not avail,
the god, in rage (for him, quite usual—
indeed too natural—for, after all,

he was the wind that gusted from the north),
rebuked himself: "I get what I deserve!
my arms and rage, ferocity and force,
my menaces—all these I've given up;
instead I've tried persuasion, pleas and prayers—
and who'd call this my most congenial course?
Yes, force is sure to win what I want most:
with force, I drive the sullen clouds; with force
I rock the sea, I fell the knotted oaks,
pack hard the snows, and pound with hail the earth.
When in the open sky—my battlefield—
I face my brother winds, the force I wield
makes heaven's center thunder; hollow clouds
erupt, and flaming lightning bursts, leaps out.
And when, through crevices, I penetrate
the earth and, having reached the deepest caves,
with my emphatic back, heave hard against
the vaults that arch those vast convexities,
I terrify the Shades, the whole world quakes.
To win my wife, I should have gone that way.
I pleaded with Erectheus—hoped he'd be
my father-in-law—but I should, with deeds,
have made him such."

                It was with words like these—
and others no less threatening—that he
now shook his wings; and as they beat, a blast
swept over all the earth; and it convulsed
the vast sea-surface, too. Then Boreas
put on his dusty cloak; across the slopes
and peaks, he trailed his mantle as he rushed
across the earth; concealed by his dark cloud,
he wrapped the terror-stricken Orithyia
within his tawny wings. He bore her off;
and as he flew, he felt the flames of love
gain force on force; he did not curb his course
across the air until he'd reached the north,
the lands and city of the Cicones. □ □ □

Latin [686–710]

There, in the north, Athenian Orithyia
became the bride of glacial Boreas
and, in due time, a mother; she gave birth
to twins, two sons, who in all else were like
their mortal mother but inherited
their father's wings; though these—so it is said—
did not appear at birth. As long as Zetes
and Calais did not show beards below
their reddish locks, the boys lacked plumage—but
as soon as both, upon their cheeks, began
to show blond hairs, two wings began to sprout
on either side, the sort that birds display.
And when the twins' boyhood gave way to youth,
they sailed off with the Argonauts to seek—
in the first ship to cross the unknown deep—
the golden radiance of the gleaming fleece.

Latin [711–21]

BOOK VII

NOW, IN THE SHIP they built at Pagasa,
the Argonauts were furrowing the sea.
They had already seen the Thracian seer,
King Phineus, dragging out his final years
in endless blindness. Boreas' twin sons
had eased his sufferings: they'd driven off
the Harpies, women-birds who tortured him;
in recompense, the old king helped them chart
the way to Colchis. After many trials,
led by the hero Jason, they had reached
the rapid current of the muddy Phasis.
There, when they went to King Aeëtes, claiming
the Golden Fleece he had obtained from Phrixus,
the king agreed to yield the fleece they sought—
but only on his terms: he set three tasks,
horrendous tests that Jason had to pass.

Meanwhile the raging flame of love has struck
Medea, daughter of the king: when she,
who struggled long against that passion, sees
that reason cannot win again her frenzy,
she says:

       "Medea, you are doomed to fail:
the force you face must be some deity.
I wonder if this power (or something like it)
is not the power known to men as love.
Indeed, why do the terms my father set
seem harsh to me? But then . . . they are just that!
Why do I dread the death of one whom I
have seen but once—a first and only time!
What led to this? Why am I terrified?
Come, quench the flame that burns your virgin breast—
would you, unhappy girl, could do just that!
If it could blaze no more, I would be healed.
Instead, despite myself, a force that I
have never known before impels me now:
my longing needs one thing; my reason seeks

Latin [1–20]

another. I can see—and I approve
the better course, and yet I choose the worse.
Oh, why do you, the daughter of a king,
burn for a stranger? Why, why must you dream
of wedding one whose world is alien?
You can, in your own land, find one to love.
The fate of Jason—life or death—depends
upon the gods. But I do hope he lives—
a hope that would be rightful even if
I did not love him! After all, what wrong
has Jason done! How could one be so cruel
as to ignore his noble birth, his youth,
his worth! But even if he lacked all these,
would Jason's face alone not be enough
to stir one's heart? At least, my heart—the heart
he has entranced. If I don't take his part,
he will be blasted by the bulls' hot breath,
and then face foes that he himself begets—
sprung from the very soil that he will sow—
or else fall prey to the voracious dragon.
If I let him become their victim, then
I must confess that I'm a tigress' daughter,
who carries steel and stones within her breast.
And why don't I look on as Jason dies—
why would that spectacle defile my eyes?
Why not incite the bulls, and savage foes
the earth engenders, and the sleepless dragon?
O gods, forbid that! . . . Yet, why do I pray?
I have to act! But shall I then betray
my father's kingdom—be the one to save
this foreigner (I only know his name—
and nothing more), who then can sail away
without me, once he has escaped the fates,
and marry someone else, while I remain
alone—to face the penalty I'll pay?
If he is capable of that, if he
can choose another woman over me,
then let him—so ungrateful—die! But no . . .

Latin [20–43]

but no, his aspect is so kind, his soul
so noble, and his form so gracious—I
need have no fear of fraud: he won't forget
my merits. And, in any case, he'll pledge
himself to me before I act: I'll have
the gods as witnesses—a solemn pact.
Why be afraid, when all is sure and safe?
Begin to work—don't wait—do not delay!
Jason will owe an endless debt to you:
a sacred marriage bond will join you two;
in all the towns of Greece there will be crowds
of mothers hailing you as savior!
Shall I, borne by the winds, sail off, desert
my sister, brother, father, my own gods,
my native land? Indeed my father is harsh,
my land is barbarous; and on her part,
my sister sides with me, my brother is young—
still but a boy; and I, within my heart,
can count upon the greatest of the gods.
I don't abandon great things; I sail toward
greatness: I'll gain much fame for having saved
the young Achaeans; I shall learn the ways
and manners of a better land than mine,
of cities whose renown has reached these shores,
of countries known for culture and the arts;
and I shall gain the man I'd not exchange
for all the gold the world may hold: the son
of Aeson. As his wife I shall be known
as the most blessed of women, whom the gods
most cherish; I shall touch the very stars!
And yet . . . there are reports of certain peaks
(I don't know how they are called) that in midsea
collide and clash; and I have heard men speak
of dread Charybdis, bane of sailors—she
who, girt with greedy hounds, barks in the deeps
of the Sicilian straits! I may face these—
but even as I clasp my Jason, he
will shield me as we cross the long sea tracts.

Latin [43–67]

I shall fear nothing, held in his warm grasp;
and if I fear, it won't be for myself
but for my husband. But, Medea, can
you hide your guilt beneath the gilded name
of 'matrimony'? See instead the shame
you'll face—while there's still time, escape disgrace:
the fate that waits if you commit that crime!"

Such were Medea's words. At last she sees
the righteous path and duty, modesty:
defeated now, her longing beats retreat.

But when Medea, having curbed her ardor,
felt stronger and sought out the ancient altar
of Perse's daughter, Hecate—a shrine
concealed by forest shadows—on her way
she saw the son of Aeson; and love's flame,
which had been spent, again began to rage.
Her cheeks grew red; fire spread across her face:
and just as a small spark that has been hid
beneath a veil of ashes can be fed—
and grow—beneath a breath of wind, and thus
regain the force that it had lost, her love,
now weak—one could have called it languishing—
rekindled when, along her way, she saw
the captivating form of Aeson's son—
who chanced, that day, to be even more graceful
than usual: her trance was pardonable.

She saw him, and she stared as if this were
the first time he was ever seen by her;
dismayed, she thought her gaze had found the face
of a divinity; her eyes were fixed.
But when the stranger started speaking and—
even as he held fast Medea's hand—
with his soft voice implored her help and pledged
that he would marry her, Medea wept
and said: "I am aware of what I do;

Latin [67–92]

if I'm undone, the cause is surely not
my ignorance, but love. You shall be saved;
but when that's done, maintain the vow you made."
He swore by all the holy mysteries
of Hecate—the triform goddess he
supposed was in that grove—and by the Sun,
who sees all things, the father of the one
now destined to become his father-in-law—
and by his triumphs over such great dangers.
His oath convinced her: she believed the stranger.
And so, without delay, the Greek received
from her the magic herbs of Hecate;
and having learned the proper use of each,
delighted, he went back to his own dwelling.

When Dawn has banished all the glittering stars,
the crowds move toward the sacred field of Mars;
they throng the heights that ring the combat ground.
The king himself has come; in purple robes,
among his retinue, he sits enthroned;
his ivory scepter is conspicuous.
And now the bulls, with their bronze hooves, charge out.
From adamantine nostrils, they breathe flames;
as they exhale, the meadow catches fire.
And even as a well-stoked furnace roars,
or as a limekiln hisses when they pour
fresh water on the lime and it dissolves
and starts to boil, so do the bulls now roar
with whirling flames pent in their chests and throats.
Yet Jason moves ahead. The bulls are grim;
their horns with iron tips are leveled at him;
they paw the dusty ground with their forked hooves;
they fill the field with bellows and hot smoke.
His Argonauts are terrified, but he
(his herbs are powerful indeed) draws near;
untroubled by the gusts of heat, he dares
to stroke their hanging dewlaps with his hand.
He thrusts the bulls beneath a yoke, compels

Latin [92–118]

those beasts to pull a massive plow, to furrow
a field that never felt a plow before.
The Colchians are baffled, but his men
urge Jason on with mighty shouts—and then,
from the bronze helmet, he draws out snake's teeth
and scatters them on the plowed field as seed.
These teeth had first been steeped in potent venom;
earth softens them; they grow, take on new forms.
Just as a fetus gradually takes,
within its mother's womb, a human shape,
acquiring harmony in all its parts,
and only sees the light that all men share
when it is fully formed, so here, the likeness
of men, perfected in the pregnant earth,
sprang from the soil; and what is even more
miraculous, each man was armed and clashed
his weapons at his birth.

               But then this dread
assailed the Greeks; they saw these warriors set
to cast their sharp shafts at young Jason's head.
The Argonauts grew pale; their courage failed.
Even Medea, who had kept him safe
from every menace, feared for Jason's fate:
alone, he must withstand so many foes—
she, too, grew pale and chill; about to faint,
she sat; and fearing that her gift of herbs
might not be strong enough, she chose to add
a spell, a chant drawn from a secret source.
But Jason, who had hurled a massive stone
into the ranks of his attackers, turned
the fray away from his own self; instead
they raged against each other, and the brothers
sprung from the earth met death in civil war.

The Greeks, exulting, crowd around the victor,
embracing Jason eagerly. You, stranger—
Medea—would embrace the victor, too,

Latin [119–44]

but are restrained by modesty, although
that would in truth have been no curb to you—
it was your public name that held you back.
But you're allowed your secret joy; you watch
in silence, thanking magic and the gods
who are the source of those compelling arts.

Now one ordeal alone still waits for Jason:
he has to put to sleep the wakeful dragon,
the horrid guardian of the golden tree—
the tri-tongued, crested serpent with hooked teeth.
And when the son of Aeson sprinkles him
with juices from a hypnagogic herb,
and three times over has pronounced the words
that bring calm sleep, that quiet troubled seas,
that curb the rivers' flow—the dragon's eyes
shut tight: they meet with sleep for the first time.
The hero Jason gains the Golden Fleece;
and proud of what he's won, he also takes
another prize: the girl, whose magic gave
the victory to him, becomes his bride.
And he sails home—Medea at his side.

————————

And on their sons' return, in glad thanksgiving
the mothers and the aged fathers bring
their offerings and burn incense on the altars,
and sacrifice the victim they had vowed,
a bull with gilded horns. But in that crowd,
one man is missing: Jason's father, Aeson;
now close to death, the long years weigh him down.
And Jason says: "Dear wife, to whom—I know—
I owe my own salvation: it is true
that you have given everything to me;
your merits can't be tallied; they exceed
all I could ever have relied upon.
And yet, if you now can (and spells and chants

and magic may accomplish even this),
please take some portion of the years I'll live
and, since I am still young, assign that share
to my dear father." And he adds his tears.
His filial piety has moved Medea—
his generous request; and she—whose soul
is so unlike the soul of Jason—calls
to mind her own Aeëtes, left behind.
But she does not betray that sentiment.
She answers: "Husband, how can you permit
such sacrilege to issue from your lips?
Do you believe I have the power to
prolong another's life, depriving you
of years? May Hecate forever hold me back
from that—and what you ask is, too, unjust.
And yet there is a gift more marvelous—
and, Jason, I shall try to grant you that.
I'll try to lengthen Aeson's life—but not
by shortening your days. For magic arts
will be the means I use—if Hecate
will help me realize this daring feat!"

The moon was three nights short of rounding out
its horns. But when its circle was complete
and shone in full upon the earth, then she,
in a loose robe, barefoot, her hair uncombed
and unadorned, went out to wander through
the silences of midnight. Men, birds, beasts—
were all held fast by deep tranquillity.
The hedges did not murmur, and the leaves'
not stir; the humid air was motionless.
Only the stars were glittering—and she
stretched out her arms toward them; three times she turned
around, around; three times, upon her head,
she poured fresh river water; and three times,
Medea opened wide her lips and wailed;
then, as she knelt on the hard ground, she said:
"O Night, true guardian of secret rites;

Latin [167–92]

o golden stars, who, when the flames of day
retreat, emerge with the moon's rays; and you,
o three-formed Hecate, who are aware
of our endeavors, you who shield and shelter
the chants and arts of sorcery; and, Earth,
who offer to magicians potent herbs;
you breezes, winds, and mountains, rivers, lakes;
and all you forest gods and gods of Shades—
be my allies! It's with your help that I,
at will, as the bewildered banks stood watch,
have turned back river currents to their source.
My spell can still the swollen sea and stir
calm seas; I can expel and can convene
the clouds; I can disperse or summon winds.
My incantation burst the serpent's throat;
I can uproot and move the rocks, the oaks,
the forests; I can make the mountains quake,
earth bellow; and I can command the Shades
to leave their tombs. And even you, o Moon,
I can draw down from heaven's heights, although
the clanging bronze of Temesa tries so
to ease your agony; my song makes pale
even the chariot of my grandfather,
the Sun; my venom frightens even Dawn.
It's you who, to assist me, dulled the flames
of those bronze bulls; you bent their stubborn necks
beneath the curving plow; and you compelled
the serpent's sons to war among themselves;
it's you who made the watchman yield to sleep
for the first time; and so the Golden Fleece,
once he had been bewitched, went back to Greece.

"Now I have need of juices to renew
the life of an old man, so that he can
regain his youth, the years that he first knew.
I know that you will help me; it is plain;
the stars are glittering—and not in vain;

. . .

Latin [192–217]

and not in vain—drawn by the yoked winged dragons—
a chariot is now at hand."

                    Indeed
a chariot had been sent to serve her needs—
a chariot from the sky. On mounting it,
Medea stroked the dragons' bridled necks,
then shook the light reins with her hands and soared
on high: below her lay the vale of Tempe
in Thessaly; she steered her serpents toward
the sites she knew so well: she scanned the heights
of Ossa and of Pelion, of Othrys,
of Pindus and the taller peak, Olympus;
and when she found an herb that served her purpose,
Medea plucked it from the roots or cut
the stem with her curved pruning-hook of bronze.
She also culled her herbs on riverbanks:
on the Apidanus and the Amphrysus;
and you, Enipeus, were not left untouched,
nor were Peneus and Sperchios, just
as Boebe's reedy banks were also plucked.
And from Anthedon, town that faced Euboea,
she culled an herb that gave new life, a grass
not yet well known for what it did to Glaucus,
whose body it transformed. Nine days, nine nights
had seen Medea travel: driven by
winged dragons, she had searched through every land.
That done, the sorceress came home again.
And though those herbs had touched no dragon, just
the odor was enough: the dragons sloughed
their aged skin—they were renewed, transformed.

On her return, Medea stopped before
she crossed the threshold of her house: she sought
no other roof than heaven's spacious vault.
She kept her distance, and with turf she built
two altars: on the right, to Hecate;
and on the left, to Youth; and these she wreathed

with boughs from the wild woods, dark forest leaves.
Then, not far off, she dug two trenches: these
were meant to catch the blood of two black sheep
that she now sacrificed; she plunged the knife
into their throats; the wide pits overflowed.
Then, from one goblet, on the blood she spilled
pure wine and, from a second cup, warm milk;
and she intoned her spells and called upon
the deities who rule the underearth:
the Monarch of the Shades and she whom he
had stolen as his bride, his dark realm's queen.
Medea begged for time: she asked that they
not sever Aeson's soul too hastily
from his exhausted body. After she
had pacified the gods with these entreaties
and murmured prayers, Medea had the body
of the decrepit king borne out beneath
the open sky; then, with her incantation,
into deep sleep she plunged the aged Aeson
and stretched him out, as one would a cadaver,
upon a bed of grass. She called on Jason
to leave; she had the servants sent away—
warned all to turn aside their eyes—lest they
profane the secret rites. They all obeyed.

Now, left alone, Medea—with her hair
disheveled, like a bacchant—round the pair
of blazing altars, circles; and she soaks
the many-headed torches that she grips
in the dark blood of sacrificial pits
and, at the altar fires, lights these brands.
Then she proceeds to purify the body
of the old king: three times with fire, three
with water, and three times with sulfur, she
cleanses his flesh of all impurities.

Meanwhile a potent potion boils and seethes
and foams within a brazen pot, for she

Latin [242–64]

is now concocting roots that she had plucked
in a Thessalian valley, brewing these
with the most pungent juices, flowers, and seeds.
To these, she's added stones from the far East,
and sands the Ocean washed up on the beach,
and hoarfrost gathered when the moon was full;
and filthy wings—flesh still attached—of screech-owls;
together with the guts of a werewolf,
which has the power to change its savage snout
and show a human face. Nor was that brew
without the liver of a long-lived stag,
the thin and scaly skin of Libyan snakes,
and—added to all these—the head and beak
of a crow whose life spanned nine full centuries.

When the barbarian sorceress—with these
as well as countless other nameless things—
had readied what she needed to complete
the gift she'd promised to the dying king,
she stirred it with a stick of olive wood,
a bough long since dried out; she took great care
to mix the bottom and the top together.
And when that olive stick had stirred around
within that pot, at first the wood grew green;
but soon it sprouted leaves—and suddenly
it blossomed with plump olives. And wherever
the hollow pot had splattered foam and froth,
and warm drops fell onto the ground, the soil—
as if in springtime—bloomed and showed soft grass.
As soon as she saw this, she drew her sword
out from its sheath and cut the old man's throat;
and after letting his stale blood run out,
she filled his veins with all that she had brewed.
When Aeson, through his lips or through his wound,
had drunk this potion, he was soon renewed:
his grayness disappeared, his beard and hair
turned black again; the look of long neglect,
his senile scrawniness and pallor fled;

Latin [264-90]

the wrinkles on his flesh filled out; his limbs
reclaimed the energy that had been his.
And Aeson is bewildered; he recalls
that this was his own self in days gone by—
some forty years before.

                              Now, from the sky,
Bacchus had seen this dazzling prodigy;
and he concluded that his nurses could
regain—this way—the beauty of their youth.
And from Medea he received this gift:
the secret of the potion she had mixed.

That fraud might have its day in full, Medea
pretended that she'd quarreled with her husband,
and fled, a suppliant, to Pelias' palace.
He, too, like Aeson, was weighed down by age;
and so, it was his daughters who received
Medea—and in little time, she had
ingratiated them through guile and craft;
and when she came to speak of her own deeds,
she cited as her greatest feat the fact
that she had freed from his senility
old Aeson, Pelias' brother; hearing this
told by Medea with such emphasis,
the girls, beguiled, were led to hope that she,
in that same way, could help their father find
again the youthful years he'd left behind.

This is what they beseech: they want this gift,
assuring her that she herself can fix
her recompense. Medea does not speak:
as if in doubt, she pauses, seems to weigh
her answer; they are anxious, in suspense;
at last, with sham solemnity, she says:
"I'd have you gain still greater confidence

Latin [291–309]

in what I want to do—my gift to you:
my potions will transform your oldest ram,
the leader of your sheep, into a lamb."

Straightway, they had that shaggy ram—that sheep
exhausted by his many years—led out:
they tugged him by the horns that curved around
his hollow temples. With a knife she'd brought
from Thessaly, Medea pierced his throat
(and from his wizened flesh such scant blood flowed—
her blade was scarcely stained). The sorceress
then plunged his carcass into a bronze vat
and added potent potions, herbs that shrank
his limbs and burned away his horns—his years.
And from within that vessel one could hear
a tender bleating; and what soon appeared
brought wonder to them all: a lamb leaped out
and went in search of udders plump with milk.
Astonished, Pelias' daughters felt that they
could trust Medea's promise: they insist—
with still more eagerness—upon that gift
for Pelias.

Three times the Sun had loosed
its steeds into the Spanish sea, and stars
had plunged into the waves of Ebro's stream.
On that fourth night, the stars were glittering
when the deceptive daughter of Aeëtes
began to boil a caldron of fresh water
to which she added herbs that had no power.
Meanwhile, Medea's magic melodies
and chants had put to deathlike sleep the king
together with his watchmen: now his body
was slack; and just as she had bid them do,
his daughters crossed the threshold of his bedroom
and there, beside Medea, ringed his couch.
She said: "Why do you hesitate? Act now!
Take up these swords and drain the old blood out,

Latin [310–33]

that I may fill his veins with vibrant blood.
Your father's life and youth depend on you.
If you have filial love for him, then prove
your hopes are more than empty gestures: do
this service for your father; let your blades
expel the rot and rid him of foul age!"

Spurred by the witch's words, each girl was keen
to be most pious through impiety—
most pure by rushing to impurity.
And yet no daughter dared to watch as she
brought down her blade: all turned their eyes away;
backs turned, they hacked; their savage strokes were blind.

And Pelias, though he was streaming blood,
propped on his elbow, raised himself; with swords
around him, half his flesh in shreds, he tried
to get up from his bed. Then, as he stretched
his pale arms toward his daughters, Pelias cried:
"What are you doing? What has prompted you
to take up arms against your father's life?"
The daughters faltered: hands and hearts drew back.
He'd have said more—had not his throat and speech
been cut short by the sorceress, who cast
his shredded flesh into the boiling vat.

And if Medea had not soared on high
with her winged dragons, she'd have had to pay
a bitter price. But she flew through the sky
above the shaded peak of Pelion,
and over Othrys and the famous heights
that saved Cerambus' life in ancient times
(upon the wings the nymphs had given him,
by flight on high, he had escaped the waves
that surged when the earth's mass had been submerged
by the great flood in good Deucalion's days). □ □ □

Latin [334–56]

Upon her left, as she passed Pitane,
she saw the long stone image of the dragon;
and she passed Ida's grove where Bacchus hid—
beneath the feigned form of a stag—the ox
his son had stolen; and the site where Paris
lay buried underneath the shallow sands;
where she who was transformed to Maera spread,
with her strange barking, terror through the land;
and Cos, the city of Eurypylus,
where women sprouted horns while Hercules
and his invading ranks withdrew; and Rhodes,
the island dear to Phoebus; and the town
where the Telchines lived—Ialysus—
until they were submerged by Jove because
their gaze infected anything they saw:
despising them, Jove called on Neptune's aid
and drowned them all within his brother's waves.

And next she saw the lake of Hyrie
within the vale of Cycnus, famous for
the swan that had appeared so suddenly.
There, Cycnus, a capricious boy, was served
by Phyllius, who trained wild birds and tamed
a savage lion—all of these he gave
as gifts to Cycnus; but when he was asked
to tame a wild bull and fulfilled that task,
fond Phyllius refused to give that bull
to Cycnus, who'd so often spurned his love.
Offended, Cycnus cried: "But you will wish
that you had given me this gift!" and leaped
down from a towering cliff. And all were certain
he'd fallen, but he hovered in the air
on snow-white wings: he had become a swan.
His mother, Hyrie, was not aware
that he'd been saved: she shed so many tears
that she dissolved, became a lake that bears
her name. Nearby lies Pleuron; it is there
that Combe, Ophius' daughter, had escaped

Latin [357–83]

her sons' death-dealing blades: she flew away
on fluttering wings.

                And then the sorceress saw
Latona's sacred isle, Calaurea,
whose king and queen were transformed into birds.
And to the right Cyllene lay, the peak
where fate would have depraved Menephron mate
with his own mother—the incestuous way
of wild beasts. When Medea looked far back,
she saw the river-god Cephisus weep
for his dear grandson, whom Apollo changed
into a plump sea-calf; and she could see
Eumelus' house, the home of one who mourned
his son, who now lived in the air, transformed.

At long last, borne upon her dragons' wings,
Medea came to Corinth's sacred spring.
Here, when the world was born—so we are told
by ancient legends—mortal bodies sprang
from mushrooms risen in the wake of rain.

And it was here, in Corinth, that Medea
now took atrocious vengeance, killing Jason's
new wife: the sorceress burned her with poison,
then fired the royal halls; the seas that bathe
the two sides of the Isthmus saw the flames.
That done, the blood of her own infants stained
her sacrilegious sword. And she escaped
her death by fleeing Jason's upraised blade.

Borne by the dragons of the Sun, she fled
for refuge to the citadel of Athens.
(This height had seen three metamorphoses:
you, Phene, one most just, became a bird
and soared beside old Periphas, changed, too;
and Polypemon's daughter also flew
with her new wings.) Medea was received

Latin [383–402]

by Aegus (welcoming that fugitive
was quite enough to blame him); but as if
that act were not enough, he wed the witch.

———————

Soon Theseus came to Athens; though King Aegeus
had fathered Theseus, he had never known
his son, whose courage now had pacified
the Isthmus bathed by seas on both its sides.
Medea wanted Theseus dead, and so
she brewed a potion with a plant she'd brought—
long since—from Scythia's shores: a lethal herb
spewed from the teeth of Cerberus—they say.
There is a cave whose shadowed entranceway
lies at the end of a down-sloping path
along which Tiryns' hero, Hercules,
dragged Cerberus in chains of adamant:
the hound was furious; his eyes could not
support the light, the glare of naked day;
and tugging loose, his three heads barked as one
and, barking, sprayed the green fields with white foam.
This slaver, so men say, coagulated
and, nourished by the rich and fertile ground,
became a plant that had the power to poison,
an herb that grows and thrives upon hard stone,
a plant the peasants call aconitum
(in Greek the word for whetstone is *akóne*).

Now Aegeus, whom Medea had deceived,
was just about to have his own son drink
this brew, as if he were an enemy.
As Theseus, unaware of what they brought,
within his hand held high the fatal cup,
his father recognized the sign embossed
upon the ivory hilt of Theseus' sword
and, from his dear son's lips, dashed down the cup.

. . .

Latin [402–23]

Medea fled her death: she hid herself
within a cloud she conjured with her spells.

But Aegeus, happy that his son was saved,
was still dismayed: how close was their escape
from an abomination! Now he gave
the gods abundant gifts; he kindled fires
upon the altars; and the sturdy necks
of bullocks wreathed with garlands felt the ax.
And the Athenians—so it is said—
have never known a day more glad than that.
The joy was shared by common folk and elders:
they banqueted together; wine inspired
their artful songs in praise of Aegeus' son:

"O mighty Theseus, it is you who filled
all Marathon with wonder when you killed
the Cretan bull; and if in Cromyon
the fields are safe and farmers now can till
with no fear of the awful sow, they owe
that gift to you; and Epidaurus must
thank you if it is free from Vulcan's son,
that bandit, Periphetes, with his club;
and on Cephisus' banks, you felled the fierce
Procrustes; in Eleusis, Ceres' city,
you struck down Cercyon; you shattered Sinis,
whose massive power had horror as its end,
the giant who could twist tree trunks and bend
pine tops down to the ground—his catapults
to rend and fling on high his victim's bodies.
And it was you who freed Alcathoe,
the citadel of Megara, by killing
the bandit Sciron; now we go in safety
along that coastal road. Both land and sea
refused that brigand's bones; and it is said
that strewn about so long, those bones grew hard
and formed the cliffs now called Scironian Rocks.
Were we to tally all your feats and years,

Latin [424–48]

your years would be exceeded by your deeds.
Great Theseus, now we pray on your behalf;
for you, in gratitude, we drain these drafts."

Throughout the royal halls, the people throng;
applause and prayers for Theseus echo loud.
In all of Athens, gloom has been unhoused.

And yet (since joy indeed can't be complete,
and happiness is always marred by griefs)
King Aegeus, glad to have his dear son back,
still had his cares. For Minos now prepared
to war on Athens. He had many men
and many ships, but he was most equipped
with anger: he was bent on just revenge,
retaliation for his son, Androgeos,
who had been killed by the Athenians.
But first he sailed in search of allies, combing
the seas with his invincible, swift fleet.
He gathered to his cause Astypalaea
and Anaphe, the first by force, the last
by promises; low-lying Myconos
and, too, Cimolos, with its chalky fields;
the fertile Syros and the flat Seriphos;
and Paros' marble cliffs (the isle that Arne
had sacrilegiously betrayed; and she
became the bird—with black feet and black wings—
that, to this day, delights in golden things).
But Gyaros, Oliaros, and Tenos,
and Andros, Didymae, and Peparethos,
the island rich with gleaming olives—all
refused to help the Cretan fleet. And Minos
sailed left: he headed for Oenopia,
the realm of Aeacus. Oenopia
had been its ancient name; but Aeacus
called it Aegina, honoring his mother.   □   □   □

Latin [449–74]

A crowd rushed out to see a man so famous.
The king's three sons received him: Telamon,
the eldest; and his younger brother, Peleus;
and Phocus, the third-born. And Aeacus,
solemn and slow beneath the weight of years,
came, too: he asked what had brought Minos here.

Compelled to think of his own grief as father,
Minos, the ruler of a hundred towns,
sighed deeply as he answered: "For the sake
of my dead son, I'm set on waging war.
I ask you to support my righteous cause:
there is a tomb I'm anxious to console."
But Aeacus, Aesopus' grandson, said:
"You ask in vain: my city can't do this.
In truth there is no land with stronger ties
to the Athenians than our Aegina:
we are their close allies." Turning aside
to leave dejectedly, Minos replied:
"And you will pay most dearly for that treaty."
He thought that, at this point, the better course
was threatening war, not waging it: his men
had best save their full force—to shatter Athens.

The Cretan fleet was still within eye's reach
of those who lingered on Aegina's walls,
when to the friendly port an Attic ship—
full sail—rode in with Cephalus, who brought
a message from his land to Aeacus.
Although much time had passed since they had last
seen Cephalus, the sons of Aeacus
were quick to recognize him; and they clasped
his hand and led him to their father's palace.
The hero, still a formidable man,
retained the signs of one who'd been most handsome;
he entered with an olive branch in hand;
and at his side—he was the senior presence—

Latin [475–99]

there came, one to the right, one to the left,
young Clytus and young Butes, sons of Pallas.

When they'd exchanged the greetings that precede
such meetings, Cephalus conveyed the plea
that he had brought from Athens: he beseeched
the aid of the Aeginians, invoking
the treaty of alliance signed long since
by their forefathers. And he added this:
King Minos was a threat to all of Greece.
He made his case with eloquence and grace.
And even as his left hand leaned upon
the pommel of his scepter, Aeacus
replied: "There's no need to entreat; we're allies.
Take help at once; whatever fighting force
this island has, is yours; we do not lack
resources: I can count on ample ranks
for our defense—and our attacks. I thank
the gods: these are good times; I can't deny
what you Athenians have asked of us."
"I hope this happy state of things may last,
and may your isle grow still more populous!"
said Cephalus. "Indeed, on coming here,
I was most pleased to see young men so fair,
so matched in years. Yet I was struck by this:
many of those I'd seen on my last visit
are missing now."

———

                    And even as he sighed,
in sadness the Aeginian replied:
"Would I could tell you of the end without
recounting the beginning! But I speak
directly—bones and ashes, corpses, these
are what became of those your memory seeks!
In taking them, death took much of my realm.
The plague was sent by Juno in her rage

Latin [499–523]

against the people of the isle that bore
her rival's name, Aegina. A fierce scourge,
at first it seemed a sickness nature caused,
one to be fought with the physician's art;
but medicine was thwarted—nothing helped.
To start, thick darkness fell upon the earth;
beneath the mantle of the clouds, the heat
was stifling; when the waxing moon had reached
its full orb, joining horns for the fourth time,
then, thinning, had undone its fourth full orb,
the torrid south-wind breathed its lethal breath.
The pestilence infected lakes and springs;
and—thousands upon thousands—serpents swarmed
across the untilled fields, contaminating
our streams with poison. The infection's force
was first felt by the dogs, the birds, the sheep,
the oxen, and wild beasts. The wretched farmer—
dismayed—saw his stout bulls collapse midway
into the furrows. Of itself, the wool
falls from the bleating sheep; their flesh is prey
to ulcers; and the fiery horse, that once
was celebrated for his breakneck runs
along the dusty course, can win no more:
his glory gone, he moans within his stall;
the death he faces is anonymous.
The boar forgets his rage; the stag can't trust
his speed; the bears do not assail strong herds.
Now torpor takes all things. The woods, the roads,
the fields are filled with fetid carcasses;
the stench infects the air; let truth be told,
however strange it seems: even the dogs,
even the greedy birds and the gray wolves
won't touch the rotting corpses; pus and stench
spread far and wide the raging pestilence.

"The plague then gains still greater strength, attacks
the wretched countryfolk, and it holds sway
within the city walls. It first inflames

Latin [523–54]

the guts: the outer sign of that disease
is redness and a panting, fiery breath;
the tongue grows swollen, rough; the burning jaws
hang open to the scorching air; men gasp
and swallow heavy air. No one can bear
to lie upon a bed, and none can stand
a covering of any kind; face down,
each lies upon his belly on the ground,
but earth provides no coolness to the flesh;
it is the soil that gathers heat instead
from the hot bodies. None can offer help,
ease the disease; the plague is pitiless,
assailing even those who try to heal—
the doctors' craft rebounds against their selves.
For he who stays more close to the diseased
and cares for them most faithfully will meet
his fate more speedily. And when they see
that hope of ever being healed is gone
and death is inescapable, the sick
obey their own desires, caring not
if what they do is harmful—after all,
nothing can help them. And chaotically,
unchecked, they crowd around the springs and streams
and spacious wells. Their thirst is never quenched
till life itself is spent—they drink till death.
And many, bloated, cannot lift themselves
out of the springs and streams—and so are drowned.
But even with cadavers lying there,
some of the sick still seek—and drink—those waters!
As for the wretched who are still at home,
they can't endure their beds; and they leap up
or, if they are too weak, will just roll off
their mattresses onto the ground—and all
desert their houses. Home is hateful now:
not knowing what caused this disease, they blame
their narrow dwelling places for the plague.

▢   ▢   ▢

Latin [554–76]

"You could have seen the half-dead roam the streets
as long as they could stand, while those too weak
lay stretched along the ground; there they would weep;
their straining eyes looked up—a final plea—
their arms stretched toward the sky; and then they breathed
their last beneath the hanging heaven's shroud—
here, there—wherever death had found them out.

"What did I feel? How, how could I not hate
all life—not long to share my dear friends' fate?
Wherever I would turn my gaze, men lay
along the ground, as acorns when one shakes
the oak or rotten apples when boughs sway.
You see the temple with its long stairway;
that shrine is Jupiter's. Who did not bring
unto those altars useless offerings?
How often did a husband, even as
he prayed for his dear wife, a father as
he pleaded on his son's behalf, meet death
before those cruel altars—with a bit
of unused incense still within his hand!
How often did the bulls that they had brought
collapse before the blade had done death's work—
just as the priest pronounced the sacred words
and poured pure wine between the victim's horns!
And I, for my own sake and for my land
and my three sons, was offering a bull,
when suddenly—although no knife at all
had struck—the victim bellowed loud and fell;
it scarcely stained the knife with its scant blood.
The guts were too infected to allow
true signs, the warnings of the gods, to show:
the wretched plague had reached the viscera.
And at the sanctuary's doors I saw
abandoned corpses; and along the altars,
to render death more hateful, some had used
a noose to end their lives: with death they drive
away their fear of death—it would arrive

Latin [576–605]

in any case, but they would have it haste.
And those dead bodies are not borne away
with customary rites: the city gates
are too strait for so many funerals!
Unburied bodies weigh upon the ground
or else—without the gifts one would expect—
are heaped upon high pyres. All respect
is gone; men brawl for spots where they can cast
cadavers—and steal flames to burn their corpses.
There's no one to shed tears: the children's souls
and husbands' roam unwept, the young, the old—
no space is left for graves, no wood for flames.

"Struck by this storm of sorrows, I cried out
to Jove: 'If what is said is truly told,
and you embraced the daughter of Aesopus,
Aegina, and are not ashamed—great Father—
to be my forebear, then restore to me
my people—or let me, like them, be buried.'
He answered with these signs, a lightning flash
and thunder—his assent to my request.
I said: 'I note the omens you have sent:
I hope they signal your accord—your pledge.'

"Nearby there chanced to stand a rarity:
sacred to Jove, an oak whose crown was vast
beyond all measure; that great tree had grown
from seed belonging to Dodona's grove.
Here we caught sight of ants that filed along
a track they'd traced upon the wrinkled bark.
They were seed gatherers who bore great loads
within their tiny jaws; I was amazed
to see how many ants there were. I said:
'O gracious Father, fill the emptiness
of my dear land with citizens who match
the number of these ants.' The tall oak swayed;
. . .

Latin [605–29]

its branches rustled, though there was no wind.
My body shuddered; my hair stood on end;
despite my fear I kissed the ground, the tree;
I did not dare speak of my hope, and yet
that longing in my soul was dear to me.

"Night fell; sleep overcame my weary body.
Before my eyes the selfsame oak appeared,
as vast as I—awake—had seen: its boughs
bore just as many beings; then the tree
swayed as it had and scattered on the ground
the ranks of those seed gatherers, who grew
in size so suddenly, so constantly.
With chests erect, they rose up from the ground
and stood upon stout feet: their fragile forms,
their many paws, their blackness—all were gone;
their limbs had human shape. And then sleep left.
On waking, I rebuked myself for such
an idle vision, and I blamed the gods
for bringing me no help. But my ears caught
a muffled roar within the palace—sounds
that seemed so unfamiliar: human voices.
And while I thought this, too, must be in dream,
my dear son, Telamon, as he rushed in,
threw wide the door and cried: 'Come see a thing
beyond all hope and all imagining!
O Father, follow me!' I left the hall;
and just as they'd appeared within my sleep,
so did I see a file of human beings—
men whom I recognized. And drawing near,
they greeted me as king. To Jove I gave
the gifts I had promised him; and to the men
just born, I portioned out my town, my lands
that had been stripped of their inhabitants.
And I called my new subjects Myrmidons—
for *myrmex* [ant] recalls their origin.
You've seen their outer guise; within, their ways
remain what they had been: a frugal race

Latin [629–56]

of patient workers, men who gather gains
with zeal—and keep all they accumulate.

"These men—alike in age, alike in courage—
are those who'll follow you to war as soon
as Eurus, gracious wind that brought you here
(for Cephalus indeed was helped by Eurus),
has given way to Auster."

                                    And long hours
were filled with talk of this and other matters.
And then day's end was spent in banqueting—
and night in sleep.

                        The golden Sun's bright rays
had risen: Eurus still was blowing hard,
and the Athenians' homeward run was blocked.
Joined by the sons of Pallas, Cephalus—
their elder—went to wait on Aeacus.
But deep sleep still held fast the king. It's Phocus,
a son of Aeacus, who welcomes them
upon the threshold, while his brothers, Peleus
and Telamon, are busy marshaling
the troops that will wage war. And Phocus leads
the visitors to a secluded place,
a handsome inner space where they can wait.

———

And as they sit together, Phocus sees
the lance that Cephalus is carrying:
its point is gold, its shaft from strange tree.
At first, young Phocus speaks of this and that,
but in the middle of such small talk, asks:
"I study woods and wild game with much care,
yet I am puzzled by the shaft you bear:
of what wood is it made? If it were ash,
it would be blond; and cornel would show knots.

Latin [656–78]

I don't know where it comes from, but my eyes
have never seen a javelin so fine."
And one of Pallas' pair of sons replied:
"Even the beauty of this lance can't match
the wonder of the way in which it acts.
When it flies off, it catches—not by chance—
whatever mark it tracks; then it flies back,
with no guide but itself—a bloodied shaft."
And then the Nereid's son, young Phocus, asked
just why that shaft was so miraculous
and who had given it to Cephalus.
And this was the Athenian's reply
(though when it came to telling what he paid
to get that gift, he held his tongue, ashamed),
a tale he told as tears burst from his eyes,
even as he remembered his dead wife:

"This spear that you, son of a goddess, see
(however hard it is to lend belief
to what I say), compels me now to weep
and will yet make me weep in time to come,
if fate allows my life to be prolonged.
This shaft destroyed my precious wife—and me.
Would that this gift had never been received!
My Procris, who was Orithyia's sister
(and you may well have heard of Orithyia,
whom Boreas had carried off), was far
more graceful and more gracious than her sister:
she was a richer prize for ravishment.
It's Procris whom her father joined to me;
it's Procris who was joined to me by love.
Men said that I was happy—and I was.
But such good fortune did not please the gods;
for if it did, I'd still be happy now.

"No more than two months after we were wed,
when I, at break of day, as darkness fled,
had spread my nets to catch the antlered deer,

the golden goddess of the dawn, Aurora—
who'd reached Hymettus' ever-flowering peak—
set eyes on me: she carried me away
against my will. The simple truth is this—
I only pray the goddess will forgive
my telling it: my only love was Procris.
Aurora may indeed be marvelous
at break of day, with her rose-colored blush;
and she may be the keeper of the gates
between the light and night; Aurora sips
celestial nectar—but I wanted Procris:
she was the one on whom my heart was bent,
the one who was forever on my lips.
I kept on speaking of the sanctity
of marriage, of the joys that she and I
had known so recently, of the dear ties
that had been knitted with my cherished bride
upon the couch that I had left behind.
The goddess felt the goad of my laments;
she shouted: 'Stop your whining! You can keep
your Procris! But if what my mind foresees
is true, you will regret your loyalty!'
Enraged, she sent me back to my dear wife.

"Along the road to Athens, as I weighed
Aurora's warning, I became afraid
that Procris had betrayed her marriage vows.
Her loveliness, her youth might well abet
adultery; but on the other hand,
her probity was proof against that threat.
But I had been away—and I had stayed
with one quite famed for infidelities;
in any case, we lovers fear all things!
So I decided to torment myself,
to test her honor and her faithfulness.
Delighted by my doubts, Aurora helped
my plan; she changed my face. In that new guise
(I felt the difference), unrecognized,

Latin [702–23]

I entered Athens, Pallas' sacred town.
There were no signs of guilt within my house,
only an air of chaste expectancy
of waiting for the absent lord's return.
It took a thousand wiles, astute deceit,
for me to gain the presence of my Procris.
The sight of her so captivated me
that I was almost ready to retreat
from any test of her fidelity.
It was so hard to hold myself in check—
not to embrace my wife, not to confess
the truth. She grieved; but there will never be
a woman who can match the loveliness
of Procris standing there in her deep sadness,
her longing for the husband snatched from her.
How often my petitions were repelled;
how often she replied: 'I save myself
for one alone; wherever he may be,
it's he who'll share my joy!' Could any man
whose mind was not awry have failed to see
in that, firm proof of her fidelity?
But I was still not satisfied. I kept
insisting (harming only my own self);
for just one night, I promised countless wealth;
and then I added gift on gift—until
I forced her to the point where she might fall.
At that, I shouted: 'He who faces you
is one who, sad to say, is not a true
adulterer! Beside you now, it's I—
your husband—whom you see! And it is these—
my own eyes—that have spied your treachery!'
My wife did not reply; in silence, she—
ashamed—abandoned our insidious house
and her disloyal husband. My offense
led to her hate for all the race of men;
she roamed the mountain slopes—she was intent
upon the skills for which Diana cares.
She'd left me: in my loneliness the flame

Latin [723–47]

of love burned even more—deep in my bones.
I begged for pardon, and I recognized
that I had sinned; I, too, if tempted by
such splendid gifts might well have set aside
my scruples and succumbed. Once I'd confessed
and she had no more need to seek revenge
for her offended honor, she came back;
and then, in love and fond accord, we spent
sweet years together.

           "And as if the gift
of her own self was not enough, she gave
as gift to me a hound she had received
from her Diana, who had said: 'This beast
will outrace all the rest.' And to that,
she added this: the javelin I carry.
The fate of that first gift was so prodigious
that it will stun you. Would you hear it now?

"When the dark riddle that the Sphinx had set
was solved by Oedipus (no Theban's wits—
until he came—had ever passed her test),
the monstrous Sphinx leaped headlong from a cliff:
there—enigmatic prophetess—she rests,
dead even to the questions she had asked.
But kindly Themis—do be sure of this—
would never let such action go unpunished.
And so she sent another pest to plague
the Thebans: a ferocious fox that filled
the countrymen with terror, threatening
their herds and their own lives. And to their aid,
we came, young warriors, from the lands nearby.
We ringed their fields with nets to trap the fox,
but she leaped over them—across the top.
Then we unleashed our hounds to track her down,
but she—swift as a bird—outraced the pack.
So all my comrades asked me to release
the gift hound I'd received: his name was Laelaps.

Latin [747–72]

For some time now, he'd strained against the leash—
his neck was tugging hard. I set him free—
and we lost sight of him, such was his speed:
the warm dust showed the imprint of his feet,
but Laelaps' self was nowhere to be seen.
No pellet from a sling, no slender shaft
sent flying from a Cretan bow, no lance
has ever flown more swiftly than Laelaps.
There is a hill whose summit overlooks
all the surrounding fields; I reached the top;
from there I watched a most uncommon chase:
the fox seems to be caught, but now she slips
away—just when the hound has firmed his grip.
The wily fox seeks no straight-line escape
but twists and turns to trick his jaws, to blunt
the force of his attack. He's at her heels;
he is as fast; he seems to catch her, yet
he has not caught her: as he bites, his teeth
snap shut on empty air. I now prepared
to use my javelin: I balanced it
in my right hand; my fingers tried to slip
into the loop; my eyes were turned aside
from that strange chase, and when I lifted them
again to take aim with my javelin,
amid the fields I saw a miracle,
two marble statues: one in flight, whereas
the other statue barked—you could have said.
Some god—if any god was there to watch—
had surely seen the pair so closely matched
that neither of the two could win that test."

Here Cephalus broke off his tale. But Phocus
asked: "Why did you accuse the javelin?"—
at which the teller told how it had sinned.

"O Phocus, sorrow has its origin
in joys. First I shall speak of my delights:
how fine a thing to call back blessed times!

Latin [772–97]

In those first years, o son of Aeacus,
I was delighted with my wife, and she
was happy with her husband. Each of us
cared for the other, a fond covenant.
For even if she could have wedded Jove,
she would have chosen me as her dear love;
as for my heart, no other woman could
have tempted me—not even Venus' self;
in our two hearts there burned one equal flame.

"At that hour of the day when the first rays
of sunlight touch the summits, I was used
(as young men often are) to hunt for game.
I would set out alone: I wanted no
escort, no servants and no horses, no
keen-scented dogs, no knotted hunting nets.
I had my javelin—enough defense.
But when I'd had my fill of killing game,
I'd go to seek some cool spot in the shade,
just where a breeze blew up from the deep valleys.
Light winds are what I wanted in that heat;
I prayed for them to free me from fatigue.
I cried out: '*Aura*, come!' (so—I recall—
I'd often chant, as if it were a spell);
'come, dearest *aura*, find your tender way
into my chest; I beg you to relieve—
as you know how to do—this scorching heat.'
And then I may have added words as sweet
as those before (fate may have prompted me),
words that I would repeat insistently:
'You are my chief delight; you comfort me,
refresh me; it's because of you I love
the woods, the solitary glades; my lips
are never weary of your gentle breath.'
Someone—I know not who it was—had lent
his ears to all these ambiguities;
and he mistook the *aura* that—again,
again—I had invoked, for some nymph's name,

Latin [798–823]

a nymph who had provoked in me love's flame.
That rash informer hurried to my wife
to tell her of my inexistent crime:
to her he whispered every word he'd heard.
And love is credulous. Struck down by grief—
so I am told—she fainted. When she gained
her senses—slow in coming back—she wept,
said she was wretched; and her long lament
mourned her betrayal; in her misery
over a sin that never was, she feared
a nullity, a name without a body;
poor Procris grieved as if she had indeed
a rival. Yet, from time to time, she felt
some doubt and hoped that she had been mistaken;
she would reject the tale of the informer,
refusing to condemn her own dear husband
if she'd not seen him sin with her own eyes.

"The next day dawned; and when Aurora's light
expelled the night, I sought the woods again.
My search for game went well; and as I roamed,
I said: 'O *aura*, come, soothe my fatigue . . . '
But suddenly, before I followed that
with my next word, I thought I heard a sort
of groan. But I continued: 'Dear one, come!'
This time some leaves fell—a faint rustling sound.
I thought some beast had stirred, and then I cast
my speeding javelin. The mark it met
was Procris; as she clutched her wounded breast,
she cried out. And I recognized the voice
of my own faithful wife; headlong I rushed,
as if gone mad, to where my Procris was.
I found her dying, even as she tore
her bloodstained robe in her attempt to draw
out of the wound the very shaft that she
herself had given me—the wretched me.
Upon my arm I lifted up—most gently—
the body dearer to me than my own;

Latin [824–48]

and tearing from her breast a piece of cloth,
I bound the cruel wound; I tried to staunch
the blood; I begged her not to perish, not
to leave me in my misery forever.
Then, with her final effort, near her death,
these were the last few words that Procris said:
'Oh, for the ties that join us, for the gods—
those of the sky and those to whom I go—
for any good I may have done for you,
and for the love that brought my death—a love
that I still bear you as I near my end—
I beg of you: do not let Aura take
my place as wife upon our wedding bed.'
And only then did I first understand
what caused the dreadful error. I explained—
but of what use was explanation now?
Her limbs fell slack; what meager strength she had
fled with her blood. So long as she could look
at anything, my Procris looked at me;
and when her sad soul breathed its last, her breath
fell on my lips. And yet she seemed content
in death: her face had gained serenity.''

These were the things that, even as he wept,
the hero called to mind. The others shed
their share of tears. Just then King Aeacus,
with his two other sons and the fresh ranks
of soldiers they had mobilized, came in.
And Cephalus received those well-armed men.

BOOK VIII

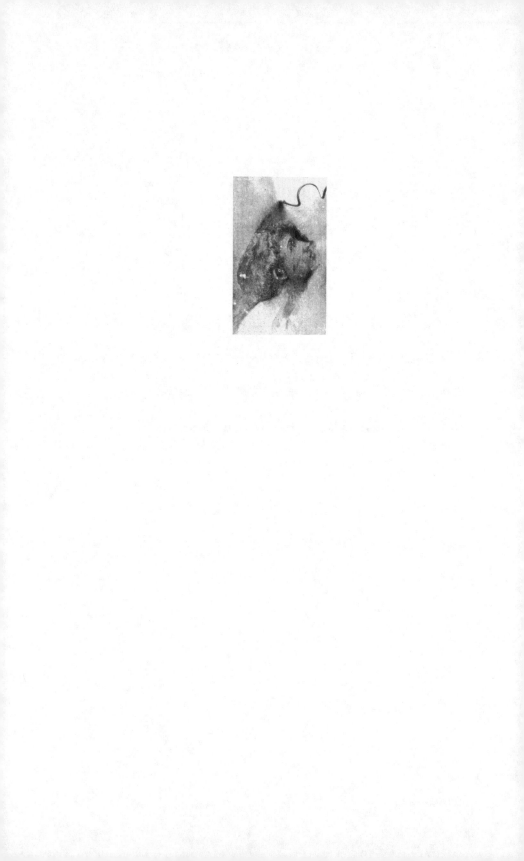

NOW LUCIFER, EXPELLING NIGHT, revealed
the light of shining dawn; as Eurus fell,
the damp fog lifted. Gentle Auster helped
the glad return of Cephalus and all
of his new allies to their longed-for port:
they reached Piraeus sooner than they'd hoped.

Meanwhile, the city of Alcathous,
where Nisus now was king, was under siege
by Minos; he was devastating all
the coast of Megara. King Nisus had,
amid the gray hairs growing on his head,
a gleaming purple tuft: on this alone,
there hung the safety of his realm, his throne.

Six times the new moon's crescent horn had risen;
the fate of Megara was still uncertain;
for Victory—on wings of indecision—
flew now to one, now to the other camp.

There was a tower—the tower of the king—
that rose up from the walls of Megara:
upon those walls Apollo had set down
his golden lyre, and within those stones
his music lingered. Scylla, Nisus' daughter,
in peaceful days, climbed often to this tower;
and now, with war at hand, she went there still
to watch the savage feats and trials of Mars.

By now the siege had lasted long, and she
had learned to recognize the names of chiefs,
their weapons and their battle dress, their steeds
and Cretan quivers; but the one whom Scylla
knew best—far better than she should—was he
who led the siege: Europa's son. She deemed
King Minos handsome if he chose to keep
his head concealed beneath a crested casque;
and if he bore a bright gold shield, then that

Latin [1–27]

gold shield delighted Scylla. If he cast
a pliant shaft—his sinews taut and tense—
she marveled at his mix of strength and craft.
And if he bent the curving bow whose shaft
was fitted to the string, she would have sworn
that it was Phoebus' self whose hands held fast
those arrows. But when Minos showed his face
without a casque of bronze and, in his cloak
of purple, rode his milk-white stallion graced
with an adorned caparison, and gripped
the foaming bit, then Scylla almost went
insane: she said how happy was the lance
that his hands touched, how glad the reins he clasped.
If she, though but a girl, could only speed
her way among the ranks of enemies!
If she, down from that tower's top, could fling
herself into the Cretans' camp, or else
throw open Megara's bronze gates—indeed
whatever thing might meet her Minos' needs!

And even as she sat and watched the white
tents of the Cretan king, young Scylla cried:
"I cannot tell if I should welcome or
should mourn this lamentable war! I grieve
that Minos, he who has my love, must be
my enemy! But if there had not been
this siege, he'd never have been known to me.
If he just took me hostage, he'd win peace;
he could give up this war—and then I'd be
in Minos' company. And if your mother,
Europa, was as splendid as you are,
then Jove indeed was right to burn for her!
If I had wings, I'd ride across the air
and then—thrice happy—stand within the camp
of Minos: I'd reveal myself, my love,
and ask him how much dowry it would take
to win him as my husband! Just so long
as he does not demand the citadel

Latin [27–54]

of my own land! Oh, yes, I would give up
that wedding, if I thought it must be bought
by treason! On the other hand, the victor
can often prove to be a man of peace—
and there is little wrong with such defeat.
The war that Minos wages is quite just:
his son was murdered—it's revenge he wants;
his cause is strong, his army has great force,
and I believe that he will triumph; but
if what awaits my city—its sure fate—
is loss, should it be Mars to break our walls,
or should it be my love? It is far better
for him to win without a massacre,
without delay, without his having paid
one drop of his own blood. I would at least
be rid of fear that someone—unaware—
might pierce your chest, my Minos—unaware,
I say, for is there any man who'd plan
with cruelty to cast an evil lance
at you, if he, in truth, knew who you were?
I like this scheme: I'm set now to consign
myself, my homeland, and my dowry—I
will end this war. But if my wish is just
a wish, that's not enough. The watchmen guard
the entrances; the king, my father, keeps
the gateway's keys; yes, he and only he
prevents my plan; unhappy me, I fear
just him. O gods, would that I had no father!
But then, is everyone not his own god?
Fortune rejects the prayers of the halfhearted!
Another girl, afire with love like mine,
would well before this have destroyed—with joy—
whatever obstacle stood in love's way.
And should another's strength be more than mine?
Through fire and sword, I'll dare to go—although
there's no need here for fire, nor for sword:
my father's lock of hair will be enough;
that purple tuft is far more dear to me

Latin [54–79]

than any gold, for it alone can be
my blessing—giving me what I most need."

As Scylla said these things, night fell—the chief
healer of cares. But as the shadows grew,
within the girl audacity grew, too.
The hour of rest had come, when sleep invades
hearts that are weary with the cares of day.
Now Scylla steals into her father's room
in silence and—how vile a crime!—tears off
the fatal tuft; she grips that obscene loot;
then, quick to hurry off, she exits through
the gates; and striding past the Cretan troops
(she is so sure that what she's done will win
their favor), she confronts the king of Crete.
The sight of Scylla startles him. She says:
"It's love that drove me to this act. Now I,
King Nisus' daughter, Scylla, would consign
into your hands, my home, my native land.
For this I ask you just one recompense:
yourself. This purple lock is my love-pledge;
this is not hair that you receive: it is
my father's head." She showed the sinful gift;
she held it high, and then she offered it.

The king recoiled; and shocked by that outrage,
he cried: "May you, who have disgraced our age,
be banished by the gods from all their world!
May neither land nor sea have place for you.
And I, at least, will surely not allow
a monster of your sort to reach the isle
of Crete, my world, the cradle of great Jove!"

That said, as soon as he'd imposed just laws
on the Megarians—and Minos was
an upright man—he set his homeward course:
he had the hawsers of the fleet unloosed;
the oarsmen sped his ships adorned with bronze. ☐ ☐ ☐

Latin [79–103]

When Scylla saw the Cretan fleet afloat
and saw her sin had won her no reward,
when she had prayed till she could pray no more,
with outstretched hands, incensed, enraged, insane,
her hair disheveled, wild, the girl exclaimed:
"Where do you flee, abandoning the one
who brought you victory? Beyond my own
dear home, more than my father, what I chose
was you. Where do you flee? It was my sin
that let you win—and did that sin not earn
some merits? Have you scorned my gift and spurned
my love—forgotten that my fate and hopes
depend on you alone? Where shall I go?
I am a derelict. Shall I return
to my own city? It is overthrown.
And even if it stands, to me it's closed:
I am a traitor. Or shall I return
to face my father, he whom I bestowed
on you as gift? My people hate me so,
and with good reason; and our neighbors know
that others, too, may do as I have done.
I am shut out from all the world, unless
you open Crete to me. But if you choose
to bar this, too, and to abandon me—
ungratefully—along this shore, Europa
is not your mother: you must be the son
of an Armenian tigress, or Charybdis—
forever lashed by Auster's blasts—or Syrtis,
the treacherous. You are no son of Jove—
your mother was not tricked by a false bull;
that tale they tell is but a lying fable:
the bull who fathered you indeed was true—
a savage beast who needed more than heifers.
O father Nisus, punish me! Delight
in my despair, you walls that I betrayed!
I know that I deserve my wretched state;
I'm only fit for death. But I should die
beneath the hands of those whom my foul crime

Latin [104–29]

has wronged. Why should you, Minos, claim the right
to punish me when, through my sin, you've won?
For both my country and my father, it
was sin; for you, it was a benefit.
She is indeed a worthy wife for you—
she who, in her adultery, deceived
a savage bull: she used that shape of wood
and bore a monstrous fetus in her womb:
half-man, half-beast. Do my words reach your ears,
or, thankless Minos, do the winds that bear
your ship away, bear, too, across the air—
the empty air—my words? I do not wonder—
no, no—that your Pasiphae preferred
that bull to you: your bestiality
was worse than his. But now, what misery
is mine! He's told his crew to speed away;
the surge churned by his oars is loud, and I—
together with my shores—am left behind.
But none of this will help! In vain you try
to cancel from your mind the gifts that I
gave you. Against your will, I'll follow you
and, clinging to the curving stern, I shall
be drawn across the sea's long surge and swell."

As soon as she had finished, Scylla dived
into the waves and, following the fleet
(her frenzy gave her force), she found the ship
of Minos, and the girl held fast to it—
she was a hateful comrade. When her father
caught sight of her (he now was hovering
above her in the air on tawny wings—
yes, he had just been changed into an osprey),
he rushed to tear at her with his hooked beak
as she hung at the stern. Her grip grew slack;
and terrified, she fell, and yet did not
touch down along the surface of the sea:
the air, though light, seemed to sustain her body.
She found that she had feathers; as a bird,

Latin [129–50]

her name is Ciris (drawn from the Greek verb
keirein, "to cut"), for she had shorn the tuft.

———————————

As soon as Minos, disembarking, touched
the soil of Crete, he sacrificed to Jove
the hundred bulls he owed; his palace walls
were soon adorned with trophies, spoils of war.
But now the foul obscenity that shamed
the family of Minos grew: the strange
half-human and half-beast, the monstrous child
of Minos' queen, the living proof of vile
adultery. And so the king decides
to place the shame that stains his marriage far
apart from Minos' house: he wants to hide
the monster in a labyrinth, where blind
and complicated corridors entwine.
The famous builder, Daedalus, designs
and then constructs this maze. He tricks the eye
with many twisting paths that double back—
one's left without a point of reference.
As in the Phrygian fields, the clear Meander
delights in flowing back and forth, a course
that is ambiguous; it doubles back
and so beholds its waves before they go
and come; and now it faces its own source,
and now the open sea; and so its waves
are never sure that they've not gone astray:
just so did Daedalus, within his maze,
along the endless ways disseminate
uncertainty; in fact the artifex
himself could scarcely trace the proper path
back to the gate—it was that intricate.

And it was in this labyrinth of Crete
that Minos jailed the monstrous Minotaur,
the biform bull-and-man. And twice the king

gave him Athenians to eat—these, each
nine years, were picked by lot to feed the beast.
But at the third return of those nine years,
the beast was killed by Theseus, Aegeus' son.
He, helped by Ariadne, Minos' daughter,
was able to retrace his steps: she gave
a thread to him, which he would then rewind,
and so he found the entrance gate again—
a thing that none before had ever done.
Without delay he sailed away to Naxos.
He'd taken Ariadne with him, yet
he showed no pity: on that shore he left
the faithful girl. And Ariadne wept
till Bacchus came; that god was warm and fond,
and he embraced the girl; through him she won
a place in heaven as the Northern Crown—
Corona—an eternal constellation;
for from her brow, he took her diadem
and sent it up to heaven. Through thin air,
it flew, and in its flight, its gems were changed:
they blazed as flames—but its crown-shape was saved.
Now Ariadne's diadem is placed
between the Gripper stars, which hold the Snake,
and those that show the Kneeling Hercules.

But Daedalus was weary; by this time,
he'd been exiled in Crete too long; he pined
for his own land; but he was blocked—the sea
stood in his way. "Though Minos bars escape
by land or waves," he said, "I still can take
the sky—there lies my path. Though he owns all,
he does not own the air!" At once he starts
to work on unknown arts, to alter nature.
He lays out feathers—all in order, first
the shorter, then the longer (you'd have said
they'd grown along a slope); just like the kind

Latin [170–91]

of pipes that country people used to fashion,
where from unequal reed to reed the rise
is gradual. And these he held together
with twine around the center; at the base
he fastened them with wax; and thus arranged—
he'd bent them slightly—they could imitate
the wings of true birds.

              As he worked at this,
his young son, Icarus, inquisitive,
stood by and—unaware that what he did
involved a thing that would imperil him—
delighted, grabbed the feathers that the wind
tossed, fluttering, about; or he would ply
the blond wax with his thumb; and as he played,
the boy disturbed his father's wonder-work.

When Daedalus had given the last touch,
the craftsman thought he'd try two wings himself;
so balanced, as he beat the wings, he hung
poised in the air. And then to his dear son,
he gave another pair. "O Icarus,"
he said, "I warn you: fly a middle course.
If you're too low, sea spray may damp your wings;
and if you fly too high, the heat is scorching.
Keep to the middle then. And keep your eyes
on me and not on Helice, Bootes,
or on Orion's unsheathed sword. Where I
shall lead—that's where you fly: I'll be your guide."
And as he taught his son the rules of flight,
he fitted to the shoulders of the boy
those wings that none had ever seen before.
The old man worked and warned; his cheeks grew damp
with tears; and with a father's fears, his hands
began to tremble. Then he kissed his son
(he never would embrace the boy again);
and poised upon his wings, he flew ahead,
still anxious for the follower he led

Latin [*191–213*]

(much like the bird who, from her nest on high,
leads out her tender fledglings to the sky).
He urges on his son, saying he must
keep up, not fall behind; so he instructs
the boy in flight, an art most dangerous;
and while the father beats his wings, he turns
to watch his son, to see what he has done.

A fisherman, who with his pliant rod
was angling there below, caught sight of them;
and then a shepherd leaning on his staff
and, too, a peasant leaning on his plow
saw them and were dismayed: they thought that these
must surely be some gods, sky-voyaging.

Now on their left they had already passed
the isle of Samos—Juno's favorite—
Delos, and Paros, and Calymne, rich
in honey, and Labinthos, on the right.
The boy had now begun to take delight
in his audacity; he left his guide
and, fascinated by the open sky,
flew higher; and the scorching sun was close;
the fragrant wax that bound his wings grew soft,
then melted. As he beats upon the air,
his arms can get no grip; they're wingless—bare.

The father—though that word is hollow now—
cried: "Icarus! Where are you?" And that cry
echoed again, again till he caught sight
of feathers on the surface of the sea.
And Daedalus cursed his own artistry,
then built a tomb to house his dear son's body.
There, where the boy was buried, now his name
remains: that island is Icaria.

□   □   □

Latin [213–35]

———————

While Daedalus was burying the corpse
of his ill-fated son, a chattering partridge,
lodged in a muddy ditch, caught sight of him.
The bird knew Daedalus at once: he beat
his wings and seemed to chirp maliciously—
a bird that was indeed a novelty,
till then, the only partridge ever seen—
but one who knew how guilty you had been,
o Daedalus, when you connived against him.

That bird had been your sister's son, a boy
whom she—not knowing what his fate would be—
confided to your care, that you might teach
your arts to one so young and yet so keen:
a twelve-year-old, alert and shrewd. Indeed,
on noting how a fish's spine was shaped,
the boy cut out, along a sharpened blade,
a row of teeth, inventing—thus—the saw.
He also was the first to twin a pair
of metal arms joined by the hinge they shared;
and while the first stood firm—erect and central—
the second, moving arm described a circle.

And Daedalus, in envy, threw him headlong
down from Minerva's sacred citadel
and—lying—said he'd fallen. But Minerva,
who favors those with ingenuity,
caught up the boy before he struck the earth:
while he was in midair, the goddess clothed
his form with feathers; he became a bird.
And though the speed that always marked his wits
passed into both his wings and feet—so swift—
his name remained; it did not change: Perdix—
or Partridge—is the name the bird retained.
And yet that bird will never fly too high
up from the ground, nor does he build his nest

Latin [236–57]

among the branches or along the treetops.
All partridge eggs are laid along hedgerows.
That bird recalls its ancient fall, and so
it shuns the high and always seeks the low.

Now Daedalus exhausted, spent, at last
landed near Aetna—and, a suppliant,
entreated Cocalus, a clement king,
to shield and shelter him. The king agreed;
he readied all his troops, lest Minos seek
revenge—invading Sicily from Crete.

By this time, Athens was at last relieved;
for thanks to Theseus, there was no more need
to send the wretched tribute down to Crete.
And they adorn their shrines with festive wreaths
and call upon Minerva, warrior-goddess,
and Jove together with the other gods;
to these they offer sacrificial blood
and gifts and fragrant incense.

　　　　　　　　　　　Theseus' name
had spread through all the towns of Greece, for Fame
is quick: she speeds from place to place; now all
who dwell in rich Achaea seek the help
of Theseus when they have to face great perils.
And even Calydon, although she had
her Meleager, asks—a suppliant—
for Theseus' help. That land had been attacked
by a huge boar, who served Diana's ends—
he was the instrument of her revenge.

They say that Oenus, king of Calydon—
since there had been so rich a harvest season—
had offered the firstfruits of grain to Ceres,

wine—Bacchus' gift—to Bacchus, and to blond
Minerva, her own flowing olive oil.
And after all the harvest gods were honored,
the homage that the other gods deserved
was also paid. But Calydon forgot
one deity—they say—Latona's daughter:
they burned no incense on Diana's altars.

Gods, too, are stirred by wrath. "We shall not let
this outrage pass without due punishment,"
Diana cried; "they'll say we were not honored,
but they'll not say that we were unavenged."
So, into Oeneus' land, the goddess sent
a boar—so massive he could even match
the bulls of green Epirus: he surpassed
the bulls of the Sicilian fields. His eyes
were glittering with fire and blood; his neck
was bold, erect; his bristles were as stiff
as rigid spears; his giant flanks were flecked
with hot foam as he grunted, hoarse; his tusks
could match an Indian elephant's; his mouth
flashed lightning; and his breath, in passing, scorched
the boughs; and now he tramples fledgling corn,
and now he means to make the farmers mourn—
to reap but tears: he ruins ripened ears.
In vain the threshing floor, the granary
await the grain that seemed a certainty.
He ravages the vines weighed down by grapes;
he strips the ever-leafy olive trees
of boughs and fruits. And he attacks, enraged,
the herds; no watchman and no hound can face
that boar; no bull can keep the cattle safe.
The people flee the fields; they only feel
secure behind the city walls. And then
a band is brought together, picked young men
who stand with Meleager to defend
the fields of Calydon—they want renown:
the twin sons born of Leda, she whose mate

Latin [274–301]

was Tyndarus—one of these sons is famed
as boxer and the other as a horseman;
and Jason, artifex of the first ship;
and Theseus and Pirithous, whose friendship
was close; and Thestius' two sons; and Lynceus
and speedy Idas, sons of Aphareus;
and Caenus, not a woman anymore;
the fierce Leucippus and Acastus, peerless
lance thrower; Dryas and Hippothous;
and Phoenix, son of Amyntor; and Actor's
twin sons; and Phyleus, who had come from Elis.
Nor did the great Achilles' father miss
this expedition, nor did Telamon,
nor Pheres' son, nor Iolaus, come
from the Hyantians' land. Eurytion,
unflagging, and the one whom none outraced,
Echion, also joined this mighty chase—
as did the Locrian, Lelex of Naryx;
and Panopeus and Hippasus and Hyleus;
and Nestor, at that time, still in his prime;
as well as sons sent by Hippocoön
from ancient Amyclae; Penelope's
father-in-law; and from Arcadia,
Ancaeus; and the famous augur, son
of Ampyx; and the son of Oecleus—he
had yet to suffer his wife's treachery;
and, too, Tegean Atalanta, glory
of Mount Lycaeus' woods in Arcady.

Atalanta's robe was fastened at the neck
by a smooth brooch; her hair was simply dressed,
caught up in just one knot; her shafts were stored
within an ivory quiver, which she wore
on her left shoulder; as she moved, the arrows
would jangle; Atalanta held her bow
in her left hand. And her beguiling face
was, for a girl, quite boyish; for a boy,
it had a girlish cast—one could have said.

Latin [301–23]

And Calydon's great warrior, Meleager,
was stricken at the very sight of her
(although a god forbade that love); he nursed
his flame in secret, saying: "Oh, how blessed
that man will be, if ever she consents
to take a husband!" But the hunt prevents
his saying more—as does his modesty.
His task impels—he feels the urgency.

Up from the plain, ascending to the peak
from which the sloping fields below were seen,
there rose a mighty forest dense with trees—
no ax had touched it through long centuries.
The hunters reached these woods; some stretched out nets,
and some unleashed the hounds, while others tracked
the footprints on the soil; for they were keen
to face the danger, foil their enemy.
There was a hollow where rainwater drained,
with pliant willows at its marshy base,
and soft swamp-grass and osiers; there, beneath
the tall bulrushes, grew low-lying reeds.

Roused from his marshland den, the charging boar
drives straight into the hunters, like a flash
when cloud banks clash. His rush lays low the plants;
the tree trunks crash. The young men shout; their hands
are steady; each is poised to cast his lance,
whose broad head glints. The boar does not relent:
he rips each hound that blocks his frenzied path;
his sidelong blows, too, smash the barking pack.

Echion was the first to fling his shaft;
his aim was off, and so his lance head glanced
against a maple trunk. The second cast
seemed set to pierce the monster's massive back,
as one would wish, but overshot the boar—
Jason of Pagasae used too much force.
Then Mopsus, son of Ampyx, cried: "If I

Latin [324–50]

have always honored and do honor you,
o Phoebus, let this shaft be sure, exact!"
The god did grant his plea—as far as he
was able to: the boar was struck indeed
but was not wounded. Even as it sped,
Diana had wrenched off the iron head:
the wooden shaft struck home—but with no tip.

The beast is furious, incensed: he seems
like lightning, all afire; his eyes cast sparks;
his chest breathes flames; and as a giant rock
flung from a catapult flies at the walls
or at the towers where the soldiers crowd,
so he—his force is deadly—rushes at
the band of hunters: two, his charge knocks flat—
Eupalamus and Pelagon—they're snatched
to safety by their comrades. But his tusks
are fatal when they strike Enaesimus,
son of Hippocoon; he'd turned to run,
when he was hit behind the knee, hamstrung,
his tendons giving way. And even Nestor
might well have died before the Trojan War,
had he not used his long lance-pole to vault
into the branches of a nearby oak;
and from that place of safety, he looked out
and saw the enemy he had escaped.
Against that trunk, the boar began to rub
his tusks: enraged, he threatened death and then,
with his hooked weapons freshly whetted, struck
and ripped the thigh of mighty Hippasus.

Now Leda's twins, the brothers who had not
as yet been set into the sky as stars,
rode up: they both were most conspicuous—
both riding horses whiter than the snow,
both brandishing fine shafts that—ominous—
shook at each step. They would have struck the beast,
that bristly boar, had he not turned to seek

Latin [350–76]

the thick woods, where no lance or horse could reach.
One—Telamon—did follow, but too keen,
too rushed, he took no heed and stumbled on
a jutting root—and so, along the ground,
he fell headlong. While Peleus helped him up,
the girl from Tegea notched a rapid shaft,
then sent it flying from the bow she'd bent.
The arrow grazed the top of the boar's back
and stuck beneath his ear; his bristles showed
some flow of blood—though slight. While her success
made Atalanta glad, her joy was less
than Meleager's; for he was the first
to see the blood, the first to point it out,
to say: "It's only right that you receive
the honor due such signal bravery!"

The men grew red with shame; each hunter spurred
the other; taking courage from the clamor,
they cast their shafts at random; the confusion
of lances hindered careful aim; they missed
the mark. Then the Arcadian Ancaeus
(his frenzy is to be his doom) cried out,
as he drew close with his two-headed ax:
"Young men, make way for me: it's time you learned
that nothing women wield will ever match
a weapon that is wielded by a man.
Yes, let Latona's daughter do her best:
I know Diana surely will protect
this beast with her own weapon; even so,
it's my right arm that now will lay him low!"
So did he bluster, puffed and arrogant;
his two hands lifted up his two-edged ax;
he stood on tiptoe, tall, and then bent back;
his arms were poised to strike. But he is rash:
the boar foresees his move and plants
two tusks into the spot where death comes fast:
Ancaeus' groin is struck—its upper part.
The hunter falls; his blood-soaked guts slide out;

Latin [377–402]

the ground is drenched with dead Ancaeus' gore.
Pirithous, the son of Ixion,
with pike in hand, was rushing toward the boar.
But Theseus cried: "Stay clear of him! You are
more dear to me than my own self; you are
a part of my own soul. And I say, halt!
To battle at long range is not a fault,
no cause for shame: the stout Ancaeus paid
for rashness." So he said, and then he cast
a heavy shaft. Though he had balanced it
with care and could have scored a deadly hit,
along its path it met a leafy branch.
And then the son of Aeson flung his lance;
but as it sped ahead, it struck—by chance—
a sorry barking dog—an innocent.

A better fate awaits the son of Oeneus:
two lances leave his hand—the first one lands
upon the ground; but then the other shaft
strikes home—midway along the monster's back.
The hunter does not wait: the wounded beast
is frenzied, whirling round and vomiting
fresh blood and foam—and Meleager goads,
provokes, incites his enemy, and strikes
between the shoulders with a gleaming pike.
The shouts and the applause are fervid now;
all want to press his hand—his comrades crowd;
astonished, they admire the massive beast
who stretches over so much ground; they still
don't feel quite sure enough to touch the boar—
they simply dip their lances in his gore.

Then Meleager, with his foot upon
that deadly head, to Atalanta said:
"O Atalanta, share with me this trophy,
and share the glory of this victory!"
With that, he gave the girl his spoils: the stiff
boarhide, with rigid bristles, and with this,

Latin [402–28]

the snout and the tremendous tusks; the gift
delights her, as does he who's given it.

But all the rest are envious: a murmur
of protest runs through that great band of hunters.
Two sons of Thestius, the hero's uncles,
advance with arms outstretched; their shouts are loud:
"Yes, you are beautiful, but do not count
on one so lovesick; he can't help you now."
From her they snatch the trophies, and from him
those brothers take away the right to give.
But he whom Mars holds dear won't stand for this;
gnashing his teeth, enraged, he cries: "You thieves
of others' glory, watch—and learn from—me
the drastic difference between mere speech
that blusters, and the act itself—the deed."
Then, with his uncles caught off guard, he plunged
his impious iron in Plexippus' heart.
The other brother, Toxeus, on his part,
is torn: he would avenge his brother's death
but fears the very fate his brother met—
and now indeed but little time is left
for hesitation: Meleager warms
again—in Toxeus' blood—the shaft still warm
with blood he'd drawn from Thestius' other son.

———————

Althaea, grateful for the victory
of Meleager, her dear son, was bringing
gifts for the gods into the sanctuary;
she saw them carry in her brothers' bodies.
Althaea beat her breast; she filled the city
with sad laments; she changed her gilded dress
and now wore black. But when she learned who was
the author of their death, she left behind
her tears and mourned no more; her heart was bent
on vengeance. □   □   □

Latin [429–50]

               Years ago, when she still lay
upon her childbirth bed, Althaea saw
the Fates, three sisters, place a log upon
the hearth; and even as the sisters spun
the threads of her son's life with their firm thumbs,
they sang: "We now assign the selfsame span
of life unto this log and you, newborn."
Their chant was done; the goddesses were gone.
At once the mother snatched the blazing brand
out of the fire and drenched it in fresh water.
For all the years, that piece of wood lay hid
within the house, in the most secret place.
O Meleager, saving it had saved
your life!

               At last, Althaea fetches it;
she calls for knots of pitch-pine and for splits
of kindling—then the cruel fire is lit.
Four times she is about to toss that log
onto the fire; four times she checks herself.
Within Althaea, mother wars with sister;
those two names tear apart her single heart.
First she grows pale with fear of what she plans,
a crime so foul; but then her seething wrath
inflames her eyes with its own color, red.
Now she appears to be most menacing—
a horrid thing—and now you'd swear that she
was merciful. When savage frenzy dries
her tears again, Althaea cries. She's like
a ship that, driven by the wind and by
a current running counter, is the prey
of both and—in uncertainty—obeys
two forces: so was Thestius' daughter torn
by counterforces; she, at times, is calm
but, having calmed, is prey to wrath once more.
But then the sister in her overcomes
the mother; she decides she must appease
with blood her brothers' Shades; impiety
is now her piety. And, when the flames

Latin [450–77]

gain force, Althaea cries: "Oh, may this pyre
consume the flesh of my own flesh!" Her hand
is pitiless; she grips the fatal brand;
and in despair, before that mournful hearth,
she stands and says:

            "May you three goddesses
of vengeance, you, the Furies, turn your eyes,
as witnesses, to this infernal rite!
Now I, through this, my crime, avenge a crime.
Death is to be atoned by death; let sin
to sin be added; and add burial
to burial; my wretched house will end
in all these many mournings, these laments.
Would it be right to leave an Oeneus free
to celebrate his dear son's victory,
when Thestius is left without his sons?
Far better for them both to weep at once!
O you, my brothers' souls, you, new-made Shades,
accept this honor that—to you—I pay;
accept the deadly offering I make—
it is so dear, so costly—for your sake:
the evil fruit my womb has reaped. And yet—
why must I be so quick? Forgive, forgive,
my brothers: I'm a mother, and my hands
can not complete what they began. I know
that he deserves to die, but must it be
a mother who's the author of his death?
But if he is not punished, he'd be left
alive, a victor, puffed up with success.
Would he become the king of Calydon
while you were underearth, handfuls of ash,
chill Shades? No, no, I never could bear that.
Then let him die—that murderer—and drag
to ruin all his father's hopes, this realm,
and his own fatherland. . . . But then . . . but then,
where's my maternal love? And parents' care
for their own sons? Where are the pains I bore

Latin [477–500]

for nine long months? If you had only burned
to death when you were born—and I had faced
that sorrow then! My gift has let you live—
the log I saved; you earned the death you meet;
what you now pay for is your own misdeed.

Give back the life I gave you twice: at birth
and when I hid the brand—or send me, too,

just as you sent my brothers—to the tomb!
I would—but cannot—act. Could I but choose!
My eyes can only see my brothers' wounds—
the sight of slaughter! But the name and love
that are a mother's shatter my resolve.
What misery is mine! The victory
is yours, my brothers—sad, but it must be;
but once the one I sacrifice has gone
along the way you took, allow me, too,
to follow you."

  That said, she turns her back,
so that she need not see the fated brand
she flings into the flames with trembling hand—
the brand that gives or seems to give a groan.
The fire—against its will—performs its role:
it catches and consumes the cursed wood.
Far off—and unaware of why he's scorched—
poor Meleager burns in that same flame:
his guts are parched, he feels a hidden source
of heat; his heart, his courage can support
his agony—but he laments this sort
of death—so bloodless, so inglorious.
He thinks of one who died of wounds, Ancaeus,
and calls him fortunate. And at the last
he calls on his old father, on his brothers
and pious sisters, and upon the woman
who shared his bed; and he may have invoked
his mother. Pain and fire gain fresh force,
but then grow weaker, and at last die out
together. Slowly, his soul's breath is lost;

Latin [500–524]

it slips away into thin air, and just
as slowly, on the embers, white ash forms
a veil.

    And grief lays low great Calydon.
The commoners and nobles weep; the young
and old; the matrons who had made their homes
along the banks of the Evenus mourn—
they tear their hair and beat their breasts. And Oeneus,
his father, prone upon the ground, defiles
his white hair and his aged face with dust;
he's lived too long, he says—his life was cursed.
As for Althaea, she had killed herself
by then: as soon as she had learned her son
was dead, she plunged a blade into her guts—
as punishment.

    But I can scarcely tell
in full the wretched sisters' lamentations—
not even if some god had given me
a hundred mouths and just as many tongues,
consummate skill, and all of Helicon.
Those sisters have forgotten all decorum;
they beat their breasts till they are livid, bruised;
and while their brother's body still is there,
they warm the corpse, caressing it again,
again; they kiss their brother, kiss the bier;
and when he's burned to ashes, they take up
those ashes by the handful, pressing them
against their breasts; and after time has passed,
and Meleager has his tomb, they cast
themselves against that mound; entwined around
his name incised in stone, the sisters drench
his name with tears.

    Diana was content.
Her work was done: the goddess was avenged.
At last, Parthaon's house had reached its end.

Latin [524–43]

And now, to comfort Meleager's sisters
(except for Gorge and the great Alcmena's
daughter-in-law), she gave their bodies feathers;
and then she thinned their arms into long wings
and changed their mouths to horny beaks. And when
their new shape was complete, Diana sent
the sisters out to fly—as guinea-hens.

Meanwhile, the son of Aegus, having done
his share to help the hunt in Calydon,
was heading home to Athens but was blocked
by heavy rains that swelled the Achelous:
he could not cross the stream. The river-god,
while warning him against the waters' course,
told Theseus: "Please take shelter in my house,
you famous son of Athens; for the course
my current takes is far too ominous:
those roaring, rolling waters are quite used
to bearing off stout trees and giant rocks.
I've seen great stables standing on those shores
and seen them carried off—livestock and all;
against such surge, the bullocks' power failed,
the helpless horses' speed did not avail.
And when the snows along the mountain slopes
have melted, this—my torrent—often swallows
the bodies of young men in its wild whirlpools.
Rest here; wait till the waters ebb and find
their normal channel, and the banks confine
the current." Aegeus' son, convinced, replied:
"I welcome both your house and your advice,
o Achelous." And he went inside.

The room that Theseus entered had dark walls
of porous pumice and rough tufa, while
the floor was damp and soft with moss; the panels
sunk in the ceiling alternated conchs

Latin [543–64]

and purple shells. By now the sun had crossed
two thirds of its day-course. The son of Aegeus,
together with some comrades from the hunt,
reclined. Pirithous lay here; and there
lay Lelex, the Troezenian warrior,
whose temples showed his age—a bit of gray;
as well as others whom the river-god
would honor, too, with hospitality—
a guest as great as Theseus made him happy.
At once barefooted nymphs set out the feast—
there was abundance; when the meal was done,
they served the wine in jeweled cups.

                              Then Theseus,
greatest of heroes, looking toward the sea
that lay far off, beyond the river's mouth,
pointing his finger, asked the river-god:
"What is that island there? What is it called?
And is it just one isle? It's hard to tell:
it's so far off." And this was the response:
"What you see there is not one isle but five;
it is the distance that deceives your eyes.
And that you may be less astonished by
Diana's answer to the grievous slight
she suffered, hear my tale. Those isles were once
five Naiads. They had sacrificed ten bulls;
and to their festal dance, they had invited
the rural gods; but to that sacred rite,
the nymphs forgot to ask one guest: yes, I
was not invited. I swelled up with rage,
just as my waters swell when they rampage:
my flood was high and horrible; my waves,
my impetus ripped woods from woods, and fields
from fields; my waters swept the nymphs away,
together with the site on which they stood;
borne past the river's mouth and out to sea,

Latin [564–87]

they finally remembered me. My waves
joined with the sea to tear away a piece
of land and form five parts—the isles you see
among those waters: the Echinades.

"But if you look beyond—and carefully—
there's still another isle you can detect,
apart from all the rest: it's dear to me—
the sailors call that island Perimele.
I loved the girl who bore that name; I took
away, by force, my love's virginity.
Hippodomas, her father, was not ready
for this; and so he hurled his daughter down
from a sheer cliff into the deep, to drown.
I caught her—I supported her, that she
might swim. I cried: 'O you who were assigned—
by lot—the wandering waves, the kingdom second
to none but heaven; you, who bear the trident,
I pray you, Neptune, now to help this nymph;
her father's cruelty would have her drown;
concede some place to serve as shelter, or
make of the nymph herself a place'—I still
was speaking, when I saw the girl transformed;
for as she floated, land—it was new made—
embraced her limbs and grew more solid till
my Perimele had become an isle."

The river-god was done. The miracle
that he'd recounted stirred the hearts of all
but one—Pirithous, Ixion's son.
He found his friends too gullible; he scorned
such tales; he mocked the gods; he disbelieved
and doubted most ferociously: "But these
are fictions: Achelous, you concede
too much if you allow the gods to be
so powerful, if you think they can give

Latin [587–615]

and take away the forms of things." Such words
shocked all that company—no one concurred;
and Lelex, he who was the most mature
in mind and years, began to tell this tale:

"The power of the heavens is immense
and limitless; whatever gods may wish
is soon accomplished. I have evidence
for this: my tale will help to credit it.

"Among the Phrygian hills there stands an oak
together with a linden; round them both
a low wall runs. And I have seen this spot,
for Pittheus sent me there (his father, Pelops,
before he came to Troezen, ruled in Phrygia).
Close to that spot, there is a stagnant marsh;
a place that once had welcomed crops and men,
it now has water birds—loons and marsh hens.
And Jupiter came there in mortal guise;
and with his father, though he'd set aside
his wings, came Mercury, Atlas' grandson,
with the caduceus, his wondrous wand.
They asked for shelter at a thousand doors;
and at a thousand they were shunned and spurned.
But one house took them in: a modest place,
its roof was thatched with simple straw and reeds.
And, in that hut, there lived an aged woman,
the pious Baucis, and with her, Philemon,
as old as she was; they were wed when young
within that hut; and there they had grown old,
serene in poverty, not seeing it
as taint or tarnish, something to be hid.
You need not ask who was the master, who
the servant in that house, for only two
lived there—that pair commanded and they served.
And when the two gods from the sky arrived,
they stooped on entering—the door was low.
The old man, setting out a bench on which

his Baucis had been quick to spread rough cloth,
invited them to sit, to rest their limbs.
The coals of yesterday were covered by
warm ashes; Baucis, raking these aside,
now fanned the coals and added leaves, dry bark;
then, on her hands and knees, with all the breath
she had, she breathed new life into the hearth.
That done, from underneath the roof, she took
wood splits and dried-out twigs and broke them up
into still smaller pieces—small enough
to set beneath a little copper pot.
She took the greens Philemon had brought in
from their well-watered garden; and she cleaned
a cabbage, lopping off the outer leaves.
Meanwhile her husband used a two-tined pole
to spear a chine of smoked ham hanging from
a rafter's blackened beams and, slicing off
a modest portion of that well-kept pork,
he put it in the boiling pot to cook.
And they beguiled their waiting-time with talk—
and readying the table. Baucis shook
a cushion made of marsh grass, placing it
upon the dining couch, with feet and frame
of willow wood. And over this they draped
the cover the old couple kept for feast days;
but even this was worn and plain, a cloth
quite in accord with such a willow couch.

"The gods recline. Old Baucis, with her skirts
tucked up—and hands that shook a bit—sets out
the table; one of its three legs was short—
but then the piece of broken pottery
she jams beneath the shorter leg adjusts
the slant—at last it's level. And with green
mint leaves, old Baucis wipes the table clean.
She offers dappled olives—green-and-black—
the berries frank Minerva cherishes;
wild cherries, pickled fruits of autumn, kept

Latin [639–65]

in lees of wine; endive and radishes;
and curdled cheese; and—taken from warm ashes—
some very delicately roasted eggs.
And all of this is served on earthen dishes.
That same rich ware is matched by the embossed
wine bowl they have set out with beechwood cups

whose cracks and holes were patched with yellow wax.
And soon the steaming ham and cabbage come
from off the hearth; and wine of no great age
again is served, then set aside: the space
is needed for the final course—dried dates
and nuts and figs and plums and purple grapes
straight from the vine, and fragrant apples heaped
in ample baskets; and the centerpiece—
a comb of honey that is pale and clear.
And to all these are added liveliness,
good cheer, kind faces—willing, generous.

"Meanwhile the aged couple noticed this:
the wine bowl, which had served so many cups,
seemed to replenish its own self, fill up
again, again with welling wine. Dismayed—
this sight was unbelievable—afraid,
both Baucis and the old Philemon prayed
with hands—palms up—to heaven, begging pardon
for food so meager, and so scant a welcome.
Then they got set to kill their only goose,
the guardian of their poor patch of land—
they planned to serve it to their godly guests.
But that was no slow goose; he tired out
the aged couple as he flapped about;
he slipped the chase until at last—it seems—
he landed safely, near the deities.
And then the gods told Baucis and Philemon
that they were not to kill the goose. They said:
'We're gods indeed; your sacrilegious neighbors
have earned the punishment they will receive,
but you'll be saved from that catastrophe.

Latin [665–91]

And now, come, leave your hut, and go with us
to the tall peak that you can see far off.'
They both obeyed, and taking up their staffs,
they made their slow way up the mountain path.
When they were just a bowshot from the top,
they turned around and saw, below, a swamp
that covered everything—but their own hut.
And while the aged couple watched, amazed,
and weeping for their neighbors' fate, that hut
in which they'd lived so long—a home that was
small even in their eyes—became a temple:
in place of those forked poles that had sustained
the roof, now marble columns stood; the straw
now gleamed with gold; carved panels graced the doors;
and on the ground there stretched a marble floor.
Then Jove, the son of Saturn, said with calm:
'You, just old man, and you, his worthy wife,
tell me what you desire most.' Philemon
spoke briefly to his Baucis, then declared
unto the gods their choice, the wish they shared:
'We want to be your priests, to guard your shrine;
and since, for such long years, we two have lived
in harmony, we pray that the same hour
in which one dies, may also take the other,
that I may never see her sepulcher
and she may never have to bury me.'
Their wish was honored. And as long as life
was granted them, they served within the shrine.
But weary with their long, long years, one day
as they were standing near those sacred steps,
recounting times gone by in that dear place,
old Baucis saw that boughs were covering
Philemon, even as the old Philemon
saw his dear Baucis covered by green boughs.
One treetop covered both their faces now;
but they—as long as they still could—called out
in unison, 'Farewell, dear mate, farewell . . .'
until at the same instant, bark had sealed

Latin [691–718]

their lips. And Phrygian farmers still will show
two trunks that stand beside each other, two
that once were Baucis' and Philemon's bodies.

"These things were told to me by sound old men
who had no need to trick me, to invent.
And, too, I saw the oak and linden wreathed
with votive flowers; and I even set
such garlands on the boughs myself. I said:
'May those the gods have loved become divine;
may those who have revered, now be enshrined.' "

Lelex was done. And all were moved by both
the teller and the tale: the one most stirred
was Theseus; and since he was curious
to hear still other marvels that the gods
had brought to pass, the river-god, his host,
now propped upon his elbow, told his guest:

"O Theseus, bravest hero of them all,
some who have suffered change, always retain
their newly given shape. But there are some
who have the power to take on many forms:
and Proteus, you who live within the sea
that clasps the earth, indeed are one of these.
For men have seen you as a youth, a lion;
you've been a raging boar; you've been a serpent
men fear to touch; at times you have won horns,
become a bull; you've often seemed a stone
or seemed a plant; sometimes you've had the guise
of flowing water, seemed a stream; at times
you have been fire, water's opposite.

"And Erysichthon's daughter, she who wed
Autolycus, possessed such powers, too.
Her father scorned the gods: he was a scoffer

who never burned an offering at their altars.
And—so it's said—he even went so far
as to profane the sacred grove of Ceres,
for sacrilegiously he brought an ax
to fell her venerable trees. An oak,
immense and ages old, rose at that spot—
so huge, it seemed to be itself a grove.
It was adorned with fillets, votive tablets,
and garlands—offered gratefully by those
whose prayers had been fulfilled. Beneath this tree,
the Dryads danced at their festivities.
And often, hand in hand, they circled round
its holy trunk, however broad it was—
indeed its girth spanned fifteen full arm's-breadths;
it took some fifteen nymphs to circle it.
In height and in the number of its leaves,
this one oak stood to all the other trees
as each of these stood to the grass beneath
its shade. But this did not deter the son
of Triopas: he gave his men the ax
and ordered them to fell the sacred oak.
But seeing them shrink back, that profane wretch
snatched up the ax and shouted: 'Even if
this tree were not just Ceres' favorite
but her own self, its leafy crown would now
be toppled to the ground!' He was about
to strike the trunk aslant with his poised ax,
when, trembling, Ceres' oak tree groaned aloud;
its leaves and acorns paled—and its long boughs.
And when that cursed stroke had hacked the trunk,
out from the wounded bark, blood gushed; just as
it gushes from a sacrificial bull
who falls before the altar, his neck smashed.
They all are petrified—just one man tries
to stop the sacrilege, to check the ax.
But Erysichthon stares him down and says,
'This blow will pay you for your holy zeal!'
and, turning from the tree, he aims his ax

Latin [740–68]

at that bold man and slices off his head.
Then, as he pounded, blow on blow, against
the oak tree, from within the trunk, these words
emerged: 'I am the nymph most dear to Ceres;
I live beneath this bark; now, at my death,
I prophesy—and this leaves me content:
your punishment indeed is imminent.'
But Erysichthon does not halt his work;
and at the end, the oak—which sways beneath
the countless blows, and then the tugging ropes—
collapses, crushing many other trees.

"The ruin of the grove and their own loss
have stunned the Dryad sisters; dressed in black,
the mourners go to Ceres, begging her
to punish Erysichthon. She consents;
and so the lovely goddess nods her head,
then blights the fields already ripe with grain
and plots this punishment (her plan is one
that would stir pity if compassion were
not inappropriate for such a sin):
the goddess would have him devoured by Famine.
But since great Ceres cannot visit Famine
directly (Fate forbids those two to meet),
she called upon a lesser goddess, one
who haunts the slopes, a rustic Oread.
And Ceres said: 'In frozen Scythia,
the farthest borderland is barren, sad:
a land that has no harvests and no trees.
That is the home of sluggish Cold and Pallor
and Terror and gaunt Famine: find the last
of these, and tell her she must hide within
the stomach of that sacrilegious wretch.
No matter how abundantly he feeds
his belly, Famine must not meet defeat:
however copious my fruits may be,

Latin [769–92]

she's not to slacken as she wars with me—
it's Famine who must win the victory!
That land is far, but do not be afraid.
My chariot is yours to ride, and take
my dragons. Guide them high across the sky.'

"She gave the nymph the reins. And through the air,
drawn by her borrowed chariot, she came
to Scythia; she landed on the peak
of a bleak mountain (called the Caucasus),
unyoked the dragons, and, in search of Famine,
saw her within a stony field, intent
on tugging at scant grass with teeth and hand.
Her hair was straggly and her eyes deep-sunk;
her face was pale; her lips were wan and stale,
unused; her jaws were rough with scurf; her skin
so hard and thin, one saw through to her guts;
her dry bones jutted from her hollowed loins;
she had no belly, just the empty space
where bellies often are; you would have called
her chest suspended, since its only peg
was her frail spine; her thinness made her joints
protrude: her kneecaps swelled, her ankles bulged
incredibly. And when the Oread
caught sight of her, the nymph fulfilled her task:
she told to Famine what the goddess asked
(but did it from afar—she did not dare
to get too close). And soon, though she had kept
her distance and had just arrived, she felt—
or thought she felt—the pangs of hunger start.
At that, the goddess mounted, turned about,
and rode the dragons back to Thessaly.

"Though Famine's work and Ceres' are opposed
forever, Famine did as she was told:
she used the wind to wing her through the air.
She flew straight to the sinner's house; she reached
his room, and while he lay—limbs slack, asleep

Latin [793–817]

(for it was night)—she held him fast and breathed
her very essence into him: she reached
his mouth, his throat, his lungs; his hollow veins
were filled with hunger now. Her mission done,
she left the fertile regions of the world,
returning to her customary cave,
her home along the barren northern waste.

"Soft sleep still cradles in its peaceful wings
the sinner. In his dreams he needs to feast:
he champs his jaws on nothing, grinds his teeth
on teeth, and—wearying his gullet—feeds
on fictive and deluding fare—on air.
And when he wakes from sleep, that need to eat
is wild, incendiary as it sweeps
across his avid jaws and burns his guts.
He cannot wait; he calls on all that sea
and land and sky—the world's great buttery—
can now provide; his tables may be heaped
with everything, yet he cannot find peace;
amid the feast he seeks still other feasts;
what could have satisfied entire cities
leaves him still famished, for the more he eats
the more he wants. Just as the sea receives
the rivers of the earth, but then can drink
still other streams that flow from distant parts;
and just as a devouring fire will not
reject more fuel, but feeds on countless logs,
becoming more voracious with each gift:
so for the sinner Erysichthon's lips,
each banquet only adds to what he's missed.
For him, food calls for food, glut calls for glut;
his being full amounts to emptiness.

"Now hunger and his belly's bottomless
abyss have thinned his rich inheritance;

Latin [818–44]

yet even then his hunger gnaws no less
ferociously, his maw cannot relent.
At last, his patrimony swallowed up—
it is within his guts—all he has left
is his own daughter, she who merited

a better father. He is penniless—
and so he sells her. She's a noble girl;

her spirits cannot suffer this disgrace;
she does not want to be a master's slave.
And so, along the sea—over the waves,
her palms are stretched—a suppliant, she prays:
'I beg of you, save me from slavery,
you, who have stolen my virginity.'
Such was her plea to Neptune: it was he
who took her once by force. And now he grants
her prayer. The god transformed the girl so that
her master, who had seen her just before
and tracked her to the seashore, finds instead
a male, dressed as a proper fisherman.
Her master, staring at that figure, says:
'Oh, you there, with the bit of bait that hides
your dangling hook, who ply and guide that rod,
so may the sea stay calm for you, the fish
among the waves be trusting, and not notice
the hook until they've bitten—but I must
ask this: Where did that girl who was just here—
that girl with shabby clothes and straggly hair—
yes, where could she have gone? I saw her on
this shore; and past this point the footprints stop.'
She understood that she had been reprieved
by Neptune's gift, and happy to be asked
for news about herself, she gave this answer:
'Whoever you may be, please pardon me,
but I have never turned aside; my eyes
have always watched these waters: I am bent
on what I'm doing. And if you should doubt
my words, so may the sea-god favor all
my skills, I swear to you that I alone—

Latin [844–67]

no man, no woman other than myself—
set foot upon these sands.' And he believed
her words: he turned and left the beach—deceived.

"That done, the girl resumed the form she had
before; but when he saw he had a daughter
whose shape could alter, Erysichthon sold her
again, again—to master after master.
And she would easily escape: she'd take
shape after shape: now she became a mare,
a bird, a deer—and, through these changes, she
saw to her avaricious father's needs,
with food that he did not deserve. At last,
when his disease became so virulent
that it consumed whatever stores he had—
and lack could only make his sickness worse—
the wretched Erysichthon then began
to rend his flesh, to bite his limbs, to feed
on his own body.

———

                    "But must I indeed
spend so much time on metamorphoses
of others? I myself have often changed
my shape—although the forms that I may take
are limited. At times I show myself
just as you see me now; at times I am
a snake; and then I can become a bull,
the chieftain of the herd, who vaunts and flaunts
his horns. Though 'horns' by now is not exact;
I had two once, but only one is left:
as you, young men, can see, my forehead lacks
one of my weapons." Here the river-god
removed his wreath of simple reeds and showed
his wounded brow. His words were done. He groaned.

Latin [868–84]

BOOK IX

AND THESEUS, HERO dear to Neptune, now
asked Achelous why he groaned and how
his brow had lost a horn. The river-god
bound up the wreath of reeds that ringed his head
to hide the wound he'd suffered. Then he said:

"You've set a melancholy task for me:
who wants to tell the tale of his own defeat?
But I'll recount the story step by step,
and—after all—there was no stain, no shame
in fighting as I fought; that battle brought
much glory to me; even in my loss,
there's solace—I had faced so great a victor.
You may have heard men speak of Oenus' daughter,
fair Deianira—sought by many suitors.
I joined the crowd that hurried to the house
of Oenus; like the rest, I hoped to win
that lovely girl. As soon as we went in,
I said: 'Parthaon's son, I want to be
your son-in-law.' And so said Hercules;
and when the rest—reluctant to compete
with two like us—withdrew, he made his plea:
if Deianira married him, then she
would be Jove's very own daughter-in-law;
as for himself, there were the famous tests
that Hercules had met—the labors set
by his stepmother, Juno. In rebuttal,
I made my case: 'It surely would be shameful
for any god to give way to a mortal'
(in those days Hercules had not as yet
been made a god); 'and I who stand before you
am master of a river that winds through
·your realm. With me you'd have a son-in-law
who was no stranger here, come from afar,
but one of your own countrymen, a part
of your own kingdom. And in truth I hope
that I shall not be penalized because
I have not earned the hatred of Queen Juno,

Latin [1–22]

and she, to punish me, has not imposed
hard tasks. And you, Alcmena's son, now boast
that you are sprung from Jove. But either he
is not your father, and your claim is false;
or it is true, and you were born in sin.
And so, to make a father out of him,
you make your mother an adulteress.
Admit your tale of Jove is fiction, or
confess that you were mothered by a whore!'

"These were my words, but Hercules had long
been glaring at me; and he could not curb
his hot rage any longer. His brief words:
'My brawn is better than my tongue. You win
in speech, but I can beat you with my blows.'
He—frenzied—charged at me. Just now I'd been
so swaggering that I could not retreat;
I stripped down, throwing off my coat of green.
I hold my arms out; poised, I tense my hands
to grab him when and where I get the chance.
He stoops to gather up some dust, a clutch
he flings at me; in turn, the tawny sand
now yellows him. He tries (or seems to try)
to grip me by the neck and then to catch
my darting legs—yes, Hercules' attack
aims everywhere. But I have too much bulk;
my weight foils his assault, just as a rock
assailed by roaring surge stands firm, intact.
We disengage, then—once again—we clash;
each holds his ground, for neither would fall back;
foot against foot, hand against hand, we strain;
bent forward with my chest's full weight, I push
my brow against his brow. So have I seen
strong bulls collide in battle when they strive
to win the fairest heifer as their prize;
and on the valley slopes, the terrified
herd waits to see who'll win, who is to gain
the victory and reign as king. In vain,

Latin [22–49]

Alceus' grandson tried to push away
my chest—three times; but at the fourth attempt,
he shook me off, broke free of my arms' clutch,
and struck with so much force that I spun round
(I said I'd tell the truth—at any cost).
And then he landed on my back—and clung
with all his weight. I'd not enhance my fame
by telling lies about the force I faced,
and so you can believe me when I say
I felt as crushed as if a mountain lay
upon my back. And yet I found the strength
to insinuate my arms—they dripped with sweat:
I broke his massive hold; but he won't let
my breath come back; and even as I pant,
he switches to a stranglehold—he chokes
my neck. And so at length my knees were pressed
into the ground; face down, I bit the sand.

"I could not match his force; I had to call
upon my crafty arts; I changed myself;
becoming a long snake, I slid away.
But when he saw my supple body twist
and coil and menace with the savage hiss
of my forked tongue, the mighty Hercules
just laughed. He mocked my cleverness, my tricks:
'But that was cradle work for me: a babe,
I conquered snakes. It's true you might outdo
all other dragons; but, poor Achelous,
how could you, just one snake, lay any claim
to size if set against the monstrous Hydra
of Lerna? From each wound I would inflict,
the Hydra gained new strength: if one cut off
one of its hundred heads, its neck would just
sprout two new heads. Out from that monster branch
fresh serpents at the death of any head;
it thrived upon the blows I struck—and yet
I won against the Hydra, and I ripped
that monster open when I'd mastered it.

Latin [50–74]

What can you hope to do with shifts and tricks?
You are a bogus snake, a counterfeit
with borrowed weapons, with a form that is
precarious, a mask.' Such—his disdain.
And then his fingers, as if they were chains,
pressed hard upon my throat; I felt as if
a pincers had me in its grip: in anguish,
I tried to free my jaws from his firm clutch.

"I'd lost as river-god; I'd lost as snake;
all that was left to try was my third shape:
so I became a savage bull and—changed—
took up the fight again. Upon my left,
he threw his arms around my neck; and as
I ran full speed, he let himself be dragged;
and finally he forced my hard horns down
into the ground; and in the swirling dust,
he laid me low. But that was not enough;
for as he clutched one horn—and it was tough—
he wrenched it off—he tore it from my brow;
I bear that mutilation still. The Naiads
filled up that horn with fruits and fragrant flowers;
they made of it a sacred thing. And now
Abundance—gracious goddess—uses this,
the Cornucopia, as her motif."

The river-god was done; and now a nymph
dressed like Diana in a tucked-up tunic,
with long hair flowing over both her shoulders,
came in, to serve us our dessert: the fruits
of autumn, the exquisite fruits that we
admired in the ample horn of plenty.

Firstlight has come; and when the mountain peaks
are struck by rays of sun, the young men leave;
they do not wait until the stream finds peace,
the calm of an untroubled course: they part
before the flood has beat its full retreat.

Latin [75–96]

And Achelous sinks his rustic face
and head, which lacks one horn, beneath the waves.

————————

Although the god had lost his handsome horn
and had his forehead marred, he still was sound
in every other way. And he could hide
his scar with wreaths of weeds or willow boughs.
But you, ferocious Nessus, who were struck
with love for Deianira, lost your life:
a flying arrow pierced you through the spine.

In fact, while Hercules, the son of Jove,
was heading back to Tiryns with his bride,
he reached the rapid flow of the Evenus.
The river, swollen by the winter rains,
had risen; eddies swirled—impetuous—
defying any who might dare to cross.
As Hercules, with no fear for himself
but anxious for his bride, stood on the banks,
the centaur Nessus, sturdy and adept
at fording such a stream, drew near and said:
"O Hercules, I can take care of her
and get her safely to the other shore,
while you—whose daring can't be matched—swim over."
And Hercules entrusted to the centaur
fair Deianira; she was trembling, pale,
afraid of the Evenus and of Nessus.
The Theban, although he was weighted down
with both his quiver and his lion's skin
(for he had tossed his club and curving bow
onto the other shore), cried out: "It seems
that I am destined to contend with streams;
then let me conquer this one, too." He plunged;
he did not try to find the calmest point—
and spurned whatever help the current might
have offered him.   □   □   □

Latin [96–117]

And now he had just reached
the other shore; as he retrieves the bow
that he had thrown across, he hears outcries—
it is his wife, for he can recognize
her voice; and he sees Nessus sneak away;
he's carrying off the girl; he has betrayed
his trust. And Hercules cries out: "You beast,
where do you think your feet can carry you?
It's you I'm talking to—you biform Nessus!
Hear what I say: don't prey on what is mine!
And if you've no respect for me, remember
the ever-whirling wheel that chains your father,
the price Ixion paid for his adulteries!
In any case, however much you trust
the half of you that is a speeding horse,
you will not get away: I'll wound you yet—
not with my feet but with this fatal shaft!"

His action fit these final words: he shot
an arrow and it caught the fugitive
right in the spine—and drove deep, coming out
through Nessus' chest; and as the centaur wrenched
the barbed tip out, blood spurted from both wounds—
the front, the back; and in that blood was mixed
the Hydra's venom—Hercules had dipped
his arrows in that poison after he
had killed the beast of Lerna. Nessus knew
of this, and to himself he murmured: "I
shall not die unavenged." And then he gave
his tunic soaked with his envenomed blood
to Deianira as a gift; he told
the girl whom he had tried to carry off
that his hot blood would serve to spur the love
of Hercules, if it should ever wane.

□ □ □

Latin [118–33]

Much time had passed; the mighty Hercules
had filled the world with word of his great deeds;
and Juno's hatred now was at its peak.
Just then, as Hercules was journeying
back home from his Oechalian victory,
he halted at Cenaeum's promontory;
and there, upon Jove's altar, he prepared
to sacrifice in gratefulness. But Rumor,
forever babbling, had already reached
your ears, o Deianira. Rumor loves
to mix the true and false; she can take off
from something slight and swell it with her lies;
and now to you she said that Hercules
was passionately drawn to Iole.
The loving wife, believing Rumor's story
and overcome by news of that new love,
at first gives way to tears—her misery
finds its release in weeping constantly.
But soon she says: "Why weep? For should she see
my tears, my rival surely would be pleased;
and she will be here shortly; I must find
some scheme, some plan—with speed, while there's still time—
before this stranger has usurped my bed.
Shall I complain, decry—or simply grieve
in silence? Shall I stay or should I leave
for Calydon? Should I desert this house
or, if there's nothing more to do, at least
defy that concubine? But if I can
remember, Meleager, that I am
your sister, and devise a fierce revenge
and show just what a wounded woman's wrath
can do, and cut my rival's throat—what then!"

These schemes were but a part of what her mind
was conjuring. At last she did decide
upon this plan: to send to Hercules

Latin [134–53]

the tunic that was soaked in Nessus' blood,
so that it might revive her husband's love.
And to her servant Lichas she consigned
this tunic; and he hurried to Cenaeum,
for there, with suasive words, she said he was
to take it, as a gift, to her dear husband.
As she is not aware that what she sends
can only bring her ruin and lament,
so Lichas does not know just what he bears.
And Hercules, in turn, is unaware
that what he has received is steeped in venom:
the Hydra's horrid poison. He puts on
the tunic Deianira sent from home.

It is the fatal tunic that he wears,
as there, upon Cenaeum's marble altars,
he kindles fires, and offers incense, prayers,
and pours wine offerings to Jupiter.
The fire's heat set free the venom's force,
and through the limbs of Hercules it coursed.
At first his famous courage checked his groans,
but when the savage pain had grown too great
to be endured, he overturned the altars
and filled the woods of Oeta with his cries.
He tries to tear the tunic off his flesh;
but where he tugs, the fatal garment shreds
his skin and—this is horrid to retell—
sticks to his limbs, and can't be ripped away,
however hard he strives, or—eating through
the flesh—lays bare his massive bones and sinews.
The blood of Hercules is hissing now,
as does an incandescent metal bar
when plunged into a pool. The greedy fire
cannot be checked as it consumes his guts,
and all his body drips with blue-gray sweat;
his tendons crackle, scorched; his marrow melts—
the deadly heat within is just too much
for Hercules to stand. A suppliant,

Latin [153–75]

he lifts his hands up toward the stars and shouts:
"Come, Juno, feast upon my agony!
Yes, feast and, from the height of heaven, see
my torment and content your cruel heart!
But if my fate can even wake some pity
in my worst enemy—that is, yourself—
then rid me of my life: my soul is weary
of suffering; I hate my life—born only
to labor. Death will be a gift to me—
a gift that a stepmother might well give.
Is it for this that I have killed Busiris,
who desecrated all the shrines of Egypt
with strangers' blood? That I deprived the fierce
Antaeus of his force by lifting him
up from his mother Earth? For this that I,
in Spain, was unafraid of Geryon,
the shepherd with three heads—and did not fear
your three heads, too, o Cerberus? My hands—
were you the hands with strength enough to bend
the horns of the stout bull that Neptune sent,
the hands that cleansed the stables of Augeias,
Stymphalus' marsh, the woods of Mount Parthenius?
The golden girdle of the Amazon—
who won it on Thermodon's shores? Who won
the apples guarded by the sleepless dragon?
Am I the one whom neither centaurs nor
the boar that savaged Arcady could conquer?
The man who made it useless for the Hydra
to grow anew with every blow, to show
redoubled force? And when the king of Thrace,
who fed his horses human flesh, had filled
their bins with butchered corpses, did not I
cleanse all those feeding bins and kill both him
and his stout stallions? These are mine—the arms
that choked the giant lion of Nemea;
and mine, this nape that has sustained the sky.
The savage wife of Jove is weary now
of setting tasks for me, though I am not

too tired to perform them. But I face
a strange affliction: neither force nor arms
of offense or of defense offer help.
The fire devours me; stealing through my lungs,
it feeds on all my limbs. Meanwhile Eurystheus—
be sure—is safe and sound! And are there those
who still believe the gods exist!"

He spoke
these words and then, along the mountain slopes
of towering Oeta, dragged his wounded self,
just as a bull will carry in his flesh
the shaft that struck him, though the one who shot
that barb has fled. And Hercules now moans,
now roars, now tries anew to tear to shreds
the tunic; and he topples trees, and vents
his wrath against the hillside boulders, and
with arms outstretched, implores his father's heaven.

But—suddenly—the hero catches sight
of Lichas: he is cowering, terrified;
within the hollow of a rock, he hides.
And Hercules, with all the rage his pain
has stored, cries out: "O Lichas, is it you
who gave this deadly gift to me: are you
the author of my death?" Pale, Lichas trembles
in fear; he stammers timidly; he pleads
for pardon. But while he's still stammering
and trying, suppliant, to clasp the knees
of Hercules, the hero seizes him;
and whirling him around three and four times,
he flings him far—a toss with greater force
than any missile from a catapult—
out, into the Euboean. As he flies
high, through the air, the servant petrifies.
Even as rain—they say—grows more compact
when swept by icy winds, and turns to snow;
and those snow flakes, still soft, as they are whirled,

Latin [199–221]

condense—and thicken into solid hail:
so, cast into the void by those stout arms,
frozen with fear, his body drained of sap,
dry Lichas is transformed into hard stone.
This is the way the tale—of old—was told.
And even now, in the Euboean sea,
a low shoal rises up, above deep eddies,
and keeps the traces of a human form.
And just as if this rock were sentient,
seamen are careful not to step on it;
and Lichas is the name they've given it.

But you, the far-famed son of Jove, cut down
the trees that grew on towering Oeta's slopes;
and having heaped a pyre for yourself,
you order Philoctetes, Poeas' son,
to set a torch beneath; and it is he
who will receive your bow, your spacious quiver,
your arrows—fated shafts that are to see
the Trojan kingdom for a second time.
The eager flames have caught the heap of logs;
and you, atop the pyre, spread the skin
of the Nemean lion; there, supine,
you rest your neck upon your club, recline
as if you were a banquet guest who finds
himself among the brimming cups of wine,
a guest whom garlands crown.

                Upon all sides,
the fire rages, roars, and rises toward
the limbs of Hercules who—peacefully—
awaits them without fear. And now the gods
are anxious and dismayed; they are afraid
of what will happen to the earth's defender.
And Jove, the son of Saturn, sensed their fear
and spoke to them serenely: "I am glad,
o gods, to see just how concerned you are;
and I indeed, within my deepest heart,

Latin [222-44]

am pleased to be the father and the lord
of subjects who respond so gratefully—
and I can see how, too, my progeny
can count on your affection. Although he
has earned this by himself, through his great deeds,
I, too, now feel—and owe you—gratitude.
In any case, don't let your faithful hearts
be stirred by needless fear—just disregard
those flames. For Hercules, who overcame
all things, will also overcome the flames
you see; he'll only feel the force of Vulcan
within the part his mother gave to him.
His other part—the seed he owes to me—
is his eternally; it cannot be
consumed; it knows no death; there is no flame
that can destroy it. When his earthly days
are done, I'll welcome his eternal portion
into the heavens; as for that decision,
I trust that it will gladden all the gods.
Yet, if there's anyone—yes, anyone—
who's grieved to see my making Hercules
a god, though that dissenter may begrudge
the prize that Hercules has won, he must
admit: the prize is merited—and so,
approve my action, even though it goes
against his will." The gods gave their assent.
And even Juno, royal wife of Jove,
seemed to accept his speech in peace; her face
betrayed no grief—except for his last words:
he'd singled out his wife; she felt the hurt.

Meanwhile, whatever Vulcan could destroy,
he did. Though Hercules' immortal part
remained, he was unrecognizable;
for nothing of his mother's image now
was left; the traces that he kept were Jove's.
Just as a serpent, when it sheds its skin
casts off old age and is resplendent in

Latin [245–67]

its glittering scales and now, made new again,
rejoices; so did the Tyrinthian,
when he had put aside his mortal limbs,
attain new power in his better part,
for he began to seem more large, more tall—
majestic, godly, grave and venerable.
Now Jove, his father, the all-powerful,
rode down to earth and wrapped him in a cloud
and, in his four-horse chariot, carried off
his son and set him in the sky among
the bright stars. Heaven now was heavier
on Atlas' shoulders.

                But Eurystheus' rage
did not abate: he nursed his bitter hate
for Hercules and all his race, harassing
his offspring. And Alcmena, faced with that—
and with so many other cares—was anxious;
the only one with whom the queen could share
these cares was Iole, who now was married
to Hyllus, son of Hercules. The will
of Hercules had brought about this wedding;
and Hyllus, to fulfill his father's wish,
had welcomed Iole both to his bed
and to his heart; and now, with noble seed,
the girl was pregnant. And the old Alcmena—
just as old women will—was now recounting
to Iole the feats of Hercules
and the vicissitudes of her long life.
She started out by saying: "May the gods
be gracious to you, and your labor pains
be shortened when you call upon Lucina,
the goddess who sustains all fearful mothers
in their travail, although when Hercules
was born, she made that hour harsh for me,
yes, hard indeed—that Juno might be pleased.

Latin [267–84]

For when his hour of birth was imminent,
the sun was just about to touch the tenth
sign of the Zodiac; my womb was heavy
with Hercules, one fated for such toil:
my belly was so large that you could tell
that Jove himself was father of this child.
By then, the fierce pangs were unbearable;
even as I tell this, my limbs grow chill
with horror: that pain lives in my recall.
For seven nights and days I was in torment;
exhausted by the pain, a suppliant,
I called upon Lucina and her three
attendant goddesses of birth's travail.
She came indeed—but had already schemed
with cruel Juno: they were both in league
against me, and Lucina meant to give
my life to Saturn's daughter as a gift.
She sat before the door, upon the altar;
and listening to my moans, the goddess crossed
her left knee with her right, and then laced tight
her fingers, locking them around her knees;
so did Lucina block delivery.
She also chanted spells beneath her breath;
with them, too, birth—which had begun—was checked.
I labored, mad with pain; in vain I cursed
ungrateful Jove; I longed to die; my words
would move the hardest stones to tears. Around me
the Theban women also pleaded, prayed:
they tried to give me strength to meet this test.
Now one of my attendants was Galanthis,
a blond-haired girl of humble family,
one quick to get her work done—dear and caring.
She sensed that something strange was happening,
something that Juno had devised and schemed;
and as she came and went and passed the entrance,
she saw the goddess seated on the altar
with her laced fingers locked around her knees.
Galanthis said: 'Whoever you may be,

congratulate my mistress. She is happy.
Argive Alcmena has just given birth;
the mother and her son are doing well.'
At that, the goddess of childbirth leaped up,
dismayed, and her locked fingers drew apart.
The knot was now undone; and I gave birth.
They say that, at that point, Galanthis jeered:
she laughed at the deluded deity.
And as she laughed, the savage goddess caught
Galanthis by the hair and dragged her off,
along the ground; the girl tried to get up—
but then the goddess kept her on all fours
and changed Galanthis' arms into forefeet.
In her new shape, Galanthis kept her old
quickness; her back still kept her color—blond;
it was her form that changed. And since her mouth's
deceptions helped me to give birth, Galanthis—
transformed—gives birth to younglings through her mouth.
And still, just as before, it is our house
that is her home: she is a weasel now."

Such were Alcmena's words, and then she moaned,
remembering her faithful serving-girl.
And as Alcmena grieved, this was the way
her daughter-in-law spoke:

                       "What moved you so
is, after all, a change of form that struck
someone outside our family. But what
if I should tell the stupefying tale
of my own sister? Though—to speak—I must
contend against the tears that choke my words.
For Dryope, her mother's only child
(our father had me from another wife),
was famous for her beauty, unsurpassed
among the women of Oechalia.　□　□　□

Latin [312–31]

After the loss of her virginity
(against her will) to Delphi's deity,
Andraemon married her—and he was happy.
But one day Dryope was visiting
a lake whose sloping shoreline formed a sort
of inclined beach, which at its top was crowned
with myrtle shrubs. She came not knowing what
would be her fate: and—what is even more
disturbing—she had come to gather garlands
as offerings to the nymphs. My sister bore
a welcome weight, her infant son, not yet
one full year old; and at her breast she nursed
the boy with her warm milk. Not too far off,
there grew a water-loving lotus plant,
with buds whose hue resembled Tyrian purple;
its branches promised to show berries soon.
And from this lotus, Dryope had plucked
some blossoms to delight her infant son;
I thought I'd do the same (yes, I was there)
but stopped when I saw drops of blood that dripped
down from the blossoms as the branches shuddered.
The truth (slow-witted rustics would explain—
but later, much too late to help) was this:
once, lewd Priapus was in hot pursuit
of Lotis, and in order to escape,
the nymph had changed into this plant: her name—
though not her form and features—had remained.
My sister did not know of this; afraid,
she tried to hurry from that place; she prayed
unto the nymphs, but now her feet were stayed
like roots within the ground. She tried to shake
earth's grip, but it was just her upper limbs
that moved. The bark climbed slowly from below
and gradually covered all her loins.
When Dryope saw that, she tried to tear
her hair, but leaves were all she clutched: her head
had flowered now with boughs. The boy Amphissos
(the name that his grandfather Eurytus

Latin [331–57]

had given him) could feel his mother's breasts
grow stiff; however hard he sucked, he drew
no milky fluid. I myself was there,
o dearest sister, at your cruel end
but could not help you; I brought all my strength
to bear: I clasped you, trying to delay
the trunk, the branches on their upward way;
and yes, I wanted, too, to disappear
beneath that bark with you.

          "And now Andraemon
and her sad father, Eurytus, have come
to search for Dryope. It's Dryope
they seek, and I show them the lotus plant.
They kiss the warm wood; prone along the ground,
they clasp the roots of their dear plant. By now,
dear sister, just your face remains unchanged;
and tears rain down upon the leaves that sprout
from your poor body. But as long as she
can speak, as long as her poor lips allow
her voice to pass, my sister tells her sorrow:

" 'If even sorry wretches have the right
to be believed, I swear upon the gods
that I did not deserve this horrid end.
I have no fault yet suffer punishment.
In life I injured no one: if I lie,
may I be parched with drought and lose my boughs,
be cut down by the ax and burned to ash.
But take my baby from his mother's leaves;
entrust him to a nurse. And see that he
comes often to my tree and takes his milk
and plays beneath these branches. When he learns
to speak, be sure to teach my son to greet
his mother. Let him say in sadness: "She
is here—my mother hides within this trunk."
But keep him far from pools; and he must not
pluck any flowers from trunks; and any bush

Latin [357–80]

he sees—he must remember this—may be
the body of a goddess. Now farewell,
dear husband; you, my sister; and my father.
If you still feel fond piety for me,
protect my branches from sharp pruning hooks,
my leaves from browsing sheep. I'm not allowed
to lean toward you; instead, reach up, receive
my kisses for as long as I can give them,
and lift my little boy up to my lips.
Now I can say no more. The soft bark creeps;
it twines around my white neck, hiding me:
I'm sealed beneath its fold. There is no need
to close my eyelids with your hands: just let
the bark—and not your act of piety—
now veil my dying eyes.' Both life and speech
were done in one same instant. And for long,
the new-made leaves and boughs of the transformed
body of Dryope still kept their warmth."

———————

As Iole told this amazing story,
Alcmena (she herself was weeping) dried
the tears of the young girl. But soon lament
was banished by a singular event.
For Iolaus had appeared upon
the high threshold; but now he seemed so young—
the down upon his cheeks was faint indeed—
one almost could have said he was a boy;
his face had been restored to what it was
long years ago. For Juno's daughter, Hebe,
became the wife of Hercules when he
was taken to the sky as deity;
and Hercules had asked of her this gift
for his dear nephew. Hebe granted it;
but when she tried to swear that, after this,
she would bestow such gifts on no one else,
Themis the prophetess checked Hebe's vow:

Latin [381–403]

she spoke of things to come, and she foresaw
that change of age would also be bestowed
upon the children of Callirohe:
"O Hebe, do not vow in vain. At Thebes
a civil war is raging: Capanaeus
shall only be defeated by the force
of Jove himself—a lightning bolt; the pair
of dueling brothers, Polynices and
Eteocles, each at the other's hand,
shall die; the prophet shall be swallowed by
the earth alive; within the world below,
he'll see the spirits he had once controlled;
and to avenge his death, his son, Alcmaeon,
shall be at once both just and criminal—
and kill his mother. Stunned by what he's done,
exiled from both his reason and his home,
he shall be hounded by his mother's ghost
and by the Furies. King Phegeius
shall offer refuge to the fugitive,
who then shall wed the daughter of the king
and give to her the necklace that had bribed
his mother. But gone mad again, he'll wander
away and take as second wife the daughter
of Achelous. She, Callirohe,
shall ask him for the necklace. When he seeks
to take it back from his first wife, he'll meet
death at Phegeius' hands. Callirohe
shall then implore great Jove to grant at once
adulthood to her sons—they are still young—
so that the death of the avenger not
go unavenged too long. Moved by her plea,
Jove shall himself apply the powers of Hebe
(who is both his stepdaughter and his daughter-
in-law): Callirohe's young boys shall be
made men before they have reached puberty."

When Themis—she who knew what was to come—
had finished prophesying, many gods

Latin [403–19]

began to murmur and to agitate,
to ask why others could not benefit
from that same gift—the change of age. Aurora
complains about her husband's age; mild Ceres,
about Iasion's white hairs; and Vulcan
seeks the rejuvenation of his son,
his Erichthonius; and Venus, too,
wants her Anchises' life to be renewed—
the future worries her. There's not one god
who does not plead for some dear favorite's cause.
The tumult grows—a loud, seditious surge—
until Jove opens up his lips to urge:
"Come now, show some respect! Have you gone mad?
Does any one of you believe that he
can undo destiny? The will of Fate
permitted Iolaus to regain
the youth he had lived through—to change his age.
And it is Fate—and not ambition or
their warlike skills—that will allow the sons
Callirohe has borne to leap at once
out of their infancy—to turn adult.
You, too, depend on Fate; and (if that helps
to reconcile you) so do I myself.
Consider my own sons: if I could change
his age, dear Aeacus would not be bent
beneath the bitter burden of his years;
and Rhadamanthus, too, would now appear
as an eternal youth; as Minos would—
his many years weigh hard upon him, too:
he cannot govern as he used to do,
and he's disprized, defied." The words of Jove
persuaded them: no god could now complain;
for the exhaustion of old age was plain
in Rhadamanthus, Aeacus, and Minos.

□   □   □

Latin [419–41]

Now, even Minos' name alone, when he
was in his prime, could terrify great cities.
But he had grown infirm with age—afraid
Miletus, son of Phoebus and Deione,
proud of his parentage and youthful strength,
would head an insurrection, take his place.
Though he was sure of this, he did not dare
exile the youth. But on your own, Miletus,
you sailed off in a rapid ship across
the waves of the Aegean; on the coast
of Asia, at the mouth of the Meander,
you built a city that still takes its name
from you, its founder. Even as you wandered
along the river's winding banks, you found
Cyanee, the daughter of Meander,
whose course so often turns back on itself.
Her body was stupendous; you knew her.
The nymph gave birth to twins, Byblis and Caunus.

The fate of Byblis teaches us indeed
that when girls love they should love lawfully:
for Byblis loved her brother, Phoebus' grandson,
but with a love that was not sisterly.

In fact, the girl at first was unaware
of what fire burned in her; again, again,
she kissed her brother, twined her arms around
his neck—but she could see no sin in that;
she did not know that love can play the part
of simple fondness—she deceived herself.
But step by step, her love takes its own path;
and now, when she prepares to see her brother,
she dresses with great care: she is too eager
for him to find her fair; and if another
more lovely than her own self visits Caunus,
Byblis is jealous. But she does not know—

Latin [441–64]

not even now—the nature of her throes:
for though she does not plead or pray or wish
for a fulfillment, hidden fires burn
within. Now she begins to call him lord;
she hates those names that speak of their shared blood;
she'd have him call her "Byblis," not "dear sister."
And yet, when she's awake, she does not dare
to let her obscene hopes invade her soul.
But when she's sunk in peaceful sleep, again
the girl can see the one she loves; and when
their bodies meet, she blushes in her sleep.
When sleep retreats, the girl lies still for long
and, thinking back on what she'd seen in dreams—
her mind beset by doubts—begins to speak:

"What misery is mine! What does it mean,
this vision in the silence of the night,
this scene I'd never want to see in daylight?
But why this dream? Yes, he is fair indeed—
even unfriendly eyes would grant him that;
he pleases me, and I could love him if
he weren't my own brother; he would be
most worthy of me. To my grief, I am
his sister! Yet, if I, awake, do not
attempt such things, then let me see that dream
again in sleep—the same beguiling scene.
In dreams, no one can see you, and delight
does not seem feigned. O Venus, tender mother,
with your winged Cupid at your side, what joy
was mine! How true it seemed—so full, so deep,
it reached my marrow! Memory is sweet,
although the pleasure that I had was brief
and Night too quick to leave—she must have envied
what we were doing. Oh, if I could change
my name, o Caunus, and your father gain
so fine a daughter-in-law, even as mine
would gain in you so fine a son-in-law!
Oh, if the gods had only let us share

Latin [464–90]

all things in common—but for our parentage!
I'd have you born of higher lineage!
Instead, my fairest Caunus, you'll beget
a son by someone else whom you will wed;
for me, who had the evil fate to share
your father and your mother, you will be
no more than brother. All we'll have in common
is what has blocked our love. But then, these scenes
that I have often dreamed—what do they mean?
Do dreams have any weight at all? I call
upon the blessed gods to curb my love. . . .
Yet . . . yet . . . it is the gods themselves who wed
their sisters: Saturn married Ops, his kin
by blood; and Tethys married Oceanus;
and he who rules Olympus married Juno.
But gods have their own laws: why do I try
to seek another measure for the rites
of humans? Heaven's ways are different.
I can expel this passion from my heart
before I've taken that forbidden course—
but if I lack such force, may I die first!
And as they lay me—dead—upon the couch,
and I lie there, stretched out, may Caunus come
to kiss my lips! But, after all, not one
but two must will such things. What pleases me
may be what he would deem depravity.

"And yet the sons of Aeolus were not
ashamed to wed their sisters. Why do I
bring this to mind? Why do I cite such things?
Where am I veering now? Have done, have done
with these obscene, foul fires; let me love
my Caunus as a sister should. And yet
if he had chanced to be the first of us
to feel this flame, I might have seconded
his frenzy. And, if I would not have scorned
his wanting me, should I now seek him out?
And can I speak to him—confess in full?

Latin [490–514]

Urged on by love, indeed I can. Or if
my shame won't let me speak, I still can write
a secret letter, and the love I hide
will be revealed to him."

And she decides
on this: her mind had wavered—but she likes

this plan; and now she lifts herself and leans
on her left elbow, as she says: "Let him
decide! Let me confess this insane love.
Ah me, where am I bound? What flames erupt
within my mind?" And she begins to write,
composing words with care, though her hand shakes.
Her right hand grips the iron stylus, while
her left holds fast a slab of wax—as yet
untouched. And she, unsure, begins; she writes,
then cancels; traces letters, then repents;
corrects, is discontent, and then content;
picks up the tablets, lays them down; and when
they are at rest, she picks them up again.
She knows not what she wants; about to act,
she cancels her resolve. Upon her face
audacity is plain—but mixed with shame.
She has already written "sister" on
the tablet but decides to blot it out.
She cleans the wax and then inscribes these words:

"Here one who loves you wishes you good fortune,
that fortune she will never gain unless
you grant it to her. I'm ashamed—yes, yes—
I am ashamed to tell my name. One thing
I've wanted so: to plead my cause but hide
my name—I did not want to let you know
that I am Byblis till I could be sure
that what I want—and hope for—was secured.
In truth, the signs of my heart's wound were clear.
I was so pale, so drawn, so prone to tears;
I sighed but showed no cause; and often I

Latin [515–38]

embraced you, and my kisses were indeed—
had you but noticed them!—not sisterly.
But I, despite a wound so harsh, so deep—
for fiery frenzy burned within me—tried
by every means (the gods will testify)
so long against tremendous odds: I sought
to flee—in misery—from Cupid's shafts.
You'd not have thought a girl could bear that task.
But now I'm overcome, I must confess:
it is your help that—trembling—I must ask.
You are the only one who can decide
if I'm to be delivered or destroyed:
it's you who now must choose. No enemy
beseeches you but one who, though already
close-linked to you, longs for still closer ties.
Let those who are our elders seek and find
what is permitted; let them analyze
the niceties of law—the wrongs, the rights.
But we are young: it is audacity
that's opportune in love. We've yet to learn
what's licit: we think nothing is forbidden;
we take as our examples the great gods.
Our father is not harsh; we are not blocked
by scruples for our good name; fear cannot
curb us. In fact, what need we fear? We'll hide
our meetings under the sweet names of sister
and brother. I am fully free to meet
alone with you, to speak in secret—we
already kiss, embracing openly.
What's missing still, can easily be reached.
Have mercy on the one who has confessed
her love—who'd not have written this unless
the ardor driving her had been relentless.
Don't let them write upon my sepulcher
that I have died because of you."

                            Her tablets
were full; she had no more on which to trace

Latin [538–65]

her futile message. Byblis had to run
the last line she inscribed along the margin.

At once she seals her sinful words: she takes
her ring, which she can only wet with tears
(her tongue is much too dry to moisten it),
and presses it into the wax. Ashamed,
she calls a servant; when he hesitates,
she uses honeyed words to urge this task:
"O you, who've been so faithful, take these tablets
to my . . ." and here the girl paused long before
she added, "brother." As she handed them
to him, the tablets slipped; down to the ground
they fell. That omen troubled her, and yet
she sent them on. The servant left and, when
he found a moment that was suitable,
consigned to Caunus that confessional.

Her brother is astonished, furious;
he flings aside the tablets, just half-read,
and even as he finds it hard to check
his hands—he wants to beat the servant—says:
"Be off, before it is too late, foul pimp,
you filthy go-between for lust and sin;
for if your death would not mean my disgrace,
your life would be the price I'd make you pay!"

The messenger runs off—he's terrified—
to tell his mistress of that fierce reply.
And when you hear that Caunus has repulsed
your love, pale Byblis, you are petrified;
your body is invaded by chill frost.
But when her mind has been restored, the force
of frenzy, too, returns; and though her voice
finds speech is hard indeed, these are her words:

"This is what I deserve! Why did I rush
to bare my wound, my love? Why did I trust

Latin [565–86]

a letter—sent in haste—to bear what's best
left secret? There were better ways to test
his bent: with ambiguities and hints—
I could have spoken. To avoid the risk
of his not seconding what I so wished,
at first I should have kept my sails close-reefed,
seen what the wind was like, and faced the deep
only when I was sure I had safe seas;
but now I've spread my sails, and they are filled
with winds I did not chart before I sailed.
So I am wrecked upon the shoals; the surge
has ruined me, and I can't change my course.
But I, in truth, had been forewarned: that omen—
was it not clear that I must not pursue
my love when those wax tablets slipped and fell,
as I was just about to send them off?
Did that not mean my hopes had fallen, too?
I should have waited for a later day
or sacrificed my hopes—although delay
and not denial is the better way.
The god himself had warned me, and the signs
were clear—had I not been out of my mind.
In any case, I should not have relied
on tablets; to divulge my frenzy I
could have confessed it to him face-to-face:
he would have seen my tears, my loving gaze;
I could have told him more than I inscribed,
have thrown my arms around his neck, despite
his protests; and if I was still denied,
I could have seemed like one about to die,
and sunk down to his feet, embracing them
and, stretched along the ground, have begged for life.
I'd have used all these means: if taken singly,
each might be useless; but they would succeed
if I employed them all together—he
could not resist. And, then again, perhaps
some fault lies with the servant I had sent.
He must have made the wrong approach; the time

he chose was—I am sure—inopportune;
he did not wait until my brother's mind
was free of other cares. That hurt my cause.
For, after all, my brother was not born
of some fierce tigress; there is no hard flint,
no rigid iron, and no adamant
within his heart; nor did a lioness
give suck to Caunus. I can conquer him!
I will not let him be. As long as I
still have some breath of life, I'll try—and try
again. Although I know the best course was
never to have begun, what I have done
can't be annulled; and since I have begun,
the next best choice is, stay until I've won.
For even if I should renounce my hopes,
by now he can't forget how rash I was.
And if I should desist, I would seem heedless
or—worse—insidious, as if I'd tried
to tempt and trap him. And in any case,
I'd seem to him no more than one enslaved
by lust—not one who has indeed obeyed
this god who has deployed his tyrant force
to subjugate and to inflame my heart.
In sum, I cannot act as if I'd done
no wrong: I wrote to him; I sought him out—
and sought what's sinful. Even if I stop
at this point, he can't think me innocent.
The way is long if I'd fulfill my hopes;
but to sin more, there's little way to go."

Such were her wavering words; unsure, disturbed,
her mind is torn by doubts: while she repents
of what she's done, she wants to try again.
And now the helpless girl has lost all sense
of measure; and she pleads again, again
with Caunus, who rejects, rejects, rejects—
until at last, relentlessly harassed,

. . .

Latin [612–33]

he flees his native land and her foul pleas
and, in a foreign land, founds a new city.

And now Miletus' daughter, in despair,
loses her mind completely; Byblis tears
her robes and bares her breasts and beats her arms—
in frenzy. Byblis openly declares
her sacrilegious love; she rages, raves.
Then, having lost all hope, the girl forsakes
her country, leaves the home that earned her hate;
she wants to track the fugitive: she takes
the path her brother took when he escaped.
And, Bacchus, even as in Ismarus
your devotees, excited by the thyrsus,
each third year celebrate your bacchanal,
so now, along broad fields, near Bubassus,
the matrons see the wailing Byblis rave,
delirious. The warlike Leleges,
the Lycians, and the Cares see her frenzy.
And she'd already left behind the Cragus,
the Limyre, and Xanthus' stream; she crossed
the wooded ridge where fierce Chimaera lived—
that monster with a fire-breathing midriff,
whose head and chest showed her as lioness,
but bore a serpent's tail. Beyond those woods,
you, Byblis, weary of your long pursuit
of Caunus, fell; and there you lay—your hair
streamed out along the hard ground, and your face
was buried in the fallen leaves. Again,
again, the Lelegeian nymphs attempt—
so tenderly—to lift her up; again, again,
they try to teach her how to cure her love;
they offer words of comfort, but she can't
respond. She lies there; with her nails she grasps
the green grass; and the meadow now is damp
with Byblis' streaming tears. Upon this flow
of tears—they say—the Naiads then bestowed
this gift: it never dries. What greater gift

Latin [633–58]

could they have given Byblis? Just as pitch
drips from a slashed pine-bark; or as, from rich,
drenched earth, bitumen oozes, sticky, thick;
or as, beneath the west wind's gentle breath,
the waters winter froze now melt beneath
the sun; just so is Byblis changed at once
into the tears she shed; she has become
a fountain that, within those valleys, still
retains unto this day its mistress' name:
just at the foot of a dark ilex tree,
the never-ending fount of Byblis streams.

———

Word of this prodigy might well have stirred
all Crete—its hundred towns—if Crete itself
had not—so recently—produced its own
great miracle: when Iphis changed her form.

In Phaestus, close to Gnossus' royal city,
there lived a man called Ligdus. Though the son
of humble parents, Ligdus was freeborn.
And like his lineage, his property
was modest; but he'd lived most honestly—
he bore no stain, no blame. And when his wife
was just about to have their child, he turned
to her with these admonitory words:
"There are two things for which I pray: the first,
that you may suffer little in childbirth;
the second, that your child may be a boy.
Our means are meager—girls require more.
So, if by chance (I pray it not be so)
you bear a female, I would have you know
that (hateful as it is—and may the gods
forgive me) I shall have her put to death."
Such were his words. They both were bathed in tears:
he who had ordered this, and she who must
obey. Though Telethusa, his dear wife,

Latin [658–82]

entreated Ligdus not to set such limits
upon the birth they both had longed for so,
she prayed in vain. He would not change his course.

And now the hour of birth drew close; her womb
was full—a burden she could hardly bear—
when at midnight she saw—or thought she saw—
an image in her dreams: before her bed
stood Isis and her train of deities.
Upon her forehead she bore lunar horns
and, round her head, a yellow garland—stalks
of wheat that had been wrought in gleaming gold;
and she had other signs of royalty.
Beside her stood the barking god, Anubis;
sacred Bubastis; Apis, in his cloak
of many colors; and Osiris' son,
who checks his voice and, with his finger on
his lips, urges our silence. There were sistrums;
and there, at Isis' side, Osiris, he
who always is longed for; and the Egyptian
snake swollen with his soporific venom.
And Telethusa, who saw all of this
as if she were awake, heard Isis say:
"O Telethusa, you, who worship me
so faithfully, can set aside despair:
there is no need to heed your husband's order.
And once Lucina has delivered you,
don't hesitate to let your newborn live.
I am the goddess who, when called upon
for help and hope, bring comfort: I respond.
No, I am not a thankless deity."
Her counsel ended here. The goddess left.

The Cretan woman rose up from her bed,
rejoicing; stretching out her blameless hands
unto the stars, she prayed—a suppliant—
that what she'd seen in dreams would be confirmed.
Her labor pains grew more intense, and soon

Latin [682–704]

she'd given easy birth: a girl was born.
Now, to deceive her husband, Telethusa
gave orders to the nurse (for she alone
knew of this guile) to feed the newborn child
and to tell everyone it was a son.
And Ligdus thanked the gods, and to the child
he gave the name of Ligdus' father: Iphis.
And Telethusa was most pleased with this:
it was a name that suited male or female—
a neutral name, whose use involved no tricks.
No one unmasked the pious lie. She dressed
her Iphis as a boy—and whether one
assigned them to a daughter or a son,
the features of the child were surely handsome.

Some thirteen years had come; thirteen had gone.
O Iphis, now, for you, your father found
a bride, the blond Ianthe—there was none
among the girls of Phaestus who had won
more praise for the perfection of her form.
Her father was a man of Crete, Telestes.

Iphis and she were equal in their age,
their beauty; and the two of them were trained
by the same tutors; they had learned—together—
the basic rudiments of arts and letters.
In sum, they had shared much; and so when love
had struck their unsuspecting hearts, they both
shared one same wound—but not with equal hopes.
Ianthe waits impatiently to wed;
she longs for what was promised and accepted,
her wedding one she takes to be a man;
while Iphis is in love with one she knows
is never to be hers; and just for this,
the flame is still more fierce; and now she burns—
a virgin for a virgin. It is hard
to check her tears.

□   □   □

Latin [705–26]

"What end awaits me now?"
she says. "I am possessed by love so strange
that none has ever known its monstrous pangs.
If heaven meant to spare me, then the gods
should have done so; and if the gods' intent
was to destroy me, then the means they chose
could have been natural—a normal woe.
Cows don't love cows, and mares do not love mares;
but sheep desire rams, and does are drawn
by stags. And birds, too, follow that same norm;
among the animals, no female wants
a female! Would I could annul myself!
Yes, it is true that all monstrosities
occur in Crete; and here Pasiphae
has loved a bull. But even that is less
insane than what I feel; for, after all,
she was a female longing for a male.
Yet she was able to attain her goal:
when she appeared in heifer's guise, then he—
deceived—appeased her with adultery.
But how can I be helped? For even if
the world's most cunning minds were gathered here,
if Daedalus himself flew back to Crete
on waxen wings, what could he do? Nothing—
no learned art—can ever make of me
a boy. And it cannot change you, Ianthe.

"Why then not summon all your mettle, Iphis?
Return to your own self; extinguish this
flame that is hopeless, heedless, surely foolish.
For you were born a girl; and now, unless
you would deceive yourself, acknowledge that:
accept it; long for what is lawful; love
as should a woman love! What gives most life
to love is hope; it's hope that lets love thrive—
but it is hope of which you are deprived.
No guardian keeps you from her loving touch;
no jealous husband keeps a sleepless watch,

and no harsh father; nor would she herself
deny you what you seek; yet you cannot
possess her. Though all things may favor you,
though men and gods may help in your pursuit,
you can't be happy. Even now there's no
desire of mine that's been denied; the gods
have been benevolent—they've given me
as much as they could give; and what I want
is what my father and Ianthe want,
and what my future father-in-law wants.
It's nature, with more power than all of these,
that does not want it: my sole enemy
is nature! Now the longed-for moment nears,
my wedding day is close at hand: Ianthe
will soon be mine—but won't belong to me.
With all that water, we shall thirst indeed.
Why do you, Juno, guardian of brides,
and you, too, Hymen, come to grace these rites
at which there is no husband—just two brides?"

Her words were done. Meanwhile the other virgin,
whose passion matches Iphis', prays, o Hymen,
that you be quick to come. But Telethusa,
who fears the very thing Ianthe seeks,
delays the date; at times she feigns some illness
and often uses omens seen in dreams
as an excuse. But no pretext is left,
and now the wedding day is imminent—
indeed it looms tomorrow. She removes
the bands that circle her and Iphis' heads;
with hair unbound, she holds the altar fast
and pleads: "O Isis, you who make your home
in Mareota's fields and Paraetonium
and Pharos and the Nile, whose waters flow
to seven mouths, I pray you, help us now
and heal the fear we feel. O goddess, I
have seen you: yes, I saw and recognized
you and your regal signs—your mighty band

Latin [752–77]

of gods, the torches, and the sistrums' sounds—
and I can still remember your commands.
If my dear daughter is alive, if I
have not been punished, we owe all of this
to your advice, your gift. Take pity, Isis:
we two indeed have need of you." Her words
were followed by her tears.

                              The goddess seemed
to shake her altar (and Osiris had
in fact done that): her temple doors had trembled;
one saw the glitter of her crescent horns;
one heard the clash and clatter of her sistrums.
Still not completely sure, yet glad to have
such hopeful auguries, the mother left
the temple. Iphis walked behind her, but
her stride was longer than it was before,
and her complexion darker; she was more
robust; her features had grown sharper, and
her hair was shorter, without ornaments.
You are more vigorous than you had been,
o Iphis, when you still were feminine—
for you who were a girl so recently
are now a boy! So, bring your offerings
unto the shrines; set fear aside—rejoice!

They bring their offerings, and then they add
a votive tablet, one on which they had
inscribed these words: "These gifts, which Iphis pledged
as girl, are paid by him as man." And when
the first rays of the next day's sun again
revealed the wide world, Venus, Juno, and
Hymen assembled: marriage flames were lit,
and the boy Iphis made Ianthe his.

Latin [777–97]

BOOK X

BUT HYMEN HAD TO LEAVE the isle of Crete.
Clad in his saffron-colored cloak, he cleaved
the never-ending air until he reached
the home of the Cauconians in Thrace;
for he had heard the voice of Orpheus,
who was to wed—who pleaded for his presence.
He came—but came in vain. He did not bless
the rite with sacred utterance; his face
displayed no joy; he brought no hope, no grace.
Even the torch he held kept sputtering:
eyes teared and smarted from the smoke; no flame,
however much he shook that brand, would blaze.

The start was sad—and sadder still, the end.
The bride, just wed, met death; for even as
she crossed the meadows with her Naiad friends,
she stepped upon a snake; the viper sank
its teeth into her ankle.

Orpheus wept

within the upper world; but when his share
of long lament was done, the poet dared
to cross the gate of Taenarus, to seek
his wife among the Shades consigned to Styx.
Among the fluttering clouds, the phantom forms
of those who had been buried, he drew close
to both Proserpina and Pluto, he
who rules the dead, the joyless kingdom's king.
Then Orpheus plucked his lyre as he sang:

"O gods who rule the world beneath the earth,
the world to which all those of mortal birth
descend—if I may speak the truth to you,
without the subterfuge that liars use,
I've not come here to see dark Tartarus,
nor have I come to chain the monster-son
Medusa bore, that horror whose three necks
bear bristling serpents. This has brought me here:

Latin [1–23]

I seek my wife: she stepped upon a viper,
a snake that shot his venom into her
young body, robbing her of years of life.
I'll not deny that I have tried: I wish
that I had had the power to resist.
But Love has won; to him I must submit.
Within the upper world, he has much fame,
but I'm not sure if here that god has gained
renown—though I do hope so; if the tale
they tell of an abduction long ago
is not a lie, why then you, too, do owe
your union to the force of Love. And now
I pray you, by these fearful sites and by
the silences of this immense abyss,
reknit the severed threads, restore the life—
undone too quickly—of Eurydice.
For all of us are yours to rule by right;
our stay above is brief; when that is done,
we all must—sooner, later—speed to one
same dwelling place. We all shall take this way:
our final home is here; the human race
must here submit to your unending sway.
She, too, will yet be yours when she has lived
in full the course of her allotted years.
I ask you only this: lend her to me.
But if the Fates deny my wife this gift,
then I shall stay here, too, I won't go back;
and you can then rejoice—you'll have two deaths."

The bloodless shades shed tears: they heard his plea,
the chant the Thracian had accompanied
with chords upon his lyre. Tantalus
no longer tried to catch the fleeing waves;
Ixion's wheel stood still—entranced, amazed;
the vultures did not prey on Tityus' liver;
the Danaids left their urns; and Sisyphus,
you sat upon your stone. It's even said
that, moved by Orpheus' song, the Furies wept—

Latin [23–45]

the only tears the Furies ever shed.
Nor could Proserpina, nor he himself,
the ruler of the lower world, refuse
the plea of Orpheus of Rhodope.

They called Eurydice. She was among
the recent dead; as she advanced, her steps
were faltering—her wound still brought distress.
The Thracian poet took her hand: he led
his wife away—but heard the gods' command:
his eyes must not turn back until he'd passed
the valley of Avernus. Just one glance
at her, and all he had received would be
lost—irretrievably.

              Their upward path
was dark and steep; the mists they met were thick;
the silences, unbroken. But at last,
they'd almost reached the upper world, when he,
afraid that she might disappear again
and longing so to see her, turned to gaze
back at his wife. At once she slipped away—
and down. His arms stretched out convulsively
to clasp and to be clasped in turn, but there
was nothing but the unresisting air.
And as she died again, Eurydice
did not reproach her husband. (How could she
have faulted him except to say that he
loved her indeed?) One final, faint "Farewell"—
so weak it scarcely reached his ears—was all
she said. Then, back to the abyss, she fell.

And when that second death had struck his wife,
the poet—stunned—was like the man whose fright
on seeing Cerberus, three-headed hound
enchained by Hercules, was so complete
that he was not set free from fear until,
his human nature gone, he had become

Latin [46–67]

a body totally transformed—to stone.
Or one might liken Orpheus instead
to Olenus, who took the blame himself
for his Lethaea's arrogance when she—
unfortunately—boasted of her beauty:

Lethaea, you and he were once two hearts
whom love had joined; but now you are two rocks
that Ida holds on its well-watered slopes.

But then—when he had found his speech once more—
the poet pleaded, begging Charon for
a second chance to reach the farther shore;
the boatman chased him off. For seven days,
huddled along the banks of Styx, he stayed;
there he shunned Ceres' gifts—he had no taste
for food; he called on desperation, pain,
and tears—with these alone he could sustain
himself. But after Orpheus had arraigned
the gods of Erebus for cruelty,
he left; he sought the peak of Rhodope
and Haemus' heights, where north winds never cease.

Three times the ever-wheeling sun had come
to Pisces' watery sign. Three years had gone;
and Orpheus, in all that time, had shunned
the love of women; this, for his misfortune,
or for his having pledged his heart to one—
and to no other—woman. That did not
prevent their wanting him; and many sought
the poet—all those women met repulse
and grief. Indeed, he was the one who taught
the Thracian men this practice: they bestow
their love on tender boys, and so enjoy
firstfruits, the brief springtime, the flowers of youth.

□   □   □

Latin [67–85]

There was a hill and, on that hill, a glade,
an ample span of meadow grass, a plain
that was endowed with green but had no shade.
Yet when the poet, heaven-born, would play
on his resounding lyre, shade on shade
would seek that glade. Together with the tree
of the Chaonians, these came to listen:
the tall and leafy oak, the tender linden;
the poplar, shape that suited Helios' daughters;
the willow, most at home near flowing waters;
the virgin laurel, beech, and brittle hazel;
the ash, so fit for fashioning spear shafts;
the silver-fir with its smooth trunk, the myrtle
with its two hues, and the delightful platan;
the maple with its shifting colors, and
the water-loving lotus, evergreen
boxwood, as well as slender tamarisk;
and with its deep-blue berries, the viburnum;
and bent beneath its acorns' weight, the ilex.
You, ivy, with your feet that twist and flex,
came, too; and at your side came tendrils rich
with clustered grapes, and elm trees draped with vines;
the mountain-ash, the pitch-pine, the arbutus
red with its fruits, the pliant palm, the prize
of victors; and that pine which tucks its boughs
up high to form its shaggy crown—the tree
dear to the mother of the gods, Cybele,
if it be true that Attis, for her sake,
shed his own human form, that he might take
the stiff trunk of that pine as his new shape.

The cone-shaped cypress joined this crowd of trees:
though now a tree, it once had been a boy—
the boy beloved by the god who makes
the bowstring and the lyre's strings vibrate.

For, sacred to the nymphs who make their home
on the Carthaean plain, a stag once roamed—

Latin [86–110]

a stately stag whose antlers were so broad
that they provided ample shade for him.
Those antlers gleamed with gold; down to his chest,
a collar rich with gems hung from his neck;
upon his forehead, dangling from thin thongs,
there was a silver boss, one he had worn
from birth; against his hollow temples glowed
pearl earrings. And that stag forgot his own
timidity and, without fear, approached
the homes of men; he let his neck be stroked
by all—yes, even those he did not know.
But, Cyparissus, it was you to whom
he was most dear. You, handsomest of all
the Ceans, let him out to pastures new
and to the waters of the purest springs.
Now you weave varied garlands for his horns;
or, seated like a horseman on his back—
now here, now there—you ride him joyfully
with purple reins that guide his tender mouth.

But once, at high noon on a summer day,
when, heated by the sun's most torrid rays,
the curving claws of the shore-loving Crab
were blazing on the grassy ground, the stag
lay down to rest, to seek cool woodland shade.
And it was then that, accidentally,
a javelin's sharp shaft—it had been cast
by Cyparissus—pierced the stag; the wound
was fierce, the stag was dying: and at that,
the boy was set on dying, too. Oh, Phoebus
tried words that could console the boy: indeed
he urged him to restrain his grief, to keep
some sense of measure. But the boy did not
relent; he moaned still more; he begged the gods
to grant this greatest gift: to let him grieve
forever. As his lifeblood drained away
with never-ending tears, his limbs began
to take a greenish cast; and the soft hair

Latin [110–38]

that used to cluster on his snow-white brow
became a bristling crest. The boy was now
a rigid tree with frail and spiring crown
that gazes on the heavens and the stars.
The god, in sadness, groaned. He said: "I'll mourn
for you, and you shall mourn for others—and
beside the mourners, you shall always stand."

Such was the grove that gathered round the poet.
In that assembly of wild beasts and birds,
the Thracian singer sat. He tried the chords:
he plucked them with his thumb; and when he heard
that, although each note had a different sound,
it stood in right relation to the rest,
he lifted up his voice. This was his chant:

"O Muse, my mother, let my song begin
with Jove (he is the king of every thing).
I've often sung his power before: I've told
the story of the Giants; in solemn mode
I chanted of those smashing lightning bolts
that on Phlaegrean fields were hurled by Jove.
But now my matter needs more tender tones:
I sing of boys the gods have loved, and girls
incited by unlawful lust and passions,
who paid the penalty for their transgressions.

"The king of gods was once afire with love
for Phrygian Ganymede and hit upon
a guise that, just this once, he thought might be
more suitable than being Jove himself:
a bird. But of all birds, he thought that one
alone was worthiest; the bird with force
enough to carry Jove's own thunderbolts.

Latin [138–58]

Without delay Jove beat the air with his
deceiving wings, snatched up the Trojan boy.
And even now, despite the wrath of Juno,
he still fulfills his role: the page of Jove,
the boy prepares Jove's nectar, fills his cups.

"And you, too, Hyacinthus, would have been
set high within the sky by Phoebus, if
your wretched fate had not forestalled his wish.
Yet, in your way, you are eternal now:
whenever spring has banished winter and
the rainy Fish gives way before the Ram,
it's then you rise and flower once again
where earth is green. My father loved you more
than he loved any other; even Delphi,
set at the very center of the earth,
was left without its tutelary god;
for Phoebus went instead to visit you
in unwalled Sparta, on Eurotas' banks,
neglecting both his lyre and his shafts.
Not heeding who he was—his higher tasks—
alongside you, the god did not refuse
to carry nets, to hold the dogs in leash;
he was your comrade on rough mountain peaks;
and lingering beside you, he could feed
his flame of love.

          "And now the Titan sun
was at midpoint—between the night to come
and one that had already gone. And Phoebus
and Hyacinthus shed their clothes, anoint
their bodies; gleaming with smooth olive oil,
the two are set to see which one can cast
the discus farther. Phoebus is the first
to lift and poise the broad and heavy disc,
then fling it high; it bursts across the sky

Latin [159–79]

and rends the clouds along its path. Its flight
is long: at last, the hard earth feels its fall,
its weight—a throw that shows what can be done
when strength and skill are joined. The Spartan boy
is reckless: risking all for sport, he runs
to pick the discus up. But the hard ground
sends back the heavy bronze; as it rebounds,
it strikes you in the face, o Hyacinthus!
You and the god are pale: the god lifts up
your sagging form; he tries to warm you, tries
to staunch your cruel wound; and he applies
herbs that might stay your soul as it takes flight.
His arts are useless; nothing now can heal
that wound. As lilies, poppies, violets,
if loosened as they hang from yellow stems
in a well-watered garden, fade at once
and, with their withered heads grown heavy, bend;
they cannot stand erect; instead they must
gaze at the ground: just so your dying face
lies slack: too weak for its own weight, your neck
falls back upon your shoulder. 'Sparta's son,
you have been cheated,' Phoebus cries; 'you've lost
the flower of your youth; as I confront
your wound, I witness my own crime—my guilt,
my grief! It's my right hand that has inscribed
your end: I am the author of your death.
And yet, what crime is mine? Can play, can sport
be blamed? Can having loved be called a fault?
If I could only pay for what I've done
by dying for or with you—you are one
so worthy! But the law of fate denies
that chance to me. Yet I shall always have
you, Hyacinthus, in my heart, just as
your name shall always be upon my lips.
The lyre my fingers pluck, the songs I chant,
shall celebrate you; and as a new flower,
you'll bear, inscribed upon you, my lament.
And, too, in time to come, the bravest man

shall be identified with you—Ajax'
own letters, on your petals, shall be stamped.'

"As he spoke these true words, the blood that had
been spilled upon the ground and stained the grass
is blood no more; instead—more brilliant than
the purple dye of Tyre—a flower sprang;
though lily-shaped, it was not silver-white;
this flower was purple. Then, not yet content,
Phoebus—for it was he who'd brought about
this wonder that would honor Hyacinthus—
inscribed upon the petals his lament:
with his own hand, he wrote these letters—AI,
AI—signs of sad outcry. And Sparta, too,
is not ashamed to have as its own son
a Hyacinthus; they still honor him
each year, just as their fathers always did:
the Hyacinthia, their festival,
begins with an august processional.

"But if you ever chance to ask the city,
so rich with metals—Amathus—if she
would lay proud claim to the Propoetides
as daughters, she'd refuse to claim that brood.
And she is just as ready to disown
those other old inhabitants of hers
whose foreheads were disfigured by two horns—
from which they also took their name, Cerastes.
Before their doors, there used to stand an altar
of Jove, the god of hospitality;
a stranger—ignorant of what had caused
the bloodstains on that altar—might have thought
that was the blood of sacrifices brought
for Jove—of suckling calves or full-grown sheep
from Amathian herds. In fact it was
the blood of guests! Incensed, the generous

Venus was ready to desert her Cyprus,
to leave her cities and her plains. 'And yet,'
she said, 'these sites are dear to me, these towns—
what crime is theirs? What evil have they done?
This sacrilegious race—they are the ones
to pay the penalty for profanation:
exile or death—or else a punishment
midway between their death or banishment.
Can that be any penalty except
a change of form?' But even as she asked
that question, wondering what shape is best,
her eyes fell on their horns. These can be left—
so she reminds herself; and she transforms
their massive bodies into savage bulls.

"And the obscene Propoetides had dared
to stir the wrath of Venus: they declared
that she was not a goddess. And—they say—
this was the penalty that Venus made
those girls of Cyprus pay for their outrage:
they were the first to prostitute their grace,
to sell their bodies; and when shame was gone
and they could blush no more, they were transformed
(the step was brief enough) into hard stones.

"Pygmalion had seen the shameless lives
of Cyprus' women; and disgusted by
the many sins to which the female mind
had been inclined by nature, he resigned
himself: for years he lived alone, without
a spouse: he chose no wife to share his couch.

"Meanwhile, Pygmalion began to carve
in snow-white ivory, with wondrous art,

Latin [229–48]

a female figure more exquisite than
a woman who was born could ever match.
That done, he falls in love with his own work.
The image seems, in truth, to be a girl;
one could have thought she was alive and keen
to stir, to move her limbs, had she not been
too timid: with his art, he's hidden art.
He is enchanted and, within his heart,
the likeness of a body now ignites
a flame. He often lifts his hand to try
his work, to see if it indeed is flesh
or ivory; he still will not admit
it is but ivory. He kisses it:
it seems to him that, in return, he's kissed.
He speaks to it, embraces it; at each
caress, the image seems to yield beneath
his fingers: and he is afraid he'll leave
some sign, some bruise. And now he murmurs words
of love, and now he offers gifts that girls
find pleasing: shells, smooth pebbles, little birds,
and many-colored flowers, painted balls,
and amber tears that the Heliades
let drop from trees. He—after draping it
with robes—adorns its fingers with fine gems,
its neck with a long necklace; light beads hang
down from its ears, and ribbons grace its breast.
All this is fair enough, but it's not less
appealing in its nakedness. He rests
the statue on the covers of his bed,
on fabric dyed with hues of Sidon's shells;
he calls that form the maid that shares his couch
and sets its head on cushions—downy, soft—
delicately, as if it could respond.

"The day of Venus' festival had come—
the day when, from all Cyprus, people thronged;
and now—their curving horns are sheathed with gold—
the heifers fall beneath the fatal blows

Latin [248–72]

that strike their snow-white necks; the incense smokes.
Pygmalion, having paid the honors owed
to Venus, stopped before the altar: there
the sculptor offered—timidly—this prayer:
'O gods, if you indeed can grant all things,
then let me have the wife I want'—and here
he did not dare to say 'my ivory girl'
but said instead, 'one like my ivory girl.'
And golden Venus (she indeed was there
at her own feast-day) understood his prayer:
three times the flame upon her altar flared
more brightly, darting high into the air—
an omen of the goddess' kindly care.
At once, Pygmalion, at home again,
seeks out the image of the girl; he bends
over his couch; he kisses her. And when
it seems her lips are warm, he leans again
to kiss her; and he reaches with his hands
to touch her breasts. The ivory had lost
its hardness; now his fingers probe; grown soft,
the statue yields beneath the sculptor's touch,
just as Hymettian wax beneath the sun
grows soft and, molded by the thumb, takes on
so many varied shapes—in fact, becomes
more pliant as one plies it. Stupefied,
delighted yet in doubt, afraid that he
may be deceived, the lover tests his dream:
it is a body! Now the veins—beneath
his anxious fingers—pulse. Pygmalion
pours out rich thanks to Venus; finally,
his lips press lips that are not forgeries.
The young girl feels these kisses; blushing, she
lifts up her timid eyes; she seeks the light;
and even as she sees the sky, she sees
her lover. Venus graces with her presence
the wedding she has brought about. And when
the moon shows not as crescent but as orb
for the ninth time, Pygmalion's wife gives birth

Latin [272–97]

to Paphos—and in honor of that child,
Cyprus has since been called the Paphian isle.

———————

"And Paphos' son was Cinyras, a man
who, if he'd not had children, might have found
some happiness. The tale I now would sing
is dread indeed: o daughters, fathers, leave;
or if your minds delight in listening,
do not put trust in me, do not believe
the truth that I will tell; or if you must
believe it, then believe the penalty
that punishes such acts. In any case,
if nature can permit so foul a sin
to see the light, I do congratulate
this region of the world, my Thracian race;
I'm grateful that we are so far away
from lands where such obscenities take place.

"Panchaea's land is rich in balsam and
in cinnamon and unguents; and its trees
drip incense, and its soil has many flowers.
What need had it for myrrh? Did it deserve
so sad a plant? O Myrrha, Cupid had
no part in your undoing—for he says
his arrow did not strike you; he declares
his torches innocent. The firebrand
and venom-swollen snakes were brought from Styx
by one of the three Sisters: she did this
to crush you. Yes, to hate a father is
a crime, but love like yours is worse than hate.

"Young lords from every land, the noblest men
from all the Orient, have sought your hand;
among all these, choose one as your dear husband.
But, Myrrha, there is one who can't belong
to those from whom you choose. □ □ □

Latin [297–318]

                         "And she, in truth,
knows that; she strives; she tries; she would subdue
her obscene love: 'Where has my mind led me?
What am I plotting? Gods, I do beseech,
and, too, I call upon the piety
I owe my parents: check my sacrilege,
prevent my sinning—if it is a sin.
Parental piety does not exclude
such love: the other animals pursue
delight and mate without such niceties.
There's nothing execrable when a heifer
is mounted by her father; stallions, too,
mate with their daughters; and a goat can choose
to couple with his child; the female bird
conceives from that same seed which fathered her.
Blessed are those who have that privilege.
It's human scruples that have stifled us
with jealous edicts; law is envious—
what nature would permit, the law forbids.
And yet they say that there are tribes in which
the mother mates with her own son, the daughter
with her own father, and the loving bonds,
so reinforced, make families more fond.
But I—to my misfortune—was not born
among those tribes; instead I am—forlorn—
denied the very man for whom I long.
But why do I keep coming back again,
again, to this? I must dismiss such thoughts:
blot out my lust. Yes, Cinyras deserves
much love—but as a father. Were I not
his daughter, I could lie with him; but since
I'm his, he can't be mine; and that close link
dictates my loss. If I were but a stranger,
I would have had some chance. But now I want
to leave my native land: nothing but flight
can save me from so foul a flaw. And yet
I stay: this evil ardor holds me here,
that I may gaze at Cinyras, and touch

Latin [319–43]

and speak to him, and give him kisses if
I cannot hope for more. Would you transgress
beyond that? Can you let such sacrilege
incite you? Do you know what holy ties
and names would be confronted by your crimes?

Would you be your own mother's rival and
your father's mistress? Would you want to be
a sister to your son? Your brother's mother?
And those three Sisters, don't they make you fear?
Their hair is wreathed with serpents, and they bear
barbaric brands when they appear before
the eyes and faces of unholy souls.
Come now, your body's still unstained: do not
debauch your soul with lust, defile the code
of nature with a lawless mating. Though
you will it, nature will not have it so;
for Cinyras is pious in his ways,
a man of virtue. Would that he were prey
to my same frenzy, to that passion's sway!'

"These were her words. Now Cinyras, confused,
does not know what to do: the suitors crowd—
so many worthy men. He calls upon
his daughter to select the one she wants,
and he lists all their names. At first, the girl
is silent: staring at him, she's in doubt;
and warm tears veil her eyes. Her father thinks
these tears are simply signs of modesty,
forbids her weeping, dries her cheeks; and then
he kisses her. She takes too much delight
in this; and when he asks what kind of man
she'll have her husband be, she answers: 'One
like you.' Not understanding what is hid
beneath her words, he praises her for this:
'And may you always be so filial.'
When she hears him say 'filial,' the girl
lowers her eyes: she knows she's criminal.

□ □ □

Latin [343–67]

"Midnight: now sleep sets cares and flesh to rest.
But Myrrha does not sleep: she cannot check
the fire that feeds on her; she is held fast—
her madness does not slack; first she despairs
and then is set to try; she is ashamed;
but though she longs, she cannot find a plan.
As, when the axes strike the massive trunk,
the tree will waver at the moment just
before the final blow: one does not know
which way it is to fall; upon all sides
men now rush off—so, too, enfeebled by
so many blows from many sides, the mind
of Myrrha leans this way, then that. At last
it seems no thing can check her love, bring rest,
except for death. On death she now is set.
She rises from her bed: she ties her belt
around a ceiling beam—to hang herself.

" 'Dear Cinyras, farewell,' his daughter moans,
'I hope you come to know why I would die.'
Then she begins to run the cord around
her pallid neck. They say her murmurs reached
the ears of her old nurse, who faithfully
stood watch before the door of her dear charge.
The nurse leaps up at once; on opening
the door, she sees her Myrrha readying
the tools of death; in one same moment, she
cries out and beats her breast and tears her dress
and snatches off the rope from Myrrha's neck.
And only after that, the nurse takes time
to weep, to clasp her Myrrha, and to ask
why she was driven to the noose. The girl
is silent, speechless; staring at the ground,
she's sorry her attempt at death was foiled—
she was too slow. But her old nurse insists:
she bares her white hairs and her withered breasts;
she calls on all the days and nights she'd spent
on Myrrha in the cradle, and she begs:

Latin [368–93]

what grief had brought her Myrrha to this pass?
But Myrrha turns aside those pleas; she groans.
The nurse is set on finding out, and so
she promises not only to hold close
the secret but to help her: 'I am old,
but I'm not useless. If it is a stroke
of madness that afflicts you, my dear girl,
I know a woman who has charms and herbs
to heal you; and if anyone has cast
an evil spell upon you, magic rites
can purify you; and to cure your plight,
you can bring offerings, a sacrifice
unto the gods, and so appease their wrath
if they, in anger, led you to this pass.
I've thought of all that could have brought distress.
This house can only bring you happiness:
yes, all things here go well; your mother and
your father are alive and prosperous.'
As soon as she has heard those words, 'your father,'
the girl sighs deeply; but the nurse—although
she has begun to sense that Myrrha's soul
is sick with love—does not as yet suspect
a passion so profane. And stubbornly,
she probes: she wants to hear in full the cause
of Myrrha's pain—whatever it might be.
She hugs the tearful girl to her old breast
and, holding Myrrha in her frail arms, says:
'I know, I know: you are in love. But set
your fears aside; you'll find that I can help;
and I shall keep your secret; Cinyras
won't hear a word of this. But, come, confess.'
The frenzied girl breaks loose and, on her bed,
collapses, helpless; as she sinks her head
into the cushions, Myrrha cries: 'Don't seek
the source of this! Stop probing, I beseech!
The thing you want to find is my foul crime!'

□   □   □

Latin [393–413]

"At that, the girl's old nurse is horrified.
And as she stretches out her hands that shake
with years and fears, the old nurse falls; prostrate
before the feet of her dear girl, she pleads
and menaces: she threatens to reveal
the noose, the try at suicide—but then
she promises to help if Myrrha will
just tell the truth about her secret love.
The young girl lifts her head; against the breast
of her old nurse, it's many tears she sheds.
Again, again, she tries—she would confess—
but checks her voice; ashamed, she hides her face
within her robes and sighs: 'How happy you,
my mother, are beside the mate you chose.'
And Myrrha says no more; she only moans.
Then through the nurse's body, to the bone,
a shudder lances, sharp and cold (she knows,
she knows); her white hair stiffens on her head;
she tries with warning word on word to rid
the girl from that dread love; and Myrrha knows
the nurse's pleas are just; but she is set
on death if what she wants cannot be had.
At this, the nurse says: 'Live, for you will have
your . . .' Daring not to utter 'father,' she
falls still; but then—before the gods on high—
she vows to keep the promise she had made.

"And now, their bodies clothed in snow-white robes,
all pious wives were honoring the feast
of Ceres; her first fruits, the ears of wheat,
were bound in garlands as an offering
on these, the days they celebrate each year.
This was the time when women, for nine nights,
shun union with their husbands; any touch
of man is banned. Cenchreis, the king's wife,
has joined the throng; she shares these secret rites.
When, in her wretched zeal, the old nurse finds
that Cinyras is drunk with wine, deprived,

Latin [414–38]

without his lawful wife, she tells the king
that a young girl is now in love with him;
but she does not reveal the girl's true name—
the girl whose beauty she is quick to praise.
And when he wants to know the young girl's age,
she says, 'the same as Myrrha's.' When he tells
the nurse to fetch that girl, she runs to find
her Myrrha and, 'My dear, we've won,' she cries;
'you can rejoice!' The wretched girl is stirred,
and yet her joy is not complete; a sad
foreboding grips her heart, but she is glad:
the virgin's mind is torn by such discord.

"The hour when all is silent now is here.
And, seen between the stars of the two Bears,
Boötes, veering downward with his wain,
inclines his guide-pole. Myrrha makes her way
to her misdeed. The golden moon now flees
the sky; black clouds conceal the stars; the night
has lost its flaring lights. The first to hide
their faces at the shameless sight were you,
o Icarus, and dear Erigone,
your daughter, she whose holy love for you
won her a starry place—her sacred due.
Three times young Myrrha stumbles on her path,
an omen telling her she should turn back;
three times the screech-owl, with his eerie chant,
warns her. But still the longing daughter moves
ahead; her shame is muted by the black
of night. Her left hand grips her nurse hard fast,
and with her right she gropes and probes. At last
she's at the threshold, opening the door;
and now she is inside the room. Her knees
are trembling; and as blood and color flee,
her face is pale; her courage leaves; as she
draws closer to her crime, her fears increase;
the girl repents of her audacity:
she would turn back if she could go unseen.

Latin [438–61]

As Myrrha hesitates, her old nurse takes
her hand; she draws her toward the high bed's side—
consigns her to the king and says: 'Take her,
o Cinyras; she's yours.' And she unites
those two in dark damnation. Cinyras
obscenely welcomes to his bed the flesh
of his own flesh; he helps her to defeat
her virgin's shame; he sets her fears at ease.
Perhaps because she is so young, the king
calls timid Myrrha 'daughter,' even as
she calls him 'father'; so do they complete
their sacrilege; they name their guilt in speech.

"Filled with her father, Myrrha leaves that room;
she bears his impious seed within her womb.
And on the second night, again they lie
together; so it went, time after time,
until the father, keen to recognize
the girl he'd held so often, carried in
a lamp—and saw his daughter and his sin.
Struck dumb by grief, he pulls his gleaming sword
out from its sheath, which hung along the wall.

"And Myrrha fled. The night was kind; the shades
and darkness favored her; the girl escaped
her death; she crossed the open fields; she left
palm-rich Arabia and Panchaea's lands.
Nine times the moon had shown its crescent horns,
and still she wandered on. At last she stayed
her weary steps in the Sabaeans' land.
Her womb was heavy now—so hard to carry.
Not knowing what to hope for—torn between
her fear of death and the fatigue of living—
she gathered up her wishes and beseeched:
'Oh, if there is some god to hear the plea
of one who knows that she is guilty, I
accept the death that I deserve. But lest
I, in my life, profane the living and,

Latin [462–85]

in death, profane the dead, do banish me
from both these realms; transform me, and deny
both life and death to me.'

                                    "And some god heard
the girl confess her guilt: her final plea
was answered. As she spoke, the earth enclosed
her legs; roots slanted outward from her toes;
supported by those roots, a tall trunk rose.
Her bones became tough wood (although her marrow
remained unchanged); her blood was turned to sap;
her arms became long boughs; her fingers, twigs;
her skin was now dark bark. And as it grew,
the tree had soon enveloped her full womb;
then it submerged her breasts and was about
to wrap itself around her neck; but she—
impatient—met the rising bark: she sank
down, down, until her face was also bark.
Her flesh had lost the senses it once had,
but she still wept—and, trickling down the tree,
tears fell. But even tears can gain long fame:
myrrh, dripping from that trunk, preserves the name
of Myrrha, mistress of that tree; and she
will be remembered through the centuries.

"But when the misbegotten child had grown
inside the wood, it wanted to come forth
to leave its mother. Halfway up the trunk,
the pregnant tree was swollen; all the bark
was taut with that full burden. But the pain
and pangs could not find words; though this is birth,
there is no speech that can beseech Lucina.
And yet the tree trunk bends and moans in labor;
the bark is wet with fallen tears. Lucina
takes pity: standing near the groaning boughs
she lays her hands upon them, even as

Latin [486–511]

she speaks that spell which shepherds safe childbirth.
At that, the tree trunk cracked, the bark was torn;
the tree delivered what had weighed it down;
a living thing, a wailing boy was born:
Adonis. And the Naiads set him on
the tender meadow and anointed him
with myrrh, his mother's tears. And even Envy
would praise his beauty, for indeed his body
is like the naked Cupid artists paint.
And to remove the only difference,
just add a quiver to Adonis or
remove the quiver from the Cupid's form.

"The flight of time eludes our eyes, it glides
unseen; no thing is swifter than the years.
Yes, he who is the son of his own sister
and his grandfather, was but recently
enclosed within a tree. But recently
a newborn, then a handsome baby boy,
Adonis has become a youth, a man;
his beauty now surpasses what he was,
inflaming even Venus' love, and thus
avenging that dread fire—incestuous—
which Venus made his mother, Myrrha, suffer.
And this is how that vengeance came about.

"One day, as Cupid, son of Venus, kissed
his mother, unaware, he scratched her breast:
an arrow jutting from his quiver chanced
to graze her. Though the goddess felt the prick
and pushed her son aside, the wound was far
more deep than it had seemed to her at first.

"And Venus now is taken by the mortal
Adonis' beauty: she no longer cares
for her Cythera's shores; she cannot spare

the time to visit sea-encircled Paphos
and Cnidos, rich with fish; and she neglects
her Amathus, the city rich with ores.
She even finds the skies too tedious:
she much prefers Adonis. She stays close
to him; it is with him she always goes;
and she, who always used to seek the shade—
there she could rest at ease and cultivate
her beauty—now frequents the mountain slopes,
the woods, the rocks beset by spiny thorns;
as if she were Diana, Venus keeps
her tunic tied above her knees. She spurs
the hounds and chases after game: that is,
those beasts whom it is safe to hunt—the hares
that leap headlong, the stags with branching horns,
or does. But she is careful to avoid
stout boars, rapacious wolves, bears armed with claws,
and lions stained with blood of slaughtered herds.
Adonis, she would warn you, too, to stay
away from those fierce beasts: 'Be bold,' she says,
'when you approach the timid animals,
those who are quick to flee: but do not be
audacious when you face courageous beasts.
Dear boy, do not be reckless when the risk
involves me, too; don't let me lose you just
because you wanted glory; don't provoke
those animals whom nature has armed well.
Your youth, your loveliness—the many things
with which you have enchanted even me—
don't move the lion or the bristling boar,
don't touch the eyes and hearts of those fierce beasts.
Those boars have lightning in their curving claws;
the tawny lion's wrath is wild and raw—
I do indeed detest that race.' At this,
he asked her why, and she replied: 'Adonis,
you'll hear the answer now: an ancient crime—
which had a monstrous outcome. But since I
am weary now—you see, I'm not quite used

Latin [530–54]

to such hard labors—let us profit by
the poplar, here at hand; its shade invites,
and here, along the grass, we can recline.
I want to rest beside you.' She stretched out
along the ground and held him close—for he
had stretched out, too. And pillowing her head
upon his chest, the goddess—even as
she mingled kisses with her words—began:

———

" 'You may have heard of Atalanta: one
who, when she ran, would beat the fastest men.
That was no idle rumor, for she won
in truth. And, too, you would have found it hard
to say if she was worthier of praise
for her amazing speed or splendid grace.

" 'Now she had gone to ask the oracle
about a husband: "No, you have no need
of any husband"—so the god replied—
"you must shun any marriage. This advice
will not be taken; though you stay alive,
you will have lost yourself." Then, terrified
by what the god had said, she lived unwed
within the shadowed forests; to hold off
the crowd of her insistent suitors, she
set harsh conditions for her matrimony:
"Whoever hopes to have me," so she said,
"must first defeat me in a footrace; bed
and wife are what await the man who wins;
for all of those who are too slow, it's death
they'll get. These are the terms of this contest."
Yes, she showed little pity; but her beauty
was so entrancing that, despite the terms
that Atalanta set, a reckless crowd
of suitors came to race that fateful course.

□   □   □

Latin [554–74]

" 'Of those who took their seats to watch the race,
one was Hippomenes. He had exclaimed:
"Can anyone be fool enough to risk
his life to gain a wife?" So he condemned
those young fanatics' love. But when she sheds
her clothes and shows her splendid form (much like
my own, or what your beauty, too, would be
were you a woman), then Hippomenes,
astonished, lifts his hands and cries: "Forgive me,
you whom I just rebuked! I did not know
the value of the prize you wanted so."
And even as he praises her, love grows:
his hope, that none would outrace Atalanta;
his fear, that some young suitor now may win—
and this spurs jealousy in him. "But why
don't I risk, too? Why not compete?" he cries;
"the god helps those who dare." Hippomenes
is pondering this course, when she flies by
as if her feet were wings. She seems to speed
as swiftly as a Scythian arrow, but
the young Aonian is even more
astonished by the splendor of her form—
a grace that is enhanced as she competes.
She wears gold sandals on her rapid feet;
her hair is fluttering over her white shoulders
as, at her knees, the ribbons with white borders
are fluttering; and all her young, fair body
is flushed with rose, just as a purple awning
within a marble hall will lend white walls
a darker hint, a veil, a shadowed tint.
The stranger notices all this; and now
they cross the finish line; and she has won;
a victor, she receives the festal crown
of garlands. The defeated suitors go
with heavy groans, to pay the deaths they owe.

" 'And yet Hippomenes is not dismayed
and not delayed by their sad fate. He makes

Latin [575–601]

his way to her; eyes fixed upon her face;
"Why seek such easy glory, why outrace
such sluggish men?" he says. "Contend with me,
for then, if fortune gives me victory,
your losing to so grand an enemy
would not bring shame to you. For I can claim
Megareus of Onchestus as my father,
and he had Neptune as grandfather: thus,
I am the great-grandson of one who rules
the waters; and my worth does not belie
my lineage. And if I meet defeat,
for having outraced me, Hippomenes,
you'll gain unending fame." And as he speaks,
the eyes of Atalanta take him in
most tenderly. Oh, does she want to win
or does the virgin long to lose to him?

" 'So Atalanta wonders, inwardly:
"Is there some god who, wishing to destroy
fair youths, has willed the ruin of this boy
and prods him now to seek me out as wife
and risk his own dear life? Were I to judge,
I'd hardly say that I was worth that much.
It's not his self that stirs me—it's his years:
he's young—and yet he's bold, a fearless soul!
He's young, yet he can claim that he is fourth
within the line of sons descended from
the monarch of the seas! And he loves me
and wants so much to marry me that if
an evil fate should foil him, he will live
no more! No, stranger, leave while you still can;
forget this savage marriage; wedding me
means sure fatality. No woman would
refuse to marry you; you'll surely find
a wiser girl to welcome you. But why
must I, who've sent so many to their deaths,
feel such distress for you? He can take care
of his own self. Then let him perish, too,

Latin [601–24]

since, after all, the death of those who wooed
was not enough to warn him off; he must
be weary of this life. But that would mean
he died because he wished to live with me;
is that a just, a seemly penalty
to pay for having loved? My victory—
if I should win—is not a thing to envy.
Yet that is not my fault. Can't you renounce?
But if you're mad enough to try, I would
that you might be more swift than me. Yes, yes,
his gaze, his face have charm and tenderness.
Ah, poor Hippomenes, I would that you
had not set eyes on me. You were so worthy
of life. If I were just more fortunate,
if wretched fate had not forbidden me
to marry, you would be the only one
with whom I'd ever want to share my couch."
Such were her troubled words; a neophyte
whom Cupid now has touched for the first time,
indeed she loves—but knows not that she does.

" 'But now the people and her father—all
call for another trial—as usual.
Hippomenes, a son of Neptune's race,
prays urgently to me: "O Venus, may
I count upon your favor as I dare
to face this test; and may you treat with care
the love that she has stirred in me." His plea
was gentle, and it was a gentle breeze
that bore that prayer to me. And I confess,
it moved me—but so little time was left.

" 'There is a field the Cypriots have called
the field of Tamasus; within that isle
there is no place more fair. In ancient times
that field was set aside as sacred site:
a holy place they added to my shrines.
Within that field there grows a tree with leaves

Latin [624–47]

of gold; its crackling branches also gleam
with tawny gold. And when his gentle plea
reached me, I was, by chance, returning from
that sacred site—my hands were carrying
three golden apples gathered from that tree.
Invisible to all but him, I drew
close to Hippomenes; I taught him how
to use the apples. Blaring trumpets now
announce the race's start: and from their crouch,
those two flash out; they skim the sandy course
with flying feet. Indeed, one might have thought
that she and he could even graze the sea
yet leave their feet still dry; or speed across
a field of standing rain and leave the stalks
untouched. Applause and shouts are loud; the crowd
cheers on Hippomenes, and some cry out:
"Go, go; this is the time to take the lead,
to give it all you have, Hippomenes!
Don't spare your speed! Don't slack—and you will win!"
It's hard to say if this applause brought more
delight to Megareus' heroic son
or Scheneus' virgin daughter. As they sped,
how many times did she, about to pass
Hippomenes, relent and gaze at length
upon his face until, at last, she raced
ahead—reluctantly? And now his throat
is weary: he is parched; he pants, and yet
the run is long, the goal is still far off.
And finally, he drops the first of those
three golden apples. Even as it rolls,
she is enchanted by the gleaming gold;
she veers off course to pick it up. The crowd
applauds Hippomenes, who takes the lead.
But she recoups her loss; a surge of speed—
once more the girl has gained the lead. And when
he throws the second apple, she retrieves
that apple, too, but passes him again.
The final stretch is all that's left. He pleads:

Latin [647–72]

"O goddess, giver of this gift to me,
do stand beside me now." With all the force
of youth he throws the gleaming golden fruit—
obliquely, distantly—off course. The girl
seemed hesitant—uncertain of her choice:
to let it lie or pick it up. But I
compelled her: she went off; she picked it up.
So she lost time—and, too, the weight of three
gold apples hampered her. So that my story
not take much longer than that race, I say
she was outstripped; the winner led away
his prize, his wife.

          " 'But now, Adonis, I
must ask you this: did I not merit thanks
for all I did? Did I not earn sweet incense
to honor me? But he forgot completely:
I had no incense and no thanks from him.
At that offense, my wrath was spurred; and lest
in time to come I ever suffer such
a slight again, I saw that I would have
to make them serve as an example: I
incited my own self against that pair.
One day, they chanced to pass before the shrine
that, to fulfill a vow that he had pledged,
Echion built: a temple for Cybele,
the Mother of the gods, a shrine that stood
concealed within the shadows of deep woods.
The pair had journeyed long; they needed rest;
and I ignited him: Hippomenes—
such is my power as a deity—
was struck with an indecent, sudden need
for Atalanta's body. Near that shrine,
there was a cavelike cell where little light
could filter; it was vaulted by soft rock,
the pumice of that place—a sacred cave,
where men had venerated deities
for age on age, beyond all memory:

Latin [672–93]

indeed a priest had set within that cell
the wooden statues of the ancient gods.
Hippomenes, on entering that cave,
was quick to desecrate the sacred place
with lust. The hallowed statues turned away
their eyes; the Mother goddess, turret-crowned,
was set to plunge the obscene lovers down
into the waves of Styx. But then that seemed
too slight a penalty: instead, she wraps
their necks in tawny manes; their fingers take
the shape of cunning claws; their arms are changed
to legs; their weight moves forward to their chests;
and they grow tails that sweep along the ground;
their faces harden now; they speak in growls,
not words; the wild woods are their mating place.
As lions, they strike terror into all;
but they indeed are tame when, yoked, they draw
Cybele's chariot: they champ tight bits.

" 'Avoid those beasts, dear boy, and any sort
of animal that will not turn its back
and flee from you but, ready to attack,
stands firm, chest forward; no, I would not have
your daring damage you and ruin me.'

―――――――――

"So did the goddess warn Adonis; then
she yoked her swans, rode off across the air.
But daring is not keen to heed such warnings.
By chance, Adonis' hounds had caught a scent
that led them to a wild boar's hidden den;
the trail was sure. The boar was roused
out of the woods: Adonis' spearhead caught
the boar—a slanting thrust. With his curved snout,
the savage beast worked free—he had torn out
the spearhead stained with his own blood. The chase
is on: he charges at Adonis now.

Latin [693–714]

The youth, in fear of his own life, runs hard,
but he is caught: the boar sinks his long tusks
into Adonis' groin; he fells him—and
the boy lies prone along the yellow sands.

"On her light chariot, Venus, who was drawn
across the middle air by her winged swans,
had not reached Cyprus yet; she heard, far off,
the dying boy—his moans. She turned around
her white swans and rode back. When, from the heights,
she saw him lifeless there, a bleeding corpse,
she leaped down to the ground. And Venus tore
her hair, and—much unlike a goddess—beat
her hands against her breast. She challenged fate:
'But destiny does not rule all. Adonis,
your memory will live eternally:
each year they will repeat this final scene—
your day of death, my day of grief, will be
enacted in a feast that bears your name.

" 'I shall transform your blood into a flower.
If you, Proserpina, were once allowed
the metamorphosis of Mentha, when
you changed that nymph into a fragrant plant—
the mint—can anyone begrudge me if
I change the form of Cinyras' dear son?'
That said, she sprinkled scented nectar on
his blood, which then fermented, even as
bright bubbles form when raindrops fall on mud.
One hour had yet to pass when, from that gore,
a bloodred flower sprang, the very color
of pomegranates when that fruit is ripe
and hides sweet seeds beneath its pliant rind.
And yet Adonis' blossoms have brief life:
his flower is light and delicate; it clings
too loosely to the stem and thus is called
Anemone—'born of the wind'—because
winds shake its fragile petals, and they fall."

Latin [714–39]

BOOK XI

SUCH WERE THE SONGS of Orpheus: with these
the Thracian poet charmed the woodland trees
and souls of savage beasts; even the stones
were held in thrall by Orpheus' tender tones.

But now the Thracian women—all had cast
the hides of beasts around their frenzied breasts—
down from a high hilltop, spied Orpheus
as he attuned his lyre and his sweet voice.
And one of these—hair streaming loose beneath
light winds—cried out: "He's there! The man who dares
to scorn us." Through the air she hurled her staff
against Apollo's poet; it was meant
to smash his singing mouth; but since its tip
was wreathed with leaves, it left a glancing mark,
a hit that did no deadly work. At that,
another woman cast a stone; but as
it cleaved the air, it yielded to the spell
of his enchanting voice and lyre: it fell
at Orpheus' feet as if compelled to seek
forgiveness for its mad audacity.

But nothing now can check the wild attack;
fanatic Fury whips their rage. In truth,
the song of Orpheus could have subdued
all of their weapons; but his lyre is drowned
by shrieks and caterwauls, the raucous sounds
of drums and twisted Berecynthian flutes,
bacchantes pounding hands, and strident howls.
And so, at last, the stones were stained with blood,
the blood of one whose voice could not be heard.

Then the bacchantes chose to slaughter first
the countless birds, the serpents, and the throng
of savage beasts—all who were still spellbound
by Orpheus: the trophies he had won,
the living proof of his triumphant song.
Then, with their gory hands, those women turned

Latin [1–23]

to Orpheus himself. They circled him
as birds will do when they catch sight—by day—
of some nocturnal bird of prey. The poet
was like the stag who, in a spectacle,
is doomed to die by morning light, when dogs
surround him in the bounds of the arena.
Some women, rushing at him, hurled their staffs,
their thyrsi wreathed with green leaves—hardly meant
to serve this purpose. Others cast thick clods,
and some flung branches ripped from trunks, while rocks
served others. And to stock the armory
of frenzy with true weapons, there—nearby—
by chance yoked oxen plowed the soil; not far
from these, well-muscled, sweating peasants toiled.
And when those peasants saw the women rush,
when they caught sight of the fanatic crowd,
those peasants fled at once, and on the ground
they left behind their tools. Deserted fields
were strewn with mattocks, heavy shovels, hoes.
The women—crazed—rushed off, picked up those tools;
and having torn apart the oxen—who
had menaced with their horns—they hurried back
to kill the poet. He, with arms outstretched,
for the first time spoke words without effect;
for the first time his voice did not enchant.
And they—in desecration—murdered him;
and from that mouth whose speech had even held
the stones and savage beasts beneath its spell—
o Jupiter—the soul, with its last breath,
was driven out.

       The birds, in mourning, wept,
o Orpheus—the throngs of savage beasts,
and rigid stones, and forests, too—all these
had often followed as you sang; the trees
now shed their leafy crowns—as sign of grief,
their trunks were bare. They say that even streams
were swollen; yes, the rivers, too, shed tears;

Latin [23–48]

Naiads and Dryads fringed their veils with black
and left their hair disheveled. Orpheus' limbs
lay scattered, strewn about; but in your flow,
you, Hebrus, gathered in his head and lyre;
and (look! a thing of wonder) once your stream
had caught and carried them, the lyre began
to sound some mournful notes; the lifeless tongue,
too, murmured mournfully; and the response
that echoed from the shores was mournful, too.
Borne by your seaward flow, they leave their own
dear Thracian stream; they're carried to the coast.
And there, a savage snake attacked the head
that had been cast onto that foreign shore—
a head still drenched and dripping, damp with spray.
But Phoebus intervened: just as that snake
was set to bite, the god froze his spread jaws,
converting him to stone just as he was:
with open mouth.

        The Shade of Orpheus
descends beneath the earth. The poet knows
each place that he had visited before;
and searching through the fields of pious souls,
he finds Eurydice. And there they walk
together now: at times they are side by side;
at times she walks ahead with him behind;
at other times it's Orpheus who leads—
but without any need to fear should he
turn round to see his own Eurydice.

But Bacchus would not leave that crime unscourged.
His grief was great; and to avenge the loss
of Orpheus, the poet who had sung
of Bacchus' sacred mysteries, the god
at once bound fast with twisting roots all those
who'd shared in such a crime. And when their toes

Latin [48–71]

were lengthened, Bacchus thrust them tight and hard
into the solid ground. Just as a bird
whose claw is caught within the cunning trap
a fowler set, can feel it's gripped, and flaps
and flutters but, while struggling, only draws
the snare still tighter: so each woman was
held fast within the soil; and when she sought,
in fear, to free herself, the pliant root
gripped even harder every time she shook.
When any woman asked where were her toes,
her nails, her feet, the tree bark simply rose:
she watched it climb along her tender thighs;
she tried to beat those thighs in sign of grief,
but all she did was pound against a tree.
Her breast and shoulders now were wooden, too;
you could have taken—not mistakenly—
her arms to be the boughs of an oak tree.

But not content with that, Bacchus now left
the Thracians; and with finer devotees,
he reached the vineyards of his own Timolus,
his Lydian land on the Pactolus' banks,
although that river's flow and bottom sands
were not yet precious, golden—such as men
would envy. There, his customary satyrs
and his bacchantes crowded round him—but
Silenus was not there. Some Phrygian farmers
had found him stumbling with the weight of years
and wine; they made him captive, bound him fast
with vines; that done, they led him to King Midas,
who'd been instructed in the rites of Bacchus
by Thracian Orpheus and by Eumolphus
of Athens. And when Midas recognized
his friend and old companion in those rites,
he welcomed him at once; and he decreed
a festival—to last ten days and nights,

Latin [71–96]

all in a row—to honor old Silenus.

But now, for the eleventh time, the rise
of Lucifer has driven from the sky
the stars of night. And Midas has arrived,
with joy, in Lydia, to reconsign
Silenus to his cherished protégé:
his foster-son, the god whom he had trained.

And Bacchus, glad to see his teacher safe,
rewarded Midas so: the god would give
to Midas anything that he might wish
(a gift both flattering and—if one picks
unwisely—perilous). The king made this
sad choice: "Do grant that anything that is
touched by my body turns to yellow gold."
That prayer was granted by the god, and so
Bacchus discharged the fatal debt he owed.
And yet the god was sad, for he had hoped
the king would ask for something more than gold.

But Midas was delighted; quite content,
he went his way and, on his path, began
to touch this thing, then that—so he could test
the truth of Bacchus' promise. It was hard
to trust his own eyes, but when he had bent
a green twig hanging from a low oak branch,
the twig was turned to gold. And, too, a stone
that he had picked up from the ground soon showed
the color of pale gold. He touched a clod;
beneath the spell his finger held, that soil
became a chunk of gold. He plucked dry stalks
of wheat, and what he harvested was gold.
He held an apple he'd picked off a tree:
you'd say it came from the Hesperides.
And if a towering pillar felt his touch,
at once he saw it glitter. Even when
he bathed his hands, and limpid water ran

Latin [96–117]

down from his fingers, Danae might well
have been beguiled. Beside himself, gone wild,
he dreamed that everything had turned to gold.

As he rejoices, Midas' servants set
his table—high with meats and with no lack
of toasted bread. But when he reaches out
to touch the gifts of Ceres, they grow hard;
and if, with avid teeth, he bites a piece
of meat, where they have bit that piece, his teeth
meet yellow gold. He mixes some pure water
and wine of Bacchus, Midas' benefactor;
and in his mouth it's liquid gold that floats.
Amazed by his incredible mishap,
a wretch among such riches, he detests
what he had hoped to get; he cannot stand
those treasures. There's no heap of food that can
appease his hunger, and he burns with thirst—
his throat is parched. And, just as he deserves,
he's tortured and tormented now by gold.
Lifting his hands and gleaming arms to heaven,
"Forgive me, father Bacchus; I have sinned,"
he cries; "but do have mercy, I implore;
release me from the specious fate I sought."

The gods are capable of kindness: since
King Midas recognized that he had sinned,
Bacchus restored his former state to him;
the god retrieved the gift that, after all,
he'd only given to make good his word.
He said: "Lest you be left within the clutch
of gold, the trap that you so rashly sought,
go to the river near the mighty town
of Sardis, and then walk upstream till you come,
as you ascend the hillside, to the source;
there, place your head beneath the fountain's spray,
just where its jet is fullest; you must bathe
your body there—and wash your sin away." □ □ □

Latin [117–41]

So Bacchus ordered, and the king obeyed.
He reached the source; and even as he bathed,
the waters—from the human form they washed—
took on the force that once lay in his touch:
the power to transform things into gold.
Even today, along Pactolus' shores,
the fields—which still receive the precious seed
from that old vein—are glittering, pale and cold:
the stream that soaks the soil is streaked with gold.

And Midas, hating riches, now frequents
the fields and forests; and he honors Pan,
who always makes his home in hillside caverns.
But Midas' wits are what they always were—
not sharp; his mind, as it had done before,
seeks stupid things that are to do him harm.

The mountain-mass of Tmolus rises steep;
its peak looks out upon the distant sea;
upon one side its height slopes down to reach
the town of Sardis; on its other flank
lies small Hypaepa. There, one day, while Pan
was charming tender nymphs with melodies
and light cadenzas piped on shepherd's reeds
held fast with wax, he dared to scorn the songs
Apollo sang, if set against his own.
Too rash, he now was matched—unequally—
against Apollo. Tmolus was to be
the judge; and so that tutelary god
was seated on his ancient mountaintop.
To hear, he shook his ears free from the trees.
To wreathe his dark green hair, he wore oak leaves;
around his hollow temples, acorns hung.
Then, facing Pan, the shepherd-god, he said:
"This judge is ready for you; go ahead."
And Pan, upon his rustic reeds, began
to play, entrancing Midas (who by chance
was there) with his barbaric shepherd's airs. □ □ □

Latin [142–63]

When Pan was done, the sacred Tmolus turned
his face toward Phoebus' face; and as he turned,
his forests followed him. The god-of-Delos'
fair hair was wreathed with laurel of Parnassus;
his mantle, steeped in purple dye from Tyre,
was long enough to sweep the ground. His lyre,
inlaid with gems and Indian ivory,
was held by his left hand; and in his right
he held the plectrum. Even in his stance
he seemed a master artist. With a thumb
adept, consummate in its craft, he plucked
the strings; and Tmolus, moved by notes so sweet,
declared defeat for Pan and his rude reeds.

And all approved the sacred mountain-god's
decision. Only Midas—no one else—
protested, said the verdict was unjust.
Apollo cannot suffer that affront:
he can't allow such stupid ears to vaunt
their human shape; and so he made them longer,
and added gray and shaggy hair as cover,
and made them, at their base, unstable, loose,
so that they could be moved. But just that part
was changed: all else retained its human cast.
This was the only punishment of Midas:
to wear the ears of a slow-moving ass.
He had to hide his shame, his horrid blot;
and so, around his temples, Midas wrapped
a purple turban. But the slave who cut
the king's hair when it was too long, found out.
He did not dare reveal what he had seen;
yet he was keen to speak of the disgrace—
he was not one to keep it to himself.
So, leaving Midas, he went off to dig
a hole within the ground; and into this,
he murmured—all his words were soft and low—
what he had learned. Then, covering that hole,
he buried what he'd said; that done, he stole

Latin [163–89]

away in silence. But above that hole,
a stand of swaying reeds began to grow;
and when a year had passed, those reeds stood tall,
and they betrayed the servant who had sown
his secret there; for as the soft south wind
stirred them, they spoke his buried words, made known
King Midas' shame—the ass's ears he'd grown.

Avenged in full, Latona's son can leave
the slopes of Tmolus. Now Apollo cleaves
the limpid air; before his flight has reached
the straits of Helle, daughter of Nephele,
he comes to earth.

                    Between two promontories—
right of Sigeum, left of those deep seas
that ring Rhoeteum—stands an ancient altar
to Jove the Thunderer, author of all
the oracles. From there Apollo saw
Laomedon beginning to build walls
for his new city, Troy. And he could tell
how hard those labors were, what means—not small—
were needed to complete those awesome walls.
At that, together with the god who bears
the trident, ruler of the swollen sea,
he took on human form and, for the king
of Phrygia, built those walls; it was agreed—
before they had begun—that they'd receive
the payment for their finished task in gold.

The work was done. But false Laomedon
defaulted on his debt: they did not get
the gold he owed; with perjured words he swore
that he had never promised a reward.
The sea-god answered: "You will pay for this!"
And he bent all his waters' force against

Latin [189–208]

the shores of Troy the miserly; the flood
made all of Troy seem like a sea; it seized
the farmers' crops and buried fields beneath
the surge. And even that was not enough,
for Neptune ordered them to offer up
Hesione, the daughter of the king;
they had to chain her fast to a hard reef
as prey for some fierce monster of the deep.
But she was saved by Hercules, who then
asked for the horses they had promised him
as payment. And again a task was left
unrecompensed. And he waged war against
twice-faithless Troy as punishment for that:
he, Hercules, the victor, razed their walls.

His ally in that war was Telamon.
He, too—when they had won—received a prize:
Hesione—he gained a royal bride.
Alongside Telamon there also fought
his brother, Peleus; he, however, was
already famous as the man who'd won
a goddess as a wife: indeed, his father-
in-law inspired no less pride in Peleus
than his grandfather did: more than one mortal
could boast of having Jove as his grandfather,
but only Peleus had as wife a goddess.

It was old Proteus who had prophesied
to Thetis: "Goddess of the waves, conceive—
for you will bear a boy; and when he's reached
his prime, he will outdo his father's deeds;
and men will celebrate his name and fame
as one who puts his father's might to shame."
That prophecy made Jove most cautious: though
within his heart an ardent fire glowed
for Thetis, goddess of the sea, he shunned

Latin [208–26]

her arms, her couch; if Thetis bore a son
whom he had fathered, earth would harbor one
more mighty than himself. And so he bid
his grandson, Peleus, son of Aeacus,
to take the place of lover in his stead,
to seek and wed that virgin of the sea.

There is a bay in Thessaly that curves
much like a sickle; two protruding arms
of land enclose a cove that could indeed
serve as a harbor if it had more depth.
Instead, the sea lies shallow on the sands.
The shore is firm, and footsteps leave no trace;
there is no seaweed there to slow one's pace—
one does not sink or slide. Beyond the beach
there is a grove of myrtles that can boast
bicolored berries thick upon the bough.
There is a grotto in that grove, and though
one cannot say with certainty that art
or nature was its maker, what it shows
seems more like artist's work. It was this grotto
that often served you, Thetis: naked, you
would ride your bridled dolphin to that cave.
There, overcome by sleep, you lay, when he
surprised you, seized you; but—though he beseeched—
you would not yield to him; and so he tried
to force you, twisting both his arms around
your neck. If you'd not been adept in all
the arts of transformation, your honed skills,
he would have had his way; but you were now
a bird—and though he gripped a bird, he still
held fast; and now a tree, whose trunk might well
have crushed him—yet his clutch did not relent.
And so, as your third change, you chose to take
a spotted tigress' shape. That was too much:
afraid, the son of Aeacus let go.

▢   ▢   ▢

Latin [226–46]

Then Peleus left that cave: he went to pray,
to pour wine-offerings upon the waves,
to bring entrails of sheep, to burn incense,
to ask the sea-gods' aid. At his behest,
old Proteus, the seer of Carpathus,

rose from the sea's abyss to tell him this:
"O son of Aeacus, you will possess
the bride you so desire. There is but
one thing that you must do: when she lies down
in her cool cavern, while she is too numb
with sleep to notice anything, you are
to tie her with tenacious cords and knots.
And when she wakes, don't falter; though she takes
a hundred lying shapes, hold fast, be firm
until she has regained her own true form."
Now Proteus was done; he hid his face
beneath the waters, and he let a wave—
as it flowed back—enclose his final words.

The Sun was sinking low; his chariot sloped
down to the western sea; and now the fair
sea-goddess sought her grotto; there she slept
upon her customary couch. And when
she woke, she found her virgin body gripped
by Peleus—he'd attacked. At once she took
shape after shape, until she felt her limbs
were bound hard fast; her arms were pinioned, tied
apart and wide, one to each side. At last,
she moaned and said: "You never could have won,
had you not had a god as your ally."
At that, she took on her own form; as Thetis,
the goddess yielded to the hero. Peleus
embraced her; he fulfilled his dream, and she
was pregnant with the seed of great Achilles.

□   □   □

Latin [247–65]

And Peleus was a happy father and
a happy husband—one completely blessed
if he had not, by fatal accident,
killed Phocus, his half-brother. And for that
bloodstain, his father's house was barred to him;
and he sought refuge in the land of Trachin.
There, Ceyx, son of Lucifer, was king;
there, not by force or acts of blood, he reigned
with all his father's radiance in his face.
But at the time when Peleus reached his realm,
the king was sad, unrecognizable,
in mourning for the loss of his own brother.

His journey had been long, his cares were many;
when Peleus came to Trachin, he was weary.
Outside the walls, within a shaded valley,
he left the flocks and herds he'd taken with him:
with but few men, he entered Ceyx' city.
As soon as he was given leave to see
King Ceyx, he came forward; suppliant,
he held an olive bough that had been wrapped
in woolen bands whose borders veiled his hands,
as he announced his name and lineage.
The one thing that he hid was his own crime;
and, to explain his flight, he told a lie.
And then he pleaded for a chance to find
some way, in town or country, to provide
a new life for himself. The king was kind:
"This realm is hardly inhospitable;
its gods are open even to the humble,
o Peleus. There's not only our goodwill,
there are your own rich merits: you can claim
much fame—and are a grandson of great Jove.
Don't waste your time on pleas; you will receive
all that you seek; and everything you see
is yours to share and use. If only we

Latin [266–88]

could offer greater joy to meet your needs!"
Here Ceyx wept. And Peleus and his men
asked for the cause of his profound lament.

———————

———————

This tale was his reply: "Indeed you may
believe that he, the bird who lives on prey
and terrifies all other birds, was always
a feathered thing—but he was once a man.
The spirit's bent and bias are so constant,
that even then he was ferocious, set
on battles, always keen for violence.
His name—Daedalion; and he was born,
like me, of Lucifer, the one who summons
Aurora and is, too, the last to leave
the sky. I care for peace: tranquillity
and family have been most dear to me;
but what my brother loved was savage war.

"He had a daughter, Chione—most lovely;
and though she had just reached her fourteenth year,
the marriageable age, she was already
sought by as many as a thousand men.
Both Phoebus and the son of Maia chanced
to set their eyes on her at the same time.
While Phoebus was returning from his Delphi,
and Mercury from his Cyllene's peak,
the two at once were struck by ardent love.

"The first put off until nightfall his hope
of having Chione; but Mercury
could not endure delay, and with his wand
that brings on sleep, he touched the virgin's lips.
That wand has too much force: the girl submits,
in deep sleep, to his godly violence.
Then, when night scattered stars across the sky,
Phoebus approached in an old woman's guise;

Latin [288–310]

and from fair Chione he gathered more
of those delights that had been reaped before
by Mercury. Nine months had come, had gone;
from seed that had been planted by the son
of Maia, shrewd Autolycus was born:
a connoisseur of wiles and guiles, an heir
who passed off black as white and white as black,
he fully matched his father's art and craft;
whereas Apollo's son (the birth was twin)
was Phillamon, much famed for lyre and song.
But though the lovely girl had borne two sons
and pleased two mighty gods and could claim one
so brave as father and a star so bright
as her grandfather—did the girl derive
delight or profit? For we often find
that fame does not bring fortune. Certainly
her glory spelled the end of Chione.
The girl was rash enough to say that she
surpassed Diana's beauty: she found flaws,
unpleasing features, in the goddess' form.
Incensed, the goddess cried ferociously:
'If not my features, then my flawless deeds
will please you!' And, at once, she bent her bow,
drew back the string, and sped the arrow off;
it pierced the guilty tongue. The tongue fell still:
the voice, the words she tried to utter found
no exit. Even as she tried to speak,
her life, together with her blood, took leave.
What misery was mine—an uncle's grief!
How many words of comfort did I speak
to my dear brother! But just as the reefs
respond to the low murmur of the sea,
so did my brother then respond to me:
all he could do was mourn for Chione.
And when her body burned upon the pyre,
four times he tried to leap into the fire;
four times they thrust him back. In frenzy, he
rushed off headlong across the trackless fields,

Latin [310–34]

like a young bull whose neck is stung by wasps.
And even then he seemed to me to run
more swiftly than a human being can.
No one could catch him; keen to kill himself,
he raced up to Parnassus' peak—and leaped
down from a cliff. Apollo, pitying
my brother, made of him a bird with wings
that sprouted suddenly; and he received
a hooked beak and curved claws; but he did keep
the courage that he had before—and force
that seemed more great than body can support.
And now he is a hawk, befriending none;
all birds endure his savage indignation—
himself aggrieved, he makes all other mourn."

While Ceyx, son of Lucifer, told this
amazing story of his brother's fate,
Onetor, Peleus' Phocian cowherd, dashed
into the palace, panting. "Peleus, Peleus,"
the cowherd cried, "I carry dreadful news!"
And Peleus urges him to tell in full,
whatever news he brings: so, too, the king
of Trachin, terrified, waits anxiously
for tidings from those trembling lips. Then he,
the cowherd, tells his story: "I was driving
the weary oxen to the curving beach.
Just then, along his course, the Sun had reached
his highest point, a point from which he saw
behind him just as much as lay ahead.
Some oxen stretched out on the yellow sands
and watched the ample surface of the sea;
and some roamed here and there—quite lazily;
and others swam, their necks above the water.
Close to the sea a shadowed temple stood;
it did not gleam with marble and bright gold;
it's hidden by thick trunks, in ancient woods—

a shrine for Nereus and his Nereids,
the god and goddesses who guard that sea
(a sailor was the one who told me this,
while, on the sandy shore, he dried his nets).
Nearby, backwaters of the sea had formed
a marsh enclosed by thickset willows' shade.

And from that marsh a monstrous beast burst out,
a wolf who crashed ahead, who trampled, loud,
and filled with terror all the countryfolk;
his jaws were deadly, flecked with foam, blood-soaked;
his blazing eyes were fiery red. Though rage
and hunger spurred him on, rage was foremost.
Indeed, he did not stop to fill his maw,
to quell his savage hunger and devour
the cattle he had killed; but out of hate
he mangled all the herd—yet did not feast.
And some of us, in trying to defend
the herd, fell, too, beneath his fatal jaws.
The shore, the shallow water, and the swamp
were loud with bellowings and red with blood.
But now, do not delay! Don't hesitate!
Before we have lost everything, let's rush
to arms—to charge the monster—all of us!"

So said the countryman. But Peleus' loss
seemed not to touch him deeply: what he brought
to mind was this—his crime, his having killed
the son of the sad Nereid: this wolf
was sent by Psamathe; the slaughtered herd
had served as sacrifice to Phocus' Shade.

The king of Trachin now commands his men
to put on armor; all must take in hand
their deadly lances; he himself prepares
to hunt the wolf with them. But when his wife,
Alcyone, is roused by loud outcries,
she rushes from her room—her hair is still
uncombed and so accents her disarray;

Latin [361–85]

she throws herself upon his neck, she prays
with words and tears, imploring him to stay:
there is no need for him to join the rest;
it is enough for him to send out aid—
and doing so, he can be sure to save
himself and her: in sum, two lives in one.
And Peleus, hearing this, says: "Queen, your fears
move me; yes, they are seemly; but be sure,
they can be set to rest. You have my thanks
for offering your help; but I don't wish
strange monsters to be met by weaponry.
There is, instead, a proper remedy:
I must pray to the goddess of the sea."

Above the citadel a tall tower rose,
a tower at whose top there always blazed
a signal fire that offered welcome aid
to weary ships. This was the spot they reached.
From there, in sad dismay, they saw the beach
strewn with dead cattle, and the savage beast,
his muzzle and his shaggy hair blood-soaked;
hands stretched out to the shore and open sea,
the son of Aeacus prayed fervently
to Psamathe, the sea-blue nymph, that she
might set aside her wrath—might shower mercy.
But Peleus' prayer did not stir Psamathe.
Instead, it was his wife, the goddess Thetis,
who, interceding for him, led the nymph
to pardon Peleus, son of Aeacus.

But though he had been ordered to retreat,
the wolf has found the taste of blood so sweet
that, frenzied, he persists—until the nymph,
as he held fast a heifer he had ripped,
changed him to marble. But his body kept
the shape and stance it had—in all respects,
except its color: just its stony hue
reveals that he's no longer wolf but statue—

Latin [386–406]

that need be feared no more. And yet the fates
did not wish exiled Peleus to remain
in Trachin; so the nomad left—and came
at last into Magnesia, the land
of King Acastus, the Haemonian.
And it was there that Peleus, at the hands
of good Acastus, was completely cleansed
of his bloodguilt.

        Meanwhile, King Ceyx, still
perturbed by these strange things—his brother's fate
and then the singular events of late—
wants to consult a sacred oracle;
for oracles can comfort men in trouble.
He wants to leave for Clarus (on that isle
Apollo has a shrine): the sanctuary
in Delphi was—just then—impossible
to reach, for under impious Phorbas,
the Phlegyans had sacked the sacred city.
But you, Alcyone, his trusted wife—
it is to you that Ceyx first confides
his plan. A sudden chill invades your bones;
your face grows pale as boxwood; and your cheeks
are wet with tears. Three times she tries to speak;
three times her face is tear-streaked as she weeps.
At last, though sobs still interrupt her plea,
she utters her affectionate entreaty:

"What fault of mine has turned your mind awry?
Your care for me was once the first of things—
where has that gone? My dearest one, are we
so distant now that you can tranquilly
leave your Alcyone alone? Long journeys—
do those intrigue you now? When I am far,
am I more dear to you? But I should hope
that you will go by way of land. At least—

Latin [406–25]

although I grieve—I will not have such need
to fear: I'll suffer but without despair.
It is the sea that haunts me: there is terror
in the drear image of its endless waters.
Lately, I saw some planks along the beach,
the shattered remnants of a wreck at sea;
and often I've seen tombs that bore a name,
although, within those tombs, nobody lay.
And do not let illusions cozen you:
the father of your wife may be the son
of Hippotas—yes, Aeolus is one
who holds the winds as prisoner and may,
whenever he so wills it, calm the waves.
But once the winds, unleashed, have reached the deep,
they can be curbed no more; there is no land,
there is no tract of water to withstand
their power: no thing then is safe from them.
They can harass the highest clouds of heaven;
and when contending winds collide, impact,
wind batters wind, and then red lightnings flash.
(As a child, I often saw those winds within
my father's house—I know them—and be sure
the more I know of them, the more I fear.)
But if no plea of mine can change your plan,
if you in truth must leave, then take me, too,
dear husband; let me journey out with you.
The storms will batter both of us, and I
will only have to fear what meets my eyes.
As one, we shall endure whatever comes;
as one, we'll sail the sea's immensity!"

The words and tears of Aeolus' dear daughter
have deeply moved the son of Lucifer:
he feels in full the fire of love for her.
And yet he won't renounce his voyage out
by sea, nor would he have Alcyone
share any of the dangers he might meet.
He tries, with many suasive words, to ease

her frightened heart. But she cannot agree.
At that, he adds these words, the only pledge
that calms his loving wife, wins her consent:
"There's no delay that won't seem long to us;
yet by my father's radiant fires, I promise
that if my fate permits me to return,
you are to see me home again before
the moon has twice filled all of her white orb."

Alcyone, on hearing Ceyx' vow,
is filled with hope that he'll return; and now
he tells his men to launch his ship at once,
with proper gear to meet its every need.
When she has seen that done, Alcyone—
as if she could foresee what is to come—
shudders anew, sheds tears, embraces him,
and, desperate, at last with sad voice says
farewell, then falls as a dead body falls.

And now, though Ceyx would have liked to linger,
his keen young men are quick to cleave the water;
aligned in double rows, with measured strokes,
back to their sturdy chests they draw their oars.
Alcyone lifts tearful eyes: she sees
her husband standing at the curving stern;
he signals first; with waving hand he greets
his wife, and she replies with other signs.
And when the shore is long since left behind,
and faces can't be seen by loving eyes,
she scans the sea as best she can, until
the ship recedes from sight. And when it fades,
her eyes, still watchful, seek the far-off sail
that flutters at the summit of the mast.
When even that is gone, she hurries back
in desperation, to her room—and there
she throws herself upon the empty bed.
The room, the bed renew her drear lament;
she thinks upon the part of her that left. □ □ □

Latin [448–73]

The ship had left the harbor, and the wind
was rattling through the rigging. They drew in
their oars and let them dangle at shipside;
they ran the yard high up the mast; to catch
each breath of quickening breeze, all sails were spread.
By now the ship had traveled slightly less—
or one might say, no more—then half her course:
the land they'd left and land they headed toward
were both far off. Night fell; the rough seas swelled
with foaming whitecaps, Eurus' gusting force
grew ominous. "Haul down the yard at once,"
the captain shouted; "tight reef all the sails!"
He shouted, but his sharp command is drowned
by blustering winds: the storm advances now—
no human voice is heard; the surge is loud.
But even so, some sailors, on their own,
now stow the oars, some seal up the oar holes;
some reef the sails while others now bail out
the waters flooding in: they pour the sea
into the sea—all this, confusedly.
The storm redoubles force; the winds wage war
ferociously; they churn the angry waters.
The captain, too, is fearful; even he,
despite his skill, is helpless in these seas.
And there is uproar everywhere: the howls
of men, the creaking rigging, and the roar
of wave on wave, and thunder from the sky.
The surge is mountainous; it seems to rise
to heaven, where it sprays the clouds with spume;
now, sweeping up the bottom of the sea,
the waves take on the tawny hue of sand;
and now they are as black as waves of Styx;
and then, from time to time, as they spread out,
the waves are white with the resounding foam.
And like the surge, the ship of Ceyx, too,
is in the grip of chance, of sudden shifts;
now lifted high, as from a mountain peak,
she seems to look below, into the deep

Latin [474–504]

of valleys, lowest Acheron's abyss;
now, driven down, hemmed in by surge that twists,
from pools as deep as Styx—on distant skies
so far above—she seems to set her sights.
Huge combers often crash against her sides,
as battering rams or catapults can strike
a savaged citadel with massive thuds.
And even as fierce lions gain new force
just when they launch their final, frantic rush
against poised spears, so, when contending gusts
lash hard, the waters charge in wild assault
against the hull and tower over it.
The wedges now give way; the hull springs leaks;
the surge has stripped the covering of pitch,
and gaping seams let fatal waves pour in.
The clouds have burst; great torrents now cascade;
one would have thought that all the skies had fallen
into the sea, while swollen waves had risen
into the sky. The downpour soaks the sails,
and all the waters—sea's and heaven's—mingle.
Not one star shines. The night is doubly dark—
with its own shades and shadows of the storm;
and yet, from time to time, the dark is torn
by flashing lightning bolts; and one can watch
the waves glow red beneath the lightning's glare—
and see just how those waves invade the hull
(by now, they don't sweep through the seams but leap
directly). As an eager soldier seeks
to scale the walls of a beleaguered city
and, after failing many times, succeeds
at last and, all aflame with love of fame,
leaps over that great wall and finds himself
the only one among a thousand men:
just so, when some nine waves have tried to leap
across the hull's high sides, it is the tenth
that, surging even more ferociously,
assaults the weary hull without a let
until its overwhelming fury lifts

Latin [504–32]

that wave across the sides on to the deck—
the wave has won; the hull is overcome.
And thus, in this invasion of the ship,
while one part of the sea is still without,
the other part already is within—
a time of terror, such as grips a town
when some assail the ramparts from without,
while other fighters rage inside the walls.
Both skill and courage fail; no thing avails;
each wave is like another headlong death.
Some cannot check their tears, and some are mute.
One sailor cries that those indeed are blessed
who die on land and earn a burial;
another prays and begs the gods to help,
stretching his arms—in vain—up toward the sky,
though there is nothing he can see on high.
One calls to mind his brothers and his parents;
another fastens on his house, his children;
and each recalls what he has left behind.

But Ceyx thinks of his Alcyone;
it's she alone for whom he longs—and yet
he's happy she is far away from this.
If only he could see his native coast,
could turn his eyes, for one last time, upon
his home! But Ceyx does not know just where
his own dear country lies: the sea is so
tumultuous; and clouds as black as pitch
conceal the sky; the night is doubly dark.
A twister lashes at—and cracks—the mast;
the rudder, too, is smashed. A wave,
triumphant—proud of all its spoils and prey—
heaves high, looks down upon the other waves,
until—as if one were to tear away
Mount Athos or Mount Pindus from its base—
it falls headlong and, with its crushing weight,
sends down the ship. And almost all the men,
caught in the vortex, never rise again.

Latin [532–59]

But some do cling to the dismembered ship's
torn planks. And with the hand that once had gripped
the scepter, Ceyx clutches at a remnant
and calls—in vain—upon his father and
father-in-law; but above all, his lips
call on his wife, Alcyone; he thinks
again, again of her—his memories
are like an eddy; he implores the waves
to bear his body to a shore where he
may yet be seen by his Alcyone
and she, with love, may bury his dead body.
And as he swims, each time the surge permits
his mouth to open, she is on his lips:
the name—"Alcyone, Alcyone"—
of one so distant. And he murmurs it
even beneath the waves, when he can't lift
his weary head. At last, a jet-black mass
of churning water arches overhead,
above the other waves, and then it breaks—
and buries him. The Morning Star—that dawn—
is dim and dark: you never would have known
that he was Lucifer—since he could not
desert his station in the sky, he wrapped
his face in thick clouds.

        In the land of Ceyx,
his wife, who'd not yet heard of the disaster,
counts off the nights; already she prepares
the festive clothes that he and she will wear
at his homecoming—conjuring a thing
that never is to be. Devotedly,
she offers up incense to all the gods;
but Juno is the one she honors most,
and Juno's shrine is where she always goes
to pray for Ceyx—one already dead:
she asks that her dear husband may be kept
free from all harm and injury, that he
come home to his Alcyone, and meet

Latin [559–81]

and love no other woman on his journey.
Of those three things Alcyone implored,
only the last request was granted her.

But Juno found it hard to hear these pleas—
these prayers for the dead; that she might free
her altar from the unclean hands of one
whom death has touched with loss, she called upon
her faithful Iris: "Trusted messenger,
go quickly to the drowsy house of Sleep,
and have him send Alcyone a dream,
an image that appears in Ceyx' shape
and shows him dead and tells of his true fate."
Such were her words; and Iris, in her cloak
that shows a thousand colors, arched across
the sky in rainbow guise. She went to seek
the palace of King Sleep, well-hid beneath
its covering of clouds.

          A cavern stands
close to the land of the Cimmerians:
a hollow mountain shelters many deep
recesses of that cave; and sluggish Sleep
lives there, in secrecy. No sun can reach
within—none of its rising, noontime, or
its setting rays; there fog and vapors pour
up from the earth: it is crepuscular.
No crested cock keeps vigil there, no crows
to summon bright Aurora; there is no
watchdog to break the silence with his barks,
no goose, who's even more alert than hounds.
One hears no cattle low, no roaring beasts,
no sound of branches rustling in the breeze;
there is no clattering of human speech.
That place belongs to silence—but for this:
out from the bottom of the stony cave,
the stream of Lethe flows; and as its waves
traverse the gravel bed along their way,

Latin [581–604]

their gentle murmuring invites to sleep.
The entranceway is graced by many beds
of flowering poppies and the countless herbs
from which damp night distills her hypnagogic
elixir to spread sleep across dark earth.
Lest any turning hinge might creak, there is
no door in all that house; no watchman waits
along the threshold. In the central space
a couch of ebony stands tall—black, too,
the feather mattress and the heavy blanket.
The god himself sprawls there with languid limbs;
and there, upon all sides, arrayed around him,
in many miming shapes, lie futile Dreams,
as many as a harvest's ears of wheat,
as many as the leaves upon the trees,
or as the grains of sand cast on the beach.

No sooner had the virgin Iris made
her way into that room (she brushed away
the Dreams that blocked her path), than all that space,
that sacred dwelling place, was filled with light:
the splendor of her cloak undid the night.
And Sleep, whose eyes were heavy, found it hard
to open them and, when he propped himself,
sank back again and knocked his chin, nodding
against his chest, until at last he shook
himself free of himself and, rising up—
his elbow served as his support—asked her
(for he indeed knew who she was) just why
she had come; and Iris answered him: "O Sleep,
the gentlest of the gods, it's you who bring
repose to everything; you offer peace
unto the soul; you banish cares; you soothe
our bodies worn with labor; you refresh
our bodies, so that we can face new tasks;
it's you, o Sleep, of whom I now ask this:
do tell a Dream, one of that band who knows
just how to mime true forms, that he must go

Latin [604–27]

to Trachin, town where Hercules was born;
before Alcyone, have him appear
as one who was shipwrecked, and have him wear
the features of King Ceyx. So says Juno."
Her mission done, she left; for she could not
withstand that cavern's soporific force.
As she felt sleep invade her limbs, she fled.
386
Along the curving rainbow arch by which
she'd passed before, she now retraced her steps.

King Sleep was father of a thousand sons—
indeed a tribe—and of them all, the one
he chose was Morpheus, who had such skill
in miming any human form at will.
No other Dream can match his artistry
in counterfeiting men: their voice, their gait,
their face—their moods; and, too, he imitates
their dress precisely and the words they use
most frequently. But he mimes only men;
for it's another Dream who can become
a quadruped, a bird, or a long snake:
that Dream the gods call Icelos—but when
he's named by common mortals, he's Phobetor.
And still another brother Dream can claim
quite special gifts: his name is Phantasos;
the forms that he assumes deceive, intrigue:
the shapes of earth and rocks, and water, trees—
in sum, of lifeless things. And there are Dreams
who show themselves by night to kings and chiefs,
while others roam among the common folk.
But the old god sets all of these aside;
and of his many sons, he takes this one
to do what Thanaus' daughter said he must—
and as I said, that Dream was Morpheus.
That done, the god gives way to drowsiness;
he hides his head beneath his thick black blankets.

□   □   □

Latin [627–49]

Now, quick to leave the cavern, Morpheus
flies on his noiseless wings across the darkness.
And soon he reaches Trachin. There he sheds
his wings: he takes the face and form of Ceyx
and, like a pale cadaver—not a shred
of clothing on him—stands beside the bed
of the dejected wife. His hair is drenched,
his beard is soggy; dripping from his head
are heavy drops. Over the bed he bends;
his face is wet with tears. As Morpheus cries,
he says: "Sad wife, oh, do you recognize
your Ceyx? Or has death disfigured me?
Look carefully; you'll see who I must be.
Yet I am not your husband but his Shade.
Alcyone, it is in vain you prayed—
I'm dead. Don't let delusion leave you prey
to barren hopes: I can't come home again.
The south wind caught my ship on the Aegean;
he tossed her with his tempest force—she sank.
Again, again, my lips cried out your name
as I was thrust below and drank the waves;
I am no messenger whom one can doubt—
what you hear now is not some vague report.
It's I myself, the one who was shipwrecked,
who tell you here—directly—of my death.
Come, then, shed tears, and put on mourning dress;
don't let me go unhonored by lament
down into Tartarus, that barren land!"

And Morpheus employed a voice so like
her husband's, that he could not be denied.
Even his tears seemed true; and as he moved,
his gestures were the gestures Ceyx used.

Alcyone, still in her sleep, began
to mourn and weep; she tried to reach her man
with outstretched arms; she wanted to embrace
his body, but it was thin air she clasped.

Latin [650–75]

She cried: "Wait, wait for me! Where do you flee!
Let me go, too, with you!" Her own loud plea
and Ceyx' image woke the anxious wife;
and, first, she looked around to see if he
whom she had seen just now was at her side.

Her servingwomen, startled by her cries,
had brought a lamp into her room. But she
could not find him; she beat her cheeks, then ripped
her robe off from her chest, and rent her breasts;
and she tore at her hair—she took no care
to loose it first; and to her nurse, who asked
what was the cause of such despair, she cried:
"Alcyone is done! She's done! She died
together with her Ceyx. Cast aside
consoling words! He's shipwrecked! He is dead!
I saw him, and I knew him, and I tried
to hold him in my outstretched hand; I tried
to clasp and—as he left—to hold him back.
It was a Shade, but it was his true Shade—
my husband's Shade. Yes, yes, his face did lack
the life that it once had, its radiance.
Poor me, I saw him pale and naked and
with hair still damp. A sorry sight, he stood
just here, just at this point" (and here she bent
to see if there were still some trace of him).
"This is what I had feared; I foresaw this—
that's why I begged him not to leave me, not
to trust the winds! But since you left to die,
you should at least have had me at your side.
It would have been far better for me then;
no instant of my life would have been spent
away from you; then, too, we'd not have met
death separately. For now, though I am here,
I've died; though I am here, I, too, contend
with waves; and although I am not at sea,
it is the sea that swallows me. Indeed,
my heart would be more savage than the sea,
were I to strive to live still longer, try

Latin [676–703]

to overcome—to last beyond—this grief.
But I won't try; I won't leave you alone;
at least this time, sad Ceyx, I shall come
along with you; this time I'm your companion.
And if we're not entombed in the same urn,
at least the letters of our epitaph
will join us; if my bones don't touch your bones,
at least my name will touch your name." But grief
stops speech; her words retreat before her moans;
from her sad heart, all she can draw are groans.

When morning came, she went down to the shore,
to that same place where she had gone before
to see him sailing off. She lingered there
and murmured: "But this very spot is where
he loosed that cable, and this spot is where
he kissed me at his parting." Even as
she called to mind each scene and watched the sea,
she saw, far off, along the waves, that something
was floating—and it could well be a body.
At first, she was not sure just what it was;
but when the surge had pushed it somewhat closer—
though still far off—it was becoming clear
that, in that sea, there was indeed a body.
She did not know whose corpse it was; and yet
Alcyone was moved, for he was shipwrecked;
and she took pity on him, just as one
will pity an unknown: "Unhappy man,
whoever you may be—unhappy wife,
if you indeed are married." And the body,
thrust forward by the waves, came closer still;
and even as she watched it, she grew more
bewildered. It was closer now to shore,
and closer, closer still—now she was sure:
it was her husband. "It is he!" she cried;
she tore her cheeks, her hair, her robe; she stretched
her trembling hands toward Ceyx, as she said:

. . .

Latin [703–27]

"O dearest husband, is it thus that you,
so wretchedly, at last return to me?"

Along the shore, there stood a long breakwater:
the work of man, it broke the waves' onslaught
by sapping it before it gained full force.
And there she ran and leaped into the surge.
That she could reach that mole was in itself
a miracle: in truth, Alcyone
had flown to that high spot with her new wings.
With these, she beat the yielding waves and skimmed—
poor bird—the combers' crests; her mouth—by now
a slender beak—gave forth such sounds as seemed
to come from one who knew lament and grief.
And when she reached the silent, lifeless body,
she threw her newfound wings round his dear limbs;
she tried to warm him with her kisses, but
in vain—her beak was hard, her kisses cold.

Did Ceyx feel the kisses that she gave?
Or was it just the motion of the waves
that made the drowned man seem to lift his face?
Men were unsure. But this must be the truth:
he felt those kisses. For the gods were moved
to pity, changing both of them to birds—
at last. Their love remained; they shared one fate.
Once wed, they still were wed: they kept their bond.
They mate; they rear their young; when winter comes,
for seven peaceful days Alcyone—
upon a cliff that overlooks the sea—
broods on her nest. The surge is quiet then,
for Aeolus won't let his winds run free:
he keeps them under guard, so that the sea
maintain the peace his fledgling grandsons need.

□   □   □

Latin [727–48]

An old man, as he watched that pair of birds
fly over broad expanses of the sea,
was praising Ceyx and Alcyone,
who loved each other so enduringly.
And one who stood nearby—or it may be
the same old man himself—then told this story:

"And that bird, too, the one whom you can see
skimming the sea—the one whose legs are slender"
(he pointed to a long-necked, swift merganser,
a fervent diver) "is of royal birth.
His forebears, if you want to hear in full
his line from its beginning down to him,
were Ilus and Assaracus and he
whom Jove stole, Ganymede; and then came old
Laomedon and Priam, king who ruled
in Troy's last days. And Aesacus himself
was Hector's brother: if he had not suffered
so strange a fate while he was still quite young,
he might have won as much renown as Hector—
though Hector was the son of Dymas' daughter,
while Aesacus was born—so it is said—
of Alexiroe, who had as father
Granicus, the horned river-god; and she
gave birth to Aesacus most secretly,
at wooded Ida's base. He hated towns
and kept away from regal banquet halls;
he lived on solitary mountain slopes
and in the simple countryside; he went
to visit Troy but rarely—an assembly
from time to time was quite enough for him.
And yet his Trojan heart was hardly crude—
nor steeled against soft love: he would pursue
Hesperie, whose father Cebren was
a river-god. For Aesacus had seen
that nymph along her father's banks as she

Latin [749–69]

was drying her long hair beneath the sun.
When she saw him, she fled, just as the hind
will flee the tawny wolf, or a wild duck,
too far from her own customary marsh,
will flee if she is startled by a hawk.

The Trojan races after her, as swift
with love as she with fear. But now the nymph
is bitten by a serpent who had hid
within the grass; just as Hesperie passed,
he struck her foot with his hooked fangs and left
his venom in her veins. And when her life
was spent, so was her flight. In his despair,
her lover clasped her lifeless form and mourned:
'I should not have pursued you: I repent.
But I could not imagine this. To win
our race, I'd not have paid this price. Poor girl,
it's two of us who killed you: yes, the wound
came from the snake, but I had caused the race.
I am more guilty than he is—and I,
to make amends for your death, offer mine.'

"That said, down from a seaside cliff whose base
the waves had worn away, the Trojan leaped
into the sea. But Thetis, taking pity,
received him gently, softening his fall;
and as he floated on the waters, she
clothed him with feathers: she did not concede
to him the death he'd sought so eagerly.
The lover now is furious: he sees
that he, against his will, is forced to live
and that his soul, so eager to desert
its wretched site, is not allowed to leave.
So with the newfound wings upon his shoulders,
he lifts himself and then again falls back;
his fall is softened by his feathers. Frenzied,
he dives headlong, dives deep; it's death he needs;
he seeks, reseeks a fatal path. His love
had made him lean; between his joints, his legs

Latin [770–93]

are slender still, as is his neck; his head
is distant from his body. And indeed
he loves the water still, and since he dives
beneath it, he is called the diving bird—
*mer*ganser—always wanting to sub*merge*."

BOOK XII

BUT FATHER PRIAM, since he did not know
that Aesacus was still alive, although
in feathered form, mourned for his son. In vain—
before an empty tomb on which the name
of Aesacus had been inscribed—the honors
the dead are due were paid to him by Hector
and all his other brothers.

                    Only Paris
was missing from the mournful rites; for he
was not at home just then—he'd gone to Greece.
A little later, he returned indeed:
he brought a stolen wife together with
a war that lasted long. A thousand ships
pursued him: at his back, the many clans
of Greece, the ranks of all Pelasgians
had massed. That mighty band would soon have won
quick vengeance, if they had not met rough storms.
When set to sail from Aulis, rich with fish,
the port of the Boeotians, their fleet
was blocked by tempest winds that made the sea
impassable. And to appease the gods,
as Danaans always do, they carried out
their rituals: the ancient altar now
was blazing with the fires kindled for
a sacrifice to Jove. Just then they saw—
even as it climbed up a sycamore
that stood nearby the place that served their rites—
a blue-green serpent. In that treetop stood
a nest that held eight fledgling birds. All these
he seized—just as he did the mother: she
was circling round her nestlings frantically.
His greedy jaws soon swallowed them. The Greeks
watched this with wonder. Calchas—son of Thestor—
the augur who had always read the future
correctly—cried: "O Greeks, we shall be victors;
rejoice, for Troy will fall—but only after
a long and wearing war." And as a sign

Latin [1–21]

that it would last nine years, the birds were nine.
Entwined around the trees' green boughs, the snake
was changed to stone; and even to this day
that stone retains a coiling serpent's shape.
But Nereus' rage does not relent; untamed,
he churns the waves and winds: he won't permit
the fleet of war to sail from Aulis' port.
And some suspect that Neptune's very self
had stirred the surge, that he might save the walls
of Troy—which he had built. But Thestor's son
does not agree: he knows the truth, and he
does not conceal it: Agamemnon slighted
Diana when he killed her sacred stag;
and to appease the virgin goddess' wrath,
the Greeks must offer up a virgin's blood.
Now pity yields unto the public cause,
and kingship overcomes a father's love;
Iphigenia stands before the altar,
among attendants all in tears. But just
about to spill such dear chaste blood, Diana
relents: she screens the scene with a dark cloud;
and at the climax of the sacrifice,
amid the pleas and outcries of the crowd,
the goddess substitutes—they say—a hind
in place of the young virgin of Mycenae.

That victim was more seemly: once the hind
was sacrificed, Diana and the sea
both felt their wrath appeased; with winds astern,
a thousand ships sailed off and, after long
and troubled sailing, reached the Phrygian shores.

———————

There is a borderland, a place where three
realms meet: the earth, the heavens, and the sea—
the home of Rumor, high upon a peak.
From there, whatever happens anywhere

Latin [21–41]

is seen; and in that palace, any word
that's ever spoken in the universe
is heard by ears that wait, alert. And though
her house has endless entrances and boasts
a thousand apertures, no thing can close
those openings: there are no doors. And so,
that house—by night, by day—is never shut.
Since every part is built of sounding brass,
each word that's spoken in the world rebounds:
the brass vibrates, repeating every sound.
No quiet and no silence can be found;
and yet there is no clamor—just the soft
murmur of voices, as of rolling waves
when heard from far away, or like the last
faint rumble of a distant thunderclap
when Jove has spurred dark clouds to clash. A crowd—
forever coming, going—fills the halls;
and mingling with the true, the false reports—
in thousands—babble, wandering about;
some fill their idle ears with chatter, some
relay to others things they've heard: the sum
of clishmaclaver grows; to tales retold
each teller adds his own fresh furbelow.
Here is Credulity; here, heedless Error,
unfounded Joy, and Consternations, Fears,
sudden Seditions, and the hissing words
of unknown whispers. She—Rumor—knows
all that is done within the heavens and
on sea and land; throughout the world she probes.

Now it is Rumor that has spread the word
that ships are drawing close to Phrygia's shores,
a fleet that's carrying sturdy warriors.
And, thus, the disembarking Greeks were not
an unexpected foe. The Trojans block
the Greeks' advance; they pin them to the coast.
Before the fatal lance of Hector, you,
Protesilaus, were the first to fall.

Latin [42–68]

The Danaans, in those first encounters, pay
a heavy price, as Hector's prowess takes
a deadly toll: the many he has slain
add glory to his name. But Trojans, too,
lose many men: they learn what Greeks can do.

400

The shores of the Sigeus had grown red;
for Cycnus, Neptune's son, sent down to death
a thousand men. And now Achilles pressed
ahead—he rode his chariot, he stretched
battalions on the ground with his stout lance
made of the wood of Pelion. He searched
among the Phrygian ranks for Cycnus or
for Hector; it was Cycnus whom he met
(he had to wait till nine years passed before
he clashed with Hector). Then, as he urged on
his white-necked stallions straining at the yoke,
straight at the enemy Achilles drove.
His stout arm lifted high his lance; he cried:
"Whoever you may be, young man, you die;
but take this solace: you are slaughtered by
Achilles of Haemonia." His words
were followed by his heavy spear: his throw
was accurate, straight to the mark, and yet,
his pointed spearhead struck without effect—
it bruised the chest, as would a blunted shaft.
"O goddess' son"—such were the words of Cycnus—
"yes, I have heard that you were born of Thetis;
why be amazed to see me stand unscathed?
You see this casque with plumes of tawny horsehair,
you see the hollow shield my left arm bears—
well, I need none of this in my defense:
I only wear these arms as ornaments—
even as Mars when he wears battle dress.
Were you to strip me of this armor, I
should still escape unscathed. I can defy

Latin [68–93]

your claims: my mother was no Nereid;
my father rules both Nereus and his daughters;
he's Neptune—and indeed the whole expanse
of sea is subject to his firm command."
So Cycnus spoke, and then he hurled his lance
against Achilles; and its tip held fast
the hero's curving shield; and then, through brass
and through nine layers of oxhide, it passed;
but when it reached the tenth, the spearhead stopped.
Achilles shook that weapon off, then cast
another quivering shaft with his stout hand.
But Cycnus' body still was left intact,
unharmed: and even with another shaft—
the third—the Trojan was not wounded yet,
although he took no steps to shield his flesh.
At that, Achilles raged just like a bull
that rushes through the wide arena when,
with deadly horns, he charges hard against
the crimson cloak that has provoked his wrath
and finds that cloak eluding his attack.
Achilles checked his weapon—lest by chance
the tip had been dislodged, slipped off the shaft—
but no, the wooden lance still held it fast.
"Is then my hand so weak?" the Grecian asked.
"Has it lost—all at once—the force it had?
For surely I've been strong before—when I
led the attack that razed Lyrnesus' walls,
or when, because of me, both Tenedos
and Thebes, the city of Eetion,
ran crimson with the blood of their own men,
and the Caicus' flow ran red with those
I killed along its shores; and Telephus—
twice over—felt my spearhead's fatal force.
But here, too, on this beach, there are these heaps
of corpses I have made and I can see.
My right hand had—and still has—potency."
That said—almost as if in disbelief
of what had happened earlier—Achilles

Latin [93–115]

hurled hard his lance against a lowly Lycian,
a soldier called Menoetes; and he pierced
his breastplate and his chest beneath. Menoetes
now clattered headlong on the solid ground,
a dying man. Achilles plucked his shaft
out from the warm wound as he cried: "This hand,
this spear have brought me victory: I hope
that he whom I had failed to fell before,
may feel their force—and with the same result."
That said, he cast his ash-wood shaft at Cycnus:
it headed straight; the Trojan did not dodge;
the spear struck—a resounding thud—against
the shoulder of the Trojan, on the left:
but then it bounded back as if a wall
of solid rock had checked its course. And yet
Achilles sees that where his lance had struck
there is a spot of blood; and he exults—
in vain. There is no wound. The blood he sees
is nothing but the blood that was Menoetes'.

Achilles trembles now with rage; he leaps
down from his chariot, for what he seeks
is combat hand to hand. His gleaming blade
smites Cycnus, piercing both his shield and casque—
but turning blunt when it meets his hard flesh.
The Greek has reached his limit: he holds close
his shield and, with his sword-hilt, showers blows
upon the Trojan's face and hollow temples
and, hounding Cycnus, stunning him, allows
no respite. Cycnus panics; shadows swim
before his eyes; and as he staggers backward,
he stumbles on a rock that blocks his course
across the field. With unrelenting force,
Achilles presses down against him, pins
the Trojan to the ground: he is supine.
Then, thrusting with his shield and his tough knees
against the chest of Cycnus, he unties
the thongs that bind the Trojan's casque beneath

Latin [115–41]

his chin; and now Achilles, drawing these
tighter and tighter, chokes his enemy:
he blocks his breath, the life-path soul must seek.
He starts to strip his foe, and then he sees
that underneath the armor there's no body;
for Cycnus had acquired a new form:
the sea-god changed him into the white swan
whose name the Phrygian had already borne.

This work of war, this battle, in its wake
was followed by a truce of many days:
both sides laid down their arms—no clash, no fray,
a time for rest. And while keen sentinels
stood guard around the trenches of the Greeks,
the festive day drew close: a solemn feast.
Achilles, victor over Cycnus, seeks
to placate Pallas with the heifer he
is offering to her. He sets the meat
in slabs on the warm altar; once the fragrance
in which the gods take such delight has risen
to heaven—for the rite, the gods receive
the innards—men can banquet on the rest.

———————

The chiefs, reclining on their couches, eat
their fill of roasted meats, as they appease
their worries and their thirst. No instruments—
no lyre, no boxwood flutes with many vents—
and no songs' sound. They don't need these; they pass
the night in talk, as they retell the acts
of bravery—their own, their enemies'.
Their theme is war: and they delight as each,
in turn, recalls the risks and perils met
and overcome. What else can fill the speech
of an Achilles? And if others speak
within the presence of the greatest Greek,
can anything but valor be their theme?

Latin [141–63]

Above all, they discuss his recent feat,
his fight with Cycnus and his victory.
They all consider it astonishing
that Cycnus' body never could be pierced,
that he emerged intact from every clash—
all iron blunted when it met his flesh.
Achilles' own self still was wondering,
just like the other Greeks, when Nestor said:
"In your own generation, none but one—
invulnerable—could contemn and scorn
all arms: no sword could do young Cycnus harm.
But long ago I saw a warrior,
Caenus of Thessaly, whose body showed
no wound, though he had faced a thousand blows:
Caenus, who had Mount Othrys as his home—
courageous Caenus, famed for warlike feats.
And what was even more amazing, he
was born a woman." Hearing this, the Greeks,
astonished, begged old Nestor to complete
his tale. And like the rest, Achilles asked:
"Come now, old man, so wise, so eloquent,
for all of us long so to hear the rest:
Who was this Caenus? Why did he change sex?
In what campaign, upon what field of war
did you meet him? Who was his conqueror—
if he was ever beaten?" And old Nestor
replied: "Old age has dimmed my memory,
and many things I saw in my young years
escape me now, yet there is much I can
recall; but of all things that I have seen
in war and peace, no thing clings more to me
than Caenus. And if anyone's long years
have seen great things, well then, I have no peer:
two hundred years and more have passed before me—
my life is now in its third century.

"The fairest girl of all in Thessaly
was Caenis: famous for her beauty, she,

daughter of Elatus, was sought by many:
her suitors flocked from every nearby city
and, too, Achilles, from your own (indeed
her region was the same as yours; and Peleus
might well have sought her out as wife, had not
your mother been already wed—or pledged—
to him). But Caenis had no taste for marriage.
Then—so the story goes—as Caenis strolled
along a lonely shore, the sea-god took her
by force. And Neptune, having harvested
the pleasures of his latest passion, said:
'Whatever you desire—rest assured,
you need but ask for it—will soon be yours.'
And Caenis answered: 'What I have endured
is so outrageous that I now must choose
some mighty gift as recompense: a thing
that will prevent my ever suffering
such injury again. If you but grant
that I not be a woman anymore,
you will have given all that I would ask.'
The tone in which she uttered these last words
was deeper—such as suits a male; indeed,
she had become a man. The god who keeps
the sea was quick to answer: he'd appeased
her longing—and had added one more gift,
conceding this to her: no blow might pierce
her body; and no iron weaponry
could ever kill her. Gladly, she, now 'he,'
goes off to spend his days in masculine
pursuits along the fields of Thessaly.

"Now, there in Thessaly, the Lapith king,
Pirithous, the son of bold Ixion,
had wed Hippodame. And for the feast,
a row of tables, ordered properly,
had been set out beneath green woodland trees

Latin [190–212]

that graced his grotto. He, most cordially,
had called on the ferocious centaurs born
of Cloud—Ixion's wife—to join the rest
of his fine guests, the chiefs of Thessaly.
I, too, was there, and in the royal cave
the crowd was loud upon that wedding day.
They chant the nuptial hymn; the spacious hall
is filled with smoke from fires; now the bride—
escorted by the matrons and young wives—
approaches. One sees beauty when she strides.
We said: 'Indeed, how happy you must be,
Pirithous, to win a wife so lovely.'
That greeting turned into sad irony.
You, Eurytus, the wildest of wild centaurs—
inflamed by wine—are now inflamed still more
on seeing the fair bride. Your drunkenness
compounds your lust and breeds a brouhaha.
They overturn the tables, and the feast
is in uproar: the bride is carried off,
dragged by the hair; she's snatched by Eurytus.
As for the other centaurs, each one grabs
the one that strikes his fancy or, instead,
whatever woman he can snatch—a scene
that suits a plundered city. Women shriek
throughout the house. We all leap up at once,
and Theseus is the first to cry: 'Enough!
What madness, Eurytus, drives you to this?
How dare you—while I'm still alive—defy
Pirithous! You know not what you do:
with one foul act, it's two men you attack!'
And then, to show that he had meant his threat,
greathearted Theseus pressed through that mad crowd
of centaurs, and set free the newlywed.
But Eurytus was silent: no reply
that he might make could ever justify
his savage act; instead, with arrogance,
he charged courageous Theseus; with his fists
he pounded at his face and noble chest.

Latin [212–34]

By chance, an ancient massive vat, adorned
with forms in high relief, stood close at hand;
and Theseus, rising to full height, seized this
and hurled it at the face of Eurytus.
Then from his mouth and wounds the centaur spouts
both blood and brains alike: he vomits wine
and, stumbling, falls on the damp ground—supine.
His biform brothers, when they see him die,
go wild; and all, as in a chorus, cry:
'To arms! To arms!' They are urged on by wine;
the onslaught starts with flying cups and frail
oil flasks and curving basins—these served well
for feasts but now are war and slaughter's tools.

"The first who dared defile the inmost shrine
was Amycus, Ophion's son: he stripped
the sanctuary of its votive gifts.
He rushed to snatch a candelabrum thick
with glittering lamps: he lifted it on high,
as if it were the ax with which one strikes
the white neck of a bull in sacrifice.
With that, he smashed the face of Celadon,
the Lapith: one could hardly recognize
the face that Amycus had crushed. The eyes
slid from their sockets, and the facial bones
were shattered, and the nose was so thrust back
it ended in the middle of the palate.
But Pelates of Pella wrenched away
a table leg of maple and, with that,
felled Amycus—straight through the centaur's chest
his chin was driven; even as he spat
his teeth and his dark blood, the Lapith smashed
again—he sent the centaur to the Shades
of Tartarus. Gryneus stood nearby;
he watched the smoking altar with mad eyes,
and then, 'Why can't we use this, too!' he cried.
At that, he lifted up the giant mass,
its fires still burning; and that centaur cast

Latin [235–61]

the altar straight against the Lapith ranks:
it crushed Orion and crushed Broteas.
(Orion was the son of Mycale;
they say that with her magic chanting she
had often drawn the moon's horns down to earth,
although those horns moved most reluctantly.)
Exadius avenged those deaths: 'Just wait
until I find a weapon—then you'll pay,'
he cried—and snatched the antlers of a stag
that hung, a votive gift, on a tall pine.
The forked-tip antlers gouged Gryneus' eyes:
one eyeball stuck upon the pointed horns;
the other slid down to his beard and hung
within the clotted blood below his chin.

"Then, from the altar, Rhoetus snatched a brand
of white-hot plum-wood; from the right he smashed
Charaxus' temples—and the tawny hair
that crowned the Lapith blazed—a blinding flash,
like dry grain set afire; within the wound,
the blood was scorched—one heard a horrid hiss,
the kind that iron, glowing red, emits
when, from the forge, it's lifted by the smith
with curving tongs and plunged into a vat:
it sizzles as the water turns lukewarm.
As eager fire devours his shaggy hair,
the wounded Lapith tries to beat it back;
then from the ground, he rips the threshold's slab
and lifts it shoulder-high, a stone that could
strain even an oxteam. Its very mass
won't let him hurl it far enough to catch
his enemy: instead, it crushes his
own friend, Cometes, who stood close to him—
too close. And Rhoetus—he's beside himself
with joy—explodes: 'Yes, I can only hope
the rest of you can show the strength he showed.'
With that same brand, half-burned, again he strikes
Charaxus' wound; then, with insulting thrusts,

Latin [261–87]

three and four times he beats the Lapith's skull
until the bones, disjoined, sink deep into
Charaxus' brains, reduced to watery gruel.

"Triumphant, Rhoetus rushes to attack
three more: Evagrus, Corythus, and Dryas.

When Corythus, whose cheeks are veiled by his
light beard—his first—is felled, Evagrus taunts:
'What glory can you gain from slaying one
who's but a boy?' But Rhoetus won't permit
another word to issue from those lips:
into that mouth he thrusts—ferociously—
the flaming brand that puts an end to speech;
and through that open mouth, the flames now reach
into Evagrus' chest. And Dryas, you—
so fierce—are what the centaur next pursues.
He whirls his firebrand above his head,
but this attack does not end like the rest.
Even as he exults in all the deaths
that he has caused, you, Dryas, taking up
a charred stake, strike him hard, just at the point
where neck and shoulder join. And Rhoetus groans
and, struggling, tugs the stake out from hard bone;
and now it is his turn to flee; he's soaked
in his own blood.

   "These others also fled:
Orneus, Lycabas, and Medon—wounded
in his right shoulder. They were joined by other
retreating centaurs: Thaumas and Pisenor
and Mermeros (one who so recently
had beaten all who raced against him, now,
encumbered by a wound, is forced to slow);
and Pholus, Melaneus, and the boar-hunter,
stout Abas; and the augur, Astylus,
who'd warned his fellow centaurs to refrain
from battle with the Lapiths—but in vain:
his comrades did not heed his augury.

Latin [288–307]

To Nessus, who—afraid of wounds—had fled
together with him, Astylus had said:
'You need not flee: the bow of Hercules—
that is the fate that you are meant to meet.'
But, Lycidas, Eurynomus, Imbreus,
Areos—none of these evaded death:
all four were felled by Dryas—his right hand
struck them in front. You, too, Crenaeus, met
death by a frontal blow; though you had turned
in flight, you did look back; and Dryas sank
a massive lance between your eyes, just where
the nose and forehead join.

              "Amid that fracas
Aphidas, unperturbed, immersed in sleep
so deep that nothing could awaken him,
reclined full-length upon the shaggy skin
of an Ossaean bear: his languid hand
still held a cup of watered wine—no lance:
he was no threat, did not attack—but that
did not prevent his death. For Phorbas saw
that young man sleeping there, far off; and through
the thong along his javelin, he drew
his finger; and as soon as he had cried,
'Go now to drink your wine that's mingled with
the waters of the Styx,' his hand let fly
his shaft of ashwood; and its iron tip
pierced through Aphidas' neck as he, by chance,
lay with his head thrown back. He died with no
alert and no awareness; black blood flowed
in spurts—out of Aphidas' throat, it gushed
over the couch and into his wine-cup.

"With my own eyes, I saw Petraeus strive
to wrench an oak tree from the ground: from side
to side he shook the acorn-laden trunk,
his arms encircling it; and now it's loose—
just one tug more. But then Pirithous,

Latin [308–30]

right through Petraeus' rib cage, cast a shaft;
its steel tip pinned the centaur fast against
the tough oak tree he'd tried so hard to wrest.

"They say that Lycus was undone because
Pirithous was stronger than he was—
and stronger, too, than Chromis, whom he crushed.
But from these victories, the Lapith king
gained less fame than he won by conquering
two other centaurs, Helops and Dictys.
The shaft he cast caught Helops on the right
and pierced his temples, through to his left ear;
while Dictys, even as he fled in fear,
chased by Ixion's son, fell headlong from
a hilltop, down its farther, sheer cliffside;
with all his body's weight, he crashed upon
an ash tree's boughs—his centaur guts adorned
the branches.

      "To avenge him, Aphareus
rushed up; he wrenched a rock from that hilltop
and tried to throw it; but the oaken club
of Theseus, son of Aegeus, caught him just
in time—and shattered his huge elbow-bone.
Then, having neither time nor patience for
finishing off the centaur's battered form,
the son of Aegeus leaped upon the back
of tall Bienor—one who till then had
not carried anything but his own self:
he dug his knees into Bienor's sides;
with his left hand, he hugged the centaur's hair;
and with his knotty club, he smashed his face
and cursing mouth as well as his tough temples.
And Theseus, with that oaken club, did in
Lycopes, skilled at tossing javelins;
Nedymnus; Hippasos, whose flowing beard
shielded his chest; and Ripheus, taller than
the treetops; and he overcame the force

Latin [330–52]

of Thereus, who along the mountain slopes
of Thessaly caught bears and brought them home
alive and snarling still.

                 "Demoleon
found Theseus' victories too much to bear.
For some time now, with all his might, the centaur
had tried to wrench a great pine from the ground
with trunk intact; unable to do that,
he broke the trunk in half and hurled it at
the son of Aegeus. But quick to draw back,
Theseus escaped that throw, because he had
received Minerva's warning—so he said
and would have had us others understand.
And yet the crashing trunk had some effect:
for it sheared off, from giant Crantor's neck,
his chest and his left shoulder. O Achilles,
young Crantor was your father's armor-bearer:
Amyntor, king of the Dolopians,
defeated in his war with Peleus, gave
that youth to him as pledge of peace and faith.
When Peleus, from far off, saw that fierce wound,
he cried: 'Crantor, so dear a boy, accept
at least this gift—to honor you in death!'
At that, with sturdy mind and steady strength,
he leveled at Demoleon his lance:
it cracked his rib cage, lodged within his chest,
and quivered there. The centaur tried to wrench
the weapon loose, yet only freed the shaft
but not the lance head—this he could not catch:
within his lungs, the pointed tip held fast.
His pain just makes his courage more intense:
Demoleon rears up, then charges at
the son of Aegeus; but the hero's casque
and shield protect his shoulders—so he checks
the centaur's trampling, clattering horse-hooves.
Now Peleus holds his lance high, then he strikes
. . .

Latin [353–76]

Demoleon with a single thrust that finds
the centaur's human and his equine chest.

"Before that, Peleus had already struck
both Hyles and Phlegraeos from far off,
and Clanis and Iphinous close up.
To these he now adds Dorylas, who wears
no spear; instead he sports a savage pair
of spreading bull's horns, fully stained with blood.
I sighted Dorylas, and I cried out
(for fury urged me on to greater force):
'Now you will see how poor a thing your horns
must be when set against my shaft of iron!'
I cast my lance. He could not dodge the shaft
but tried to fend it, lifting his right hand
to shield his forehead, where my blow would land.
The lance head pinned that hand against his brow.
The shouts were loud. But while the centaur froze,
impaled and helpless with that bitter wound,
Peleus, who stood nearby, struck from below;
he pierced the centaur's belly. Dorylas
sprang forward; his guts dragged along the ground;
and as they dragged, he trampled them; they burst;
and he, his legs entangled with his guts,
collapsed—his belly empty—to the earth.

———

"And Cyllarus, your handsome form did not
save you in that ferocious fray—if one
may be allowed to call a centaur handsome.
His golden beard had just begun to grow;
his hair was golden, even as it flowed
over his shoulders to his equine chest.
His face had features strong and eloquent;
his neck, his hands, his manly chest could match
the finest statues—just as did the rest
of all his human parts. But, too, below,

the grace the centaur's equine features showed
was flawless. And if one were to bestow
a horse's neck and head on Cyllarus—
the muscles on his chest were so robust,
his back was just so suitable as seat—
he could have served as Castor's worthy steed.
He was all black, more black than pitch, and yet
his tail was snow-white, just as were his legs.
Though many female centaurs sought him out,
no other female of the forest tribe
of those half-animals could ever vie
with fair Hylonome. And none but she
possesses Cyllarus: she honeys him;
she loves him and again, again, admits
her love, and takes fine care of her fine limbs—
within the limits that such limbs permit:
now she would smooth her long locks with a comb
now deck her hair with wreaths of rosemary,
or violets or roses; and at times
she wears white lilies; twice each day she bathes
her face within the brook that rushes down
the wooded mountainside of Pagasa;
and twice she dips her body in that stream.
She only drapes her shoulder and left side
with seemly dress, the finest wild beasts' hides.
And each requites the other's love in full:
they roam the slopes as one; as one they rest
in tranquil grottoes. And it was as one
that they had come to join the Lapith feast,
and side by side they fought. O Cyllarus,
we do not know who threw the shaft that struck
your left side, piercing you a bit below
the spot that joined your neck and chest. Your heart
was barely grazed; and yet, when they plucked out
the lance, your heart and all your body froze.
Hylonome rushed up; she helped support
his dying limbs; her hand caressed
his wound; she tried to hold back his last breath

by pressing lips on lips. And when his death
was clear to see, she murmured words too faint
for me to hear in that uproar—and then
she cast herself upon the very shaft
that had pierced him; and as she died, she clasped
her husband in a close embrace.

                       "My eyes
still see with clarity Phaeocomes,
who bore six lion-hides that he had tied
together, knotting them: enough to shield
his human and his equine halves. He threw
a log four oxen would have strained to move;
and from above, it struck and smashed the skull
of Tectaphos, the son of Olenus.

"The Lapith's dome was shattered; through his mouth
and eyes and ears and hollow nostrils oozed
his soft brains, just as curdled milk strains through
those withes of oak that countrymen will use
when making cheese—or just as soggy must
will drip when pressed down, thick, through a clogged sieve.
But when Phaeocomes stooped down to strip
the Lapith's arms (your father witnessed this),
it's my sword-thrust that pierced the centaur's guts.
And Chthonius and Teleboas, too,
fell by my blade: while one bore a forked bough,
the other bore a lance—and with that shaft
he wounded me—a scar you still can see,
however old that wound may be. Ah, yes,
they should have sent me out to Pergamum
to conquer it. For then I had the strength;
my arms could then have checked—if not surpassed—
the arms of Hector. But in those days, he
was not yet born or still in infancy:
and now it is old age that weakens me. □ □ □

Latin [425–48]

"And shall I tell you just how Periphas
struck down Pyraethus? Or how Ampyx' shaft,
although without a tip, when cast straight at
the galloping Echeclus, smashed his face?
How Macareus of Peletronia

struck Erigdupus' chest and laid him low?
And I remember how a hunting spear
that Nessus' hand had hurled was buried in
Cymelus' groin. And do not think that Mopsus,
the son of Ampycus, was only there
to serve as seer, pronouncing prophecies;
for Morphus' lance laid low biform Hodites;
and when that dying centaur tried to speak,
he found his tongue was pinned just to his chin,
just as—fast to his throat—his chin was pinned.

"By then, five centaurs had already met
their death at Caenus' hands: Antimachus
and Bromus, Elymus, and Styphelus,
and one who bore a battle-ax, Pyraemos
(though I am clear as to their names and number,
I can't recall how Caenus killed each centaur).
Now Latreus, massive in his bulk and stature,
rushed from the centaurs' ranks to challenge Caenus:
he bore the arms of one whom he had felled
and then despoiled, Emathian Halesus.
He was not young, he was not old—the age
of Latreus stood midway. Though hair was gray
upon his temples, he could still display
a young man's energy. A sight to see
and fear—he bore a shield, he bore a sword,
and also bore a Macedonian lance.
Between the Lapiths' and the centaurs' ranks,
he clashed his arms, he faced each host in turn;
while wheeling, galloping, he poured these words
upon the empty air—his boasts, his scorn:
'Must I, o Caenis, suffer one like you!
For me, you'll always be a woman, you

are nothing more than Caenis. Yes, you seem
to have forgotten that your origins
were feminine; you don't remember what
you had to do to merit this reward,
the price you paid to earn yourself this false
appearance of a man! Remember then
just what you were at birth, what you went through:
now go, take up the distaff—that's your due:
take up the basket heaped with threads, the wool
your thumb can twist: let men attend to war!'
But when he heard such boasting, Caenus cast
a lance that pierced the side of Latreus as
the centaur's flanks, in his great gallop, stretched;
and just where horse joins man, the lance head smashed.
Enraged by pain, the centaur then struck back;
his shaft caught Caenus in his naked face;
the lance recoiled, even as hailstones do
when they have struck a roof, or as a pebble
rebounds when flung against a hollow drum.
Then Latreus closes in; he tries to thrust
his sword into the hardened sides of Caenus;
but there's no point where he can pierce the Lapith.
'But you can't flee from me,' the centaur cries;
'my point is blunted, but my blade can slice
edgewise.' His long right arm then angled so
his stroke that he could hack with one great blow
across the girth of Caenus. When it hit
the Lapith's flesh, the sword blade clanged as if
it had struck marble, breaking into bits
against the toughened skin. When Caenus felt
that he had let them marvel long enough
as he stood there unharmed, he cried: 'And now
it's time to try my blade upon your body!'
He drove his deadly blade up to the hilt
in Latreus' equine chest; again, again
he turned the buried blade within the guts
of Latreus—and in wounds, inflicted wounds.

□   □   □

Latin [471–93]

"And now these biform centaurs, clamoring
and frenzied, charge at Caenus: it is he
whom all—as one—assail with sword and lance.
But when their shafts have struck, their shafts fall back;
despite their blows the Lapith stands intact,

unpierced—not one drop of his blood is shed.
A sight so strange astonishes them all.

But then the centaur Monycus outcried:
'How shameful is this sight! We, a great tribe,
are challenged by a single man—indeed
by one who is but barely man. And yet,
it's he who is a man in truth, while we
who shirk and cringe are nothing more than he
once was. What use are our tremendous limbs,
our doubled powers, and the gifts received
from nature, which combines in us two beings
who are the mightiest of living things.
I scarcely think we are a goddess' sons
or fathered by Ixion—he was one
who dared to hope that he would win great Juno,
while we have let a half-man do us in.
Come, let's heap trunks and rocks and blanket him
with mountain masses—simply smother his
tenacious soul beneath an avalanche
of forest. Let us suffocate his throat:
don't pierce him, just use weight—and crush and choke.'
That said, he chanced to find a toppled tree-trunk,
a trunk the wild south-wind had overthrown.
This, Monycus heaved straight at sturdy Caenus.
The rest were quick to do what he had done:
and soon Mount Othrys had been stripped of trees—
and there was no shade left on Pelion.

"Now buried underneath that mass of trees
their giant weight upon him, Caenus heaves
and writhes; he tries to lift that ton of rocks
upon his sturdy shoulders; but the heap
grows heavier upon his head and face;

Latin [494–517]

it's hard to breathe; he's left with little space;
beginning to give way, he can't stand straight;
he tries in vain to reach the air, to free
his body of those forests: one could see
from time to time some movement underneath
that heap—as if Mount Ida (as I speak,
you see it just beyond us) were to shake
with an earthquake. We do not know just how
he died. Some said his body was thrust down
by all that forest force to Tartarus'
deep hole. But Mopsus, son of Ampycus,
contested this: he said that he had seen,
emerging from the muddle of that heap
into the sky, a bird with golden wings
(a bird that I, too, saw—just once and then
never again). And Mopsus, sighting it—
a bird that, in slow flight, was hovering
above the Lapith ranks, with its loud wings—
with both his eyes and heart still following
its flight, cried out: 'O Caenus, it is you
I hail, the glory of the Lapith people:
you were a mighty warrior, and now
you are a bird that has no similar.'
Since Mopsus had profound authority,
his story was believed. The grief increased
our fury; we could not forget that scene—
one man against so many enemies.
Nor did we set aside our swords until—
to ease our sorrow—we, in truth, had killed
half of our centaur foes; the rest took flight,
escaping under cover of dark night."

Such was the tale that Nestor told; the war
between the Lapiths and half-human centaurs.
Tlepolemus, however, could not curb
his sorrow at the lack of any word

from Nestor on the feats of Hercules
in that great battle; so he said: "My lord,
I am amazed that you did not record
the deeds my father, Hercules, performed.
He often used to tell me of the sons
of Cloud—the centaurs he had overcome."
At this, the lord of Pylos said in sadness:
"Why must I bring old sufferings to mind?
Why must I open bitter wounds that time
had hidden, if not healed? I now confess
my hatred of your father, my deep sense
of harm and hurt he caused me. By the gods,
his deeds were glorious, beyond belief!
I would prefer to cancel—if I could—
the merits and just praise that he received,
the fame the world proclaimed (I can't deny
the truth). But we don't praise Deiphobus
or Polydamas; nor do we extol
even great Hector—who would praise a foe?
Your father was the culprit who laid low
Messene's walls; he savaged my own home
with fire and sword, while devastating both
Elis and Pylos—cities without blame.
And not to speak of others whom he slew,
we sons of Neleus numbered twelve—fine youths:
and all of us were felled by him except
for one—myself. Though all the other deaths
may have to be borne patiently, there's one
whose death still stirs astonishment—for he
was Periclymenus. The line of Neleus
begins with Neptune, and this gift he gave
to Periclymenus: the power to take,
and then to shed, at will, whatever shape
he pleased. When faced with Hercules' assault,
my brother took, in turn, so many forms:
but all those forms were vain until he changed
into the bird the king of gods loves most,
the bird that, in its claws, grips thunderbolts.

Latin [538–61]

And, with the force that only eagles own,
my brother, with his wings and curving beak
and hooked claws, ripped the face of Hercules.
But then your father aimed his bow—far too
precise—against that bird; and as it flew
to height on height, then hovered in the sky,
the arrow struck the join of wing and side.
The wound was not that deep, and yet it sliced
the sinews—they cannot respond—all flight
and movement are denied. With weakened wings
he cannot ride the air; he falls to earth;
his body presses now against the shaft
that pierced—and still hangs—from the wing. At that,
the arrow is pushed through his upper breast,
then juts out near his throat, upon the left.
Now—splendid leader of the fleet of Rhodes—
do you in truth think that I must extol
your Hercules? The vengeance that I seek
for my dear brothers stops at this: my speech,
in telling of the Lapiths' victory,
omitted the great deeds of Hercules.
This does not break the bond of amity,
Tleptolemus, between yourself and me."

Such were the graceful words of Neleus' son.
And when the old man's speech was done, the Greeks
all shared in Bacchus' precious gift once more,
then rose up from their couches. Any hours
of night that still were left belonged to sleep.

But he who rules the waters of the sea,
the trident-bearing Neptune, still feels grief—
a father's sorrow for his son, transformed
into a swan, the bird so dear to Phaethon:
he can't forget his Cycnus; he detests
the cruel Achilles; nothing curbs his wrath;

his rage is past all measure. And the war
has lasted almost ten long years by now;
and he turns to the unshorn god, Apollo:

"Of all my brother's sons, you are—by far—
the one whom I love most; you labored hard
beside me as we built (although in vain)
the walls of Troy. And now that they will fall
so soon, so doomed, don't you lament? Are you
not grieved when you recall the fighting men
who fell, defending the great battlements?
I will not name them all—but can't you see
the shade of Hector, even as they drag
his corpse around his Pergamum? Meanwhile,
the terrible Achilles, more bloodthirsty
than war itself, the one who wrecked our work,
still lives! If he would only come before me,
in reach of my own trident, by the sea,
I'd have him feel what three prongs can inflict.
But since I'm not permitted to confront
Achilles face to face, won't you instead
have him meet death by covert means—a shaft
he cannot see?"

                    The Delian agrees;
just as his uncle—and his own self—wish,
wrapped in a cloud, Apollo then is quick
to reach the Trojan ranks. There he can see,
amid that slaughter, Paris aiming shafts
from time to time against a crowd of Greeks.
Revealing his identity, Apollo
asks: "Why waste arrows killing common folk?
If you are so devoted to your Trojans,
then aim your shafts at Peleus' son: avenge
your slaughtered brothers." So Apollo said,
and then he pointed out just where Achilles
was felling many Trojans with his lance;
the god turned Paris' bow in that direction;

Latin [583–605]

and when the shaft was shot, Apollo guided
the well-aimed arrow with his deadly hand.

Since Hector's death, just this had brought the gift
of joy to the old Priam—only this.
Achilles, victor over mighty men,
now you have fallen at a coward's hands—
a ravisher who snatched a Grecian wife.
But if a woman was to take your life,
it is an Amazon you would have liked
to fell you with her double ax beside
Thermodon's banks.

             The man who terrified
the Phrygians, Aeacus' far-famed grandson,
the unsurpassable chieftain, who adorned
and shielded the Pelasgians' name, is burned.
And Vulcan, who had made Achilles' arms,
is that same god whose flames consume him now.
He is but ashes; all that's left of great
Achilles hardly fills a little urn.
Only the world can be commensurate
with such a warrior: in such a space
the son of Peleus is his own true self—
and not confined to hollow Tartarus.

Reminding us of just how great he was,
even his shield spurs warriors to war.
The Greeks contend: each hero takes up arms,
that he might bear the arms Achilles bore.
But neither Menelaus, lesser son
of Atreus; nor the greater, Agamemnon;
nor Diomedes; not the lesser Ajax,
Oileus' son; nor other mighty chieftains
dare claim the right to bear Achilles' weapons;
just two have claims upon a prize so grand:
only Laertes' son, Ulysses, and
the greater Ajax, son of Telamon.

Latin [606–25]

But to elude a task that none would envy
(reluctant to decide between those two
contenders), Agamemnon summons all
the Argive chieftains; mid–camp, they assemble.
He calls on them to choose—to end the quarrel.

BOOK XIII

RINGED BY THEIR TROOPS—who stood—the chieftains sat.
The one who rose—haranguing them—was Ajax,
the lord who bore the seven-plated shield.
Beside himself with rage—his gaze was grim—
he stared at the Sigean shore, the ships
drawn up along the beach; pointing to these,
he cried: "By Jupiter, you'd have me plead
my cause before the very fleet I saved;
and you would dare compare me with Ulysses!
But he was one who did not hesitate
to beat retreat when he was forced to face
the torches Hector threw, while I withstood
those deadly flames: the fleet was only rescued
because of me. Yes, it is far more safe
to fight with lying words than with one's hands.
But I am not at ease with speech, and he
is not the one for deeds; if one has need
to battle savagely along the field,
I am the man to call, even as he—
if it is talk you want—is quite supreme.
But I don't think that you, my fellow Greeks,
need be reminded now of all my feats—
you've seen them. Rather, let Ulysses speak
of his—for no one's seen what he has done;
the only witness he can call upon
is night. I know I'm striving for a prize
that's great indeed, but it's diminished by
the worth of my opponent. Ajax can
gain little from a prize, however grand,
if it's a thing Ulysses hopes to have.
This contest has already profited
Ulysses; he will lose, but he'll win credit:
men will remember that he faced an Ajax.

"And even if you were to doubt my courage,
it's I who claim the nobler lineage.
I am the son of Telamon, the friend
who helped the sturdy Hercules destroy

Latin [1–23]

the walls of Troy and, then, in Jason's ship,
sailed off and reached the distant coast of Colchis.
And Telamon was born of Aeacus,
who is a judge within the silent world—
precisely in the place where Sisyphus,
the son of Aeolus, must struggle with
the weight of his great stone; and Aeacus
was born of Jove—as Jove himself admits.
But I'd not use the line of my descent
as argument on my behalf, unless
I shared that line with great Achilles: he
was my own cousin; and the arms I seek
are thus a cousin's weapons. Should Ulysses,
who's born—if truth be told—of Sisyphus —
and is like him in tricks and treachery—
attempt to link the line of Aeacus
with someone alien to our family?

"Am I to be denied these arms because
I took up arms before Ulysses did—
for he feigned madness to avoid the war
and did not join until he was unmasked
by Palamedes, who was forced to drag
that coward to the war that he had shirked?
Is he to win the world's best weaponry
because he did not want to take up any?
Am I to be denied my cousin's arms,
deprived of my due honors just because
I was the first to answer war's alarms?

"Would that Ulysses had been truly mad,
or else had never had his trick unmasked,
for then he never would have joined our ranks
beneath the citadel of Troy—this man
who's only bent upon malevolence!
And then, o Philoctetes, you would not
have been abandoned on the isle of Lemnos—
as foul Ulysses urged—an act that shames us;

Latin [23–46]

and there, they say, you hide in forest dens—
even the stones are stirred by your laments.
You curse Laertes' son; you pray that he
indeed will meet the griefs that he deserves,
the lot that, if the gods exist, will be
his sorry destiny. Yes, Philoctetes
is on that isle; the chief who shared our vow
to conquer Troy, he who inherited
the bow of Hercules, is now diseased
and famished; he must count on birds to serve
as food and on their feathers as his clothes;
and he, to hunt them down, must use that bow
of Hercules; on them he spends the shafts
that had been meant to mark the end of Troy!
But Philoctetes is at least alive—
and owes that to his being left behind,
his having no Ulysses at his side.

"And Palamedes, too, if left behind,
would now be better off: he'd be alive
or would, at least, not have been put to death,
charged with a crime that he did not commit.
It was Ulysses who did not forget
that Palamedes had unmasked his madness;
he planted gold in Palamedes' tent,
as proof of the false charge he'd brought against
poor Palamedes; he pretended that
this gold was sent by Priam as a bribe
for the betrayal of the Grecian side.
So has Ulysses, using banishment
or death as means, deprived us of much strength.
This is the way Ulysses fights—and why
he's to be feared.

　　　　　"I add that, even if
his eloquence outdid the faithful Nestor's,
he never could convince me that his failure
to help old Nestor when he was in need,

Latin [47–64]

was anything but sinful. Nestor's horse
was wounded; slowed by that and by the weight
of all his years, Nestor beseeched Ulysses
for help—his friend ran off, deserting him.
And I did not invent this accusation:

ask Diomedes just how many times
he called out to his frightened friend by name,
rebuking him for having run away.
The gods watch over mortals, and their eyes
see justly. He, who had not helped his friend,
was then in need of help himself. Just as
he had abandoned Nestor, so should he
have been deserted then—he was the one
who set the precedent. He called upon
his comrades, and I came; I saw his fear
and saw his trembling; death was much too near,
too terrible for him. And even as
he lay upon the ground, I used the mass
of my great shield to cover him; and thus
(though I deserve scant praise for that) I saved
his quaking soul. If you still want this contest,
Ulysses, let's go back to that same spot:
we'll put the enemy in place again,
your wound, and your accustomed cowardice;
then you can huddle underneath my shield,
a place most safe—and there we can compete!
But just as soon as I had dragged him off,
the man who could not find the force to stand
because his wound was so disabling, ran
away—there was no wound to slow him then!

"And there is Hector. When he strides to war,
the gods are at his side. He terrifies
not only you, Ulysses; even those
who are courageous quail at his approach,
his onrush, and the force of his dread blows.
And while he was exulting in the scores
of Greeks that he had slaughtered, from afar

Latin [65–85]

I flattened him with a tremendous rock;
at that, he challenged anyone to match
his strength, and I alone sustained that test.
And in your hearts you Greeks were praying that
I be the one allotted that fierce task;
your prayers were answered. And if you should ask
how that duel ended, I was not outmatched.
And now the Trojans mount a fierce attack:
with swords and fire and Jove they move against
the Danaan fleet. Where now is mighty-mouthed
Ulysses? It is I whose chest protects
those thousand ships, the hope of your return;
award to me the prize that I deserve.
But—if I now may speak the truth—indeed,
the glory that those weapons would receive
exceeds the glory they would give to me:
their fame is linked to mine; it's they who seek
Ajax—not Ajax who seeks them. What feats
like mine were ever tallied by Ulysses?
His killing Rhesus and unwarlike Dolon;
and taking captive Helenus, the son
of Priam; and his theft of the Palladium—
but not a single one of these was done
by daylight or apart from Diomedes.

"Or, better still, why should he have these arms
at all? For he is one who wins by stealth;
he needs no weapons—he depends on snares
to catch an enemy who's unaware!
The helmet glittering with gold will just
betray his hiding place, his wily work.
And, too, Ulysses' head could not sustain
the helmet of Achilles, that great weight;
Achilles' shaft of wood, from Pelion's slopes,
might be a bit too huge—too ponderous—
for one who is no warrior. The shield,
where the vast world is carved in effigy,
is hardly suited to his timid hand—

Latin [86–111]

a left hand born for trickery and theft.
Why then, Ulysses, overreach—why seek
a prize that's sure to leave you limp and weak?
If, by mistake, the Greeks give you this gift,
the enemy will have good cause to strip
that armor from you—and no cause to fear.
Your sprinting, that one thing in which you beat
all others, since you are so cowardly,
will not be swift—when you are asked to carry
such heavy weapons. And consider this:
your shield, so little used to wars, is quite
intact; but mine—I've parried thrust on thrust—
presents a thousand rips and tears. But why
do we need words at all? Let deeds decide.
Just toss the arms of the great warrior
into the Trojans' midst; then send Ulysses
and me to get them back: who has retrieved
that armor from the enemy should be
the one who keeps those weapons: honor him!"

The son of Telamon was done. And as
he closed his case, a murmur of assent
rose from the Grecian camp. Laertes' son
stood up; he fixed his eyes upon the ground
awhile, but then he looked straight at the chiefs
and broke his silence with the gracious speech,
the eloquence expected of Ulysses:
"If things had gone as you and I had wished,
o Greeks, we would not ask who should succeed
to this extraordinary weaponry;
Achilles, you'd still have your arms, and we
would still have you. But unjust destiny
has taken him from us—from you, from me"
(his hand—here—made as if to wipe away
a tear), "and is there anyone more fit
to take the place of great Achilles than

Latin [111–33]

myself, the one who urged the great Achilles
to take his place once more in the Greek army?
But though he seems to be too slow of wit
(and what he seems, in truth is what he is),
do not let Ajax profit from that fact;
nor should my ready wits, o Grecians, count
against me, for my mind has always served
your cause. As for my eloquence—if some
is mine—what is of help to me today
has often intervened on your behalf;
don't let my quick tongue prompt resentment now—
let each man use the powers that he has.

"For I in truth would hesitate to use
the lineage of a man as proof of worth:
not ancestry—what others may have done—
has weight; it is a man's own works that count.
But since my rival claims to be the great-
grandson of Jove, then I must say my race
also begins with Jove: I'm just as close
to Jove as Ajax is. Laertes is
my father, and Arcesius was his;
and he was born of Jupiter; in this,
my lineage—unlike the line of Ajax—
there's none who was an exiled criminal.
And I can add to my nobility,
for on my mother's side there's Mercury;
a god was founder of my family
upon both sides. But I don't claim the prize—
the armor you'll assign—because of my
maternal ancestry, nor for the fact
that, unlike Telamon, my father was
not stained by his own brother's blood. Just judge
by deeds—and deeds alone: Ajax deserves
no merit for his father's having Peleus
as brother, for this test should not depend
on kinship, on one's lineage; it's only
one's worth that weighs. But if the next of kin

Latin [134–54]

are what you would insist on tallying,
why then there are two heirs: Achilles' father
is Peleus, and Achilles' son is Pyrrhus.
What right can Ajax claim? Send off these arms
to Phthia, Peleus' home, or else to Scyrus,
the home of Pyrrhus. Do you seek a cousin?
Then Teucer is as much Achilles' cousin
as Ajax is. I ask you to consider:
does Teucer claim these arms? And if he did,
would you award them to him? You would not.
Thus, it is clear that naked deeds alone
are to decide this test; and I have done
more than I can retell in this brief talk.
But let me give an orderly account:

"When Thetis, Nereid mother of Achilles,
foresaw her dear son's doom, she tricked you all;
she dressed him in the clothes of a young girl,
and Ajax, like the rest of you, was fooled.
But I slipped in—among the women's stuff
that lay about—some weapons, of the sort
to draw a man's attention. While still dressed
as girl, the hero gripped a shield and lance;
I said: 'O son of Thetis, Troy must face
her fate, her fall: it's you whom she awaits.
Why, then, delay the day when she must die?'
I placed my hands upon him, and I sent
the hero off to his heroic tasks.
So all Achilles did, you owe to me;
in truth, his deeds are mine: it is my lance
that wounded warring Telephus and then
healed him, the humbled, beaten suppliant.
The fall of Thebes is my accomplishment,
and Lesbos' fall; and Tenedos and Chryse
and Cilla—cities of Apollo—fell
because of me; to these you can add Scyrus.
Lyrnessus' walls were toppled; you might well
say that my right hand was responsible.

Latin [154–76]

And not to mention other battered walls,
it's I who gave to you the man who felled
fierce Hector: famous Hector is laid low—
and I brought that about. If I ask now
to have Achilles' arms, it's in return
for those with which I had detected him.
I gave Achilles weapons while he lived;
and now that he is dead, I ask them back.

"And when the damage done to one of us
touched every Danaan's pride, and in the port
of Aulis, on behalf of Menelaus,
a thousand ships had crowded, and we waited
so long for winds to favor us, no hint
of breeze appeared except for inshore winds.
Then Agamemnon was commanded by
the cruel oracle to sacrifice
his guiltless daughter to the fierce Diana.
But he refused to do so, clamoring
against the very gods: he is a king,
but Agamemnon has a father's feelings.
And it was I who, with my deft words, turned
his warm paternal heart to public cares.
Now I admit (and as I do so, ask
the son of Atreus to pardon this):
I had to plead a cause most difficult—
and not before the most impartial judge.
But he, at last, allowed himself to be
convinced; his people's good, his brother's needs,
and, too, the scepter we had given him—
complete command of all our men and fleet—
all these swayed Agamemnon. For our praise,
he was to pay with blood. Then I was sent
as emissary to the mother: she
was not to be persuaded; her assent
I had to win by craft. Imagine Ajax
on such a mission! We would still be stalled
at Aulis, waiting for the wind—becalmed!   □   □   □

Latin [177–95]

"And I was also sent—a daring mission—
as an ambassador to Ilium;
and I saw towering Troy's great council-hall.
It still was full of mighty warriors.
There—without fear—I carried out the task
entrusted to me; for the common cause
of all the Greeks, I pleaded: charging Paris,
I asked for the return of Helen and
of all the booty; I persuaded Priam—
and, too, Antenor, who agreed with him;
but Paris and his brothers and, with them,
all who had taken part in that great theft
were hard indeed to keep at peace, in check.
You, Menelaus, know how dangerous
that situation was, for you were there;
that was the first of many risks we've shared.

"This war is never-ending, so long-drawn:
to retell all my mind and strength have done
would run past measure. After we had clashed
in those first days, the Trojan ranks drew back:
for years on end they stayed within their walls;
we could not meet them in the open field.
And we have only faced them openly
in this, the tenth year. And in that long span,
Ajax, what have you done? You only can
wage war with weapons; how did you serve then?
Whereas for me, those waiting years were spent
in setting traps for Trojans, strengthening
the trenches, and encouraging our friends,
that they might face serenely the long tedium
as we besieged the walls of Ilium.
I showed how food could be supplied—and stores
of weapons; I was an ambassador
when that was called for.

                    "Now King Agamemnon,
beguiled by a deceitful dream, is sure

that Jove has ordered him to end the war;
so he declares that we must fight no more.
And he can easily defend his plan
by citing Jove: it is the god's command.
But Ajax certainly should not permit
such a retreat; it's he who should insist
on Troy's destruction; after all, he is
a fighter—and the time to fight has come.
And when he sees them start to sail back home,
why doesn't Ajax check them, take up arms,
and show the straggling mob what's to be done?
You cannot say this was too much to ask
of one who boasted so, who loved to brag?
Instead, what does he do? He, too, runs off.
I saw you, Ajax, when you turned your back;
I saw you—and I was ashamed. You rush
to spread your faithless sails, as I cry out:
'What are you doing? Have your minds gone wild,
my friends? You're leaving Troy when it's about
to fall? If you sail off at this late date,
what do you carry home, except disgrace?'
With these and other arguments (my rage,
my grief had made my tongue more fluent), I
call back from shore and ships the men in flight.
And Agamemnon summons our allies—
they all are still dismayed, still gripped by fright;
but even then, the son of Telamon
won't dare to say one word—his mouth stays shut—
but not Thersites, for he dares insult
the king, although—as always—it is I
who make him pay for that. Then I stand up
and urge our trembling troops to charge, to rush
against the enemy; and with my words
I reinstill the courage we had lost.
Since then, whatever bravery may seem
to be his work, indeed belongs to me—
it's I who dragged back Ajax from retreat.

□ □ □

Latin [217–37]

"And, in the end, can you name any Danaan
who praises you or wants you as his friend?
Whereas the son of Tydeus shares his plans
with me; he prizes me; he always trusts
Ulysses as a comrade: that means much—
among the many thousands who have come
from all of Greece, to be the very one
whom Diomedes chose. And even when
I was not picked by lots, I went with him;
and scorning every peril of the night
and of the enemy, I slaughtered Dolon—
who would have ambushed us, had we not caught
that Phrygian just in time. I killed him, but
before I did, I forced him to reveal
the Trojans' schemes, their treachery and guile.
By now I had learned all; I could have stopped
our spying mission on the spot—gone back
with honor to our ranks; but not content
with this, I headed for King Rhesus' tents—
I killed him and his men in their own camp.
And so, a victor, with my wish fulfilled,
I rode back in a captured chariot—
as one would do in a triumphal march—
rejoicing. If you now deny to me
the armor of Achilles (he whose steeds
Dolon had wanted as his promised prize
when he went out to spy on us by night),
then you would be less generous with me
than Ajax was when he said Diomedes
and I might share the weapons of Achilles!
And is there any need to add more feats:
must I remind you of Sarpedon's ranks,
the Lycians devastated by my blade?
For I laid low—within a lake of blood—
first Coeranos, the son of Iphitus,
and then Alastor, Chromius, Alcander,
Noemon, Halius, and Prytanis;
and I sent Thoon to his death along

Latin [238–59]

with Charops and Chersidamas and one
whom cruel fate had placed beneath my sword,
and that was Ennomos; and others fell—
less famous Lycians—there, beneath the walls
of Troy: and it was I who killed them all.
And now, my fellow Greeks, I bear these wounds
so nobly placed" (and here he bared his chest).
"Words can deceive—but here is truth indeed.
Look now! This is the chest that always fought
on your behalf! This, Ajax cannot match:
the son of Telamon has never shed—
in all these years—a single drop of blood
to help your cause; his flesh has not been touched
by any wound.

    "And what if he stood up—
just as he says—to fight for the Greek fleet
against the Trojans and the might of Jove?
He did indeed defend the fleet (and I
would not disdain the good a man has done);
but Ajax should not claim that he alone
deserves the honor others, too, have earned.
For when the Trojans were about to burn
the ships and their defender, he who thrust
the Trojans from the beaches was Patroclus
(he came dressed in Achilles' guise, and thus
he drove the Trojans back with much assurance).
And Ajax also claims that he alone
was bold enough to challenge Hector's lance;
but he forgets the king and other chiefs
and me—with all of us prepared to meet
the Trojan; if among us all, just Ajax
was picked, it's chance—the lots—he has to thank.
But how, brave Ajax, did that duel end?
For Hector left the field untouched, intact.

"What misery is mine when I recall
the day on which the shield, the very wall

and bulwark of the Greeks, Achilles, fell!
My tears, my grief, my fears did not prevent
my lifting up his body from the ground
and bearing back the hero to our camp.
I carried him upon these shoulders—yes,

these shoulders bore the great Achilles' body
and all his arms and armor—weaponry

that I now hope so fervently to carry:
I have the strength to bear that massive weight,
and I have soul enough to know how great
an honor you would then bestow on me.
Consider, if you will, Achilles' mother:
would she, the blue-green goddess of the sea,
who did so much for her dear son, aspire
to have his arms, a gift the gods have given,
a precious work of art, be worn by one
who was so rough and crude, a callous soldier?
I'm sure that Ajax never will make out
the shapes enchased by Vulcan on that shield:
the ocean, and dry land, the starry skies,
the Pleiades, the Hyades, the Bear
that never sinks into the sea; the pair
of cities, one at peace and one at war;
and, too, Orion with his gleaming sword.
He asks for arms he'll never understand.

"And what is there to say about his charge
that I evaded war and all its hard
ordeals, and did not join you at the start,
but waited? Can't he see that, charging me,
he also has to charge the great Achilles?
If it's a crime to masquerade, then I
am criminal—and so is the disguise
Achilles wore. And if delay is sinful,
I joined you well before Achilles did.
It was a loving wife who held me back;
a loving mother held Achilles back.
At first, we answered to the wants of women;

Latin [281–302]

but later we gave war our full devotion.
But if by chance I can't refute this charge,
it does not frighten me—an accusation
that I and the great hero have in common.
In any case it was Ulysses' wits
that led to the unmasking of Achilles;
but Ajax' wits did not unmask Ulysses.

"Thus, there's no need to wonder if the crude
tongue of an Ajax pours out raw abuse
against Ulysses; he insults you, too,
most shamefully. For if I am accused
of infamy for charging Palamedes—
a charge that Ajax says was false—then you,
convicting him, are hardly guiltless, too.
But, for my charges, I produced clear proof—
so clear that he could not defend himself;
and you did not depend on word of mouth—
you saw the evidence with your own eyes:
you saw his treachery—the gold, the bribe.

"And as for Philoctetes' being now
on Lemnos, Vulcan's isle, I'm not at all
responsible. It's you who must defend
that fact—you kept him there, gave your consent.
But I shall not deny that I advised
the son of Poeas to withdraw from war
and all its trials—I told him not to sail
to Troy; I thought that he should rest, to ease
his horrid suffering from the serpent's bites.
He heeded what I said, and he's alive.
I offered him that counsel in good faith;
and it brought, too, the best of cures—although,
in any case, good faith clears me of blame.
But if the augurs say that, for the fall
of Troy, we absolutely have to call
for Philoctetes, don't send me at all.
Send Ajax on that mission to the shores

Latin [302–21]

of Lemnos: he's the right ambassador.
His eloquence will surely soften up
the hero, driven mad by pain and rage;
or else, if Ajax' words cannot persuade
the madman, Ajax is astute enough
to find some other way to bear him off
from Lemnos—and to bring him back to us.
But then again, if I should fail to show
concern for you, the Simois will flow
backward, and Ida's slopes will lose their growth
of foliage, and Greeks will offer aid
to Troy before the feeble mind of Ajax
will ever bring your Philoctetes back.
Yes, you detest my friends, my kings—indeed,
all Greeks; yes, you hate me, harsh Philoctetes,
and heap your countless curses on my head,
and long to clutch me in your suffering hands,
that you might drink my blood; you pray that just
as you were in my clutches, I may be
in yours: and yet, no matter what you do,
I'll seek you out and try to bring you back.
And I shall gain possession of your shafts
(if Fortune favors me), just as I got
possession of the Trojan augur when
I took him captive, making him reveal
the secrets of the god's own oracles,
the destiny of Troy they had foretold;
just as I stole the statue of Minerva
from the Palladium, her Phrygian shrine,
with Trojan enemies on every side.
And how can Ajax claim to be my match?
Without that statue—so the fates declared—
Troy never could be ours. And where is Ajax?
Where now are that great warrior's loud boasts?
Ajax, why are you terror-stricken here?
Why is it that Ulysses now can dare
to pass the watchmen and to put his trust
in night, and then, among the hostile swords,

Latin [321–43]

to penetrate not just Troy's walls but—more—
the very summit of the citadel,
to steal the goddess' image from her shrine
and, after threading through the Trojan lines,
to bear that statue back to his own camp?
If I had failed or faltered on that mission,
the son of Telamon might well have worn
in vain his seven-layered bull's-hide shield
on his left arm. That was the night I won
the very statue that had kept Troy safe:
my theft made possible her fall, her end.

"And stop your frowning and your murmurs, Ajax—
stop trying to remind us that my deeds
were not my own but done with Diomedes.
Of course he shares some credit. But you, too,
were not alone when you held up your shield
to save the allied fleet. You had a crowd
of Greeks beside you; I had only one.
If Diomedes did not know that fighters
must yield before a reasoner, that here
it is the shrewdest, not the strongest man—
however overpowering his right hand—
who is to win the prize, then he'd have sought
these arms himself; so would the other Ajax,
more modest than you are; so would robust
Eurypylus and famed Andraemon's son;
so would Idomeneus and one who comes,
like him, from Crete, Meriones; to these
add Menelaus. All these men are just
as strong as you—and on the field, their worth
is not less than your own—and yet they chose
to yield before my ingenuity.
In battle, your right hand serves well indeed;
but when it comes to thought, your head has need
of me as guide. You have brute force, while I
must weigh, foresee, and plan; yes, you can fight,
but when we must decide on the right time

Latin [343–64]

to take the field, it's always my advice
that Agamemnon seeks. While your worth lies
in nothing but your bulk, mine lies in mind.
As much as any ship's commander stands
above the oarsman, as the general
ranks higher than the simple fighting man,
so, Ajax, am I your superior.
In me, the head indeed outweighs the hand;
all of my power lies in intellect.

"And now, o Grecian chiefs, assign this prize
to one who has stood watch, who served your cause
so faithfully, so anxiously, so long;
grant me this honor as my due reward.
Our work is almost done; I have removed
the obstacles that fate placed on your path;
I've made it possible to take tall Troy,
and one can say that I have taken her.
Now, by the hopes we share, and by the walls
of Troy—walls fated soon to fall—and by
the gods, of which I stripped the Trojan side
so recently, and by the little left—
however slight—for shrewdness to effect,
if something calls for my audacity
and willingness, if you should ever think
that there is need to foil some final chance
that fate, however late, reserved for Troy,
remember me! Or if you don't award
these arms to me, give them to her!" And here
he pointed to Minerva's fateful statue.

The chiefs were moved indeed—the proof of that
lay in the victory of eloquence:
the mighty hero's arms and armor went
to the most fluent, most incisive man.

□   □   □

Latin [365–83]

Then he who had so often met and matched
great Hector, and had stood his ground against
both sword and fire and Jove's own power—Ajax,
the undefeated one, contends with that

alone which can defeat him: his own wrath.
His sword unsheathed, he cries: "At least this blade

is mine! Or will Ulysses now lay claim
to this, too? I must use it to undo
myself: so often drenched with Trojan gore,
this shaft must shed the blood of its own lord.
Let it be shown that only one alone,
Ajax, can conquer Ajax!" Then he drove
the fatal blade into his flesh (the first
and only wound that ever pierced his chest):
he struck the softest spot, to penetrate
most deeply. None could tug that weapon free.
Only his blood—at last—flushed out the sword:
the blood that soaked the verdant soil from which
a purple flower sprang, the very same
that had—long since—sprung up when Hyacinth
was wounded. On the petals one can read
these letters, "AI-AI," asking us to think
of Ajax' name and Hyacinth's lament.

Victorious Ulysses then set sail
for Lemnos, homeland of Hypsipyle
and her famed father, Thoas (it was she
who saved him when—an ancient infamy—
the wives of Lemnos massacred their husbands).
Ulysses, landing on that isle, retrieved
the arms—that is, the arrows—Hercules
had, at his death, bequeathed to Philoctetes.
And when the Ithacan brought back those shafts
and Philoctetes' self, the Greeks at last

could win the war they'd waged for ten long years.
Troy fell. And Priam fell. Miserable,
the wife of Priam, after losing all,
was fated, too, to lose her human form;
as hound, her horrid howling was to haunt

the foreign skies above the Hellespont,
where it grows narrow.

                        Ilium still blazed;
the flames were not yet spent; Jove's altar drank
old Priam's blood, a trickle—thin and scant.
Dragged by her hair, Apollo's priestess prayed
with arms outstretched to heaven—but in vain:
she's hauled away. And in the burning shrines,
besieged, the Trojan women—this last time—
embraced the statues of their homeland's gods,
until the victors dragged those women off—
rich plunder and the source of later quarrels.
And then the Greeks hurled down Astyanax
from that same tower where he'd often sat
and watched the bitter clash below: his mother
would single out his father as he fought
in fierce defense of his own honor and
the kingdom of his ancestors, their land.

Now Boreas blows fair: in the brisk breeze,
the broad sails flap; their seamen urge the Greeks
to profit from the wind; it's time to leave.
"Farewell, dear Troy," the Trojan women cry;
"they're bearing us away!" They kiss the soil;
their native land, their burning houses lie
behind them. And the last to come aboard
was Hecuba (a sorry sight): they'd found her
among her dear sons' sepulchers—she gripped
their tombs and kissed their bones. It was Ulysses
who dragged her off. And all that she could rescue
were Hector's ashes; that handful of dust
she carried in her bosom. On his tomb

Latin [403–27]

she left a clutch of white hair, ragged tress
plucked from her head—frail offering to the dead:
a few hairs and her tears.

That part of Thrace
which faced the Phrygian Troy across the straits
was populated by the Bistones.
There, Polymestor's splendid palace rose.
And to that king, young Polydorus, you
were sent in secret by your father, Priam—
to keep you far from Phrygia's raging war.
That would have been a sound idea—if
he'd not provided you with treasure—rich,
inviting booty for a greedy soul,
prize for a criminal. And when the fall
of Troy was imminent, the Thracian king
betrayed his trust, unsheathed his sword, and slit
the throat of his young charge; then, from a cliff,
into the sea he cast the lifeless body—
as if to hide the corpse could hide the sin.

The fleet of Agamemnon moored along
that Thracian coast: the wind had grown too strong—
and so he waited for the seas to calm.
There, from a giant fissure in the earth,
a sudden apparition burst: Achilles,
as awesome as he was in life. His stance
was threatening, his gaze as grim as when
he had unjustly menaced Agamemnon
with his drawn sword. He said: "O you, Achaeans,
would you sail off without remembering me?
Does all the gratitude I've earned deserve
to be interred with me? Take care! Don't leave
my tomb unhonored: if you would appease

Latin [427–48]

Achilles' Shade, Polyxena must be
the sacrifice you bring!" The ruthless Shade
had spoken, and his comrades soon obeyed.
Wrenched from her mother's arms (Polyxena
was the sole comfort left to Hecuba),
that fearless virgin, with a strength beyond
a woman's, was led out—assigned by fate,
a victim—to Achilles' tomb: they placed
the brave girl at the cruel altar's side.
She understood that this ferocious rite
was being readied now to end her life;
when she saw Neoptolemus nearby
with sword in hand, she stared hard at his eyes:
"My noble blood is yours to use!" she cried;
"I'm ready; pierce my throat or pierce my chest!"
(and these she bared). "How could you think that I,
Polyxena, would ever want to live
as someone's slave? And will you pacify
some deity with such a sacrifice?
Oh, would my mother might be spared this sight!
That is my only wish. It is for her
I worry; it is she who lessens, thwarts
my joy in death—though it is not my death
but her own life that she should now lament.
May you, I pray, stand back, that I may go
as a free spirit to the Shades below—
if what I ask is just—and do not touch
my virgin body with your rough male hands.
Whoever he may be, the one you seek
to please by sacrificing me will take
more pleasure in the blood of a free woman.
And if the final words that leave my lips
move any of you (it is Priam's daughter—
and not a prisoner—who asks you this),
give my cadaver back to my dear mother,
and ask no ransom of her. Let her tears—
not gold—pay for the right of sepulture.
For that sad right she did pay once before

with gold, too—at a time when she still could."

Such were her words. The crowd could not hold back
the tears that she herself kept well in check.
The priest—he, too, was weeping—plunged his blade,
against his will, into her proffered breast.
On weakened knees she sank down to the ground;
but to the end her spirit never failed.
And as she fell, the girl took care to veil
her body—to preserve her modesty.

The Trojan women lifted up her corpse.
They counted Priam's children—one by one,
each daughter and each son whom they had mourned:
the blood one family had shed. They moaned
for you, o virgin, and, o Hecuba,
for you: till now you were a monarch's wife,
mother of princes, emblem of the pride
of Asia—men described you in that way;
but now your fate is—even for a slave,
a captive—singularly harsh: by lot
victorious Ulysses won you, but
you are a prize he does not truly want—
he'll only take you as a prize because
you gave birth to great Hector. And how hard
it was—even for Hector—to obtain
a master for his mother! Hecuba
holds fast the body of her dauntless daughter
and sheds the tears she'd often shed before
for her beloved land, her sons, her Priam.
Into her daughter's wound she pours her tears;
her kisses cover the cadaver's mouth;
as she has done so many times, she beats—
she tears—her breast. Then, even as she sweeps
her white hairs in her daughter's clotted blood,
she says so much—of which these words were part:
□   □   □

Latin [474–93]

"My child, your mother's final grief—what else
is left for me to mourn? My child, you die:
I see your wound, my wound—another sign
that none among my children ever met
a death that was not cruel, violent.
Yet I thought you, as woman, would be safe
from steel; but now it is a fatal blade
that strikes you, woman. After having slain
so many of your brothers, he—still he—
has killed you, too. It still is he, Achilles,
who ruined Troy and felled our family!
Yes, when he died beneath the shaft of Paris
and Phoebus, I had said: 'Oh, now at least,
there's no more need to fear Achilles!'—yet
that fear should never have been put to rest.
Even his buried ashes—from the grave—
do not abate his savagery: he hates
our race. My womb has served to bring him fruit.
Great Ilium lies low; the people's sorrow
has ended in disaster—but it's done.
Only for me does Pergama live on:
my grief is still not finished. I who once
was mistress of the world, one who could vaunt
so many children and their wives and husbands,
am now dragged into exile, stripped of all
my wealth, torn from the tombs of those I love.
Penelope will have me as her prize,
as her display; and even as I slave
at spinning wool, she'll cry to all the wives
of Ithaca: 'Here's Hector's famous mother,
the wife of Priam!' After I have lost
so many, you, the only solace left
to ease my grief, have now been sacrificed
upon the tomb of our fierce enemy!
I gave birth to a funeral offering
to our destroyer. I must have a heart
of iron if I still resist, still live.
What am I waiting for? Endless old age—

Latin [494–517]

what can it hold in store? O cruel gods,
why do you let me live—unless it be
that you have saved still other griefs for me?
Who would have thought that, after Pergama
had fallen, Priam ever could be called
a happy man? But now he has been blessed
with death: dear daughter, now he does not see
your murder—in one instant he lost both
his kingdom and his life. Oh, some might say
that you, a princess, will be laid to rest
within the tomb of your forefathers. Yet
our family is not that fortunate!
The only honors you'll receive are these:
a mother's tears—a clutch of foreign dust.
We have lost all. One thing alone is left—
one reason to endure: my dearest boy,
the youngest of my sons, my Polydorus,
whom we entrusted to a Thracian king
whose land lies on these shores. But why am I
so slow to bathe your fierce wound with pure water,
your face so mercilessly splashed with blood?"

With faltering footsteps, even as she tore
her white hair, Hecuba moved toward the shore.
"My Trojan women, let me have an urn,"
the wretched woman said, wanting to draw
clean water from the sea. But then she saw
the corpse of Polydorus on the shore;
the waves had cast it up—a corpse that bore
such savage wounds, the work of Thracian spears.
The Trojan women wail, but any tears
and words of Hecuba are checked by grief:
she cannot speak. As mute as stone, as stiff,
she's stunned; she stares at what lies at her feet,
and now lifts up her grim gaze heavenward,
and now stares at his face, now at the wounds

Latin [518–43]

of her dead son as he lies there, outstretched.
But it's the wounds on which she's most intent;
it's these that fuel her anger, arm her wrath.
And once she is inflamed, she plots revenge
as if she still were queen: she images
harsh punishment. Just as a lioness,
stripped of a suckling cub, fanatically
will track her stealthy enemy, just so,
forgetful of her years but not her grandeur,
fierce Hecuba goes straight to Polymestor,
the author of that execrable murder.
She seeks a private colloquy with him:
she says that she has brought another treasure,
a hidden hoard of gold that she would like
the Thracian to consign to her dear son.
The king is caught; his customary greed
is stirred; and at a secret place, they meet—
and here he urges her with lying words:
"Come, Hecuba, be quick! Give me that hoard
you want your son to have. By all the gods,
I swear that anything you give to me,
your son will get, just as he has received
the gold you gave to me before." His speech,
his promises are false: ferociously,
she stares at him; the anger in her seethes.
Then—suddenly—she grips him; and she calls
upon the other Trojan women—all
her fellow captives—as she digs her nails
into his lying eyes; and she rips out
his eyeballs from their sockets (it is rage
that gives her strength). And then into the place
that once contained his eyes, she drives her hands,
soaked with his guilty blood: she plucks his flesh.

The Thracians, at the sight of his distress,
began—with stones and lances—to attack
the Trojan women. But she tried to catch
those stones: with a hoarse howl, she snapped her teeth.

Her jaws could only bark, though set for speech.
And one can still find in the Cherronesus
this place: the She-hound's Mound or *Kynos sema*,
the name it gained from Hecuba's sad change.
And then, for long, through all the fields of Thrace,
remembering her many griefs, she howled.
Her Trojan friends and Grecian enemies
alike were moved; all of the gods took pity—
and even great Jove's wife and sister, Juno,
was ready to concede that such great sorrow
was something Hecuba had not deserved.

And yet Aurora, though she'd always been
a friend of Trojan arms, did not lament
as one might have expected at the fall
of Ilium and Hecuba—because
the goddess was afflicted by a death
that touched her much more closely: she had lost
her own son. On the Phrygian battlefield,
beneath Achilles' shaft, her Memnon fell;
and she, the radiant one, had seen him killed.
At that, the color of the goddess paled;
daybreak did not grow bright with rose-red hues;
the jet-black clouds kept heaven from men's view.

And when the corpse was set upon the pyre,
his mother could not bear the sight; just as
she was, with hair disheveled, shorn of pride,
she threw herself at great Jove's feet and cried
these words—the plea she added to her tears:
"I am the very least of deities,
and yet I am a goddess—and as that,
I come before you. No, I do not ask
for temples, sacred days on my behalf,
for sacrifices to me—I don't pray
for altars bearing fires for my sake.

Latin [569–90]

Yet, if you were to gauge the good I do,
all I, though but a woman, bring to you
when, at the day's return, I guard the bounds
of night, you must admit that I deserve
some recompense. No, no, it is not this

for which I care, for which I come—those honors
that I may well have earned. What brings me here

is Memnon's death, my loss: in vain he fought—
bravely—to help his uncle Priam's cause;
at great Achilles' hand, he has died young.
Console my Memnon in his death: o grant,
great lord of all the gods, some gift to him,
some honor that will also soothe the wound
his mother feels.''

                Jove nodded in consent.
And Memnon's pyre crumbled in an instant,
destroyed by a great blaze; black smoke in spirals
darkened the day—just as, when rivers breed
thick fog, the sun can't penetrate the pall.
Dark ashes soared on high and, there, grown dense
and more compact, began to form one mass;
this took on shape and, from the flames, drew out
both life and heat—but not with so much weight
that it could not be winged. At first it seemed
much like a bird, and then one bird indeed
whirred with his wings; and soon his brother-birds—
a countless flock (they shared a common birth
from one same cluster)—clamored everywhere.

Three times they circled over Memnon's pyre;
three times, in unison, across the air,
their cry resounded. When for the fourth time
they'd circled, they split into two fierce flocks
that fought ferociously; in savage fury
they plied their beaks and their hooked claws; they wearied
their wings and chests in battle; and they fell,
a holocaust, down into Memnon's ashes,

an offering honoring the one from whom
they had been born—that mighty soldier, Memnon.
After the author of their family,
these wingèd beings—born so suddenly—
are called Memnonides; and every time
the sun completes his journey through twelve signs,
these flocks return to war against each other
and die, a rite that honors their dead father.

And so the other gods were stirred to pity
on seeing Hecuba compelled to bark;
but one, Aurora, was too taken up
with her own sorrow. Even to this day,
the goddess still sheds tears for her dear son:
the dew she scatters on the world at dawn.

Troy was destroyed; yet Fate did not intend
that, with her walls, Troy's hopes would also end.
And when, from burning Troy, Aeneas fled,
his shoulders bore her sacred images
and—sacred, too—Anchises, his old father,
a venerable burden. It was these—
of all his riches—that he chose to carry,
together with his son, Ascanius,
as he, the pious hero, fled the city.

He sailed out from Antandros with his fleet
of fugitives; he made his first landfall
in Thrace but left that land of criminals.
Then, with the clement winds and current, he,
together with his comrades, reached the isle
of Delos, where Apollo has his town.
There, Anius—who served men as their king
and Phoebus as his priest—welcomed Aeneas
to both the palace and the sanctuary;
he showed his city and the famous shrines

Latin [616–34]

and those two tree-trunks that Latona gripped
when she was giving birth to her dear twins.

They scattered incense on the altar fires
and then poured wine upon them. As prescribed,
they offered bullocks as a sacrifice
and burned the vitals to complete the rites.
Then, once more in the palace, they reclined
upon high couches, savored Bacchus' wine
and Ceres' gifts. "O Phoebus' cherished priest,"
pious Aeneas asked, "am I in error
or did I see a son of yours together
with four fine daughters when, some time ago,
I visited your city?" And in sorrow,
shaking his head—around his temples ran
his sacred snow-white fillets—Delos' priest
replied:

                "What you recall is right—unflawed—
o best of heroes; when you came, you saw
that I was father of five children: now
(things human are so mutable) you see,
to all effects, a man who is bereft.
Can I call on my absent son for help
when he lives so far off, upon an isle—
Andros—that takes its name from him? His land
is there, where he is king; the god of Delos
endowed him with the power of prophecy.
But to my daughters Bacchus gave a power
beyond their deepest prayers, beyond belief;
for anything they touched was turned to wheat
or wine or to the oil that we receive
from Pallas' gray-green tree—and certainly
great riches were implicit in that gift.
As soon as Agamemnon heard of this,
that pillager of Troy (we suffered, too—

Latin [634–56]

in some way—from the storm that battered you)
dragged off my daughters: using brutal force,
against their will he tore them from my arms.
And then he issued this profane command:
my daughters were to use their god-sent gift
to feed the Grecian fleet. Each girl escaped
as best she could: two daughters sought Euboea;
and two made for their brother's island, Andros.
But they were followed there by Grecian troops,
who threatened war unless my daughters were
consigned to them. Since fear had greater force
than did fraternal love, my son gave up
his sisters, destined to harsh punishment.
And yet one must forgive the fright he felt;
for, after all, his island had no Hector
and no Aeneas as its firm defenders—
those two who made it possible for you
to hold the Greeks at bay for nine long years.
They were about to chain their prisoners,
when my two daughters, lifting up their arms—
not bound as yet—to heaven, cried aloud:
'Help, father Bacchus!' And the god who'd given
so singular a gift to them, brought help—
if one may call the loss of human shape,
although it be a miracle, true aid.
And I cannot describe their change, so strange
that I have never understood it, nor
can I explain it now; we only know
the end result of my dear daughters' sorrow:
they sprouted feathers, turned to snow-white doves,
the birds Anchises' consort, Venus, loves."

With this and other tales, both host and guests
passed all their banquet time. And then they left,
to sleep. At daybreak they awoke and went
to visit Phoebus' oracle; it bid

Latin [656–78]

the Trojans to seek out their "ancient mother"—
their land of origin—and other shores
that nurtured their ancestors. Anius
was there as they embarked, and he brought gifts:
a scepter for Anchises and a cloak
and quiver for Ascanius; Aeneas
received a well-wrought cup that had been sent
to Anius by Therses, his dear friend,
whose birthplace lay along Ismenus' banks.
Therses had shipped it from Aonia—
he was the sender; and the maker was
Alcon of Hyle, who had ringed that cup
with his engravings, images that told
a lengthy story.

             There one saw a city
and seven gates: their number took the place
of "Thebes"—he did not have to carve that name.
Before the city, funeral and tombs
and blazing fires and pyres, and, in despair,
women with bared breasts and disheveled hair
were signs of a disaster. There were nymphs
who wept to see the drying-up of springs.
The trees were nude, their branches stripped of leaves;
the goats were forced to gnaw on stony fields.
Inside the wall he carved Orion's daughters:
with more than women's courage, their blades pierce
their naked necks, whose flesh does not resist.
They die to save their people from the plague;
they're borne through town—a mighty funeral;
the crowd surrounds the pyre when they are burned.
And that their line may not die out with them,
beyond, out of the virgins' ashes, rise
two youths to whom the legend gives the name
Coroni; they are shown as they parade,
leading the rites that would commemorate
the ashes from which they have sprung—their mothers'.
That was the final scene, the last relief

Latin [678–700]

he carved upon the gleaming ancient bronze.
And he adorned the rim of that wine-cup
with jutting carvings—gilt leaves of acanthus.

The Trojans, in return, gave Anius
fine gifts of no less worth than his: the priest
received a censer, a libation bowl,
and a bright crown that gleamed with gems and gold.

From Delos, mindful of the oracle,
they sought the land of their ancestor, Teucer,
an early king of Troy, who came from Crete.
But when they disembarked, the Trojans found
the climate of that island far too harsh;
and so they left behind those hundred towns—
and sailed toward Italy, Ausonian shores.
But then a tempest swept the wintry seas;
the fleet sought shelter in the Strophades.
But in that harbor there lurked treachery;
they had to flee Aiello, a foul Harpy.
As they sailed on, they passed Dulichium
and Ithaca and Samos, and the homes
of Neritos—astute Ulysses' realm.
They saw Ambracia, isle for which the gods
contended, and the statue of the judge
Apollo turned to stone, poor Cragaleus—
Ambracia, which is now so famous for
Apollo's facing shrine at Actium.
They saw Dodona's grove of speaking oaks,
and saw Chaonia's gulf where the three sons
of the Molossian ruler, Munichus,
grew wings, the only way they could escape
when brigands set the royal halls ablaze.

And then they landed on the nearby isle
of the Phaeacians, whose fields are full

of splendid orchards. Their next port—Buthrotos—
was in Epirus; there the Phrygian seer
who was a son of Priam, Helenus,
had built a replica of Troy. From him
Aeneas' men heard friendly prophecies
about their future. On to Sicily
they sailed—a land that juts into the sea
with three capes: one, Pachynus, feels the gusts
of Auster, bringing rains; while Lilybaeum
lies open to the gentle winds of Zephyr;
and, to the north, Pelorus faces both
the Bears that never sink into the sea
and Boreas. The Trojans reached the last.
Night fell; with oars and with the current's help,
the fleet made land along Messina's sands.

The straits that bathe Messina's coast are kept
by Scylla, who infests them to the east,
while to the west Charybdis never rests.
Charybdis sucks the ships into her depths,
then spews them up again; while Scylla's waist
is strange and dark and girdled by fierce dogs.

Yet Scylla wears the face of a young girl,
and if the tales the poets tell are more
than fictions, Scylla was indeed—before
she suffered such a monstrous change—a girl.
Young men would come—in crowds—to court her: she
disdained them all—then let the company
of sea-nymphs (they were fond of Scylla) hear
how she had spurned her suitors.

                       Galatea
was one of those sea-nymphs. And once, while Scylla
was combing Galatea's hair, she heard
the goddess sigh these melancholy words:

Latin [720–39]

"Dear Scylla, you are sought by gentle men:
you face no danger in rejecting them.
But I, though one of Nereus' fifty daughters,
I, who have sea-green Doris as my mother,
I, with so many sisters as my keepers,
was only freed from Cyclops' love for me
by way of unrelenting misery. . . . "

Her words were curbed by tears. But Scylla dried
those tears with her white fingers, comforting
the goddess Galatea. Scylla said:
"Dear friend, why do you grieve? You need not hide
the cause—you can trust me, you can confide."
This tale was Galatea's sad reply:

"My Acis was the son of woodland Faunus
and one of the Simeto's river-nymphs.
Both parents took much joy in such a son,
but my delight was even greater: none
but Acis knew my undivided passion.
Acis was handsome and, at sixteen years,
his cheeks were lightly marked by a soft beard.
Even as Polyphemus longed for me,
so I desired Acis—endlessly.
And should you ask what feeling had more force—
my love for Acis or my hatred of
the Cyclops—I could not reply: I was
possessed by equal powers. Generous
Venus, what force you can command! The Cyclops—
who frightens even wildest forests, demon
who brought disaster to all strangers, one
who scorns august Olympus and its gods—
now that same Cyclops feels love's mastery.
The prey of passion's force and fire, he
forgets his caves and cattle. Polyphemus,
you tend to your appearance now, you care
to see how handsome you can be, you take
a rake to comb your shaggy hair, you shave

your rough beard with a scythe, and you are pleased
to mirror your crude features in a pool,
to temper them with tenderness. Your taste
for blood, which never could be quenched, abates;
and now, along your shoreline, ships are free
to sail in safety and tranquillity.

"One day, along the coast of Sicily—
just at the foot of Aetna—Telemus,
the son of Eurymus, had disembarked.
He was an augur never known to err
in his interpreting the flights of birds.
He met foul Polyphemus. He predicted:
'That lone eye in the middle of your forehead—
Ulysses will yet steal it from you.' But
the Cyclops howled with laughter, and he scoffed:
'You, stupid seer, are wrong—for someone else
has blinded me already.' So he mocked
a warning that was true. Then Cyclops stalked
away; with his tremendous steps, he crushed
the shore, then—tired—returned to his dark grottoes.

"There is a hill that juts into the sea—
the pointed wedge of a long promontory.
Waves bathe that cliff on both its sides. The brutal
Cyclops had climbed up to the very middle;
he sat upon that hill. His woolly sheep—
though he neglected them—had followed him.
Then, at his feet he laid his walking-stick—
a pine trunk meant as mainmast for a ship.
He lifted up his flute—one hundred reeds.
And when he played his shepherd melodies,
all of the peaks could hear—all of the sea.
I, too, could hear him. In my Acis' arms
and sheltered by a rock, I heard him—far
away. I still recall the words he sang:

□   □   □

Latin [766–88]

" 'O Galatea, you are whiter than
the snowy buds upon the privet hedge;
the blossoming of meadows cannot match
your blossoming; you are more slender than
the alder, brighter than clear crystal, and
more playful than a young goat, smoother than
the seashells polished by unceasing waves,
more welcome than the sun in winter or
than shade in summer, more exquisite than
the fruit of orchards, more majestic than
the tall plane-tree, more clear and radiant
than ice, more sweet than ripened grapes, more soft
than feathers of the swan or curdled milk;
and if you did not flee from me, you would
be lovelier than a well-watered garden.

" 'Yet you—the selfsame Galatea—are
more nasty than an untamed ox, more tough
than aged oak; you are more treacherous
than waves, more slippery than willow or
white bryony, more difficult to budge
than are these boulders, more tumultuous
than torrents, prouder than a praised peacock,
more fierce than fire, sharper than the thorns,
more savage than a she-bear shielding cubs,
and deafer than the sea, and with less pity
than snakes when stepped upon; and finally—
your worst defect, the fault that I would cure—
whenever you retreat from me, you are
not only swifter than the stag that flees
from barking hounds, but swifter than the breeze
that fleets, and winds that gust. And yet—were you
to know me somewhat better—you might then
regret your having fled: you would condemn
yourself for having kept me waiting—and
would try to hold your Polyphemus fast.

□   □   □

Latin [789–809]

" 'This mountainside is mine—this living rock
serves as my grottoes' roof: there, one need not
endure the dog-days' sun, the winter's cold.
The branches in my orchard bend beneath
the weight of apples; on my trailing vines,
some of my grapes are tawny gold, and some
are purple—I want you to have both kinds.
And, Galatea, your own hands will find
tender strawberries in the shaded woods,
and cherries in the autumn, and two sorts
of plums—the purple ones with their dark juice
and plums more prized, as yellow as new wax.
If you would only marry me, you would
not lack chestnuts or fruits of the arbutus:
each tree would serve your pleasure and your use.

" 'And, Galatea, all the herds you see
are mine; and many more are wandering
across the valley, many more are safe
within the woods, or sheltered in my caves.
Were you to ask me what my flocks may number,
I could not answer you—only the poor
have need to count their cattle. But if you
should ask about their quality, you need
not trust my word: see for yourself—you judge
how, pushing past their thighs, their udders bulge.
As for the young, my lambs are in one fold,
my kids are in another—all well-warmed.
My snow-white milk is always in abundance:
some of that milk is best for drinking, some
is to be hardened by dissolving rennet.

" 'And, Galatea, when I give you gifts,
they will not be the common, easy things—
like does or hares or goats or doves in pairs
or simple birds'-nests stolen from a treetop.
What I shall give, I found among the peaks:
a pair of cubs born of a shaggy bear,

Latin [810–34]

a pair for you to play with—so alike
that each can be mistaken for the other.
I found them and I told myself: "These are
a present for my lady." Galatea,
come now and, from the blue sea, lift your head;
come now, do not disdain my gifts. Surely
I know what I look like: just recently
I saw my likeness in a limpid pool,
and what I saw I liked. Just look how huge
I am, for even Jupiter above
can claim no bigger body (since you speak
of some Jove or another who is king
in heaven). And my hair—abundantly—
pours down on my severe face, and it shades
my shoulders—just as if it were a grove.
And do not think that there is anything
ugly in rough and thick hair covering
my body: without leaves a tree is ugly;
a horse is ugly if it lacks a thick
mane on its sorrel neck; the birds are dressed
with feathers; wool enhances sheep; and thus
a man is more beguiling if he wears
a beard and, on his body, shaggy hair.
Yes—in the middle of my forehead I
have but one eye, yet that one eye is like
a massive shield. And, after all, does not
the giant sun see everything upon
this earth from heaven? And his eye is one!

" 'And do remember this: my father is
the ruler of the sea in which you live—
Neptune will be the one whom I shall give
to you as father-in-law. I ask you this:
to show a bit of pity, hear my prayer;
to you alone I kneel. I, Cyclops, who
have nothing but disdain for Jupiter—
who scorn his skies, deride his thunderbolts
that shatter everything—I do fear you,

o Nereid, for your anger is more fierce
than lightning. Yet if your contempt were meant
for all, were you to flee from every man—
I could endure your scorn. But why—instead—
do you disdain the Cyclops but accept
the love of Acis? Why do you prefer
Acis' embraces to my own? But let
him please himself and please you, too (and yet,
would he could be the one whom you reject).
But have him keep himself out of my hands!
For if he falls into my grip, that chance
will let me show my strength—just as immense
as is my body. I shall disembowel
the living Acis. I shall cast his limbs
across the fields and—that you two may mingle—
across the waves in which you live. I burn,
I burn, and my offended longing, stirred
to frenzy, rages in me more intensely:
it is as if, within my chest, I carried
a penetrating, an erupting, Aetna.
But you—you, Galatea—are unmoved.'

"These were his worthless ravings. Then he rose
(I saw it all) and—like a raging bull
who, having lost his cow, cannot stand still—
across the valleys and familiar hills,
he wandered. Then that savage being found us
unexpectedly, surprising me
and Acis. And he howled: 'My eye has seen:
this is your last sweet clasp, your final fondling.'
The howl erupting from him had the power
and size that suits a Cyclops' rage. That roar
left Aetna shuddering. I—horrified—
dived back into the nearby sea. In flight,
Acis, son of Simeto's line, implored:
'O Galatea and my family,
receive your dying Acis; let me cross
into your realm of waves and water.' Cyclops,

pursuing Acis, heaved a massive rock,
a piece of mountain that he had torn off.
Only the merest edge touched Acis, but
the corner of that rock was quite enough
to bury him completely. And the only
thing fate permitted me was to restore
Acis to his ancestral powers. Blood
flowed crimson, dark, down from the mass of rock;
but soon its crimson faded; it became
the color of a stream that early rains
have swollen; then the torrent slowly gained
more purity. The rock that Cyclops cast
now split wide open, and a tall green reed
rose through the crack; the hollow opening
within the rock resounded. Waters leaped
and—suddenly—a young man stood, waist-deep,
up from the waves; his new-sprung horns were wreathed
with supple rushes. That young man was Acis.
Though larger now, and with a dark-blue face,
Acis had certainly not been erased:
a river-god—that was his newfound shape—
a river that retained his former name."

This was the end of Galatea's story.
The company of Nereids—scattering—
now leave, to swim within the tranquil seas.

And Scylla also left—but too afraid
to face the deep, she took the shoreward way.
Unclothed, she roamed the porous sands or else,
when weary, sought some sheltered pool; and in
secluded waters, she refreshed her limbs.

But now a new inhabitant has cleaved
the waters of the deep: he'd only found
his sea-shape recently, close to Anthedon,

Latin [882–905]

a port that faced Euboea: he is Glaucus.
He reaches shore; he sees the girl; he wants
to have her; and he utters all those words
that—so he thinks—can hold her back. And yet
she flees and does not slow her flight; indeed,
her fear incites her speed; now she has reached
a mountainside that rises from the beach.
It stretches from the waters to the sky,
a massive rise that ends in one sharp peak
whose height commands a spacious stretch of sea.

It's here that Scylla stops; from this safe spot,
not sure if she is looking at a god
or at a monster, Scylla stares in wonder:
she marvels at his color, at the hair that wraps
around his shoulders, falls across his back;
and she's amazed to see the way in which,
down from the groin, he tapers—like a fish.
And Glaucus senses her dismay; he grips
a rocky spur nearby, in time to say:
"I'm not a monster or a savage beast;
dear girl; I am a god who rules the deep;
my powers as a sea-lord fully match
the claims of Proteus and Triton and
Palaemon, son of Athamas. I was
a mortal man before, but even then
deep waters were my world; my life was spent
upon the sea. Now I would draw in nets
that, in their turn, drew in the fish; and now,
seated upon some shoals, I plied my rod
and line. There is a shoreline bordered by
green meadows; water lies upon one side
and, on the other, grass and plants; there, too,
horned cattle never grazed; no quiet sheep
and shaggy she-goats ever foraged there;
and there, no bee had ever gathered pollen;
and no one ever gathered feast-day garlands;
no hand that held a scythe had ever passed.

Latin [905–30]

I was the first who ever sat upon
that turf: I dried my damp nets in the sun;
and on the shore I tallied up the fish
that I had caught by chance and those I'd tricked
and caught with my curved hooks. And now—although
I know the tale I tell will seem untrue
(but what have I to gain by fooling you?)—
no sooner had I spread my catch along
the grass, than all that crowd of fish began
to stir, to flop from side to side, and then
to move on land as if at sea. Amazed,
stopped cold, I stared as all those fishes made
straight for the water; they deserted me—
they left their new lord, leaped into the sea.
I'm stunned and stilled; it takes me long before
I probe the cause of this. Was it the work
of some god, or the juice within the grass?
'But is there any herb that has such force?'
I asked; and then I plucked a tuft of grass,
and clutching it, I let my teeth sink in.
No sooner had my throat felt that strange sap,
than—suddenly—I felt my innards shake;
within my heart I felt a fierce desire
to live another life. I could not check
that longing, and I cried: 'O earth, farewell,
I never will return to you'; I plunged
into the waves. The sea-gods welcomed me;
they took me in and asked Oceanus
and Tethys now to purge whatever was
still mortal in me. Purifying me,
they chant nine times the sacred song that frees
the body from impurities; I'm told
that I must let a hundred rivers' waters flow
across my chest. At once, from all directions,
those rivers poured their waters over me.
That much I can recall, that much I tell.
But I don't know what happened then to me.
I lost my senses; and when I awoke,

Latin [930–58]

I'd changed completely from what I had been
so recently: my body had been changed
in full, and, too, my mind was not the same.
And then I saw this dark green beard I'd gained,
this flowing hair that sweeps across long waves,
these massive shoulders and these azure arms,
these legs that merge and taper, ending in
the pointed body of a fish with fins.
And yet, what use is this astounding shape,
what good, that I have pleased the gods who rule
the sea and am myself a deity—
if all these things don't stir you in the least!"

Such were his words, and Glaucus would have said
much more, if cruel Scylla had not fled,
not left him there alone. Repulsed, enraged,
the sea-god heads for Circe's wondrous isle,
the daughter-of-the-Sun's enchanted halls.

Latin [958–68]

BOOK XIV

AND GLAUCUS THE EUBOEAN, god who haunts
the swollen surge, swam hard—he never paused—
past Aetna, heaped upon the Giant's jaws,
and past the Cyclops' fields, which know no plow
or harrow, and are rich and fertile, though
they never see yoked cattle. Then he raced
past Rhegium and Messina, towns that face
each other as they flank those narrow straits
that swallow passing ships and separate
Ausonia and Sicily.

        Now he,
with stalwart strokes, cleaves the Tyrrhenian sea
and reaches green hillsides and Circe's halls—
her palace full of phantom animals.
As soon as he's seen Circe, after she
and he have given and received their greetings,
he says: "O goddess, may you pity me,
a god. You are indeed the only one
who can (if I am worthy of your care)
give me the remedy for love's despair.
O daughter of the Sun, I know as well
as anyone the power herbs possess,
for I was changed by them. But now you'll hear
the cause of my wild frenzy: on the coast
of Italy, where it lies opposite
Messina's walls, I first caught sight of Scylla.
I won't repeat to you (I'm too ashamed)
my pleas and promises, my flattery,
my words—they all were treated scornfully.
But now, if magic chants have any force,
do let your sacred lips entrance her heart;
or if the better way is herbs, I pray—
do choose an herb whose power has been proved.
Don't cure my longing, do not heal my wound."

And Circe is familiar with such flames:
no one, in matters of the heart, falls prey

more easily than Circe (whether she
is in herself the cause of this, or else
must suffer the revenge of Venus for
the time when Circe's father was informer—
the one who spied on Venus and her lover);
and so she did not hesitate to answer:
"You'd do much better seeking one who shares
your loves, your hopes—one flame that warms you both.
One such as you should have no need to plead,
for you yourself deserve to be beseeched;
and if you would concede to me the least
of hopes, believe me, I'll indeed implore.
And to dispel your doubts, your lack of trust
in your own form and its compelling force,
I cite myself as proof: although I am
a goddess, daughter of the splendid Sun,
and have the power to enchant with song
and to entrance with potent herbs, I long
to be your own; it's you I want. Save scorn
for one who scorns you, and requite with love
the flame of one who wants you. So, at once,
two women can receive what they deserve."

So Circe tempted him. But Glaucus said:
"Green foliage will blossom in the sea,
and seaweed sprout upon the highest peaks,
before my love for Scylla suffers change
as long as she's alive." And now, enraged,
the goddess, since she cannot strike the god
himself (and, loving him, would hardly want
to hurt him), turns her rage against the girl
whom he preferred. Offended and repulsed,
straightway she pounds and minces noxious herbs,
whose juices are horrific; as she mixes
those potions, she intones infernal chants,
the spells of Hecate. Then she puts on
an azure cloak and makes her way among
a crowd of fawning beasts. She leaves her halls

Latin [25–46]

and heads for Rhegium, which lies across
the narrows from Messina's rugged rocks.
She treads the surface of the churning sea
as if she were on solid ground: dry-shod,
she reaches Rhegium.

There was a cove,
a little inlet shaped like a bent bow,

a quiet place where Scylla, at midday,
sought shelter when the sea and sky were hot;
and, in midcourse, the sun scorched with full force,
reducing shadows to a narrow thread.
And Circe now contaminates this bay,
polluting it with noxious poisons; there
she scatters venom drawn from dreadful roots
and, three-times-nine times, murmurs an obscure
and tangled maze of words, a labyrinth—
the magic chant that issues from her lips.
Then Scylla comes; no sooner has she plunged
waist-deep into the water than she sees,
around her hips, the horrid barking shapes.
At first, not able to believe that these
are part of her own body, Scylla flees;
afraid, she tries to chase off these loud dogs.
But what she flees, she carries with her self;
and as she probes her thighs, her shins, her feet,
she finds just gaping dogs in place of these,
the sort of hounds that Cerberus might keep.
Below, her body's made of these mad dogs;
for at her loins, her belly is cut short;
she stands upon the backs of beastly forms.

And Glaucus, for the love of Scylla, wept;
he fled from Circe now; he shunned the bed
of one whose herbs had been so harsh, so heartless.
But Scylla stayed, fixed in her place, and when
at last she had a chance to take revenge
on Circe, she snatched up Ulysses' men.

Latin [47–71]

She also would have swallowed all the ships
in which Aeneas crossed the narrows if,
before his coming, she had not been changed
into a rock that stands there to this day.
But even as a rock along those straits,
she still leaves passing mariners afraid.

And when, by force of oars, the Trojan ships
had safely passed both Scylla and Charybdis'
voracious vortex and had almost reached
the shoreline of Ausonia, the wind
drove them far back—onto the Libyan coast.
And there the woman who had come from Sidon
welcomed Aeneas, offering the Trojan
her heart and home; but then she could not bear
Aeneas' leaving her, and on a pyre
that she'd prepared by using as pretext
a sacred rite, she fell upon her sword;
herself deceived, she then deceived them all.
When he had left behind those new-built walls
of Carthage, founded on a sandy shore,
Aeneas visited again the land
of Eryx and hospitable Acestes,
and offered there a sacrifice to honor
his father's tomb. And then the Trojans boarded
the boats that Iris, Juno's messenger,
had almost burned; they passed the island realm
of Aeolus, and lands that smoked with fumes
of sulfur, blazing hot, and passed the rocks
held by the Sirens, Achelous' daughters.

Then, having lost his pilot, Palinurus,
Aeneas sailed along Inarime
and Prochyte, and rocky Pythecusae,
the barren island that derives its name
from its inhabitants, a pack of knaves:

Latin [72–90]

the vile Cercopes. For in fact, one day,
the father of the gods, out of his hate
for people so dishonest, fruitless, base,
transformed them into animals but shaped
their features so that they—at once—seemed both
like men and unlike men; for the Cercopes
were changed to *pithekoi*, the Greek for "monkeys."
Jove gave them shorter limbs; and as old age
will furrow faces, so he furrowed theirs;
and having clothed their forms with yellow hair,
he sent them off to dwell on that bare isle.
But first he stripped them of the power of words,
for perjury was all their tongues had served;
the only thing he left them free to utter
were harsh and hoarse complaints—their scrannel chatter.

———————

But after he had coasted past these isles
and, on his right, sailed past Parthenope,
Aeneas, turning slightly westward, found
the tomb of his melodious trumpeter,
Misenus, buried on the marshy ground
of Cumae. There, on entering her grotto,
the Trojan pleaded with the long-lived Sibyl
to let him cross Avernus and encounter
his father's Shade. The prophetess held fast
her eyes upon the ground; but then at last
the Sibyl, god-inspired, wild, possessed,
consented: "You, whose feats are so immense,
who, in the clash of weapons, showed such strength,
and, in the raging fires, such reverence—
it is an awesome thing you seek. And yet,
o Trojan, do not fear: what you have sought
you are to get; with me as guide, you'll see
Elysium and the third realm of the world—
and see the dear Shade of your father, too.
There is no path that is denied to virtue."

Latin [91–113]

Such were her words, and then she showed Aeneas—
within the forest of Persephone,
Avernus' queen—a gleaming, golden bough;
she ordered him to pluck it from the tree.

And having plucked the golden bough, Aeneas
was shown the massive structures of Avernus;
and there he met his own ancestors and
magnanimous Anchises' aged Shade.
There, too, he came to know the laws and norms
that rule the world below, and also learned
what dangers he would face in wars to come.

As, through the dusk and darkness, he climbed back,
to ease his weary steps on that hard path,
Aeneas talked to his Cumaean guide:
"Although I do not know if you're indeed
a goddess, or are simply one most dear
unto the gods, for me you'll always be
a deity; and I shall always be
most grateful; for you have permitted me
descent to death's domain, and once I'd seen
death's self, you granted me a safe return:
in recompense, when I am back again
beneath the the open sky, I shall erect
a shrine for you and offer fragrant incense."

Then, turning back to him, the prophetess
sighed deeply and replied: "I am no goddess;
mere mortals do not merit sacred incense.
Don't let your ignorance lead you awry;
know this: I could have had eternal light,
have lived forever, had I sacrificed
virginity, accepting Phoebus' love.
Such was his hope, and trying to corrupt
my modesty with gifts, he said: 'Now, just
express your wish—and that, Cumaean virgin,
will be the gift I give.' I gathered up

Latin [113–36]

a little heap of dust and, holding that,
I asked that I be granted years to match
the number of those grains; but I forgot
to ask that I stay young through all that span—
I was a fool. Yet even then he would
have given me that, too—unending youth—
if I had yielded to him. I did not.
I scorned him and I am a virgin still.
But now life's time of joy is in retreat;
old age, with tottering steps, is on its way
toward me; for many years I'll bear that weight.
In fact, it is some seven centuries
that I have lived already; and to match
those grains of dust, it is three hundred harvests
and just as many vintages that I
must see. The day will come when this long life
will leave me shriveled; worn away by age,
my limbs will shrink to trifles; no one then
will dream that I'd been loved—and pleased a god.
And even Phoebus may not recognize
the Sybil then—he even may deny
that he had ever loved me. And my life
will end—so frail, so scant. I shall become
invisible; and through my voice alone
shall I be known: that's all that fate will grant."

These were the things that Sybil told Aeneas
as they climbed upward from the depths of Styx,
emerging close to Cumae. And the Trojan,
after the proper rites of sacrifice,
sailed to the shore that had not yet received
its name, Caieta, after his old nurse.

It's on this shore that, after long, hard trials,
the weary Macareus of Neritus,
a comrade of industrious Ulysses,

Latin [137–59]

had stopped. The sight of Achaemenides,
alive and sound, amazed him. Long ago
Ulysses' men had left behind their friend—
abandoned him on rocky Aetna—when
they fled the Cyclops. And he asked: "What chance
or god has saved you, Achaemenides?
And how can you, a Greek, have journeyed here
upon a Trojan boat? Where is it bound?"

And Achaemenides, no longer dressed
in savage, shaggy fashion, in poor rags
that thorns helped pin together—he was back
to his own self—replied: "I swear this ship
is dearer to me than are Ithaca
and my own home; and I respect Aeneas
as much as I revere my father; if
I lie, may I be doomed to see once more
foul Polyphemus and the human gore
that drips down from his jaws. I never can—
however much I try—repay the debt
I owe Aeneas. How can I forget
that if I speak and breathe and see the sky
and flashing sun, it is because of him?
Aeneas kept my soul from ending in
the Cyclops' mouth; and even if I should
now leave behind the light of life, I shall
be buried in a tomb, not in the guts
of Polyphemus. What fear took my heart
(if I, in panic, still had any soul
or senses left) when I saw you sail off
across the deep, deserting me! I would
have shouted, but I was afraid my cries
might let the blind Cyclops discover me.
Indeed, Ulysses' clamor almost wrecked
the ship on which you left. I saw it all:
I saw the Cyclops tear a giant rock
off from the mountainside; I saw him toss
that rock into the sea; he did not stop—

Latin [160–82]

his massive arm kept flinging those great rocks
as from a catapult; and—I forgot
that I was not aboard—I feared those stones
would stir a wave or wind with force enough
to sink your ship. And when, at last, you fled
and, sailing off, escaped atrocious death,
the groaning Cyclops prowled the slopes of Aetna;
he groped among the woods, and since he could
not see, he often struck against sharp rocks,
and stretching out his bleeding arms, he cursed
the race of Greeks and howled: 'Oh, would that chance
might bring Ulysses or one of his men,
so I could vent my wrath—could eat his guts
and tear his living flesh with these bare hands
and inundate my gullet with his blood
and feel his mangled members shuddering
between my teeth! For then how slight a thing—
indeed no thing at all—would blindness be!'
He shouted this—and more—ferociously.

"And livid horror filled me as I watched
his face still smeared with slaughter, his fierce hands,
the empty socket of his eye, his limbs
and beard encrusted with the blood of men.
It's death I had before my eyes, and yet
it was the least of all my fears. I thought:
he'll grab me now, and he will stuff his guts
with mine; and with my mind I still could see
that scene when he snatched two of my dear friends
and dashed them three and then four times against
the ground; and like a shaggy lion, he crouched
over my comrades, bent on stuffing down
their flesh, white-marrowed bones, their innards, and
their limbs still warm; and terror took my soul;
I paled with horror as I watched him crunch
and spit out bleeding fare, and vomit chunks
of flesh mixed in with wine. Such was the fate
I pictured for my sorry self. For days

on end, I hid; at every sound, I quaked;
I was afraid of death—but longed for it.
Alone and helpless, desperate, I ate
acorns and leaves and grass: I held at bay
starvation. There was nothing to await
but suffering and death until—at length—
I saw this ship far off; and so I begged—
with signs and gestures—to be led away;
I hurried to the beach, and they took pity
on me; that Trojan ship received a Greek.
I've told my tale, dear friend; now tell me all
the trials you faced, the perils that befell
your chief, Ulysses, and the company
that sailed away with you across the sea."

Then Macareus told how, from Cyclops' coast,
they reached the isle of Aeolus, the king
whose realm is ringed by the Tyrrhenian;
and there the son of Hippotes imprisons
the winds within a bull's-hide sack; and this
Ulysses got—a memorable gift.
That visit done, Ulysses' men sailed on
nine days, spurred by the breeze that blew astern;
and now they had in sight the shore they sought,
their Ithaca. But when the tenth day dawned,
Ulysses' men, with greed and envy, thought
that sack held gold: and they unloosed the ties
that held it fast; the winds unleashed a blast
that drove Ulysses and his crewmen back—
along the very sea they had just crossed
into the port of tyrant Aeolus.
"From there," continued Macareus, "we reached
the city of the Laestrygonians,
the walls that Lamus founded long ago.
Antiphates was ruler of that land.
Ulysses sent me on, together with

two other men—an embassy to him.
But I and one of them were only saved
from his ferocity by flight; the third,
a victim, stained with blood the profane jaws
of King Antiphates. We rushed away,
and he pursued us with a vast array

of force: a mob threw rocks at us; they sank
our men; they sank our fleet. And just one ship

escaped their fatal rage, the boat on which
Ulysses and I, too, sailed off. We mourned
our dreadful losses, and we landed on
the isle that you see there—it lies far off.
And it is best to sight it from afar
and not close up—believe me, I was there.
And you, Aeneas, you who are most just
of all the Trojans, you, a goddess' son
(now that the war is finished, I've no cause
to call you enemy), pay me close heed:
do not land there; it is the home of Circe!
We, too, when we had landed on those sands,
recalled Antiphates and cruel Cyclops:
we did not want to enter unknown houses.
And we cast lots; and chance chose me and trusty
Polites and Eurylochus and one
who guzzled wine too frequently, Elpenor,
together with still others, twice-nine more:
it's we who were to visit Circe's halls.
We reached her home; we waited at the door;
a thousand wolves came forward—in that throng,
she-bears and lionesses mingled, too.
They frightened all of us; and yet, in truth,
there was no need for panic—not one beast
was bent on injury: instead, they wagged
their tails and followed us quite festively,
filing along and fawning, welcoming,
until attendant-maidens came to greet—
and lead—us through the marble halls to meet
their mistress. Circe's room was splendid: she

Latin [235–61]

sat on a solemn throne, in gleaming robes—
and over these she'd thrown a cloak of gold.
Fair nymphs and Nereids form the company
of her attendants, and they card no fleece
with agile fingers; they spin no wool threads:
instead, they're charged with sorting out her plants;
from jumbled heaps of flowers, a motley mass
of varicolored herbs, they must select
and separate each kind in its own basket.
And she herself controls the work they do;
she knows how every leaf is to be used,
how they can be combined; she is alert
to just what dose will serve. On seeing us,
when greetings had been given and received,
her face relaxed; we never could have wished
for warmer welcome. And at once she asked
her nymphs to serve us a sweet brew, a mix
of roasted barley, honey, curdled milk,
and pure wine; and in secret, Circe slipped
her juices into it—they'd never be
detected in a drink so honey-sweet.
And we accepted what we got from Circe—
from the right hand of such a deity.
As soon as we had drunk—for we were thirsty,
our lips were parched—the fatal goddess touched
the hair atop our heads with her charmed wand.
And then (despite my shame I tell you this)
I started to grow bristles—rough and stiff;
I lost the power of speech; I could emit
no words—all I could utter were harsh grunts;
I bent—my face was turned down to the ground,
and it had hardened into a rough snout;
I felt the muscles of my neck swell out;
and with the limbs that only now had held
the cup, I now left tracks along the floor.
Then I, together with the other men
(such was the power that her potions had),
was shut within a pigpen. Only one

Latin [261–86]

of us—Eurylochus, who had not touched
the offered cup—had not been made a hog.
And if he'd not escaped our fate, I'd still
be part of that pig herd, a swine with bristles;
for then Ulysses never would have learned
of that disaster from Eurylochus
and come to Circe's palace, freeing us.
For Hermes, god who brings tranquillity,
gave a white flower to Ulysses: moly—
the name the gods have given to that plant—
grows from a black root. And with that in hand,
together with the counsels Hermes gave,
Ulysses felt secure, forewarned. He came
to Circe's halls; when the insidious cup
was offered to him, and with her charmed wand,
she tried to touch his hair, Ulysses spurned
the goddess; he unsheathed his sword, and she
was terrified by that—and so she beat
retreat. And then, the two of them pledged peace
and clasped right hands, abjuring trickery;
and having been received into her bed
as husband, he asked this as wedding gift:
the bodies of his men as they had been.
She sprinkled other juices over us,
juices that she had drawn from some strange herb—
this time, they were benevolent; she struck
our heads with her charmed wand, which she reversed;
and then she chanted words that were opposed
to those that served her as a spell before.
And as the goddess chanted, we grew more
and more erect; we stood up from the ground;
our bristles fell from us; our forked feet lost
their cleft; we got our shoulders back; our arms
were ours again, and once again prolonged
with forearms. And Ulysses wept, and we,
embracing him, wept, too; we flung ourselves
around the neck of our dear chief; the first
words that we spoke were words of gratitude.

Latin [286–307]

"For one whole year we stayed in Circe's land,
and I saw much indeed in that long span
and heard of many things in tale and story.
And there's one tale that I heard privately
from one of Circe's four attendant nymphs
who helped her, as I said, by sorting herbs
for sacred spells. In fact, while Circe spent
her time alone with him—our chief, Ulysses—
that nymph showed me, within a sanctuary,
a snow-white marble statue wreathed with garlands:
it was the effigy of a young man
and—on his head—the form of a woodpecker.
And I, of course, was curious: I asked
whose effigy it was, and why he had
been honored with a shrine, and why his head
bore that carved bird. And, in reply, she said:
'Just listen, Macareus—and understand
what power my mistress has at her command:
this tale has much to teach—pay careful heed.

" 'Picus, the son of Saturn, once was king
of Latium; and he was famous for
his love of horses that were fit for war.
His form you now see there in effigy,
and you yourself can judge his manly beauty—
the image points to the reality.
His spirit matched his body—although he
was not yet old enough to have seen four
quinquennial Olympiads at Elis.
His face had fascinated all the Dryads
who lived among the hills of Latium;
the goddesses of fountains sighed for him,
as did the Naiads of the Albula
and those of the Numicius and the Anio;
the Almo, with its short course; and the Nar,
the stream that's so impulsive; and the Farfar,

Latin [308–30]

with its dark flow; and those who make their home
in Taurian Diana's wooded realm
and in the lake that lies nearby. But he
spurned all of these; he courted only one,
the nymph who—so the story goes—was born
of honest Janus' wife, Venilia,
upon the Palatine. And when her time
for marriage came, the man whom she most prized
of all the suitors was the Laurentine
Picus, and so the nymph became his bride.
Her beauty was most rare, but rarer still
her artistry in song: and for that gift
they called her Canens. With her song, she used
to move the woods, the stones; on hearing her,
wild beasts grew meek, long rivers stayed their flow
to listen, wandering birds would halt their course.

" 'One day, as with that womanly sweet voice
she sang, her husband Picus left to hunt
wild boars across the Latin fields; his mount
was an impulsive stallion. Picus bore
two javelins in his left hand and wore
a purple cloak that, at the top, was closed
by a gold brooch. And Circe, too, had come
to those same woods: the daughter of the Sun
had climbed up from the fields that now are called
Circean, after her—those fertile slopes
were richer hunting grounds for some new herbs.
And there the goddess, from behind a bush,
caught sight of the young man—and she was struck.
In her dismay, the herbs that she had plucked
fell from her hands, and through her marrow ran
fierce flames. As soon as she could—once again—
lay claim to sense and reason, she was just
about to tell him of her passion—but
his speeding horse and all the hunting band
surrounding Picus took away her chance.
At that, she cried: "But he will not escape,

not even if the wind bears him away—
if I'm indeed the one I know I am,
if there's some force my herbs can still command,
and I can count upon my spells and chants!"
That said, the goddess fashioned a feigned form:

she sent the phantom body of a boar
across prince Picus' path, before his eyes—

a boar that, seeking cover, seemed to hide
within a wood so thick with trunks and leaves
that any horse was barred from entering.
And Picus, unaware of her deceit,
without delay, pursued that phantom prey;
and leaping swiftly from his foaming horse,
on foot he ventured deep into the woods—
he hunts for what may seem but cannot be.
And seeing this, the goddess called upon
infernal sorcery, her chants and charms,
invoking obscure gods with a strange spell—
the spell that Circe used when she would veil
the face of the white moon or hide the Sun,
her Titan father, with a rain-rich cloud.
And this time, too, as Circe sings that spell,
the sky grows dark, mist rises from the soil;
astray along blind paths his men are lost,
and Picus, left alone, has no escort.
And Circe, when the time and place are right,
cries out to Picus: "O, by your fair eyes
that have made captive mine—and by your grace,
for you are fair indeed—compelling me,
though I'm a deity, to beg and plead:
requite my love; and welcome as your own
father-in-law the one whose eyes see all,
the Sun: don't scorn the daughter of a Titan."
But, ruthless, he scorned her and her entreaties:
"I am not yours—whoever you may be.
Another holds me in captivity:
I only hope that heaven lets me stay
her slave until I reach a ripe old age.

Latin [355–80]

As long as destiny allots to me
my Canens, Janus' daughter, I'll not breach
the faith I pledged to her when we were wed."
And after she'd beseeched again, again
in vain, Circe exclaimed: "But you will pay!
You won't return to Canens anymore!
The wounds a woman can inflict when she
is hurt by one she loves—you now will feel
in fact, for Circe is in love and she
is hurt—and she's a woman!" To the west
she turned two times, and two times to the east;
three times she touched the young man with her wand;
three times she chanted charms. And Picus turned
and raced away but was amazed to find
he was more swift than he had ever been;
he saw that wings were sprouting from his body.
And then, enraged to see that—suddenly—
he had been changed into a strange, new bird
within the woods of Latium, he pecked
with his hard beak at the wild oaks; his blows,
his wrath, inflicted wounds on the long boughs;
his wings took on the hue of his red cloak;
the gold that just before had been a brooch
that bit into his clothes was changed to feathers;
the band that ringed his neck was yellow-gold.
Nothing was left to him of his old self
except his name: that, Picus did retain.

" 'Meanwhile the friends of Picus, with hoarse cries,
kept calling for him through the countryside
but could not find him—they got no reply.
The one they found was Circe—it was she
who had in fact thinned out the mist by now.
And they accused her of the crime; they claimed
the right to have their ruler back again;
they readied an attack with deadly shafts.
But Circe sprinkled Picus' men with venom
and her insidious juices; and she called

on Night and all the gods of Night to come
from Erebus and Chaos; wailing long,
she summoned Hecate. And in response,
the forests—this is unbelievable—
leaped from their place within the ground; the soil
groaned, and the trees that stood nearby grew pale;
and on the pastures where her poisons fell,
the grass was stained with drops of blood; the stones
seemed to emit hoarse moans, and all the hounds
were barking; dark snakes swarmed across the ground;
one saw the thin Shades of the silent dead
flitting about. Astounded, that great crowd—
the men of Picus—trembled. Then the goddess
touched their dazed faces with her awesome wand;
and they were changed to beasts of every sort—
a wondrous change. Not one retained his form.

" 'By now the setting sun has spread its rays
across Tartessus' shores, and Canens waits
in vain: her eyes, her heart are watching for
her husband. And, by torchlight, all her slaves,
her people comb the woods and search each glade.
And though she weeps and tears her hair and beats
her breast, all this is not enough: the nymph
runs out; across the fields she wanders—wild.
Six nights and just as many dawns have seen
poor Canens as she wanders—without sleep
or food—across the valleys and the peaks.
The Tiber sees her last: on its long banks
the nymph, worn out with grief and her hard path,
collapses. There, together with her tears,
she pours out words of sorrow—muffled, faint
and yet melodious; just as the swan,
while dying, sings a mournful final song.
At last, consumed by her despair, her flesh
wasted to thinnest marrow, she dissolves
and slowly vanishes into thin air.
And yet that place preserves her memory:

Latin [404–33]

in honor of the name the nymph had borne,
the Muses called it Canens—rightfully.'

"And there were many things of just that sort
I heard about—or saw—in those long months.
Our idleness had left us sluggish, weak;
and now Ulysses ordered us to sea;
again, we were to spread our sails. And Circe,
before we left, warned us how treacherous
our paths might be, how vast the ocean was,
what dangers wait along the savage sea.
Her words—I must confess—filled me with fright;
and when we reached this beach, I stayed behind."

The tale that Macareus had told was done.
Then this brief epitaph was carved upon
the tomb in which they placed the marble urn
that held the ashes of Aeneas' nurse:

HERE I,

CAIETA, LIE:

THE PIOUS ONE,

WHOM I HAD NURTURED AS A SON,

SNATCHED ME FROM GRECIAN FLAMES AND—FITTINGLY—

ALONG THIS SHORE CREMATED ME.

And now the Trojans free their hawsers, leave
behind the grassy coast. At sea, they keep
their distance from the isle of treachery,
the home of awesome Circe. And they head
for that point where, amid the woods and mist,
the Tiber's waters pour their yellow silt
into the sea.

        Aeneas is received
by Faunus' son, Latinus; and he takes

Latin [433–49]

as wife Lavinia, Latinus' daughter—
but not without pitched battles. He must face
tenacious tribes; for Turnus, in his rage—
Lavinia had been his promised bride—
fights furiously. All Etruria
pours into Latium to join a war
that's long and rough, with victory hard sought.
Each side seeks allies to augment its force;
while many offer Turnus their support,
the Trojan camp can count on other cohorts.
Aeneas asks Evander for his help—
and not in vain; but Venulus, who went
to Diomedes' city, gains no aid
at all from that Aetolian immigrant.

In Daunus' time, the hero Diomedes
came to Iapygia, founded a great city,
and, wedding Daunus' daughter, got as dowry
the region he now ruled. But he refused
all help to Venulus, the emissary
of Turnus, and he offered this excuse:
he did not wish to place the men of Daunus
at risk, and few of his own men were left—
too few to form a well-armed corps for Turnus.

Recounting how his ranks had been reduced,
he told in full this melancholy truth:
"Oh, lest you think I'm lying, listen now
to this—for though remembering a sorrow
renews its bitterness, I'll try as best
I can to tell my trials. When Ilium
was burned, and Pergama had fed the flames
the Danaans set, Oileus' son had snatched
the virgin from the virgin goddess' altar;
and though, when Ajax raped Cassandra, he
alone deserved to pay the penalty,
Minerva's rage struck each and every Greek;
and we were scattered by the goddess, made

Latin [449–70]

to suffer lightning bolts and angry waves,
thrust into darkness, swamped by hurricanes—
the wrath of sky and sea and the immense
catastrophe of Cape Caphareus. I
won't keep you now to hear our miseries
told one by one; I'll only say of Greece
that it could even have made Priam weep.
Yes, I was able to escape the waves,
thanks to the aid of warrior Minerva.
But once again I had to leave my land;
this time, the fertile Venus made me pay
for an old wound that I had given her—
a wound she still remembered. So, in sum,
I suffered such great grief on the high seas
and, in my wars on land, such miseries,
that I would often deem most happy those
the deadly tempest drowned at Cape Caphareus.

"My men had borne the worst that wars and waves
can offer: they gave way to weariness;
they longed to see the last of voyages.
And Acmon, born to fume and flare by nature,
was filled with still more spleen by these disasters.
He cried: 'But is there anything at all
that you, my friends, cannot withstand! If Venus
should seek to heap still greater woes on us,
can she outdo what she's already done?
As long as one fears even greater hurt
is yet to come, he's vulnerable—but
when fate already has unleashed the worst,
then dread can be dismissed: when our ill luck
is at its height, despair can be packed off.
Though Venus hear my words and show her hate
for all of Diomedes' men—no matter:
to scorn her hate is our best shield against her.'

"The bitter words of Acmon only serve
to anger Venus, to revive her hurt.

But few among my faithful crew approved
of his abrasive speech. Far more reproach
our comrade; but when he attempts to speak,
his voice—together with its road, his throat—
thins out. What was his hair is feathers now;

and on his new-shaped neck, the feathers sprout,
as on his chest and back; and his forearms

show longer plumage, and his elbows curve
into long wings; a web grows on his feet,
a web that now englobes his toes; his mouth
grows stiff and horny, lengthens to a point.

"And Lycas, as he watches Acmon altered
so mystifyingly, is struck with terror,
and so are Idas, Nycteus, and Rhexenor
and Abas; as they stare, they, too, take on
the very form of Acmon. Almost all
my crew become a flying flock; they flutter
around the oars. And should you ask what sort
of birds these were, so suddenly transformed:
they were not swans, and yet they were, in kind,
much like the snow-white swans. Now you know why
I, the Iapygian Daunus' son-in-law,
find it so hard to make this city prosper:
the countryside is parched—and I am left
with almost none of my most trusted men."

So Diomedes said. And when he left
that region, Venulus went past the bay
of the Peucetians and then the lands
of the Messapians, in which he saw—
hid in a great and shadowed forest—caves
concealed by supple, slender reeds that swayed.
The half-goat Pan has made that place his home;
but long ago, it was the dwelling-place
of nymphs. But they had taken flight, afraid

Latin [496–517]

of an Apulian shepherd; in dismay—
he'd burst upon them suddenly—they ran
away; but soon, with their good sense regained,
they saw who'd chased them off and, taunting him,
they danced with agile feet—a choral dance.
The shepherd mocked them; and in mime, he pranced
with loutish steps, and added insults, spat
obscenities. His blabber did not stop
until the tree-bark cloaking him climbed up
around his neck: he's now a tree, in fact.
And from the juice and fruit one can divine
the nature of that shepherd; as a sign
of what he was, his tongue has left its mark:
the fruit of the wild olive tree is harsh;
the berries bear the trace of his rude words.

On Venulus' return, when Turnus learned
that Diomedes would not help their cause,
even without those added forces he
and his Rutulians did not relent;
and on both warring sides much blood was shed.
With avid torches, Turnus struck against
the Trojans' pine-framed ships: the waves had spared
those hulls, but now they faced a flaming threat—
a fire that fed on resin, fed on pitch,
and any other thing that nourished it;
it even climbed the towering masts, attacked
the sails; and from the curving hull's cross-planks,
smoke rose. But then Cybele called to mind
that all this timber came from her own pines;
and so the sacred Mother of the gods,
with brazen cymbals, clanging loud and harsh,
and with her brash and blatant boxwood flutes,
filled all the sky; drawn through the light air by
her team of harnessed lions, she outcried:
"O Turnus, with your sacrilegious hands

Latin [517–39]

you fling—in vain—those torches! I shall save
these ships; I'll not permit the greedy flames
to burn these pines—these parts, these very limbs—
of my own forests."

                                    As the goddess spoke,
the thunder roared, its boom announced a downpour
of rain and leaping hail: the brother winds—
Astraeus' sons—assailed the sky and burst
upon the waves and warred among themselves.
A gust from one of those three winds now helped
the nurturing Mother goddess; and she snapped
the hempen hawsers that had held hard fast
the Phrygian fleet; the ships were free; Cybele
now tilted them head down—into the sea.
The wood at once grew soft, turned into flesh;
the curving prows were transformed into heads;
the oars were changed to toes and swimming legs;
the flanking timbers, into living sides;
the keels, which line the ships midway, were spines;
the robes became soft hair; the sailyards changed
to arms. The color of the ships remained:
transformed to Naiads, they are still sea-green.

Those ships were born on rugged mountaintops;
but now, as water-nymphs, with young girls' joy
they sport among the waves they used to fear;
but in soft waters, none among the throng
of nymphs bears traces of her origins.
And yet, recalling perils undergone
in savage storms at sea, they often help,
with their supporting hands, all ships at risk
of sinking—that is, all but Grecian ships.
In fact, remembering the ruin wrought
at Troy, they hate the Greeks; and they were glad
to see Ulysses' ship with shattered planks,
and see the vessel of Alcinous
grow stiff as all its timbers turned to stone.   ▢   ▢   ▢

Latin [539–65]

After the ships were changed to living nymphs,
there was some hope that the Rutulians,
awed by that prodigy, would stop at last.
But they fought on; each side could count upon
its gods and—just as good as gods—its courage.
By now it's not the dowry of a kingdom,
and not the scepter of a father-in-law,
nor even you, virgin Lavinia,
that spurs them—it is simply victory:
for shame of giving up, they will not stop.
But Venus finally could see her son
triumphant: Turnus fell. So did the town
of Ardea; while Turnus was alive
its power won much fame. But when the flames
of foreigners had razed it, what remained
was nothing but warm ashes; yet from that
debris, a bird flew up, one never seen
before; it beat the ashes with its wings.
Its sound, its scrawny frame, its ashen hue,
all these seemed suited to a ruined town;
and so that bird still bears the city's name:
the heron is an Ardeidae bird—
its beating wings are Ardea in mourning.

By now Aeneas' piety and prowess
moved all the gods—and even Juno's self—
to set aside their ancient spleen and spite.
Iulus had grown up, his destiny
was well secured; and now the time had come
for heaven to receive the valiant son
of Cytherea. Venus had beseeched
the other gods' approval; lovingly,
her arms around her father's neck, the goddess
asked this: "You never have been harsh with me,

Latin [566–86]

dear father, and I need your kindness now,
as does Aeneas. He is of my blood,
and you are his grandfather; may you then,
in all your magnanimity, grant him
some portion of divinity—a place,
however small, in heaven. He has seen
the frightful kingdom of the dead—he crossed
the Stygian streams—and once is quite enough."
And all the gods agreed; even the queen,
Jove's wife, did not look on impassively:
she, too, consented peacefully. Jove said:
"Both you who pray and he whose cause you plead
deserve this gift from heaven: it is yours!"

Such were his words. And Venus thanked her father;
then, drawn through the light air by harnessed doves,
she went to the Laurentian shore, just where,
concealed by reeds, Numicius' winding stream
pours its fresh waters out into the sea.
She asked the river-god to wash away
and carry off, along his silent course,
into the sea's abyss, all mortal parts
of her Aeneas. And the horned Numicius,
obeying Venus, cleansed her son of his
mortality; the purest part alone
was left, and this—his sublimated body—
she then anointed with ambrosia mixed
with honeyed nectar, deifying him:
a god the Roman people called Indiges,
revered with altars and a sanctuary.

And with his father gone, Ascanius—
or Iulus, for he bore two names—became
the king of Alba and the Latin realm.
The next in line was Silvius; and then
his son, Latinus, ruled—one who bore both

Latin [587–611]

the name of his ancestor and his scepter;
and he was followed by the famous Alba;
and Epytus, his son, succeeded him.
The next to rule were Capys and Capetus;
and after them the king was Tiberinus,
who gave his name to that same Tuscan stream

in which he drowned. His sons were Remulus

and the proud Acrotas; the older one
was Remulus, who, trying to mime lightning,
was struck down by a lightning bolt. His brother,
a man who was more prudent, passed the scepter
to sturdy Aventinus, who is buried
on that same hill where he once reigned, the hill
to which he gave his name. After his death,
the people of the Palatine had Proca
as ruler—and the story of Pomona
took place in Proca's days.

         In Latium,
no fair nymph had more skill and passion than
Pomona in her love for gardens and
for trees and plants that yield fine fruit: in truth,
she owed her very name to that pursuit.
She was not drawn to streams, not drawn to woods;
but fields and branches bearing lovely fruit
delighted her. That nymph did not hold fast
a lance in her right hand; instead she gripped
a curving pruning-hook—it was with this
that she trimmed leaves grown too luxurious
and cut back branches that were too entwined;
with this she would incise the bark to graft
sap from one plant onto another's branch.
And she took care that no plant suffered thirst;
she sprinkled water on the porous roots'
entangled fibers. This was her sole task,
her love: she did not long for carnal touch.

Pomona feared the peasants' brutish ways,

fenced off her orchards, and avoided men—
she never let them in.

How hard they tried—
young Satyrs, with their dancing, leaping steps

and Pans, whose horns were garlanded with pines;
and he whose years were more than what he showed,
Silvanus; and Priapus, he whose scythes
and penis are a sight that terrifies
all thieves—they tried, but they did not succeed.
Vertumnus was the one who loved her most;
but like the rest, he, too, met brusque repulse.
How often did that god disguise himself
and, as a sturdy reaper, bring her gifts
of barley ears in baskets—and in fact,
his camouflage was perfect: he would wrap
fresh hay around his brow; one would have said
that he'd just come from turning new-mown grass.
At other times he gripped a cattle-prod
in his rough hand, and you might well have sworn
that he had just unyoked his weary oxen.
With scythe in hand, he seemed to be a man
who rakes the leaves and prunes the vines; and if
he put a ladder on his back, he seemed
about to gather apples. With a sword,
he was a soldier; if he bore a rod,
he was a fisherman. His masquerades
were many; and by way of them, he gained
an entry to her orchards and a chance
to see Pomona's haunting loveliness.
One day, when he had clapped upon his head
a gray wig and, around his temples, bound
a motley wimple to disguise himself
as an old woman, leaning on a staff,
he entered her fair orchard. When he had
admired the fruit he saw, he told the nymph:
"My, my—how skilled you are!" That said, he kissed
Pomona as no true old woman would;

Latin [636–59]

and then, his body bent, along the grass,
he sat and gazed at the autumnal boughs
weighed down by fruit. In front of him there stood
an elm whose boughs were artfully arrayed
with gleaming grapes. And after he had praised
the elm and its companion vine, he added:

"But if that trunk stood there alone, unwed
to that grapevine, in every way except
for foliage it would seem worthless—and
the vine that now embraces lovingly
the tree to which it's mated, would lie flat,
dispirited, upon the ground. That plant
has taught you nothing; you shun marriage—and
desire no one. If you'd welcome men,
the crowd of suitors who would seek you then
would far outnumber those who sought the hand
of Helen! Neither she who stirred the war
between the Lapiths and the centaurs, nor
the wife of timid—or, some say, the bold—
Ulysses ever moved as many men
as you, Pomona, could. For even now,
although you shun and scorn all those who plead,
you are the prize a thousand young men seek—
and half-gods, gods, and all those deities
who haunt the Alban hills. But if you're wise,
and would agree to a fine marriage, heed
what this old woman (one who loves you more
than all those others love you—and indeed
more than you would believe) now says: reject
those banal offers, and instead accept
Vertumnus as the one to share your bed!
I'll give you all the guarantees you want
on his account: though he may know himself,
I know him just as well. No nomad stray,
he will not wander off on vagrant ways;
he never fawns upon the highly placed;
nor is he like those many suitors who,

Latin [659–81]

as soon as they catch sight of someone new,
run off to her. I'm sure that you will be
the first and final love he will pursue,
the one to whom, life long, he will be true.
And add to this his other gifts: he's young,
and nature blessed him with a gracious form;
and he is versatile—he can take on
all shapes and miens; ask him to become
whatever form you want—and it is done.
And, too, your tastes show similarities;
you tend your fruit with love, but is not he
the first to welcome what you offer—glad
to hold in his right hand your gifts of fruit?
But now he is not bent on what your trees
may bear; nor does he care for garden herbs,
however sweet their juice: what he pursues
is you alone—and nothing else will do.
Have mercy, he is burning; act as if
the plea that you are hearing from my lips
had come from his own self. And do take care:
remember—there are gods who punish all
hard hearts: you know that Venus loathes such souls;
and so does she whose shrine is in Ramnuntes—
yes, Nemesis is one who won't forget
her anger. And that you may duly fear
the fruits of arrogance (my many years
have taught me many lessons), I shall share
an episode that all of Cyprus knows:
a tale that may persuade your heart to feel
more sympathetically, to bend, to yield:

"Young Iphis had seen Anaxarete;
while she was from a noble family,
he was of humble birth. He saw her once,
but that was quite enough: within his bones,
he felt the flame of love. And though he fought

against its force, he could not overcome
his frenzy: reason lost—and so he went
and stood before her door, a suppliant.
There, to her nurse, the lovesick youth confessed
his longing, pleading for benevolence:
he prayed that even as the nurse held dear
her charge, she would not be too harsh with him.
And one by one, he begged the many servants—
whom he'd ingratiated—to support
his cause; for often he'd consign his words
to waxen tablets, asking them to bear
his pleas and prayers to her. At times he propped
garlands against her door—wreaths wet with tears.
But she was even harsher than the sea
that surges at the setting of the Kids,
harder than iron forged in furnaces
of Noricus, or living rock that grips
the spot where it has roots, and so she mocked
her lover; with her acts, her words, she robbed
poor Iphis of all hope: she was too proud,
too cruel. That long torment was too much;
and there, before the door, he said: 'You've won;
now, Anaxarete, there is no need
for you to be disturbed because of me.
Prepare a joyful triumph, sing your songs
of victory, and wear your gleaming crown
of laurel. You have won indeed, and I
die willingly. And you can take delight
in that—you, made of iron. With that act
you will find something in my love—at last—
to praise; my death will please you; you will grant
some merit to me. But remember this:
my love for you won't end until my life
is ended; at my death, I lose two lights.
And you will not hear news of my demise
at second hand: it's I myself—yes, I—
whom you will see before you as I die;
I shall be visible—your cruel eyes

Latin [701–28]

can feast upon my corpse. But you, o gods,
if it be true that you watch mortal things,
remember me (there is no plea
my tongue can utter now); and to my fame,
add all the time you've taken from my days.'

"That said, he lifted up his tearful eyes
and pale arms to the door that, time on time
again, he'd wreathed with garlands; as he tied
a rope around the highest beam, he cried:
'O ruthless woman, is this—then—the kind
of wreath that pleases you?' He slipped his head
into the noose—and doing so, he kept
his head turned toward her room; and there he swayed
with broken neck—a lifeless, wretched weight.
His feet were dangling, twitching, and they struck
her door; and with a sound that seemed to moan,
it opened: what had happened now was clear.
The servants wailed and took the body down
and bore it to his widowed mother's house.
She clutched the cold corpse of her son, and then
she spoke the words of grief that parents speak
and led the sorry mourners in their course
through city streets; and Iphis' pallid corpse
lay on the bier as it was carried toward
the pyre. The house of Anaxarete
lay close to where the mourners had to pass,
and so that cruel girl heard their laments—
the girl on whom a god now wrought revenge.
At first uncertain, she then said: 'Let's look
at this sad funeral.' Beneath the roof,
there was a room whose window opened wide.
As she leaned out that window, catching sight
of Iphis on his bier, her eyes grew rigid;
her body lost all its warm blood; she paled;
and trying to step back, she could not budge;
nor she could turn her face aside—and soon
her body was held fast by that same stone

Latin [728–57]

whose hardness had—long since—possessed her heart.
And lest you think that I've invented this,
on Cyprus, in the town of Salamis,
the stony form of Anaxarete
still stands—a statue. Facing it, there is
a temple called the shrine of Gazing Venus.

"Pomona, my dear nymph, just keep these things
in mind, and set aside your arrogance:
wed him who loves you. And in recompense,
no late spring frost will nip your fruits in bud,
and headlong winds won't rip your blossoms off."

———————

So did the god, in an old woman's guise,
plead with Pomona—getting no reply.
At that, Vertumnus once again took on
his own true form; his masquerade was done;
he showed Pomona all his splendor, young
again—as when the radiant sun has won
its war against the clouds—victorious,
it shines with its unfettered light. Vertumnus
stood ready now to take the nymph by force;
but force was hardly needed, for his beauty
entranced her—godly beauty. Now she, too,
felt the same passion: love had pierced her through.

———————

The story of Vertumnus and Pomona
took place when Proca ruled Ausonia.
And it was Numitor who should have been
Ausonia's next king; but his false brother,
Aumalius, usurped his place as ruler:
by force of arms, he won the Latin scepter;
old Numitor did not regain the crown
till Romulus and Remus, his grandsons

Latin [758–73]

(born of his daughter, Ilia, by Mars),
came to his aid; and on the feast of Pales,
the shepherds' tutelary goddess, Rome
was founded. Tatius and the Sabines launched
their war against the city; it was then
that traitorous Tarpeia showed the men
of Tatius how to take the secret path
into the citadel; and she—for this—
was justly punished when that very force
which she had helped repaid the girl with death.
The Sabines crushed her under their heaped shields
and then, in silence, just like stealthy wolves,
assailed the sleeping sentinels; they reached
the gates that Romulus had bolted tight
with sturdy bars. But Juno's own hand loosed
one bar, and as the gate turned on the hinge,
there was no sound. The only one to notice
the fallen bar along the gate was Venus;
and she'd have closed the gate again, but gods
are not allowed to undo what was done
by gods. So Venus had to call upon
some Naiads of Ausonia, whose home
was near the shrine of Janus, in a grove
well watered by a crystalline, cool spring.
Those nymphs did not refuse what Venus asked:
they let their fountains stream and gush. And yet
the gates of Janus' shrine were still not blocked;
that flood was not enough to shut the pass.
And so, into their streams' great flow they poured
hot sulfur and ignited with hot pitch
the hollow channels where their waters coursed.
By these and other means, the blazing steam
drove down into the fountain's deepest veins;
and you, the spring that until then had vied
with Alpine cold, are able now to boast
that you're a match for fire and fierce coals!
Smoke rose from the two gate-posts; in the shape
the fountain now had taken, it delayed

Latin [774–97]

the sturdy Sabines: though the gate was open,
the Sabines could not pass; and so the Romans
gained time—enough to arm. When Romulus
attacked, and desecrating swords had shed
the mingled blood of sons-in-law and fathers-
in law, and corpses covered Roman soil,
a truce seemed best, an end to war—and yet
one that did not depend on total slaughter.
Peace was declared, and Tatius shared the crown.

When Tatius died, the Romans and the Sabines
shared one same ruler, Romulus; both tribes
were treated equally. Mars laid aside
his helmet; to the Father of both gods
and men, he said: "O Father, it is time:
the power of Rome is firm; it does not hang
upon the might of just one man. Then grant
the prize you promised me and Ilia's son,
your worthy grandson, Romulus: it's come,
the time to snatch him up from earth and set
this Roman in the heavens. Once you said,
with all the gods in council (I recall
your gracious words—inscribed upon my soul):
'There will be one you'll bear to the gray-blue
of heaven.' Let your promise now prove true."
Jove nodded in assent; he hid the sky
with his encumbering clouds; he terrified
the earth with thunder and with lightning bolts.

Mars understood these signs of the Almighty:
now free to seize his son, he leaned upon
his lance as lever; with that added thrust,
he vaulted into his huge chariot;
then, wielding his resounding lash, he spurred
his fearless horses under their cruel yoke.
Descending through the air, Mars halted on

Latin [797–822]

the summit of the wooded Palatine;
and there, where Romulus was governing
the Romans as their rightful king, Mars seized
his son; and as he bore that mortal form
up through thin air, its human parts dissolved,
just as a leaden ball that has been hurled
from a great sling dissolves midway along
its course across the sky. Now Romulus
has gained a guise more fair: he is Quirinus—
in his white toga trimmed with purple stripes,
his form is worthy of the gods' high couches.

———

His wife Hersilia was weeping for
her Romulus: she thought that he had died.
So Juno ordered Iris to descend
along her arching rainbow to console
the widow with these words: "O you, much prized
by Latins and by Sabines, were the wife
of one so great and, now that he's divine,
are still most worthy of him; do not weep,
and follow where I lead if you would see
your husband; I shall take you to that green
grove on Quirinus' hill, the slope that shades
the sanctuary of the Roman king."

Iris obeyed, and gliding down to earth
along her many-colored arch, she spoke
to Queen Hersilia as she had been told.
The widow barely lifted up her eyes
and modestly replied: "O goddess (I
do not know who you are, but it is plain
that you're a deity), lead me to him—
let me see his dear face again: if fate
allows me that alone, to see him once
again and nevermore, I'll say I've gained
the heavens as a gift." □ □ □

Latin [822–44]

At once she went
with Thaumas' daughter to the Palatine,
the hill of Romulus. And there a star
from heaven glided down to earth, igniting
Hersilia's hair: she and the star—together—
ascended, rising through the upper air.
In heaven, with familiar hands, the founder
of Rome receives his wife, transforming both
her body and her name. He calls her Hora:
as goddess, she's Quirinus' wife once more.

Latin [845–51]

BOOK XV

MEANWHILE THEY SEEK a man to meet their needs:
one to succeed so masterful a king.
But Fame foresees their choice: long since, the name
of Numa is illustrious; and he
becomes the Roman king—deservedly.

He knows his people's laws and customs—but
that's not enough for Numa: now he wants
his spacious spirit to encompass more:
he sets himself to study nature's laws.
For love of this, he leaves his native Cures;
he journeys to the town where Hercules
was once a guest. And there, when Numa asked
who'd founded that Greek town in Italy,
an elder, one who was indeed well versed
in ancient lore, replied. These were his words:

"They say that Hercules, the son of Jove,
when he had carried off the Spanish herds,
and bore these riches back, as he returned
from Ocean, stopped at Cape Lacinium.
There, as his cattle grazed on tender grass,
the hero rested after his long task
within the house—not inhospitable—
of mighty Croton. As he took his leave,
he pledged: 'In just two generations' time,
on this same spot, a city is to rise.'

"What Hercules had promised came to pass.
Two generations later, in the land
of Argos, Myscelus—Alemon's son—
was born: and in his time, there was no one
the gods loved more. One night, as Myscelus
lay deep in sleep, club-bearing Hercules
stood over him and said: 'You now must leave
your native land! Be up, you are to seek
the distant Aesar, gravel-laden stream.'
To this he added many fearful threats—
if Myscelus evaded this command. □ □ □

Latin [1–24]

"And now both sleep and Hercules retreat;
but Myscelus, on waking, still must think
in silence of the vision he had seen;
he's torn by doubt—deep in uncertainty:
a god had come, commanding him to leave;
but none in Argos, under pain of death,
may leave his homeland; law prohibits that.

"The glowing Sun now hides his shining head
beneath the Ocean, and the starry face
of shadowed Night has risen from the waves:
again, the god appears to him—the same
he'd seen before, and with the same command
and added threats for disobedience.
Alemon's son, now terrified, prepares
to leave his native land, to seek elsewhere
another home; at once the rumor runs
throughout the town; he's seen as one who scorns
the laws. When his accusers' charge is done,
indicted, wretched—even as he lifts
his face and hands to heaven—Myscelus
cries out: 'O you, whose twelve great labors won
a place for you within the sky, have caused
my misery, my guilt: I need your help!'
An ancient custom called upon the men
of Argos, in deciding sentences,
to cast their votes with pebbles—black and white:
the black condemns, the white absolves. And so
they voted now, and all the pebbles cast
into the cruel urn were black. But when
they turned the urn and poured the pebbles out,
they'd all been changed to white; and with that count,
the verdict was reversed: so Hercules
had intervened—and Myscelus was freed.

"Alemon's son now offers thanks to his
defender, Hercules; then, with kind winds,
he crosses the Ionian—beyond

Latin [25–50]

the Spartans' town, Tarentum; Sybaris;
Veretus; and the bay of Thuriae;
and Crimisa and the Iapygian fields.
Just past the lands that rim that shore, he finds
the Aesar; near that destined river's mouth,
Alemon's son at last has reached the mount
beneath which lie the consecrated bones
of Croton. Building city walls around
that spot—as Hercules had said he must—
he transfers to the town that he constructs
the name of him who lies beneath that mound."

Such were the origins—confirmed by sure
tradition—of that site and city: so
that town was founded on Italian soil.

Crotona had a man, Pythagoras,
who had been born in Samos but then fled
his island and its rulers, for he hated
all tyranny—and so had chosen exile.
Although the gods were in the distant skies,
Pythagoras drew near them with his mind;
what nature had denied to human sight,
he saw with intellect, his mental eye.
When he, with reason and tenacious care,
had probed all things, he taught—to those who gathered
in silence and amazement—what he'd learned
of the beginnings of the universe,
of what caused things to happen, and what is
their nature: what god is, whence come the snows,
what is the origin of lightning bolts—
whether it is the thundering winds or Jove
that cleave the cloudbanks—and what is the cause
of earthquakes, and what laws control the course
of stars: in sum, whatever had been hid,
Pythagoras revealed.   ▫   ▫   ▫

Latin [51–72]

He was the first
to speak against the use of animals
as human food, a practice he denounced
with learned but unheeded lips. His words:

"O mortals, don't contaminate your bodies
with food procured so sacrilegiously.
For you can gather grain, and there are fruits
that bend the branches with their weight, and grapes
that swell in clusters on the vines; there are
delicious greens that cooking makes still more
inviting, still more tender. You need not
refrain from milk, or honey sweet with scent
of thyme. The earth is kind—and it provides
so much abundance; you are offered feasts
for which there is no need to slaughter beasts,
to shed their blood. Some animals do feed
on flesh—but yet, not all of them: for sheep
and cattle graze on grass. And those who need
to feed on bloody food are savage beasts:
fierce lions, wolves, and bears, Armenian
tigers. Ah, it's a monstrous crime indeed
to stuff your innards with a living thing's
own innards, to make fat your greedy flesh
by swallowing another body, letting
another die that you may live. Amid
so many things that Earth, the best of mothers,
may offer, must you really choose to chew
with cruel teeth such wretched, slaughtered flesh—
and mime the horrid Cyclops as you eat?
Is your voracious, pampered gut appeased
by this alone: your killing living things?

"And yet that ancient age to which we gave
the golden age as name, was quite content
to take the tree-borne fruit as nourishment,
and greens the ground gave freely; no one then
defiled his lips with blood. Birds beat their wings

Latin [72–99]

unmenaced in the air; and through the fields,
hares wandered without fear; men did not snare
unwary fish with hooks. All things were free
of traps and treachery; there was no fear
of fraud; and peace was present everywhere.
But someone—he is nameless—then began
to envy lions' fare, and so he fed
his greedy guts with flesh—and sacrilege
was started. At its origins, confined
to savage beasts, the blade was justified:
our iron shed the warm blood, took the life
of animals who menaced us—and such
defense was not a profanation—but
the need to kill them never did imply
the right to feed upon them. From that seed
there grew still fouler crimes. The first to be
a sacrificial victim was the pig
because, with his broad snout, he rooted up
the planted seeds and spoiled the hoped-for crop.
The goat was also prey to punishment;
they butchered him on Bacchus' altars since
he browsed the god's grapevines. Those goats and pigs
were made to pay for what, in truth, they did;
but sheep, what did you do to merit death—
you, peaceful beasts, born to bring good to men,
you flocks whose swollen udders bear white nectar,
whose wool provides soft clothing for us—who
in life are far more useful than in death?
What evil has the bullock done—that beast
who never cheats, never deceives? Helpless
and innocent, he has unending patience.
Ungrateful—and indeed not meriting
the grain he's gathered—is the man who then,
with harvest done, when he's unyoked his friend,
would butcher him and aim his ax against
the neck that bears the signs of heavy tasks,
the neck of one who helped him reap the crop,
renewing stubborn soil. And men were not

content with that: they even made the gods
share in iniquity: the deities
were said to take delight in the destruction
of the untiring ox. The stainless victim,
unblemished and most handsome (too much beauty
brings sorrow), all adorned with gilded horns
and fillets, is arrayed before the altar
and, ignorant of what they mean, must hear
the prayers recited; and when they append
upon his head, between his horns, the ears
of grain that he helped gather, he must stand
and wait and watch his executioners.
When struck, he stains with his own blood the blade
whose flash he may in fact have seen reflected
in the clear waters of the temple pool.
At once—while he is still alive—they pull
the vitals from the victim's chest; and these
they scrutinize, to see if they can read
the god's intentions. Oh, do you, the tribe
of mortals, dare to feed upon such meat?
Can you lust so for that forbidden feast?
Stop that disgrace, I pray: heed what I say!
But if, in any case, your mouths still crave
the limbs of butchered beasts, then be aware
that you're devouring your own laborers.

"And since it is a god who urges me,
my lips will follow him devotedly.
I shall disclose my Delphi: I'll reveal
the truths of heaven, all the oracles
that highest wisdom holds. The things I sing
are mighty things our forebears did not probe,
things that have long been hidden. Let us roam
among the starry heights; yes, let us rise
above the earth—this site so dull, inert;
let clouds transport us, let us stand upon
the sturdy Atlas' shoulders; from that height,
we shall watch those who stagger far below,

Latin [127–50]

who, lacking reason, stray and stumble, those
who tremble in the face of what death holds;
but I'll dispel their fears: I shall unfold
the ways of fate. O you, bewildered race,
dismayed and terrified as you await
the chill of death! Why do you dread the Shades
and empty names that poets fabricate?
The Styx is nothing but a counterfeit,
a figment world whose perils don't exist.
Your bodies, whether they have been consumed
by flames upon the pyre or worn away
by time, can suffer nothing more, I say.
But over souls—be sure—death has no sway:
each soul, once it has left one body, takes
another body as its home, the place
where it lives on. Yes, I myself recall
that when the Trojan war was waged, I was
Euphorbus, son of Panthous; my chest
was pierced by Menelaus' heavy lance.
Not long ago, at Juno's shrine in Argos,
the city Abas built, I recognized
the shield that my left arm—in time gone by—
held high. For all things change, but no thing dies.
The spirit wanders: here and there, at will,
the soul can journey from an animal
into a human body, and from us
to beasts; it occupies a body, but
it never perishes. As pliant wax
is still the selfsame wax, so do I say
that soul, however much it may migrate,
is still the same. And thus, lest piety
suffer defeat when faced with belly's greed,
do not expel—so I, a prophet, teach—
the soul of others by your butchery:
those souls are kin to your own souls; don't feed
your blood upon another's blood.

□   □   □

Latin [150–75]

520

"Indeed,
since I am now well launched on this vast sea
and, under full sail, with kind winds, can speed,
I add: in all this world, no thing can keep
its form. For all things flow; all things are born
to change their shapes. And time itself is like
a river, flowing on an endless course.
Witness: no stream and no swift moment can
relent; they must forever flow; just as
wave follows wave, and every wave is pressed,
and also presses on the wave ahead;
so, too, must moments always be renewed.
What was is now no more, and what was not
has come to be; renewal is the lot
of time.

"You see how nights flow toward firstlight,
and how resplendent light succeeds dark night.
And when all weary things have given way
to sleep, the heavens' hue is not the same
as when bright Lucifer, on his white steed,
rides out; and still another color reigns
when, heralding the day, Aurora stains
the sky before consigning it to Phoebus.
And when that god's round shield is rising from
beneath the earth, at morning, it is red;
and it is red when, once again, it sets;
but at its zenith, Phoebus' shield is white,
for there the air is purer, and the blight
of earth—its foul contagion—is far off.
Nor can the nightly shape Diana takes
remain unchanged: the size that she displays
today will grow tomorrow or will wane.

"And then, too, can't you see the year's career
in changing chapters, four in number, like
the ages of our life? In early spring,
the year is fresh and tender as it mimes

Latin [176–202]

a little child; the plants are swollen, soft;
and though they still lack force, they do enchant
the farmers' hearts with hope. All blossoms; and
the colors of the flowers play; they dance
across the fertile fields, though stem and branch
are frail as yet. But after spring has passed,
the year is more robust: it now has crossed
to summer; it is like a strong young man;
there is no season sturdier than this,
none more exuberant, more keen, more rich.
Then autumn enters; fervor may be lost,
but fall is ripe and mild; a time midway
between our youth and age, and flecked with gray
upon the temples. Then, with faltering steps,
and shriveled, shivering, old winter treads;
now all its hair is gone—or any left
is white.

      "Just so, our bodies undergo
the never-resting changes: what we were
and what we are today is not to be
tomorrow. Once we were but simple seeds,
the germ from which—one hoped—a man might spring;
we dwelled within our mother's womb until,
with hands expert and wily, nature willed
that we not lie so cramped in narrow walls,
within our mother's bowels; she drew us out
into the open air from our first house.
Brought forth into the light, the infant lay
helpless; then on all fours, much like a beast,
he hauled his body up and, with his knees
unsteady, wobbling still, gradually,
although in need of props, stood on his feet.
Once he has gained agility and force,
he journeys through the time of youth and then
the days of middle age; when these are spent,
he glides along the downhill slope, the west
of time, the age when sunlight sets. The strength

Latin [202–28]

that once was his is undermined, upset;
so Milon, now that he is old, laments:
he weeps to see the arms that once had biceps
that rivaled Hercules' in mass and strength
but now hang flabby, slack. And Helen weeps
when, in the looking-glass, her eyes can see
her aged wrinkles; and she asks how she
could ever have been sought and carried off
as prize—not once, but twice. You, Time, as well
as envious Old Age, devour all;
with gnawing teeth, with slow and lingering
demise, you two destroy, consume all things.

"Not even things that we call elements
persist. And now I shall explain to you
(but listen carefully) what they go through.
There are four generating substances
in the eternal universe. And two,
water and earth, are heavy; drawn by their
own weight, they sink below. Whereas the air
and fire, which is purer still than air,
are weightless; and if nothing curbs their course,
those two will tend to rise on high. All four—
earth, water, air, and fire—are separate
in space, yet each is born out of the other,
and, to the other, each of them returns.
Thus earth, released from its confines, thins out,
becoming liquid; and when thinned still more,
that water is transformed to air and vapor;
and on its part, the air, released from weight,
leaps higher still, so that it takes its place
as fire, which occupies the topmost space;
but then, when fire thickens, it returns
to air, and air to water; water, when
it has coagulated, turns to earth.

"There is no thing that keeps its shape; for nature,
the innovator, would forever draw

Latin [228–53]

forms out of other forms. In all this world—
you can believe me—no thing ever dies.
By birth we mean beginning to re-form,
a thing's becoming other than it was;
and death is but the end of the old state;
one thing shifts here, another there; and yet
the total of all things is permanent.

"I think there's nothing that retains its form
for long: the world itself has undergone
the passage from the age of gold to iron.
And places also change: for I have seen
what once was solid land turn into sea,
and what before was sea turn into land.
Seashells lie distant from the oceanside;
old anchors have been found on mountain tops,
and waters flowing down the slopes have made
plains into valleys; and the force of floods
has carried mountains down into the sea;
what once were marshlands have become dry sands,
and lands that once were parched are now wet marsh.
Here nature has new fountains flow, and here
she blocks their course; the tremors of the earth
at times make rivers rush, at times obstruct
and curb a stream until it's seen no more.
The Lycus, swallowed by the yawning earth,
emerges at a point far off, reborn
in other guise; the Erasinus' flow
is swallowed by the soil and glides along
beneath the earth until it surfaces—
a mighty stream—in the Argolic fields;
and, discontent with its old banks and source,
in Mysia the Caicus changed its course;
whereas the Amenanus, bearing sands,
at times will flow through Sicily and then,
at other times—its sources blocked—dries up.
Anigrus' waters once were pure enough
to drink, but now they're better left untouched

(unless all that the poets sing is false);
for there the biform centaurs bathed the wounds
inflicted by the bow of Hercules,
when he who bears the club defeated them.
And, too, has not the Hypanis, which once
ran sweet and fresh down from the Scythian hills,
been spoiled by waters bearing bitter salt?

"Antissa, Pharos, and Phoenician Tyre—
all three were once surrounded by the sea,
but none of these is now an isle. Whereas,
in days gone by, all those who lived on Leucas
could say their homes were on the mainland, now
the sea surrounds them: Leucas is an isle.
Messina once was joined to Italy—
they say—until their common boundary
was borne off by the sea, which intervened
with waves and pushed the land away from land.
And if you searched for Helice and Buris,
Achaean towns, you'd find them underneath
the waves; with sailors as your guides, you still
can see—submerged—the sloping city walls.
Near Troezen, Pittheus' town, there is a hill
that rises from a plain that once was level—
completely flat; that tall and treeless mound
resulted from the winds' ferocious force:
for (this is terrible to tell) the winds,
imprisoned in dark caverns underground,
after they'd fought in vain for freer space
within the sky (those caves had not one cleft
where gusts could pass), puffed out; the soil was stretched,
as one inflates a bladder with his breath
or a two-horned goat's skin used as a sack.
That site still bulges, and it has the aspect
of a high hill; as time went by, it hardened.

"Though many more examples come to mind—
things I have seen or heard men tell—I'll cite

Latin [282–308]

only a few. Just think of guise on guise
that water takes. Horned Ammon, at midday
your stream is cold; at dawn and dusk it warms,
and—so they say—the Athamanians,
just when the moon has almost fully waned,
pour water onto wood to kindle flames.
And there's a river of the Cicones
that turns to stone the guts of those who drink
its waters; anything its waters touch
is changed to marble. And not far from us,
Cratis and Sybaris can make one's hair
like gold and amber. What is even more
astonishing—those waters can transform
not just the body but the mind as well.
Who can forget Salmacis' horrid pool
and, too, the lakes of Ethiopia—
those lakes that drive to madness all who drink,
or plunge them into sleep so strange, so deep?
Whoever slakes his thirst at Clitor's fount
shuns wine; abstemious, he prizes just
pure water; and the cause of this may be
those waters' power to counteract wine's heat;
or else—as people of that place insist—
when Amythaon's son, with spells and herbs,
freed Proetus' daughters from insanity,
he threw the herbs he'd used to purge their minds
into that spring; and to this day, the hate
of wine remains within that fountain's waves.
But in the land of the Lyncestians,
there is a stream with opposite effect:
whoever swallows but a moderate
amount of water there, will sway as if
he'd drunk pure wine. And in Arcadia
there is a lake (the ancients called it Pheneus)
whose waters are ambiguous: by night
it's to be shunned; drunk then, its waters are
malefic; drunk by day, they do no harm.
. . .

Latin [308–34]

The powers manifest in lakes and streams—
as you can see—are various indeed.

"In ancient days Ortygia floated freely,
and now that island has stability;
and when the *Argo* sailed, it was afraid
of the Symplegades: with crashing spray,
those rocks would pound each other, but today
the reefs are fixed and firm; they don't give way
before the winds. And Aetna, too, has changed
and will yet change again: for now it flames
with fires from sulfurous furnaces, and yet
it will not flame forever—and, in fact,
there was a time when all its flames were spent.
And to account for this, one might suggest
that earth is like a living animal:
it is equipped with many breathing-holes
to exhale flames, and it indeed can change
from time to time the paths its fires take;
for every time earth shakes, it can close caves
at one point, while it opens them elsewhere.
Or one could offer this hypothesis:
that if, within the deep caves underground
swift winds have been imprisoned, when they gust,
they drive the rocks against each other and
against the flinty matter that contains
the seeds of flame, and so the caves grow hot;
but once the winds have lost their force, the caves
will once again cool down. Or one might claim
that pitch and other things bituminous
catch fire underneath, or yellow sulfur,
which burns with slender flames. And certainly,
when, in the course of many centuries,
earth will have lost its energies and can
no longer richly feed and fuel those flames,
voracious nature then will feel her lack
of nourishment: unable to withstand
that hunger, being left to starve, she'll let
those fires starve—and Aetna will be spent.   □   □   □

Latin [335–55]

"They say that in the Hyperboreans' land,
within Pallene, one finds certain men
who, when they've plunged into Minerva's pool
nine times, emerge with bodies covered by
light feathers. I do not believe that's true;
but it is said of Scythian women, too,
that they can gain light feathers through the use
of magic potions sprinkled on their bodies.

"But if we turn to things that we ourselves
can test and trust, you'll see that any corpse
which—through long lapse of time or else because
of liquefying heat—has decomposed,
is transformed into tiny animals.
If, after precious bulls are sacrificed,
you set their carcasses within a ditch,
you'll see (it's a familiar happening)
that everywhere among the rotting guts,
the pollen-gathering bees will soon spring up;
and like the bulls from which they've sprung, those bees
are fond of fields, work eagerly, and wait
with patience for the fruits their labor brings.
While from the buried body of a horse,
the animal that shows its worth in war,
it is the hornet that is born. Tear off
the curving claws of the shore-loving crab,
and hide the rest of him beneath the sands;
then, from the buried part, a scorpion
will come and threaten you with his hooked tail.
And in the countryside, those worms that weave
white threads among the trees (as farmers see)
will change, becoming butterflies—the form
that often is depicted on tombstones.
In slimy mud, one seeks and finds the seeds
that generate green frogs: they have no feet
at first; but soon enough, the frogs receive
the legs that help them swim; and since they need
to leap, the pair in back is longer than
. . .

Latin [356–78]

the pair in front. And at their birth, bear cubs
are nothing more than shapeless flesh—mere lumps—
until the she-bear licks their limbs and gives
to them the shape—however crude—that she
herself, their mother, has. And can't you see
just how the larvae of the honeybees
have bodies without limbs when they are born
within their waxen cells, the hexagons
that shelter them? And only later will
you see the bee get feet and, later still,
get wings. And Juno's sacred bird, whose tail
is graced by many starlike shapes, as well
as that great bird who bears Jove's thunderbolts;
and Cytherea's doves—indeed all birds:
unless one knew, could anyone suspect
that these came from the inside of an egg?
Some even hold that when the spinal bones
rot in the sepulcher, the human marrow
is changed into a snake.

          "In any case,
all of these newborn bodies take their shapes
from other bodies. One alone can take
life from itself and so regenerate:
the bird that the Assyrians call phoenix.
The phoenix does not feed on seeds of grain
or plants, but on the gum of frankincense
and juice of the amomum; when his life
completes five hundred years, the phoenix flies
onto a swaying palm; and in that tree
he builds, with talons and untainted beak,
a nest among the boughs. When he has lined
this nest with yellow myrrh, slim stalks of nard,
and powdered cinnamon and cassia bark,
the phoenix stretches out and ends his days
among those fragrances. And then—they say—
up from his father's body springs—reborn—
a little phoenix, one who'll live as long

Latin [378–402]

as did his father. When with time, the young
bird gains sufficient strength to free the boughs;
he carries off the nest that had weighed down
the tall palm-tree. So, piously, he bears
what was his cradle and his father's tomb
through the thin air, until he has drawn near
the city of Hyperion; and there
he sets the nest before the sacred entry,
the doorway of the Sun-god's sanctuary.
And if you find these things amazing, strange,
consider still another striking change—
the way that the hyena alternates:
now she's a female mounted by a male,
and now becomes herself the male who mounts.
To these, I'd add the animal that feeds
on wind and air and takes its color from
the color of the things it's placed upon.
And after the chameleon, I can
point to the present that the Indians
gave Bacchus after he converted them:
the god who's crowned by vines received a gift
of lynxes: any liquid they emit
turns into stones—they say—as soon as it
meets air. And something similar: the moment
that coral meets the air, it hardens—though
it was a pliant plant when underwater.

"But day could well be done, and Phoebus plunge
into the deep sea with his weary steeds,
before my words had finished a recounting
of all the things that take new shapes. We see
that eras change: for here some nations gain
and grow in strength, there others lose the day.
So, Troy had might and men and wealth: she could
afford for ten long years to shed her blood;
now, razed, all she can show are ancient ruins—
her only riches are ancestral tombs.
Sparta was famed, and great Mycenae claimed

much might; so did Amphion's citadel
and Cecrops', too. The land of Sparta now
is worthless; proud Mycenae is laid low;
what has the Thebes of Oedipus to show
except for her own name? And what is left
to Cecrops' Athens other than her fame?
And now the rumor runs that Rome, the town
that sons of Dardanus had founded, grows;
along the Tiber's banks—the stream that flows
down from the Apennines—that city lays
the base of a great state. There, too, is change:
for as she grows, Rome is reshaped; one day
she will hold all the world beneath its sway.
They say that this is what the oracles
and augurs have affirmed; I, too, recall
that, when the fate of Troy was insecure,
the son of Priam, Helenus, assured
Aeneas, then oppressed by doubt and sadness:
'O son of Venus, if you keep in mind—
as you indeed must do—the things that I
foresee, Troy is not doomed entirely,
for you are fated to be saved. For you,
between the fire and the sword, a path
will open. You will leave; and taking up
your Pergamum, you'll carry it until
you have found fields that are indeed more friendly
to you and Troy than your own soil has been.
This, too, I can foresee: that men descended
from Trojans are to found a city, and
no city is or shall be greater than
that city—nor have any ages past
seen any greater. Through long centuries
and through her chiefs, that city will achieve
much power; but she only will become
the ruler of the world beneath one born
of Iulus' line. And he will benefit
the earth; but at the end, he'll reach the sky;
in him, the heavens then will take delight.'

Latin [426–49]

These were the prophecies of Helenus,
the things he told Aeneas—I indeed
remember them. And I rejoice to see
walls built by brother Greeks in Italy;
but, too, I'm glad that, from Greek victory,
the Phrygians are to benefit immensely,
for Rome is to become the greatest city.

"But lest I gallop far beyond my reach
and, so, forget what I had meant to teach,
know this: the heavens and all things beneath
the heavens change their forms—the earth and all
that is upon the earth; and since we are
parts of the world, we, too, are changeable.
For we're not only bodies but winged souls;
and we can dwell in bodies of wild beasts
and hide within the shapes of cows and sheep.
And so, let us respect—leave whole, intact—
all bodies where our parents' souls or those
of brothers or of others dear to us
may well have found a home; let us not stuff
our bellies banqueting, as did Thyestes.
Whoever cuts a calf's throat with a knife
and listens, without pity, to its cries;
whoever kills a kid that, like a child,
wails loud; whoever feeds upon a bird
that he himself has fed—profanely sheds
the blood of humans: such a man abets
a habit that is evil—little less
than murder. What awaits us at the end
of such a path? I say to you: just let
the bullock plow, and only meet the death
that old age brings; and let the sheep provide
the wool that shields you from the glacial blasts
of Boreas; let she-goat's teats be pressed
to give you milk. And set aside your traps
and nets and cunning lures and snares: don't trick
the birds with twigs you've limed: don't scare the deer

Latin [450–75]

into the nets with feathers hung from trees;
don't hide barbed hooks in bait set to deceive.
You can kill animals that do you harm.
But do no more than kill: don't feed on them;
instead seek only gentle nutriment."

They say that Numa, when his soul had learned
from these and others' teachings, then returned
to his own city; and when he was urged
to take the reins, he ruled the Latin state.
There, with the nymph Egeria, the wife
he'd wedded happily, and guided by
the Muses, Numa trained in sacred rites
the Latins; and to them he taught the arts
of peace—for until then, they were warlike.
And when he'd reached the end of his long life
and rule, at Numa's death his people wept:
the Latin mothers and the commoners
and elders—all were mourners. And his wife,
abandoning the city, went to hide
in the thick woods that filled Aricia's valley.

And there, her loud laments disturbed the rites
and worship of Diana (for Orestes
had brought her cult to Latium from Greece).
The nymphs who graced those woods, that lake, beseeched
Egeria to stay her tears; again,
again, they spoke consoling words; again,
again, the son of Theseus joined their pleas:

"You've wept enough," he said; "you're not alone
in suffering a fate that merits tears.
Just look at others' griefs much like your own,
and you will bear your loss with greater calm.

Latin [475–94]

Would I call on others as examples
of suffering! And yet my own sad tale
may serve as well to ease the pain you feel.

"If you have ever chanced to hear the story
of one Hippolytus who suffered death
because his father was too credulous
and took as true the lies asserted by
his vile stepmother, you'll be stupefied
to hear—though it is hard to prove—that I
am that Hippolytus. Yes, Phaedra tried
to tempt me to defile my father's bed;
but she did not succeed, and so she twisted
the truth: the daughter of Pasiphae
charged me with having urged the sin that she
herself had wanted. (Was her falsehood born
of fear that I'd inform against her, or
of her deep hurt when I repulsed her lust?)
My father trusted her and banished me,
though I was blameless; as I left the city,
he cursed me fatally. A fugitive,
I rode toward Troezen in my chariot
(I thought I could take refuge there with Pittheus).
I had already reached the coast of Corinth,
when suddenly the sea swelled up, much like
a massive mound and then a mountainside.
It bellowed, and along the crest appeared
a horned bull; through the unresisting air
he rose, chest-high, and spouted giant jets
of water from his nostrils and his mouth.
My comrades froze with fear, but I did not:
my exile was the care that filled my thoughts.
But my hot-blooded horses turned seaward;
and now their ears pricked up; for they had seen
the monster; terrified, they went berserk;
and headlong, down the steep and rocky path,
they drew the chariot in their wild dash.
I tried in vain to curb them with the reins;

the bits were flecked with white foam as I strived
to draw the slack thongs taut by leaning back.
I tugged with so much force that I'd have quelled
their frenzy, curbed their course, had not a wheel—
just where it always turns on its own axle—
struck a tree trunk: the shattered wheel broke off.
And I was hurtled from my chariot:
you would have seen my guts dragged live across
the ground, my legs entangled in the reins,
my sinews sticking to the tree, as parts
of me were carried off and parts remained—
in shreds—behind; the sound was ominous
as my bones snapped. My soul exhaled its last—
its weary—breath. And no part of my body
was recognizable: I was just one
great wound. Now can you—dare you—nymph, compare
what you have suffered with my own disaster?
I saw the sunless kingdom of the dead;
I bathed my shattered body in the waves
of Phlegethon. And if I did regain
my life, I owe it to Apollo's son,
to Aesculapius' strong medicine.
His potent herbs and healing arts restored
my life, though that aroused the rage of Dis;
and then Diana hid me in a thick,
dark cloud, lest others might resent the gift
of life that I'd received; and that I might
move safely, unmolested, she took care
to age me, adding years; and all my features
were changed: I was unrecognizable.
But she took long before deciding on
my home: she conjured Delos, conjured Crete;
but then, renouncing both, she sent me here,
enjoining me to lay aside my name,
because 'Hippolytus,' recalling horses,
would have revealed my old identity.
She said: 'You who were once Hippolytus,
from this day on are Virbius.' Since then

Latin [519–45]

I live—a minor deity—within
this wood; I hide beneath her godly sway—
I am Diana's faithful devotee."

But others' anguish did not help assuage
the sorrow of Egeria. She lay
prostrate, along a mountain's base and wept,
until Diana, seeing her bereft,
a widow torn by pious grief, took pity
on sorrowing Egeria and gave
her body liquid shape: her limbs became
the waters of a cool, eternal spring.

That prodigy astonished all the nymphs,
just as it stupefied Hippolytus—
in fact his wonder was so great, it matched
the wonder an Etruscan farmer felt
when he, amid the fields, beheld a clod
that seemed portentous—moving by itself,
with no one budging it; and then it lost
its earthly shape; it took on human form;
and opening its newborn lips, it spoke
of things that were to come. The natives called
that augur Tages, and he was the first
to teach the people of Etruria
to read the future. And Hippolytus'
amazement also matched the wonder felt
by Romulus when he saw his spear-shaft—
fixed in the ground upon the Palatine—
sprout leaves and boughs; it did not stand erect
supported by its iron tips, but by
its newborn roots; it was no weapon now;
it had become a tree with pliant boughs
that offered unexpected shade to all—
who were astonished by that miracle.

◻ ◻ ◻

Latin [545–64]

———

Or one could match Hippolytus' dismay
with that of Cipus, who was so amazed
to see his head, reflected in the waves,
with horns.

———

          Yes, when he gazed into the stream,
he saw those horns reflected—but believed
his eyes had been deceived. Again, again,
he touched his forehead with his fingers—and
the image had not lied. He stopped beside
the river (he was on his homeward way
to Rome, returning from the wars, a victor)
and, lifting eyes and arms to heaven, cried:
"O gods, what ever is foretold by this
prodigious thing, if it brings benefits,
may they be shared by my own home, the land
and people of Quirinus; but if threats
are meant, may I alone confront the menace."
So Cipus prayed; then, of green turf, he made
an altar, burning incense to placate
the gods; and he poured out wine offerings;
and after sacrificing sheep, he called
upon an augur to consult the entrails—
they still were quivering—to see what tale
they told about the future Cipus faced.
The augur, an Etruscan, read at once
the signs of things momentous—though they were
still indistinct. But when he lifted up
his sharp eyes from the innards of the sheep
and saw the horns of Cipus, he cried out:
"O king, I greet you! For it is to you,
and to your horns that Rome herself and all
the citadels of Latium will bow.
But you must not delay: the city's gates
are open wide; be quick to enter Rome.
So destiny would have you do. And once

Latin [565–84]

you have been welcomed there, you are to gain
the scepter you—in safety—will retain
forever."

But before the walls of Rome,
Cipus drew back; he turned his eyes away;
his face was grim and grave as he exclaimed:
"Oh, may the gods save me from such a fate!
For I would rather end my days in exile
than be crowned king upon the Capitol."
And then he called upon the Roman people
and venerable Senate to assemble.
He garlanded his brow with peaceful laurel
to hide his horns; then, standing on a platform
of earth heaped up by his stout soldiers, he
invoked the ancient gods—as customary—
and said: "In this assembly, there is one
who, if you do not banish him, will be
your king. I shall not name him, but he bears
this sign: upon his brow, he has a pair
of horns. The augur has declared to me
that if this man should ever enter Rome,
he will dictate your laws, enslave you all.
In truth, the gates are open; and he could
have burst into our city: but I checked
his course—though he is closely linked to me.
O Romans, keep him far from your dear city;
or shackle him—if that's what he deserves—
with heavy chains; or free yourselves from fear
by killing him—for if he gains your city,
fate says that you will suffer tyranny."
At this, a murmur rose in the assembly,
the sort that sweeps across the squat pine-trees
when boisterous Eurus whistles through them, or
the sound of far-off surge. But in that crowd
of muddled voices, there was one more loud
than all the rest: "Who is he?" They searched out
each other's forehead, looking for the horns.

Latin [584–608]

Then Cipus said: "The man you seek is found."
Then (though they tried to stop him) he removed
the garland from his brow: he showed his horns.

And all cast down their eyes; as one, they moaned
and, most unwillingly (for who indeed
could have expected this?), looked at the head
of one who was so notable a man.
And, since they would not have his head stripped bare
of ornaments that honored him, again
they wreathed his head with a triumphal garland.

They did forbid your entering the city,
o Cipus; but to you, the senators
assigned this prize, this honor: as much land
outside the walls as you could circumscribe
within a furrow that your plow, pulled by
a team of oxen, working from sunrise
until the setting of the sun, inscribed
upon the soil. And on the gates of bronze,
the entryway to Rome, they sculpted horns
like your prodigious horns—so as to keep
your name alive through all the centuries.

O Muses, you who know (and can recall,
despite the lengthy span of ages) all—
you, guardian goddesses of poets—now
reveal to me just how the island bathed
by the deep Tiber had received the cult
imported there by Aesculapius,
as an addition to the other rites
that grace the city Romulus had founded.

The air of Latium, in ancient days,
had been polluted by a fatal plague.
Cadavers, pale and rotting, lay about;

Latin [609–27]

no human effort was of use, the art
of medicine was helpless. Men grew tired
of funeral on funeral; at last
they turned to heaven for relief; they went
to Delphi, at the center of the world,
beseeching Phoebus' oracle to grant
a remedy to Rome—to put an end
to their great city's wretched pestilence.

The place, the laurel, and the god's own quiver—
all trembled; and the tripod deep inside
the sanctuary offered in reply
these words, which filled the Romans' hearts with awe:
"O Romans, what you seek should have been sought
much closer to your home. Search there. It's not
Apollo's self you need: it is his son.
Then, go and—with my blessings—seek him out."

The Roman senators were wise; and when
they heard of this response—the god's command—
and learned that Phoebus' son could now be found
in Epidaurus, they asked messengers
to board a ship and, with its windswept sails,
to reach that coast. And when the embassy
had beached the curving ship upon that shore,
they sought the elders of that Grecian town
and asked them to dispatch the god to Rome,
for he was needed in Ausonia
to end a pestilence: the oracle—
infallible—had so instructed them.

The Greek response was mixed: some elders felt
that help was not to be denied, but many
said they should keep their god at home and not
send off their tutelary deity.
As they debated this, the hour grew late,
and evening chased away the light of day;
earth's orb was cloaked by darkness; and the god

Latin [628–53]

who brings the gift of health, o Roman, now
appeared within your dreams, before your bed.
He held a rustic staff in his left hand;
and with his right, he stroked his long, thick beard,
and these words issued from his peaceful breast:
"Fear not; I'll go with you—I shall give up
my sanctuary. But observe this serpent
that coils around my staff: do not forget
just how he looks. For I shall change myself
into this serpent, but I shall be larger,
as large as suits the body of a god
when he transforms himself." And when his voice
was done, the god was also gone; and when
the voice and god were gone, sleep vanished, too;
and as sleep fled, the day's kind light broke through.

Dawn put to flight the starlight fires of heaven:
the Grecian elders—still unsure—again
assembled at the temple of the god
the Romans hoped to carry off with them.
The elders begged the god to grant some sign
of where he would prefer to have his shrine.
They had just finished, when the god himself—
in serpent form, with towering gold crests—
announced his presence with a hissing sound;
and at the center of the shrine he rose,
chest-high, to half his length; his flaming eyes
looked all around. The crowd was terrified.
The priest, his chaste hairs bound by a white band,
had recognized the deity; he cried:
"The god is here! The god! With reverence
and awe, beseech him now. Magnificent
divinity, may your appearance here
bring benefits to us, and may you help
all those who worship at your sanctuary."
Repeating what the priest had said, they all
revered the god who had revealed himself.
And the descendants of Aeneas, too,

joined with the Greeks in worshipping the god
with pious voice and pious heart; and he,
to show that he agreed to leave for Rome,
shook his tall crest; and with his darting tongue,
he hissed repeatedly. Then, gliding down
the polished steps, before he left, he turned
his eyes to look, for one last time, upon
his ancient altars, to salute the shrine
that, for so long, had been his holy home.
That done, he slid—immense—across the ground,
which people strewed with flowers as he went;
and coiling and uncoiling through the town,
he reached the harbor with its curving quay.
And there he stopped a moment, as if he
wanted to thank the throng, to bid a kind
farewell to all who'd worshipped at his shrine.
And when the serpent settled with his body
upon the Roman ship, his weight was heavy:
beneath the burden of the deity,
the keel sank deep. The Romans were most happy:
they sacrificed a bull along the beach,
then garlanded the ship; and loosening
the hawsers, they sailed off. A light wind bore
their vessel on its course. The snake-god towers:
he rests his neck upon the curving stern
and gazes down below, at azure waters.

With Zephyr's gentle winds, they sailed across
the Ionian; and when Dawn showed herself
for the sixth time, their ship had reached the seas
of Italy: they passed the promontory
far-famed for Juno's shrine, Lacinium;
they passed Scylaceum and left behind
Iapygia. To avoid Amphrisia's rocks
upon the left, and the Cocinthian crags
upon the right, they plied their oars, then passed
Romethium and Caulon and Narycia.
Then, in the seas of Sicily, they crossed

Latin [682–706]

Pelorus' straits; and then sailed by the isles
of Aeolus, the mines of Temesa,
and Leucosia; and saw gentle Paestum's
rose gardens. Next they skirted Capreae,
Minerva's headland; and Surrentum's hills
so rich with vines; and Herculaneum
and Stabiae; and the city born for pleasure,
Parthenope; and then the Sibyl's temple
at Cumae. Sailing on, they then reached Baiae
with its hot baths; and with abundant groves
of mastic trees, Liternum; and the mouth
of the Volturnus, stream whose swirling flow
bears many sands; and Sinuessa, known
for flocks of snow-white doves; Minturnae, town
that is unwholesome; and the city named
Gaeta by Aeneas for his nurse,
whom he had buried there; and Formia,
the city of Antiphates; and Trachas,
the city ringed by marshes; and the land
of Circe; and the town with hard-packed sands
along its shoreline, Antium.

                        And there
the Romans drove their ship—her sails widespread—
to land (the sea was rough); and soon the god
of Epidaurus had uncoiled himself
and, gliding in great curves and spirals, entered
his father's temple on the tawny sands.
But once the sea had calmed again, he left
Apollo's altars—he had been a guest
most warmly welcomed by his godly parent.
With crackling scales, along the shore he slid
and, furrowing a path back to the ship,
climbed up the rudder. Once again he set
his head against the curving stern, until—
past Castrum, past Lavinium's sacred land—
he reached the Tiber's mouth.

□   □   □

Latin [706–28]

                                    Along the banks,
people of every sort, elders and matrons,
rushed out to welcome him; there, too, the virgins
who tend your fires, Trojan Vesta, came
to greet him jubilantly. As the ship
moved swiftly up the river, on the rows
of altars they had built along the shores,
the burning incense crackled, and the air
was filled with fragrance; and the knives were warm
with blood of sacrificial animals.

And now the ship had entered Rome itself,
the capital of all the world. The god
lifted himself on high and, coiling round
the masthead, moved his neck from side to side
to find the place best suited for his shrine.
There is a point at which the stream divides,
to wrap around a place they call the Island.
That land lies in the center; the two arms
of Tiber are of equal length—and here
the serpent son of Phoebus disembarked:
he left the Latin ship; and taking on
his godly form again, he put an end
to grief and pestilence; and as he came—
the bringer of good health—so he remained.

That god we venerated in our shrines,
to reach the Tiber, left his land behind;
but Caesar is a god in his own city.
He'd won great triumphs in the field and worn
the statesman's toga here at home—in sum,
he had a lightning-quick, a rich career—
but more than all of this, it was his son
who earned for Caesar apotheosis,
his change into a comet, a new star.
In truth, among the deeds of Caesar, none

Latin [729–50]

deserves more glory than his being one
who fathered our Augustus. Is there more
renown in having conquered seabound Britons;
in leading his triumphant fleet along
the course of the papyrus-bearing Nile,
up all its seven mouths; in his subjecting
to Rome the rebels of Numidia,
and Juba, Libya's king; one Mithridates
after another, Pontus' mighty kings;
in celebrating certain triumphs and
in earning many more—can such renown
surpass his having had so great a son?
O gods, in naming him—Augustus—lord
of all the world, you blessed the human race
abundantly! But such a king must be
a son of more than mortal seed: you need
to take his father Caesar from this earth.
You have to make of him a deity.

When Venus saw that this would come to pass,
but that it also meant a sorry death
for Caesar, her high priest—and there were signs
that an armed plot was being organized—
she paled; and to each god she met, she said:
"See this conspiracy, the cunning web
they weave, how faithlessly they would attempt
to kill the one descendant left to me
from Iulus' line—Dardanus' progeny!
Must I forever be the only one
who has such cause for worry and affliction?
First I was wounded by King Tydeus' son,
the lance of Diomedes; then I faced
despair—I saw the walls of Troy erased;
and I have had to watch the wanderings
of my Aeneas thrust along the sea,
and had to see my own dear son descending
into the region of the silent dead;
I watched him as he warred with Turnus—or,

Latin [750–73]

if it be truth that we would tell, with Juno.
But why need I recount the ancient trials
of my descendants? What awaits me now
does not allow me to recall old sorrows.
You surely see that sacrilegious blades
are being sharpened! Stop that threat, I pray;
prevent this crime; do not let Vestal's flames
be quenched by bloodshed—with her high priest's death!"

Such were the cries of Venus in distress;
across the sky they went—useless laments.
But they did stir the gods—who could not break
the ancient Sisters' ironclad decrees
yet gave sure signs that grief was imminent.

They say the hideous crime was presaged by
the clash of arms among dark clouds, and horns
and trumpets blaring horribly. The sun's
own orb was sorrowing; the light it shed
on frightened earth was lurid. Firebrands
would often flash beneath the stars; and gusts
of rain would often carry drops of blood.
The Morning Star was blue-gray, and his face
showed russet-colored blotches; and blood stained
the chariot of Luna. The sad owl,
that Stygian bird, was heard to mourn and warn,
and ivory statues wept throughout the land;
and from the sacred woods—so it is said—
came words of menace and distressing chants.
No sacrificial victim offered hope:
when augurs read the entrails, all they saw
were signs of imminent uproar in Rome;
the liver showed a severed upper lobe.
And in the Forum and around the homes
and, too, the temples of the gods—it's told—
dogs howled by night and silent spirits roamed;
and tremors shook the city.

□   □   □

Latin [773–98]

Though the gods
had sent these omens, that was not enough
to curb the course of fate and human plots.
So unsheathed swords were to profane the shrine:
no other place was chosen for the crime—
Caesar was to be slaughtered in the Curia.
And Cytherea, learning of that act,
indeed beats at her breast with both her hands;
and now she leans to hiding the descendants
of her Aeneas in a cloud just like
the cloud that long ago had sheltered Paris
from Agamemnon's wrath and saved Aeneas
from Diomedes' sword. But father Jove
dissuades her with these words:

"Would you, dear daughter,
alone, change fate, which never can be altered?
All you need do is visit the three Sisters;
in their own home you'll find the massive archive
of all the world: those tablets, made of brass
and tough iron, have no fear of lightning's wrath
or heaven's tremors; and they can withstand—
secure, eternal—any other shock.
There you will find the fate of your descendants
engraved on metal—indestructible.
I read those tablets; I remember them;
and so that you may not be ignorant
of what the future holds, I'll now recount
all that I learned. The man whose cause you plead
has reached the term of years that destiny
assigns to him on earth! But this man's son
together with you, Venus, will yet help
his entry into heaven as a god—
a god who will be worshipped in earth's shrines.
As for his son, the one who will inherit
his name, he will sustain—alone—the weight
that will be placed on him; he will be brave—
the best avenger of his father's murder;

and in the wars he wages to that end,
I shall be at his side—his close ally.
Of him, the walls of Modena, besieged,
defeated, will ask peace; Pharsalia
will feel his force; and Macedonian
Philippi, too, will bathe in blood; the one
whose name is great will meet defeat upon
the seas of Sicily. And the Egyptian
wife of a Roman general will fall;
she will not do too well in letting all
depend upon her marriage pact—and thus
her threat to subject our own Capitol
to her Canopus will prove empty, futile.
But is there any need for me to tally
barbaric lands, and peoples who inhabit
the Ocean's shores at both ends of the world?
All habitable places on the earth
will lie beneath his sway—and, too, the sea.

"And once he has endowed all lands with peace,
he'll set his mind on civic polity:
the laws that he establishes will be
most just. He'll discipline (and he himself
will set the best example) modes and manners;
and out of his concern for future times,
for generations yet to come, he will
command the son born of his pious wife,
to bear his name and carry on his mission.
But only when he reaches Nestor's years
will he resign these tasks and then ascend
up to the starry heaven, to a place
among his kin.

       "Meanwhile, o Venus, snatch
the soul of Caesar from his murdered flesh
and make of him a star: there, from on high,
he may forever be the deified
. . .

Latin [821–41]

Caesar who contemplates our Capitol
and Forum from his sacred place, his shrine."

No sooner had Jove told greathearted Venus
these words, than she, invisible to all,
went to a place within the Senate hall
and, from her Caesar's body, took his soul;
she would not have his spirit disappear
within the air; she bears it to the stars.
As Venus does so, she becomes aware
that it is growing bright, is catching fire;
at that, she lets the soul leave her own breast.
It flies on high, beyond the moon; behind,
it leaves a long and flaming trail until—
by now, a star—it glows. From there the soul
of Caesar recognizes that the toils
and triumphs of his son are greater than
his own: and he is glad to see his son
as his superior.

But though the son
forbids us to esteem what he has done
as finer than his father's labors, Fame
(who does just what she would and can't be tamed)
will not obey that order: Fame insists
on greater glory for the son—in this,
and this alone, Fame violates his edict.
So Atreus yields before great Agamemnon,
and Theseus outstrips Aegeus, and Achilles
surpasses Peleus. And if one should seek
an instance more appropriate than these,
Saturn is less than Jove. Just as Jove rules
high heaven and controls the triform world,
Augustus rules the earth; and thus, they both
are fathers and are sovereigns.

O you, gods
who were Aeneas' comrades, you who saved

Latin [841–61]

the Trojan from the sword and from the flames;
and you, the native gods of Latium;
as well as you who fathered Rome, Quirinus;
you, Mars, invincible Quirinus' father;
you, Vesta, who maintain a sacred place
among the tutelary gods of Caesar;
you, Phoebus, joined to Vesta as a god
who watches over Caesar's house; and Jove,
who have your shrine atop Tarpeia's rock;
and all you other gods to be invoked—
most properly—by one who is a poet:
I beg you to delay beyond my death
that day on which Augustus, having left
the world he governs, will ascend on high
and there, from heaven—one no longer present
on earth—will hear the prayers addressed to him.

And now my work is done: no wrath of Jove
nor fire nor sword nor time, which would erode
all things, has power to blot out this poem.
Now, when it wills, the fatal day (which has
only the body in its grasp) can end
my years, however long or short their span.
But, with the better part of me, I'll gain
a place that's higher than the stars: my name,
indelible, eternal, will remain.
And everywhere that Roman power has sway,
in all domains the Latins gain, my lines
will be on people's lips; and through all time—
if poets' prophecies are ever right—
my name and fame are sure: I shall have life.

Latin [861–79]

AFTERWORD

THE LAST WORD of the *Metamorphoses* is *vivam*—"I shall live" or, as I've translated it, "I shall have life." On the spacious abacus of the Leakeys, the centuries in which humans have written and read would seem somewhat scant in number. But into the eighty-or-so generations between Ovid and ourselves, he is one tutelary shade who has indeed crowded a rich and ever-active afterlife. Ovid has spurred translators, emulators, exegetes, echoers, and parodists as various as Dante, Chaucer, Caxton, Golding, Shakespeare, Sandys, Milton, Dryden—a cohort that is flanked, among so many others, by the anonymous Frenchman who, around the time of Dante, massed seventy-two thousand octosyllabic lines to translate and moralize the *Metamorphoses*; by the Benedictine Pierre Bersuire, who completed his Ovidian handbook around 1340; and by the eighteenth-century Talmudist-kabbalist of Padua, Isaiah Bassani, who began a translation of the *Metamorphoses* into Hebrew (using as his base Anguillara's notable Italian translation into octaves, published in Venice in 1561), work that bore fruit in the one hundred octaves completed by Sabbato Vita Marini. And, too, Ovid's well-woven text became a haversack of images to be pilfered, resacked, and ransacked by generations of painters, engravers, and sculptors, down to Picasso and Chagall. In sum: W. R. Johnson is hardly hazarding in conjecturing that "no other poem from antiquity has so influenced the literature and art of western Europe as has the *Metamorphoses*."

For the details of Ovid's physical life on earth, the *Metamorphoses* does not provide a rewarding archive. Instead, our chief source is a poem written in Ovid's exile, *Tristia (Sadnesses)* IV, 10. From there and elsewhere we can glean the following:

Ovid (Publius Ovidius Naso) was born on March 20 in 43 B.C., a year after the assassination of Caesar. His birthplace was "Sulmo [now Sulmona], a [Pelignian] town rich in waters—which lay some ninety miles east of Rome"—across the Apennines. His brother was exactly one year older than he was; and the well-to-do family, of equestrian rank, soon sent both boys to Rome for schooling in rhetoric and law, way stations for a public career. (The Rome they went to was now, post-Actium, much less turbulent than it had been.) His brother—who died early—was inclined to the law; but Ovid's commitment to poetry was native to him and urgent, and politics was soon abandoned for a literary career (though his father had reminded him that Homer "left no worldly riches as his inheritance"). To that end, his studies in Greece and visits to Sicily and Asia Minor were much more than ritual interludes.

He won early recognition and "cultivated" Tibullus and other poets in the circle of Messalla Corvinus (though "the adverse fates did not give Tibullus time to become fast friends with me"), as well as Horace, Propertius, and others in the circle of Maecenas; but he "only caught a glimpse of Vergil." Between that entry into the poetic convivium and the years of his work on the *Metamorphoses* (which was probably composed in the decade between 2 B.C. and A.D. 8), he completed the *Amores (Loves)*, which first appeared in five books in 19 B.C., and later in three books; the first fifteen of his *Heroides (Letters of Heroines)*, to which he later added three pairs of letters in which not only the female but the male partner, too, speaks; the *Ars amatoria (Art of Love)*, with its first two books completed around 1 B.C. and the third book a year later; a lost tragedy, *Medea*; the *Remedia amoris (Remedies of Love)*; and *De medicamine faciei (On Facial Care)*, an incomplete verse manual for the cosmetic tutelage of the female complexion.

Vergil had died in 19 B.C. (Tibullus died in that same year or a year later, and Propertius in that same lustrum) and Horace in 8 B.C. (the same year in which the chief patrons of poetry, Maecenas and Messalla, died). And around the onset of what would later be called the first millennium, Ovid, now the foremost living poet of Rome, began to work simultaneously on the *Metamorphoses*, his wonder-work, which he did complete, and on the *Fasti (Calendar)*, his poetic elaborations on the feast days and recurrences in each of the twelve months of the Roman calendar—of which he completed only six of the twelve books, or months.

It was in A.D. 8 that Augustus—who had been proclaimed consul for life in 19 B.C., *pontifex maximus* in 12 B.C., and *pater patriae* in 2 B.C.—banished Ovid to Tomi (near the present-day Constantsa), on the western shore of the Black Sea, among the barbarian Getae. In *Tristia* II, 2, Ovid notes that "two accusations ruined me, a poem and a mistake." That mistake may—in some way—have had to do with Augustus' scandalous granddaughter, Julia, who, in the same year as Ovid's banishment, was herself "relegated" to the Tremiti islands (just as her adulterous mother, Augustus' daughter—also a Julia—had been banished ten years before). In any case, of that never precisely defined mistake, Ovid says, "I must be silent: I'm not so mean as to renew your wounds, o Caesar; it is enough that you have suffered once. As for the first—the charge that I became a mentor of obscene adulteries . . ."—and here Ovid launches into an elaborate self-defense, noting, on the way, that "if my work [the *Art of Love*] be read with a pure mind, one must conclude it can't harm anyone." (This banishment was technically a *relegatio*, a relegation, which—unlike exile—did not involve a confiscation of his goods or loss of civil rights. But Ovid uses both terms interchangeably in describing his misery.)

The banished Ovid left behind his third wife. We know little of the first two, but nothing in his recounting justifies any image of him as a libertine: "When I was still almost-a-boy, I was given a wife neither worthy nor useful, one who was not my wife for long. She was followed by a wife who, although without blame, did not last long in our bed. The last wife, who has stayed beside me many years, has sustained the weight of being the wife of an exile. My daughter, who twice became a mother while still young—but not from just one husband—has made me a grandfather." That third wife, who stayed behind in Rome as faithful lobbyist, tried to have Augustus' edict appealed. But neither Augustus, who died in A.D. 14, nor his successor, Tiberius (who was to rule until A.D. 37), revoked the edict. In A.D. 17 or 18, Ovid died at Tomi.

In his years of exile, Ovid produced the fifty poems of the *Tristia,* the sixty-four of the *Epistulae ex Ponto (Letters from the Black Sea),* and *Ibis,* a poem of hyperbolic invective—rounding out a total output which is more voluminous than that of Lucretius, Catullus, Vergil, Horace, and Tibullus summed together.

L. P. Wilkinson was not alone in finding "the bulk of the poems from exile . . . abject." And the exiled Ovid is surely no Dante, no Herzen, no Solzhenitsyn. But there is much that is moving in the Black Sea poems. When Goethe left Rome during his first Italian visit, a departure that he felt as exile, it was Ovid's recollection of the night in which he passed "his last moments in Rome" that echoed for the German. And it was in the *Letters from the Black Sea* that this translation had one of its chief seed-points. Since the '50s, I have been much attached to Ortygia, the old quarter of Siracusa, with its fountain of Arethusa—to Ortygia and other sites of Greek Sicily that Ovid catalogued in one of his verse letters written in exile. That letter (*Ex ponto* II, 10), addressed to his friend and fellow poet Pompeius Macer (not to be confused with the Aemilius Macer of *Tristia* IV, 10), recalls their student travels together, briefly noting matters and motifs chanted-decanted in the *Metamorphoses*. It was a portion of this letter that I translated as:

MY EYES—

when I saw Sicily—had you as guide,
There, side by side, we saw the sky ignite;
the Giant, pinned beneath Mount Etna, writhed,
vomiting flames; the cone of Etna blazed.
And then our eyes were graced by Enna's lakes,
the pools of the Palici, and the place
where Anapis' and Cyane's waves embrace.
Nearby was Arethusa; to escape
from Elis' stream, that nymph still runs her race
beneath the sea, from Greece to Sicily.

Almost a year . . . a year in Sicily . . .
a year that coursed so quickly . . . (O how slowly,
how differently, I tell the time in Tomi!)
And what I now inscribe is but a trace,
a vestige of the visions shared when we
were wanderers in Sicily: for me,
you made each pilgrim path a joyous journey.

Alongside that seed-point, there was my own shared "joyous journey" with Paul and Eileen Mariani (crossing the Apennines in search of her family's hometown in the Abruzzi), a trip on which I visited Sulmona. There was, too, my ever-growing awareness that, with all his resurrection of Vergil, Dante (as Landino had long since seen) needed Ovid as exemplar of "narrative variety." Finally, it was the author of the *Metamorphoses* whom I had invoked as benevolent, confederate spirit for my own *Savantasse of Montparnasse,* where my prelude saw him as:

> Ovidius-The-Garrulous,
> The-Copious, the Ever-Swift,
> Amir-Of-Metamorphosists,
> and Sad-Seigneur-Of-Scrutinists,

calling on his "fraternal breath" in the hope that he would "sustain, support, be staff and stead / for both The-Reader and The-Read."

"My Eyes," together with Sicilian sections of the *Metamorphoses,* formed what can now be seen as a preliminary volume, *Ovid in Sicily,* which was graced by the illustrations of Marialuisa de Romans, her fourteen *Ovidiane* paintings that were then shown at Gibellina, New York, and Lentini, the hometown of Gorgias, the centenarian Sophist who said that tragedy (and we may read "poetry") "with its myths and emotions has created a deception such that its successful practitioner is nearer to reality than the unsuccessful, and the man who lets himself be deceived is wiser than he who does not."

Ovid plays—in totally contemporary fashion—on the fictionality of deceptions-fictions. But in treating—dismantling, subverting—the epic, mythological array of gods and heroes, Ovid's arena is not the violence of Mars, the epic concentration on what Dryden called "those ungodly man-killers, whom we poets, when we flatter them, call heroes; a race of men who can never enjoy quiet in themselves till they have taken it from all the world." That violence is parodically treated in the battle of the Lapiths and Centaurs and in the Calydonian hunt; but another violence, the tumult and tribulations of love, is Ovid's essential arena. Not only heroes but hyperthyroid gods, too, are ungodly where Venus is at work. And in that arena, women and goddesses are as involved as men.

Vergil, we now feel, already had muted—questioned—Mars' credentials and pretensions; and my own translation of the *Aeneid* was completed under the aegis of Nisus' question: "Euryalus, is it / the gods who put this fire in our minds, / or is it that each man's relentless longing / becomes a god to him?" And, reflecting on the fictive character of myth, Vergil had had Aeneas exit from the underworld through the gate of ivory—of false dreams. Yet Vergil's queries, however impassioned, however insidious, are subtle; they leave room for tears (Vergil is the unmatched poet of the defeated—and Ovid does learn much from him in that area), but they leave little room for wit and none for humor.

Ovid's subversion, however, is not doled out. And at times his irreverence is almost predatory. Consider the poet Ovid describing (participating in?) the Latinized Mercury's descent onto Athens' holy procession as the young female devotees file up to Athena-Minerva's sacred slope on the holy feast day of Athens:

> *Then Mercury, who bears the magic wand,*
> *flew off on level wings. And from on high,*
> *in flight, he saw the land Minerva loves:*
> *Athenian fields and the Lyceum's grove.*
> *That chanced to be the very day on which*
> *chaste virgins celebrate Minerva's feast:*
> *upon their hands, in baskets flower-ringed,*
> *they bear their pure and holy offerings*
> *up to Minerva's hill, her sanctuary.*
> *And even as the winged god saw below*
> *the young Athenian girls returning home,*
> *he did not fly ahead but circled them.*
>
> *Just as the swift kite-hawk, on catching sight*
> *of innards when a bull is sacrificed,*
> *will wait and hover just as long as, round*
> *the altar, he can see the faithful crowd;*
> *not daring to swoop low, he yet stays close*
> *on high; he tips his wings and wheels above*

his prey—he's greedy; he is full of hope:
just so the swift god of Cyllene wheeled
in steady rings around the sacred hill.

It is as if the sacrilegious Roman were not only playing with—but preying on—Greece.

But there is one privileged area—a Prospero's isle—where Ovid is reverent: the domain of art, the fidelity of the maker to his labors. See his celebration of Vulcan's craft in the reliefs on the walls of the palace of the Sun, and of Minerva's and particularly Arachne's consummate art in their weaving contest.

Inevitably, Vulcan, Orpheus, and especially Pygmalion and Arachne emerge for us as counterfigures of Ovid's own self: the teller being told about—even as Narcissus warns us of the self-limiting career of self-love, however much abetted by the viewer's (reader's) echoing admiration.

There is, too, Ovid's reverence for the flow of rivers and surge of seas, for abundant forests, and for entrancing groves. He is the obsessed scrutinist and devotee of icons, images, apparitions discerned in each trunk and stream. He is the totemist-metamorphosist and, too, the delirious Buffon-cum-Linnaeus-cum-Vesalius of animal and plant and man—and, above all, of nomad forms, forms in movement from human to plant and animal.

I say a "delirious Buffon-cum-Linnaeus." But in a reading of the *Metamorphoses* that has been especially influential in Italy (see the essays by Italo Calvino and Piero Marzolla in Einaudi's edition of the *Metamorphoses*), J. K. Ščeglov, in 1962, tried to erase any delirium and replace it with a more unitary, centripetal view of Ovid as a cool-eyed, objective analyst-encyclopedist, using a carefully limited "assortment of abstract spatial and physical concepts, such as curvature, hollowness, hardness, liquid state, and extension . . . to decompose things into their distinctive traits . . . in order to reconstruct *ex novo* all the universe . . . to enlarge the multiplicity and variety of forms encountered in nature, with respect to our familiar world, so static and inert. . . . The characterization of things in the *Metamorphoses* recalls the exactness of the definitions of geometry and physics."

Though the sins of semiotics are not unnumerous, Ščeglov is not a sinner. But a tidy systematizing of Ovid's narrative digressions and dispersions can obscure his role as the Sad-Seigneur-Of-Scrutinists.

In that role lies the other residual yet essential reverence of Ovid, one that moves beyond art. A unity somewhat unsemiotic: all that is here is not all that semes. Ovid's fictions form a bacchanalian narrative revel, in which each element may be drunk or delirious, but which—in its endless deceptions—provides truth. (Ovid read not only his Gorgias but his Hegel carefully.)

Ovid's encyclopedism is en-lightened; but the truth of his revel is the ineluctability of mystery and the menace of debris—the fragility of meanings—in the shadowed life of human longings.

At the end of the *Paradiso,* as Dante approaches his blinding vision of the mystery of Incarnation, he puts his Ovid to amazing use in explaining his own amazement. Dante tallies on his abacus "twenty-five centuries" and aligns his wonder now with the spectacle "that startled Neptune with the *Argo*'s shadow"—the sea-god's wonder as he watched the first ship ever to cleave his seas.

Ovid is a late-late-comer among poetic mythographers. (His shelves are stacked with Homer, Hesiod, the Attic tragedians; with the Sicilian Theocritus and the Alexandrians Callimachus and Apollonius of Rhodes; with works that have since been wholly lost or are only retrievable in later compendiums; with Lucretius and Catullus in Ovid's own century; and with his enormously gifted contemporaries.) But the freight borne by Ovid's later *Argo* served Dante—and still serves us—as a prime exemplar of freshness, immediacy, and mystery.

The *copia* of Ovid, in fulfilling that role, also calls to mind (Ovid never inhibits multiple similes) the Cornucopia, the shorn horn of the river-god Achelous, a horn the Naiads have filled up "with fruits and fragrant flowers; / they made of it a sacred thing. And now / Abundance—gracious goddess—uses this, / the Cornucopia, as her motif."

Abundance is an autumnal goddess, well suited to latecomers—to whom she brings ever-recurring riches.

To abet my attempt at gathering some of that abundance, it was Henry Weinfield who—even as he was working on his volume of and on Mallarmé—did a line-by-line reading of this translation. It is to him, and to the works of James Hans, Robert Richardson and Burton Feldman, Teodolinda Barolini, Edward Nolan, Charles Ross, and—ever alert to Dryden's mullings—Steven Zwicker, that I am most grateful for close-to-home nourishment, encouragement—and badgering—as I worked on Ovid's book of changes.

And always unshelved, there were the editors (of Ovid's text and of collective miscellanies and symposia)-commentators-critics—debts too numerous to list in full. But in addition to Johnson, Wilkinson, and Ščeglov, already cited, these must needs be thanked: Franz Bömer, W. S. Anderson, Michael von Albrecht and Ernst Zinn, Hermann Fränkel, Charles Segal, Eduard Fraenkel (for his essay in the wake of Jacob Burckhardt, on Roman philhellenism), Niculae Herescu, Georges Lafaye, Franco Munari, Simone Viarre, R. Chevallier, Brooks Otis, E. J. Kenney, Charles Martindale, G. Karl Galinsky, Frederick Ahl, and Leonard Barkan—and the *Atti (Proceedings) del convegno internationale ovidiano* held at Sulmona in 1958, an anniversary year of Ovid's exile.